THE LAW OF THE LIST

The spread of violent extremism, 9/11, the rise of ISIL and movement of 'foreign terrorist fighters' are dramatically expanding the powers of the UN Security Council to govern risky cross-border flows and threats by non-state actors. New security measures and data infrastructures are being built that threaten to erode human rights and transform the world order in far-reaching ways. *The Law of the List* is an interdisciplinary study of global security law in motion. It follows the ISIL and Al-Qaida sanctions list, created by the UN Security Council to counter global terrorism, to different sites around the world, mapping its effects as an assemblage. Drawing on interviews with Council officials, diplomats, security experts, judges, secret diplomatic cables and the author's experiences as a lawyer representing listed people, *The Law of the List* shows how governing through the list is reconfiguring global security, international law and the powers of international organisations.

GAVIN SULLIVAN is a lecturer in law at the University of Kent. His research focuses on the politics of global security law and global data infrastructures, and has been published in journals such as *Transnational Legal Theory*, the *Leiden Journal of International Law*, the *American Journal of International Law* and *Environment and Planning D: Society and Space*. Gavin is a practising lawyer with experience in human rights litigation. He coordinates the Transnational Listing Project and has represented numerous individuals in delisting proceedings before the UN Office of the Ombudsperson. He is a member of the Law and Society Association, the European Society of International Law, the Socio-Legal Studies Association and the Law Society of England and Wales.

THE LAW OF THE LIST

UN Counterterrorism Sanctions and the Politics
of Global Security Law

GAVIN SULLIVAN

University of Kent

CAMBRIDGE
UNIVERSITY PRESS

CAMBRIDGE
UNIVERSITY PRESS

University Printing House, Cambridge CB2 8BS, United Kingdom

One Liberty Plaza, 20th Floor, New York, NY 10006, USA

477 Williamstown Road, Port Melbourne, VIC 3207, Australia

314–321, 3rd Floor, Plot 3, Splendor Forum, Jasola District Centre,
New Delhi – 110025, India

79 Anson Road, #06–04/06, Singapore 079906

Cambridge University Press is part of the University of Cambridge.

It furthers the University's mission by disseminating knowledge in the pursuit of
education, learning, and research at the highest international levels of excellence.

www.cambridge.org
Information on this title: www.cambridge.org/9781108491921
DOI: 10.1017/9781108649322

First published 2020

Printed in the United Kingdom by TJ International Ltd, Padstow Cornwall

A catalogue record for this publication is available from the British Library.

Library of Congress Cataloging-in-Publication Data
Names: Sullivan, Gavin, 1974– author.
Title: The law of the list : UN counterterrorism sanctions and the politics of global security
law / Gavin Sullivan, University of Kent, Canterbury
Description: Cambridge, United Kingdom ; New York, NY, USA : Cambridge University
Press, 2020. | Series: Global law series | Based on author's thesis (doctoral – Universiteit van
Amsterdam, 2017). | Includes bibliographical references and index.
Identifiers: LCCN 2019042594 (print) | LCCN 2019042595 (ebook) | ISBN 9781108491921
(hardback) | ISBN 9781108649322 (ebook)
Subjects: LCSH: United Nations – Sanctions. | Terrorism – Prevention – Law and legislation.
Classification: LCC KZ6373 .S85 2020 (print) | LCC KZ6373 (ebook) | DDC 344.05/3257–
dc23
LC record available at https://lccn.loc.gov/2019042594
LC ebook record available at https://lccn.loc.gov/2019042595

ISBN 978-1-108-49192-1 Hardback

For Nova and Aelle,
from the sky to the sea

CONTENTS

FIGURES

FOREWORD

The Law of the List is, as it promises, a study of global security law 'in motion' (p. 16). Tracing the UN ISIL and Al-Qaida listing and sanctions regime takes readers of this book from New York (home of the Security Council, the UN1267 Analytical Support and Sanctions Monitoring Team and the Office of the UN1267 Ombudsperson) to Montreal (ICAO headquarters), and from the tiny Italian tax enclave of Campione (home of Youssef Nada, an eight-year listee on the UN1267 list) to Rhode Island (site of targeted sanctions training workshops led by Brown University researchers of the Watson Institute), as well as beyond and between.

Along the way, the book skirts those dead ends by which much of the legal and political science literature on global security law – and on counterterrorist listing in particular – is littered. Not here will readers encounter familiar appeals for transparency, principle, participation or optimisation. Instead, Gavin Sullivan has delivered a masterful enactment of the kind of doubleness that Duncan Kennedy once urged upon legal scholars (borrowing from W. E. B. Du Bois) – doubleness, that is, towards the 'very institutions that nurture us and make it possible for us to fight against their complicity, our complicity, in group oppression'.[1]

Having worked as a lawyer advising clients seeking delisting, Sullivan has unusual insight into the 'novel form of global security law and governance' that he analyses (p. 7). Yet here that experiential insight is transected by a wide range of interviewees' voices, as well as by laser-sharp readings of cognate literature. The result is an extraordinarily powerful and revealing rendition of the operations of global power: operations whereby an 'almost comical' (pp. 6, 187) scramble to confront terrorist violence on the global plane has resulted in particular

---

[1] Duncan Kennedy, *A Critique of Adjudication* (Cambridge MA: Harvard University Press, 1997), p. 376.

individuals finding it 'difficult, if not impossible, to work or rent a house', with some 'likely to stay preventatively targeted forever' (p. 5).

By the book's end, the many things that I had gleaned from it were, I found, far too numerous to mention here. So, faced with this panoply, I did the expected thing. I reached for the technology of the list. Here are three things that *The Law of the List* brought home for me.

1   A List Is Not a List Is Not a List

Global security lists can, it turns out, be broken down into packets, specifically 'PNR-compatible data packets' (p. 110). Entries on such a list can have different apertures, some being more or less precise than others. Lists can be used to link people and things, even to make them 'more vibrant': intelligence services in different countries for example (p. 96). But they can also block things and break them apart, by distributing 'inadmissibility', for instance (p. 118). As the list 'works and changes as a global legal assemblage', matters of formatting and translation become crucial sites for its contestation and its elaboration (pp. 134, 112, 135).

2   A Law Is Not a Law Is Not a Law

Laws and legal institutions in this book's account are best understood as 'governance effect[s] arising from multiple conflicts between different actors', including 'across the listing assemblage' (p. 134). Global security law is generative and constitutive, not just disciplinary. Laws underpinning the sanctions regime may work as levers, yielding a 'flow of information and intelligence' (pp. 99, 190). Listing is aimed as much at the establishment of an 'equilibrium of possibilities' as it is at ruling some possibilities out preemptively (p. 86).

3   Global Security Law Has Not Been Secured

In many accounts, the global regime of counterterrorist surveillance and regulation is depicted as a near-perfect panopticon. In contrast, *The Law of the List* shows just how much irresolution riddles this regime. In this account, listing is not 'reducible to a story of invisible technocrats seeking to rule the world' (p. 129). Its techniques of preemption sit on a 'test bed', precarious atop the 'sandy foundations of diplomatic negotiation' (pp. 180, 190). The 'crucible[s] of knowledge production shaping this domain of global law' are multiple, with some of them very 'far apart' in their understandings of the phenomena with which they grapple (pp. 192, 197).

Sites of potential intervention in the making and remaking of this 'multiple object' are correspondingly many (p. 197). Global security law is getting 'recalibrated at the most granular of levels', suggesting many ways into that process (p. 275). Yet routes for reform still remain perilous and murky. Due process-enhancing improvements, such as the institution of the Office of the Ombudsperson, turn out not to align well with a 'human-rights friendly narrative' of progress (p. 220). Reform often serves to 'foreclose debate and deflect critique' (p. 221).

Out of this, a 'textured and complex topology of the global emerges' (p. 248). Across this topology, conventionally major features seem small and minor things loom large. Traditional distinctions – such as that between intelligence and evidence – collapse (p. 258). 'Conventional forms of legal knowledge', such as judicial modes of inductive reasoning, are 'destabilised and reordered'; alongside them, the list generates 'new problems and recombinant legal practices' (pp. 276–277).

And amid this hall of normative mirrors, Gavin Sullivan insists that 'there are no decisions (in the public law sense)' over which we might deploy the redemptive force of administrative law (p. 313). Counter-conduct, in this book's account, entails trying to 'mak[e] sense of the complexities of global legal ordering unfolding in the present' and by that means 'think ... how new global security regimes might be made otherwise' (p. 316).

This book's invitation to readers is to abandon those routes-to-rightfulness most commonly trodden around global security law and join its author instead in 'experiment[s] in strategic knowledge production' (p. 331). My guess is that it will resonate widely as a work of the utmost significance in the fields of counterterrorism law, international law and global governance and beyond. Read on to see for yourself.

Fleur Johns
Professor, Faculty of Law
UNSW Sydney

ACKNOWLEDGEMENTS

A book is a multiplicity and there have been many that have helped this research come to life. This work is based on my doctoral research at the University of Amsterdam, where I was privileged to have had two excellent PhD supervisors. Marieke de Goede developed this project with me from the beginning. It was her innovative work on preemptive security that inspired me to come back to university to undertake this research. Her method of combining empirical analysis with conceptual innovation is energising and left a lasting impression on how I think and write, for which I am immensely grateful. She engaged with my work critically and taught me how to publish and teach. And she allowed me to write this interdisciplinary book, without unduly pushing it in certain directions. Mariana Valverde also inspired and shaped this project in countless ways. We met through our shared love of Peter Goodrich's book, *Languages of Law*. Since then she has shown me – both through her work and continued engagement with my own research, within and beyond the PhD – what critical, dynamic and conceptually inventive sociolegal research can look like. Her body of work on the knowledge practices and spatiotemporal dimensions of legal governance is a continuing source of inspiration that runs through the different chapters of this book. She has been intellectually generous and frank, and helped me not be too wordy when I didn't need to be. I am deeply grateful for her support.

Kim Lane Scheppele and Amir Attaran both inspired me to undertake critical empirical research on global security law. They supported my early research on terrorist listing at a time when it was most needed, for which I am very grateful. Amir urged me to make whatever I do 'forensically valuable' for others seeking to understand and challenge this global regime down the line. Kim was one of the first to grasp the constitutional and political significance of the Security Council's post-9/11 'anti-terrorism campaign'. She is a friend, intellectual mentor and generously supports early career, sociolegal scholars – for which

I and many other relative newcomers in the field are grateful. Wouter Werner was an important interlocutor throughout this project, engaging critically with my research. Claudia Aradau and Fleur Johns have both been a source of intellectual inspiration and supported my work in numerous ways, whilst always pushing the boundaries of scholarship on security, technology and law. I am especially honoured that Fleur kindly agreed to write the 'Foreword' for this book.

Without the engagement of friends and colleagues in various cities this project would never been realised. In Amsterdam, where the bulk of the research was prepared, I particularly wish to thank Julien Jeandesboz (now in Brussels), Geoff Gordon, Francesco Ragazzi, Rebecca Sakoun, Florian Göttke and Merijn Oudenampsen for their support and innumerable discussions over coffee, lunch and drinks. In Canterbury, where the manuscript was finalised, I would like to thank my head of school Toni Williams for affording me time to finish this book on the job, Didi Herman for providing feedback and securing resources for research assistance in the final phases of the work and Dermot Walsh for pushing me to prioritise completion and ignore the things that didn't matter. I also thank Jose Bellido, Tatiana Flessas, Maria Drakopoulou, Alain Pottage, Connal Parsley, Donal Casey and Stephen Humphreys for their intellectual engagement, friendship and support. Alejandro Rodiles has been a friend and generous host in Mexico City. His work, and our collaborative project on informal security governance (globalassemblages.org), continues to shape my thinking on these issues in important ways.

I was invited to a number of events throughout this project that allowed me to present work-in-progress and get a clearer sense of how my research could draw from and speak to current debates. Wouter Werner at VU University Amsterdam coordinated the COST Action IS1003 International Law between Constitutionalisation and Fragmentation: The Role of Law in the Post-national Constellation, which hosted numerous workshops (in Amsterdam, Malaga, Lund, Copenhagen and Weimar) from 2012 to 2014, helped shape the contours of this book. I am grateful to Peer Zumbansen for inviting me to participate in the inspiring Transnational Law Summer Institute at King's College London in 2015 and 2016 and for showing an ongoing interest in my work ever since. Francesca Galli from Maastricht University asked me to a workshop on terrorist listing in Brussels in 2012 that helped influence Chapter 4. Deirdre Curtin invited me to a transnational law workshop at the University of Amsterdam that forced me to situate my research in relation to postnational legal theory debates.

Thanks to Susanne Krasmann and Sven Opitz for organising the Materiality of Law and Global Politics event at the University of Hamburg in 2014 that helped clarify my relation with Bruno Latour's work and allowed me to present the early draft findings of Chapter 2. Emilie Cloatre and Donatella Alessandrini from the Social Critiques of Law research group at Kent Law School invited me to present my research in 2014 and showed me that the University of Kent is an ideal place for cutting-edge sociolegal research. Thanks also to Sheila Jasanoff for critically engaging with my work on the sidelines of an Institute for Global Law and Policy event at Harvard Law School in 2015, and the Global Un-Governance workshop at the University of Edinburgh in 2019 (organised by Andrew Lang and Deval Desai), and pushing me to more clearly articulate its novelty and politics.

Enrica Rigo and Alice Riccardi invited me to Roma Tre University in 2012 and 2014 to present my research on the UN1267 Ombudsperson at different stages of development. Thanks to Morag Goodwin and Philip Paiement from Tilburg Law School for inviting me to their innovative Global Law Lab in 2016 and pushing me to clarify my global sociolegal methods more sharply. Anne Orford gave very helpful feedback on Chapter 2 at an event organised by Martti Koskenniemi at the University of Helsinki in 2017, for which I'm grateful. Claudia Aradau invited me to give a seminar at the Research Centre in International Relations at King's College London in 2018, where Didier Bigo and Vivienne Jabri gave helpful feedback. My colleagues at Kent Law School, Luis Eslava and Rose Parfitt, have worked tirelessly to organise the International Law and Politics research network at the annual Law and Society Association conference, where several draft papers from this book have been presented. Numerous others have given valuable feedback or shared ideas that made their way into this book. Thanks to Christian Bueger, Gráinne de Búrca, Gregoire Mallard, Campbell Munro, Fiona de Londras, David Chandler, Kristin Bergtora Sandvik, Eve Darian-Smith and Nehal Bhuta for their engagement.

The logistics of producing a large monograph like this are potentially overwhelming, and I'm extremely grateful to those who helped by providing research and editorial assistance along the way. Kate Wood provided initial research assistance at a critical time. Annika Weis provided in-depth research assistance during the final phases of manuscript production, for which I'm very grateful, as well as securing all the necessary permissions for the images. Marie Selwood provided careful copy-editing support, working tirelessly on my book over the summer of 2019 when she could have been enjoying the sun instead. Jonny Bunning was repeatedly able to find and send me hard-to-source materials at short notice from the USA, in situations that would have otherwise required a special trip to the British Library. And thanks to Marc Jonathan Costello for engaging with me about the ideas of the book and coming up with such a thoughtful cover design. The editors of the Global Law Series at Cambridge, and especially Morag Goodwin, have been very supportive. Morag saw intellectual value in this research early on and helped bring it to fruition. I am honoured to have my first book published in a series an innovative and timely as this one. Finola O'Sullivan and Marianne Nield at Cambridge University Press ensured a seamless production process throughout. And many thanks to the three anonymous Cambridge University Press reviewers for their detailed comments.

This research would not have been possible without all the interviewees who generously gave their time and shared their knowledge about the listing regime and its politics. I wish I could thank them personally, but I promised anonymity. I have legally represented listed persons and helped them get delisted before, during and after this book was published. This advocacy has provided innumerable insights into how the list works in practice as an unjust tool of global immiseration and control and continues to motivate my work in this area. My thanks go to my clients for allowing me to act on their behalf and being patient whilst I juggled my advocacy work alongside my university research and teaching commitments. Many thanks to Alice Riccardi (Rome Tre University) and Rachel Barnes (3 Raymond Buildings, London) for working collaboratively and pro bono with me on these cases over the years as part of the Transnational Listing Project to defend the rights of those disregarded.

Conducting global multisited research on a tight budget would have been impossible were it not for friends hosting me in different cities around the world during fieldwork visits. Special thanks to Sanjay Pinto and Avy Skolnik (in New York), Rafael Navar (Washington DC) and Aaron Chappel (formerly in Brussels), for their hospitality and engagement. This project also relies on classified US Embassy cables bravely leaked by Chelsea Manning and published by Wikileaks. My thanks and solidarity go to them for making this material publicly available, at great personal cost and in spite of the severity of the consequences that they could and likely will face through the unfolding US criminal procedure.

The PhD on which this book is based began in 2011 two months before the birth of my first daughter, Nova. At the end of 2014 my second daughter, Aelle, was born. Writing a PhD and book with two little kids is a challenge. But it is with deep love and gratitude that I thank both my extraordinary kids for being with me throughout this research. They made it harder at times by stealing my sleep and time. But they bring joy and unbridled enthusiasm and with them I experience the world differently each day. And for that I am immensely grateful. When Nova told me a character in one of her made-up stories was called 'Ever' after 'your book, because it goes on for ever', I knew it was time to end it.

Two people very close to my heart passed away during the making of this book – my mother-in-law, Guadalupe Alzaga, and my father, Peter Sullivan. Lupe lived with us in Amsterdam and the UK for the last five years of her life. She was intellectually curious, political and always emotionally supportive. Without her affective labour nurturing my kids when this project made more demands on my time, this book would never have been finished. My father made the long trip over to Amsterdam from Australia in 2017 for my PhD defence. I am the first person to go to University in my family, and so he was always very proud of my achievements. Seeing this book finally come to life would have made him extremely happy. I'm deeply sad he is gone and miss him greatly. My mum, Rhonda Sullivan, has always supported and encouraged me in what I want to do, however uncertain it may seem at the time. My sister, Tracey Sullivan, also helped along the way, including by transcribing my interviews and my sister-in-law, Carolina Fontoura Alzaga, was also immensely supportive throughout.

My deepest thanks go to my partner and accomplice, Valery Alzaga, for her unwavering support, love of learning and belief in the importance of what I'm doing. During this book project we crossed three countries, had two kids, changed careers, lost family members and cut through innumerable problems together with creativity, verve and grace. She critically engaged with and helped shape the ideas of this book in countless ways and reminded me of its underlying politics, when I had forgotten.

Finally, I wish to acknowledge the publications in which versions and parts of this book have appeared, including: Gavin Sullivan and Ben Hayes, *Blacklisted: Targeted Sanctions, Preemptive security and Fundamental Rights* (Berlin: ECCHR, 2011); Gavin Sullivan and Marieke de Goede, 'Between law and the exception: The UN 1267 Ombudsperson as a hybrid model of legal expertise' (2013) 26(4) *Leiden Journal of International Law* 833; Gavin Sullivan, 'Transnational legal assemblages and global security law: topologies and temporalities of the list' (2014) 5(1) *Transnational Legal Theory* 81; Gavin Sullivan, 'Secret justice inside the EU courts' *Al-Jazeera* (online, 19 April 2014); Marieke de Goede and Gavin Sullivan, 'The politics of security lists' (2016) 34(1) *Environment and Planning D: Society and Space* 67; and Gavin Sullivan, 'Rearranging global law: reflections on laws and societies in a global context' (2017) 13(4) *International Journal of Law in Context* 553. Financial support for this research was provided by the Dutch Council for Scientific Research (NWO), through the VIDI-grant 'European Security Culture', award number 452–09-016. All websites referenced throughout this text were current and last accessed on 15 August 2019.

TABLE OF CASES

International And Regional

Court of Justice of the European Union

C-155/79 Australian Mining and Smelting Europe Ltd v. Commission [1982] ECR 1575

T-306/01 Yusuf and Al Barakaat International Foundation v. Council and Commission [2005] ECR II-3533

T-315/01 Kadi v. Council and Commission [2005] ECR II-3649

T-228/02 Organisation des Modjahedines du peuple d'Iran v. Council of European Union [2006] ECR II-4665

C-317/04 and C-318/04 European Parliament v. Council [2006] ECR I-4721

T-125/03 and T-253/03 Akzo Nobel Chemicals Ltd and Akcros Chemicals Ltd v. Commission [2007] ECR II-3523

C-402 P and 415/05 P Kadi and Al Barakaat v. Council and Commission [2008] ECR I-6351

C-402/05P and C-415/05P Kadi and Al Barakaat v. Council and Commission [2008] ECR I-6351, Opinion of AG Poiares Maduro

T-85/09 Kadi v. Commission [2010] ECR II-5177

C-27/09 P French Republic v. PMOI [2011] ECLI:EU:C:2011:482, Opinion of AG Sharpston

C-584/10P, C-593/10P and C-595/10P Commission, Council and United Kingdom v. Yassin Abdullah Kadi [2013] ECLI:EU:C:2013:518

C-584/10 P, C-593/10 P and C-595/10 P Commission, Council and United Kingdom v. Yassin Abdullah Kadi [2013] ECLI:EU:C:2013:176, Opinion of AG Bot

T-306/10 Yusef v. Commission [2014] ECLI:EU:T:2014:141

T-127/09 RENV Abdulrahim v. Council and Commission [2015] ECLI:EU:T:2015:4

European Court of Human Rights

A and Others v. United Kingdom App. No. 3455/05 (ECtHR, 19 February 2009)

Al-Dulimi and Montana Management Inc. v. Switzerland App. No. 5809/08 (ECtHR, 26 November 2013)

Al-Khawaja and Tahery v. United Kingdom App. Nos. 26766/05 and 22228/06 (ECtHR, 15 December 2011)

Nada v. Switzerland App. No. 10593/ 08 (ECtHR, 12 September 2012)

United Nations Human Rights Committee

National

Canada

Germany

Switzerland

United Kingdom

United States

ABBREVIATIONS

AG	Advocate General
ANF	Al-Nusrah Front for the People of Levant
ANT	Actor-Network Theory
API	Advance Passenger Information
AQI	Al-Qaida in Iraq
AQO	Al Qaida and Taliban (UN Measures) Order 2006
AVSEC	Aviation Security Plan of Action
CMP	Closed Material Procedure
CSIS	Canadian Security Intelligence Service
CTC	United Nations Security Council Counter Terrorism Committee
CTED	United Nations Security Council Counter-Terrorism Committee Executive Directorate
CTTP	Countering Terrorist Travel Programme
ECJ	European Court of Justice
ECtHR	European Court of Human Rights
EGC	European General Court
EEAS	European External Action Service
EU	European Union
EUI	European University Institute
FBI	Federal Bureau of Investigation
FCO	Foreign and Commonwealth Office
FOIA	Freedom of Information Act 2000
FTF	Foreign Terrorist Fighter
GAL	Global Administrative Law
GCTF	Global Counter Terrorism Forum
GDS	Global Distribution Systems
GRF	Global Relief Fund
HRC	Human Rights Committee
IATA	International Air Transport Association
ICAO	International Civil Aviation Organization
ICCPR	International Convention on Civil and Political Rights
ICJ	International Commission of Jurists

Interpol	International Criminal Police Organization
IO	International Organisation
IR	International Relations
ISIL	Islamic State in Iraq and the Levant
LIFG	Libyan Islamic Fighting Group
NGO	Non-Governmental Organisation
OFAC	Office of Foreign Assets Control
P5	Security Council Permanent Five
PNR	Passenger Name Record
PTC	Permanent Technical Committee
R2P	Responsibility to Protect
SARPS	Standards and Recommended Practices
SCAD	Security Council Affairs Division
S/RES	Security Council Resolution
SIAC	Special Immigration Appeals Commission
STS	Science and Technology Studies
TO	Terrorism (UN Measures) Order 2006
TPN	Transnational Policy Network
UK	United Kingdom
UN	United Nations
UNCAT	United Nations Convention against Torture
UNOCT	United Nations Office of Counter-Terrorism
UNOHCHR	United Nations Office of the High Commissioner for Human Rights
UNODC	United Nations Office of Drugs and Crime
UNOLA	United Nations Office of Legal Affairs
UNSC/the Security Council/the Council	United Nations Security Council
USA	United States of America
USAP	Universal Security Audit Programme
USUN	United States Mission to the United Nations
WCO	World Customs Organization
WTO	World Trade Organization

INTERVIEWS

Primary Interviews

Interview A   Interview with former member of the UN1267 Monitoring Team, New York, November 2012

Interview B   Interview with former member of the UN1267 Monitoring Team, New York, June 2014

Interview C   Interview with former member of the UN1267 Sanctions Committee, New York, June 2014

Interview D   Interview with former member of the UN 1267 Monitoring Team, October 2013 (location omitted to preserve anonymity)

Interview E   Interview with International Civil Aviation Organization official, Montreal (via Skype), March 2014

Interview F   Interview with former member of the UN 1267 Monitoring Team, New York (via Skype), June 2014

Interview G   Interview with Watson Institute scholar, Toronto, March 2014

Interview H   Interview with former UN Secretariat official, New York, June 2014

Interview I   Interview with former member of the Monitoring Team, New York (via Skype), August 2014

Interview J   Interview with former UK Foreign and Commonwealth Office Director, London, April 2013

Interview K   Interview with the former UN 1267 Ombudsperson, Kimberly Prost, New York, November 2012

Interview L   Interview with the former UN 1267 Ombudsperson, Kimberly Prost, New York, June 2014

Interview M   Interview with member of European Commission Legal Service. Brussels, November 2012

Interview N   Interview with member of the European General Court. Luxembourg, March 2013

Interview O   Interview with member of the European External Action Service, Brussels, March 2013

Interview P   Interview with member of European Court of Justice, Luxembourg, March 2013

Interview Q   Interview with member of Council of the European Union, Brussels, March 2013

Interview R   Interview with a member of the Commission Legal Service, Brussels, October 2013

Interview S   Interview with the former UN 1267 Ombudsperson, Kimberly Prost, Den Haag (via Skype), July 2019

Additional Interviews

Interview with member of the German Mission to the UN, New York, November 2012
Interview with member of the Swiss Mission to the UN, New York, November 2012
Interview with two members of the UK Mission to the UN, New York, November 2012
Interview with member of the US Mission to the UN, New York, November 2012
Interview with lawyer representing targeted individuals, London, March 2013
Interview with former member of the UK Sanctions Unit, London, April 2013
Interview with member of the UK Foreign and Commonwealth Office Sanctions Team, London, April 2013
Interview with lawyer representing targeted individuals, London, May 2013
Interview with lawyer representing targeted entities, Washington DC, June 2014
Interview with member of the German Mission to the UN, New York, June 2014
Interview with member of the US Mission to the UN, New York, June 2014
Interview with expert from Interpol, New York (via Skype), September 2014
Interview with expert from International Air Transport Association, Montreal (via Skype) October 2014

1

The Law of the List

The United Nations (UN) was created after World War II as an inter-governmental organisation of states. The constituent instrument that created the UN and gave the Security Council its enforcement powers (the UN Charter) reflects this state-centred focus. The collective security provisions that empower the Council to determine threats to the peace and decide what enforcement action to take were aimed at preventing interstate war.[1] Economic sanctions were conceived as political measures for disciplining recalcitrant states deemed threats to international peace and security. They offered a means of intervention 'between words and war'[2] for the Council to 'deter individual states from taking matters into their own hands'.[3] Because they are imposed under Chapter VII of the UN Charter, sanctions must be implemented by all states. This extra-ordinary power was to be limited to specific and concrete threats.[4] When threats receded, the sanctions would be withdrawn.

With the Security Council in stalemate during the Cold War these powers were rarely used. During the first forty-five years of the UN's existence, sanctions were only imposed twice.[5] It was only with the post-Cold War political consensus in the Council that the potential of this powerful global tool began to be innovatively developed and explored. During the 1990s, UN sanctions were issued against Iraq, Libya, Angola, Liberia, Somalia, the former Yugoslavia, Sudan, Cambodia, Rwanda,

---

[1] Martti Koskenniemi, *The Politics of International Law* (Oxford: Hart Publishing, 2011), p. 83.

[2] Peter Wallensteen and Carina Staibano (eds.), *International Sanctions: Between Words and Wars in the Global System* (London: Frank Cass, 2005).

[3] Jeremy Greenstock, 'The Security Council in the post-Cold-War world' in Vaughan Lowe, Adam Roberts, Jennifer Welsh and Dominik Zaum (eds.), *The United Nations Security Council and War: The Evolution of Thought and Practice since 1945* (Oxford: Oxford University Press, 2010), p. 248.

[4] Paul Szasz, 'The Security Council starts legislating' (2002) 96(4) *American Journal of International Law* 901.

[5] Rhodesia (S/RES/232 (1966)) and South Africa (S/RES/418 (1977)).

Sierra Leone and Afghanistan. What were considered 'threats to inter-national peace and security' capable of justifying Council intervention were elastically reinterpreted – with sanctions imposed for promoting human rights, restoring democratic leadership and furthering arms control.[6] Non-state actors were targeted for the first time, reorientating the interstate focus of collective security. UN sanctions also started being triggered by domestic violations internal to states – encroaching on the sphere of state sovereignty long deemed the foundational and inviolable principle of world order.

This global governance activism ushered in a new rationale for security intervention based on 'global law and community values rather than international peace per se' and facilitated the Council's governance of terrorism as a novel threat.[7] After the 1998 Al-Qaida attacks on US embassies in Kenya and Tanzania, the Council adopted Resolution 1267 (1999) which required all states to 'freeze the funds and other financial resources, either directly belonging to or indir-ectly benefitting, the Taliban'.[8] The original aim was to pressure the Afghan regime to extradite Osama bin Laden and stop providing 'safe haven' to members of Al-Qaida. To facilitate this, a Sanctions Committee was set up – composed of the permanent members of the Security Council – to draft and administer a blacklist of indivi-duals and entities associated with the Taliban. After the bombing of the USS Cole in Yemen in 2000, the Council broadened the scope of the regime to anyone deemed 'associated with' Osama bin Laden or Al-Qaida.[9] According to the Committee: 'A criminal charge or con-viction is not a prerequisite for listing as the sanctions are intended to be preventive in nature'.[10] In other words, listed individuals are not targeted for acts they have done but for things designating states believe they might do in the future.

After the 9/11 terrorist attacks in 2001 the 'global war on terror' began on many fronts. States passed draconian emergency legislation, massively expanded executive powers and engaged in preemptive

---

[6] David Cortright and George A. Lopez, *The Sanctions Decade: Assessing UN Strategies in the 1990s* (Boulder CO: Lynne Rienner, 2000), p. 2.

[7] Jean Cohen, *Globalization and Sovereignty: Rethinking Legality, Legitimacy and Constitutionalism* (Cambridge: Cambridge University Press, 2012), p. 270.

[8] S/RES/1267 (1999), para. 4(b).

[9] S/RES/1333 (2000), para. 8(c).

[10] UN1267 Sanctions Committee, *Guidelines of the Committee for the Conduct of Its Work* (5 September 2018), para. 6(d).

security actions that undermined constitutional protections at home and disregarded human rights abroad. 'America', we were told, 'will never seek a permission slip to defend the security of our country'.[11] From the indefinite detention of 'enemy combatants' in Guantanamo Bay and extraordinary rendition of suspects to secret black-sites around the world to the torture and abuse of prisoners at Abu Ghraib and the military invasions of Iraq and Afghanistan, the world was given an unequivocal message by the USA and its allies: 'Either you are with us or you are with the terrorists'.[12]

Yet, despite all this unilateralist rhetoric, the most far-reaching legal developments in the global war on terror developed from the UN Security Council. New binding resolutions required states to change their laws to criminalise terrorism and terrorist financing, effecting a fundamental 'change in the legal bases of state action'.[13] The Council was transformed from an executive policing body into a new global legislator, 'imposing general and permanent obligations on states ... not tied to any particular conflict'.[14] After 9/11 the Al-Qaida listing regime was altered into something that bore little resemblance to the UN sanctions of the past. The need for any geographic connection with Afghan territory was removed, allowing the sanctions to be applied to individuals wherever they were in the world. Time-limitations were abolished, allowing listing decisions to be applied for a potentially unlimited duration.[15] Within three years the UN1267 list was radically repurposed into a preemptive legal weapon for disrupting global terrorist networks and their perceived supporters worldwide, with unprecedented powers (temporally and spatially unlimited in scope) for the Security Council to target individual terrorism suspects using secret material suggesting potential 'association with' Al-Qaida. In 2015, the list was extended once more to target the Islamic State in Iraq and the Levant (ISIL).[16]

---

[11] George W. Bush, 'State of the Union Address' (20 January 2004). Available at: wapo.st /2XqCumm.

[12] George W. Bush, 'Address to Joint Session of Congress and the American People' (21 September 2001). Available at: cnn.it/2JigZeY.

[13] S/RES/1373 (2001). Kim Lane Scheppele, 'The international state of emergency: challenges to constitutionalism after September 11' (21 September 2006), Yale Legal Theory Workshop (unpublished manuscript), p. 1.

[14] Kent Roach, *The 9/11 Effect: Comparative Counter-Terrorism* (Cambridge: Cambridge University Press, 2011), p. 32.

[15] S/RES/1390 (2002).

[16] S/RES/2253 (2015).

This book critically examines the UN ISIL and Al-Qaida listing regime as a novel form of global security law. It shows how the list works as an ordering device to render the uncertain future threats of global terrorism amenable to legal intervention in the present. I argue that the Law of the List is radically altering the relationship between national and international law and is best understood as a global legal assemblage. It is also generating new knowledge practices, governance techniques and mechanisms of preemptive security that are reconfiguring how legality works at a granular level. Understanding how law is transformed through globalisation, or how the governance of uncertainty transforms legal practice, requires grappling with the politics of expertise and seemingly mundane technical practices of problem management. Studying global security law empirically from the local sites that it inhabits provides a more dynamic and nuanced account of emergency in motion.

I first came to this research project as a practising human rights lawyer. In 2010 I moved to Germany to work with an international human rights Non-Governmental Organisation (NGO). Whilst there I wrote a public report on terrorism blacklisting and fundamental rights. That initial research opened my eyes to how radically the international legal order was being altered in response to the 9/11 attacks and how far-reaching and exceptional the UN Al-Qaida sanctions regime was. The UN Security Council was developing a unique global legal weapon that made individual terrorism suspects 'effectively prisoners of the state' without any political or legal redress.[17] After that report circulated, I was contacted by a Tunisian migrant rights organisation in France to provide legal advice to some listed individuals about their rights. After interviewing these men and learning more about their stories I decided to take their cases on. Together with a network of legal volunteers specifically assembled for the task, we engaged in the lengthy task of preparing and filing delisting applications to the UN1267 Office of the Ombudsperson. Four applications were filed over a four-year period, all resulting in delisting. Since then, more clients have been delisted and more targeted individuals have asked for our assistance.

This experience of working closely with listed individuals on these cases helped me see first-hand how unjust this regime of preemptive security governance is. People were being targeted on what appeared to be little or no grounds at all. And the consequences of being listed are incredibly severe. It is difficult, if not impossible, to work or rent a house.

---

[17] *HM Treasury* v. *Ahmed and Others* [2010] UKSC 2 (Lord Hope), para. 60.

Your finances are either frozen or under the personal control of appointed central government officials. You cannot travel. And it is a criminal offence for anyone to give you money to help you get by. To be listed is to be subjected to powerful new techniques of 'financial warfare'.[18] One official has likened the effect to a 'civil death penalty'.[19]

Once you are listed as a member of Al-Qaida, everyone from the local police chief to immigration officials disrupt your life and make it as difficult as possible. In Italy (where my clients lived) listed individuals could take up employment and earn a small amount of money to survive. But regular workplace visits and harassment from intelligence officers ensured that no one could keep down a job for long ('did you know you are employing a terrorist?'). Clients were told by intelligence officers that their listing might be discontinued only if they agreed to act as informants in their communities for the security services. All had been through criminal proceedings many years before and had been acquitted of international terrorism charges, and so were confused as to why they were being accused again. After reviewing the US Embassy cables released by Wikileaks, I found that even the state that listed them had reviewed their cases years before and concluded there was 'insufficient grounds' to keep them designated.[20] And yet here they were, many years later, targeted by the UN Security Council as members of the Al-Qaida global terrorist network. With no real possibility for legal redress and – without pro bono legal advice – likely to stay preventatively targeted forever.

Some might say this is simply the political price to be paid for preempting potential terrorist attacks. That there will always be 'false positives' in the global war against terror; that you can't make an omelette without cracking a few eggs. The 'one per cent doctrine' that gained currency with policymakers after 9/11, for example, stipulated that even 'if there is a one per cent chance of an event coming due', states needed to 'act as though it were a certainty'.[21] Intervening early on uncertain knowledge is how low probability–high consequence risks like global terrorism must be governed. It requires throwing a deliberately broad net

---

[18] Juan C. Zarate, *Treasury's War: The Unleashing of a New Era of Financial Warfare* (New York: Public Affairs, 2013).

[19] Dick Marty, Rapporteur for the Council of Europe, cited in Birgit Kruse, 'Zivile Todesstrafe' (*Sueddeutsche Zeitung*, 12 November 2007). Available at: bit.ly/30m2z39.

[20] This process is discussed in more detail later in Chapter 3.

[21] Ron Suskind, *The One Percent Doctrine: Deep Inside America's Pursuit of Its Enemies since 9/11* (New York: Simon & Schuster, 2006), p. 14.

and avoiding what one US Treasury official referred to as 'paralysis by analysis' by getting too bogged down in the legal details of individual cases.[22] In the aftermath of 9/11, moreover, governments needed to show demonstrable results. And terrorism listing enabled precisely that. In what was dubbed the 'Rose Garden strategy', the White House held press conferences every two weeks to announce new listings and show the counterterrorism progress it was making. This strategy prioritised 'speed of designation, number of designations and amount of money blocked', not preparing strong evidence to justify the listings.[23] 'It was almost comical', said former US Treasury General Counsel David Aufhauser, 'we just listed out as many of the usual suspects as we could and said. "Let's go freeze some of their assets"'.[24] Scores of people (mostly Tunisians and Algerians) were hastily added to the UN list without scrutiny or debate. As Thomas Biersteker put it, the political mood was one of global sympathy and blind trust: 'if the US wanted a designation made, so the logic went, it must have good reasons'.[25]

But for constitutional and human rights lawyers all of this was rather difficult to stomach. The ISIL and Al-Qaida list blatantly violates basic tenets of what most lawyers in the common law world understand to be due process, the rule of law and the protection of fundamental rights. One Canadian Federal Court judge likened the experience of listed persons to that of Josef K in Franz Kafka's novel *The Trial* who 'awakens one morning and, for reasons never revealed to him . . . is arrested and prosecuted for an unspecified crime'.[26] In its landmark *Kadi* decision in 2008 – arguably the most powerful rebuke of the Security Council's authority ever made by a regional court – the European Court of Justice (ECJ) tried to remedy these deficiencies by affirming that individuals have the right to be told the reasons why they are listed, and the EU must respect fundamental rights when implementing UN targeted sanctions.[27] As someone who has worked

---

[22] Zarate, *Treasury's War*, p. 36.

[23] Sue Eckert, 'The US regulatory approach to terrorist financing' in Thomas J. Biersteker and Sue E. Eckert (eds.), *Countering the Financing of Terrorism* (London: Routledge, 2008), p. 209.

[24] Cited in Ron Suskind, *The Price of Loyalty: George W. Bush, the White House and the Education of Paul O'Neill* (New York: Simon & Schuster, 2004), p. 193.

[25] Thomas J. Biersteker, 'Targeted sanctions and individual human rights' (2010) 65(1) *International Journal: Canada's Journal of Global Policy Analysis* 99, 102.

[26] *Abdelrazik v. Canada* (Foreign Affairs) 2009 FC 580, para. 53.

[27] Joined Cases C-402 & 415/05P, *Kadi and Al Barakaat International Foundation v. Council and Commission* [2008] ECR I-6351. The *Kadi* litigation is referred to extensively throughout this book and discussed in detail in Chapter 3.

QDi.138 Name: 1: SAID 2: BEN ABDELHAKIM 3: BEN OMAR 4: AL-CHERIF
Name (original script): سعيد بن عبد الحكيم بن عمر الشريف
Title: na **Designation:** na **DOB:** 25 Jan. 1970 **POB:** Manzil Tmim, Tunisia **Good quality a.k.a.: a)** Cherif Said born 25 Jan. 1970 in Tunisia **b)** Binharnoda Hokri born 25 Jan. 1970 in Sosa, Tunisia **c)** Hcrif Ataf born 25 Jan. 1971 in Solisse, Tunisia **d)** Bin Homoda Chokri born 25 Jan. 1970 in Tunis, Tunisia **e)** Atef Cherif born 12 Dec. 1973 in Algeria **f)** Sherif Ataf born 12 Dec. 1973 in Aras, Algeria **g)** Ataf Cherif Said born 12 Dec. 1973 in Tunis, Tunisia **h)** Cherif Said born 25 Jan. 1970 in Tunis, Tunisia **i)** Cherif Said born 12 Dec. 1973 in Algeria **Low quality a.k.a.: a)** Djallal **b)** Youcef **c)** Abou Salman **d)** Said Tmimi **Nationality:** Tunisia **Passport no:** Tunisia M307968, issued on 8 Sep. 2001 (expired on 7 Sep. 2006) **National identification no:** na **Address:** Corso Lodi 59, Milan, Italy **Listed on:** 12 Nov. 2003 (amended on 20 Dec. 2005, 21 Dec. 2007, 30 Jan. 2009, 16 May 2011) **Other information:** Mother's name is Radhiyah Makki. Sentenced to eight years and ten months of imprisonment for membership of a terrorist association by the Appeal Court of Milan, Italy, on 7 Feb. 2008. Sentence confirmed by the Italian Supreme Court on 15 Jan. 2009, which became definitive as of Feb. 2008. Subject to expulsion from Italy to Tunisia after serving the sentence. Review pursuant to Security Council resolution 1822 (2008) was concluded on 6 May 2010. INTERPOL-UN Security Council Special Notice web link: https://www.interpol.int/en/How-we-work/Notices/View-UN-Notices-Individuals click here

QDi.231 Name: 1: SALEM 2: NOR ELDIN 3: AMOHAMED 4: AL-DABSKI
Name (original script): سالم نور الدين امحمد الدبيسكي
Title: na **Designation:** na **DOB:** 1963 **POB:** Tripoli, Libya **Good quality a.k.a.: a)** Abu Al-Ward **b)** Abdullah Ragab **Low quality a.k.a.: a)** Abu Naim **b)** Abdallah al- Masri **Nationality:** Libya **Passport no: a)** Libya number 1990/345751 **b)** Libya number 345751 **National identification no:** national identification 220334 **Address:** Bab Ben Ghasheer, Tripoli, Libyan Arab Jamahiriya **Listed on:** 8 Jun. 2007 (amended on 13 Dec. 2011, 1 May 2019) **Other information:** Mother's name is Kalthoum Abdul Salam al-Shaftari. Senior member of Libyan Islamic Fighting Group (QDe.011) and member of Al-Qaida (QDe.004). Review pursuant to Security Council resolution 1822 (2008) was concluded on 24 Nov. 2009. Review pursuant to Security Council resolution 2253 (2015) was concluded on 21 Feb. 2019. INTERPOL-UN Security Council Special Notice web link: https://www.interpol.int/en/How-we-work/Notices/View-UN-Notices-Individuals click here

QDi.278 Name: 1: MUTHANNA 2: HARITH 3: AL-DARI 4: na
Name (original script): مثنى حارث الضاري
Title: Doctor **Designation:** na **DOB:** 16 Jun. 1969 **POB:** Iraq **Good quality a.k.a.: a)** Dr. Muthanna Al Dari **b)** Muthanna Harith Al Dari **c)** Muthanna Harith Sulayman Al-Dari **d)** Muthanna Harith Sulayman Al-Dhari **e)** Muthanna Hareth Al-Dhari **f)** Muthana Haris Al-Dhari **g)** Doctor Muthanna Harith Sulayman Al Dari Al-Zawba' **h)** Muthanna Harith Sulayman Al-Dari Al-Zobai **i)** Muthanna Harith Sulayman Al-Dari al-Zawba'i **j)** Muthanna Hareth al-Dari **k)** Muthana Haris al-Dari **l)** Doctor Muthanna al-Dari **m)** Dr. Muthanna Harith al-Dari al-Zowbai **Low quality a.k.a.:** na **Nationality:** Iraq **Passport no:** na **National identification no:** Ration card number: 1729765 **Address: a)** Amman, Jordan **b)** Khan Dari, Iraq (previous) **c)** Asas Village, Abu Ghurayb, Iraq (previous) **d)** Egypt (previous) **Listed on:** 25 Mar. 2010 (amended on 10 Dec. 2015) **Other information:** Mother's name: Heba Khamis Dari. Provided operational guidance financial support and other services to or in support of Islamic State in Iraq and the Levant, listed as Al-Qaida in Iraq (AQI) (QDe.115). Involved in oil smuggling. Wanted by the Iraqi security forces. Photo available for inclusion in the INTERPOL-UN Security Council Special Notice. INTERPOL-UN Security Council Special Notice web link: https://www.interpol.int/en/How-we-work/Notices/View-UN-Notices-Individuals click here

Figure 1.1 Excerpt from the UN1267 ISIL and Al-Qaida Sanctions List.© (2019) United Nations. Reprinted with permission from the United Nations.

before the English High Court of Justice and the UN1267 Office of the Ombudsperson I am acutely aware of their differences and the procedural protections that UN listed individuals don't have. And yet what became equally clear through my legal practice was that human rights discourse was unable to effectively speak to and challenge the novel form of global security law and governance that was emerging here.

Thinking about the list through the lens of human rights – as much of the legal literature on this issue does – allows us to see what it is not. It is not compatible, for example, with the right to fair trial and the right to effective remedy. But that still only shows us a very thin slither of what the Law of the List *is*. And it tells us little about how this novel form of preemptive security is reproduced and expanded into new domains, despite years of human rights litigation in the courts. 'Non-legality', as Fleur Johns reminds us, 'is more than the flip side or remainder of international legal work. Rather, non-legality is, in its own right, a central structuring device of international legal thought and work'.[28] That is, if we want to understand what this listing regime is and critique its modes of operation and administration of violence, we need to understand how it works as a global-ordering device; not just define it normatively and negatively in terms of what it lacks, but grasp it as what Michel Foucault calls a 'positive present' – a form of *productive power* analysed through the effects, practices, techniques and 'methods of subjugation that it instigates'.[29]

These were the experiences that provided the initial impetus for this study and give shape to its core research questions: how does the ISIL and Al-Qaida list work as a form of global security law and governance? What kind of global law is it, and how is it being made powerful? Existing accounts, as we discuss below, take the Security Council's authority for granted. How do the practices of global security listing enable that power to emerge, congeal and grow? How, in other words, is the global in global security law produced? Is the list altering national and international legal orders – if so, in what ways and with what effects? Does it inhabit the interstate and international legal system or depart from it, like other transnational governance regimes? And if it exits existing normative frames, what alternative frames might we use to describe it and understand the problems it poses? How is the global governance of transboundary problems like terrorist networks changing the role of expertise in international law and decision-making? And what can UN terrorism listing practices tell us about how law and collective security is transforming under conditions of globalisation?

The ISIL and Al-Qaida list isn't just a novel form of global law. It is also a weapon of preemptive warfare. Whilst the turn towards preemption and exceptional governance in contemporary security has been widely examined, the implications of this shift for legal practice are inadequately understood. So, this project also studies the ISIL and Al-Qaida list to understand what happens to legality when it gets tangled up with preemptive security logics and orientated towards the governance of uncertain future threats. How are preemptive security measures like the list

---

[28] Fleur Johns, *Non-Legality in International Law: Unruly Law* (Cambridge: Cambridge University Press, 2013), p. 11.

[29] Michel Foucault, *Power/Knowledge: Selected Interviews and Other Writings, 1972–1977* (New York: Pantheon, 1980), pp. 136, 96.

materially assembled, and what can this assemblage tell us about how law is changing in the face of unknown risks and threats? What legal and political tensions are created by using preemptive measures, and how are these problems negotiated or neutralised? How are exceptional governance techniques (like security listing) normalised, made durable and stretched through practice? And what can such practices tell us about the role of international law and organisations in creating and sustaining *global* states of emergency?

Having outlined the key questions that animate this study, this introductory chapter will now briefly highlight the main currents of scholarship on the ISIL and Al-Qaida listing regime. I focus on legal literature rather than sanctions scholarship in political science because my primary focus is on the politics of global security law, not improving economic statecraft or redesigning foreign policy tools to make them more effective. The chapter then outlines the analytical frameworks I use to study these problems and highlights the contributions to current debates that this book seeks to make. I then move to questions of method. I explain why this book studies global security law ethnographically, as a diverse array of knowledge practices and governance techniques assembled within and across multiple sites, rather than an abstract system of norms or Security Council decisions. I also critically reflect on my use of leaked material as an empirical resource and my own experiences as a lawyer working within the listing assemblage I am studying. This introductory chapter closes with a brief overview of the book's structure, outlining the key arguments developed in each chapter.

1.1 Four Walls of Scholarship

Given the relative novelty of this form of global security law and the conflicts it has created in the courts, a vast body of legal literature on the UN1267 sanctions regime has emerged. This scholarship is dominated by four key theoretical approaches to postnational law and governance: global constitutionalism, global legal pluralism, global administrative law and international regime theory.

Global constitutionalism suggests that governance beyond the state 'should be confined by a set of constitutional principles analogous to those developed in the national constitutional context'.[30] It seeks to

---

[30] Gráinne de Búrca, 'The European Court of Justice and the international legal order after *Kadi*' (2010) 51(1) *Harvard International Law Journal* 1, 40.

order the fragmentation of international law through *containment* via a constituent instrument (like the UN Charter) or through the *transfer* of core domestic constitutional principles such as the rule of law, separation of powers and human rights compliance.[31] There are at least three different strands of constitutionalist literature on this issue. *Strong constitutionalists* study the list from the apex of the international system (the UN) and stress the conventional hierarchy of legal rules in resolving disputes between normative orders.[32] *Soft constitutionalist* approaches are founded on the 'assumption of an international community', an 'emphasis on universalizability', and focus on 'common norms or principles of communication for addressing conflict' rather than the formal hierarchy of legal rules.[33] In this literature, regime conflicts between different legal orders (like the European Union (EU) and UN) can best be resolved through mutual interaction and a common commitment to shared normative principles (such as respect for the rule of law).[34] *Solange*-based approaches claim the deficiencies of this global listing regime ought to ultimately be resolved at the UN level.[35] But until sufficient procedural protections are put in place there, indirect review by national and regional courts – and the 'constitutional conversation' it stimulates – is both justified and necessary.[36]

---

[31] The notion of containment and transfer comes from: Nico Krisch, *Beyond Constitutionalism: The Pluralist Structure of Postnational Law* (Oxford: Oxford University Press, 2012), p. 15.

[32] Bardo Fassbender, 'Targeted sanctions and due process' (2006) 3(2) *International Organizations Law Review* 437; Christian Tomuschat, 'The *Kadi* case: what relationship is there between the universal legal order under the auspices of the United Nations and the EU legal order?' (2009) 28(1) *Yearbook of European Law* 654.

[33] De Búrca, 'The European Court of Justice', 42–3.

[34] See, for example: de Búrca, 'The European Court of Justice'; Erika De Wet, 'The role of European courts in the development of a hierarchy of norms within international law: evidence of constitutionalisation?' (2009) 5(2) *European Constitutional Law Review* 284; Turkuler Isiksel, 'Fundamental rights in the EU after *Kadi* and *Al Barakaat*' (2010) 16(5) *European Law Journal* 551; Armin von Bogdandy, 'Pluralism, direct effect and the ultimate say: on the relationship between international and domestic constitutional law' (2008) 6(3–4) *International Journal of Constitutional Law* 397, 398.

[35] This approach is modelled on the *Solange* jurisprudence of the German Federal Constitutional Court. In *Solange I* the court held it could review the constitutionality of EC law so long as EU institutions had not enacted a binding charter of rights consistent with the German Basic Law (*Grundgesetz*). In *Solange II* the court decided to no longer assert this competence because the ECJ provided a level of fundamental rights protection equivalent to the *Grundgesetz*. See BVerfG 29 May 1974, BVerfGE 37 at 271 (*Solange I*) and BVerfG 22 October 1986, BVerfGE 73 at 339 (*Solange II*).

[36] Juliane Kokott and Christoph Sobotta, 'The *Kadi* case: constitutional core values and international law – finding the balance?' (2012) 23(4) *European Journal of International Law* 1015.

Global legal pluralists take a rather different approach, rejecting the idea that the normative complexity of the global can be contained by a unified legal framework.[37] They stress 'the existence of a multiplicity of distinct and diverse normative systems', propose models for ordering global governance that stress 'the heterarchical interaction of the various layers of law', and highlight 'the likelihood of clashes of authority-claims and competition for primacy in specific contexts'.[38] So the *Kadi* case – where the EU courts indirectly reviewed global listing measures taken by the Security Council – is often celebrated as a paradigmatic example of global legal pluralism in action. *Constitutional pluralists* claim that, whilst the relation between different legal orders is properly horizontal, there is a common point of legal reference (or 'constitutional connective tissue')[39] through which conflicts can be resolved.[40] Here principles of harmonisation and practices of 'mutual embedded openness' are emphasised as means of achieving overall coherence.[41] *Systemic pluralists* take a more robust stance, by positing 'a pluralism that is positioned outside, and is to some extent opposed to, international law'.[42] They seek to move beyond the triad of domestic, regional and international law (by stressing the enmeshment of legal orders), and argue that it is politics (rather than any 'overarching, hierarchical frame') that determines the relationship between legal orders.[43]

---

[37] See, for example: Krisch, *Beyond Constitutionalism*; Paul Berman, 'Global legal pluralism' (2007) 80 *Southern California Law Review* 1155.

[38] De Búrca, 'The European Court of Justice', 38. Krisch, *Beyond Constitutionalism*, p. 23. For an overview of this literature, see: Ralf Michaels, 'Global legal pluralism' (2009) 5 *Annual Review of Law and Social Sciences* 243.

[39] Daniel Halberstam, 'LJIL Symposium vol 25–2: beyond constitutionalism? A comment by Daniel Halberstam'. Available at: bit.ly/1saeEHm.

[40] Ibid. See also: Krisch, *Beyond Constitutionalism*, p. 74; Opinion of Advocate General Maduro, Joined Cases C-402/05 P and C-415/05 P *Kadi and Al Barakaat v. Council of the European Union and Commission of the European Communities* (16 January 2008); Daniel Halberstam and Eric Stein, 'The United Nations, the European Union, and the King of Sweden: economic sanctions and individual rights in a plural world order' (2009) 46 *Common Market Law Review* 13; Cohen, *Globalization*.

[41] Halberstam, 'LJIL Symposium'. Constitutional pluralism and soft constitutionalism are therefore quite similar: de Búrca, 'The European Court of Justice', 39–40.

[42] André Nollkaemper, 'Inside or out: two types of international legal pluralism' in Jan Klabbers and Touko Piiparinen (eds.), *Normative Pluralism and International Law: Exploring Global Governance* (Cambridge: Cambridge University Press, 2013), p. 94.

[43] Krisch, *Beyond Constitutionalism*, p. 2. See also: Andreas Fischer-Lescano and Gunther Teubner, 'Regime-collisions: the vain search for legal unity in the fragmentation of global law' (2004) 25(4) *Michigan Journal of International Law* 999.

International regime theory starts from the observation that international law has fragmented into functional regimes 'such as "trade law", "human rights law", "environmental law" . . . that seek to "manage" global problems efficiently and empower new . . . forms of expertise'.[44] These legal regimes are akin to those defined in International Relations (IR) scholarship – as 'sets of implicit, or explicit principles, norms, rules and decision-making procedures around which actors' expectations converge in a given area of international relations' – but can be distinguished insofar as they are anchored to specific problems of international law and normative conflict.[45] Because of the functional nature of regimes, regime theorists tend to be preoccupied with instrumental concerns – such as improving the implementation of sanctions and finding flexible solutions to listing problems to ensure 'smooth functioning' and optimal regime coordination.[46] The protection of fundamental rights of listed persons by the courts – and their refusal to play the flexible game of regime coordination – for example, has been dismissed by regime theory proponents as a counterproductive assertion of 'peripheral hegemony'.[47]

The Global Administrative Law (GAL) movement picks up from where international regime theory leaves off, but with a more implicit constitutionalist twist. It seeks to repurpose domestic administrative principles for use at the global level to attend to the legitimacy and accountability concerns that come with fragmentation and functional differentiation of international law. The assumption is that 'much of global governance can [now] be understood as regulation and administration' unfolding in a 'global administrative space' where 'the strict

---

[44] Koskenniemi, *The Politics*, p. 331.

[45] Stephen Krasner, 'Structural causes and regime consequences: regimes as intervening variables' in Stephen Krasner (ed.), *International Regimes* (Ithaca NY: Cornell University Press, 1983), pp. 1, 3.

[46] Devika Hovell, *The Power of Process: The Value of Due Process in Security Council Sanctions Decision-Making* (Oxford: Oxford University Press, 2016). See also the various reports of the Watson Institute on Targeted Sanctions, discussed at length in Chapter 3, and the approach adopted by the High-Level Review of UN Sanctions, available at: bit.ly/2aownY2. For a critique, see: Alejandro Rodiles, 'The design of UN sanctions through the interplay with informal arrangements' in Larissa van den Herik (ed.), *Research Handbook on UN Sanctions and International Law* (Cheltenham: Edward Elgar Publishing, 2017). The quote on 'smooth functioning' comes from: Martti Koskenniemi, 'Hegemonic regimes' in Margaret A. Young (ed.), *Regime Interaction in International Law: Facing Fragmentation* (Cambridge: Cambridge University Press, 2012), p. 305.

[47] Larissa van den Herik, 'Peripheral hegemony in the quest to ensure Security Council accountability for its individualized UN Sanctions regimes' (2014) 19(3) *Journal of Conflict and Security Law* 427.

dichotomy between domestic and international has largely broken down'.[48] International Organisations (IOs), transnational regulatory authorities and novel 'hybrid public–private organizations' are exercising powers that are outside of the control of domestic legal systems and international treaty-based regimes.[49] Yet, according to GAL advocates, domestic administrative principles – such as 'principles of transparency, participation, reasoned decision-making and review in global governance' – are being used to bring procedural fairness and accountability to global governance.[50] From the World Trade Organization (WTO) Dispute Settlement Mechanism and World Bank Inspection Panel to the Basel Committee for Banking Supervision, GAL advocates argue that this 'embryonic field' of law needs to be both nurtured and studied. This approach therefore takes a rather optimistic 'better-than-nothing' approach to managing the problems of the list, getting behind the UN1267 Office of the Ombudsperson, for example, as a nascent form of GAL accountability in action.[51]

These four walls mark out the main discursive space in which the ISIL and Al-Qaida list is usually framed. Whilst they provide important insights into this global regime, they also carry analytical baggage that restrict us from addressing the key problems underpinning this book.

---

[48] Nico Krisch and Benedict Kingsbury, 'Introduction: global governance and global administrative law in the international legal order' (2006) 17(1) *European Journal of International Law* 1, 1.

[49] Benedict Kingsbury, Nico Krisch and Richard B. Stewart, 'The emergence of global administrative law' (2005) 68 (3/4) *Law and Contemporary Problems* 15, 16. For a good introduction to the GAL literature, see: Sabino Cassese, *Research Handbook on Global Administrative Law* (Cheltenham: Edward Elgar Publishing, 2016). See also: Benedict Kingsbury, 'The concept of "law" in global administrative law' (2009) 20(1) *European Journal of International Law* 23; Benedict Kingsbury and Lorenzo Casini, 'Global administrative law dimensions of international organizations law' (2009) 6(2) *International Organizations Law Review* 319; Michael S. Barr and Geoffrey P. Miller, 'Global administrative law: the view from Basel' (2006) 17(1) *European Journal of International Law* 15; Carol Harlow, 'Global administrative law: the quest for principles and values' (2006) 17(1) *European Journal of International Law* 187; Simon Chesterman, 'Globalization rules: accountability, power, and the prospects for global administrative law' (2008) 14(1) *Global Governance: A Review of Multilateralism and International Organizations* 39; Richard Stewart, 'Remedying disregard in global regulatory governance: accountability, participation, and responsiveness' (2014) 108(2) *American Journal of International Law* 211.

[50] Krisch and Kingsbury, 'Introduction', 2.

[51] The relationship between the GAL and the UN1267 Office of the Ombudsperson is explored in more detail in Chapter 3.

Legal regime discourse, for example, privileges the idioms of expertise that proliferate and become hegemonic through international legal fragmentation.[52] Its focus on technical problem-solving embeds a managerial approach to legal conflict as something self-evidently normal. Whilst it might be useful to talk about the 'effectiveness of sanctions' when interviewing officials and experts engaged in the daily work of list administration, this is a framework that takes the list for granted and obscures its underlying politics. It ignores, in other words, 'how particular normative biases and preferences come to be embedded within an international regime at any particular point in its historical trajectory' and misses 'the processes by which these normative biases are sustained'.[53] Because this book seeks to understand how preemptive security logics are transforming global legal practices, this displacement is analytically problematic. When studying international legal conflict, as Martti Koskenniemi observes, 'managerialism is not a solution. It is a problem'. It 'thinks of itself as a hill from which it is possible to see far. In truth it is a valley in which we always look in the same direction – and all the interesting questions lie behind our back.'[54]

Whilst the GAL literature identifies crucial shifts taking place in national and international law, it also brings an implicit teleology of global legal progress that sees experiments in global accountability as incremental 'steps in the right direction'.[55] The key problem with this prefiguration narrative, as David Kennedy argues, is that 'when partial efforts are seen as down payments on a better future, defects in current practice seem tolerable'.[56] As shown in Chapter 3, this makes critically analysing the governance effects and knowledge games of the UN1267 Office of the Ombudsperson difficult. In their eagerness to find empirical examples confirming the validity of their theory, GAL advocates gloss over real conflicts conditioning the emergence of global administration and so run the risk of missing the politics of what is at stake. And 'as they lead into specific proposals' for nurturing and improving nascent GAL

---

[52] This criticism is forcefully developed by Martti Koskenniemi: Koskenniemi, *The Politics*, pp. 63–75, 331–61. See also: Young, *Regime Interaction*.

[53] Andrew Lang, 'Legal regimes and professional knowledges: the internal politics of regime definition' in: Young, *Regime Interaction*, p. 113.

[54] Koskenniemi, 'Hegemonic regimes', p. 324.

[55] This argument is elaborated and developed in more detail in Chapter 3.

[56] David Kennedy, *A World of Struggle: How Power Law and Expertise Shape Global Political Economy* (Princeton NJ: Princeton University Press, 2016), p. 100.

efforts, as some scholars have done, 'they become part of those struggles themselves'.[57]

The key problem with both constitutionalist and pluralist accounts is that they almost exclusively focus on legal reasoning in the courts or authoritative legal texts as the privileged sites for studying the Law of the List. Most legal literature on this issue, for example, is concerned with debating the significance of the *Kadi* case and preoccupied with establishing whether the EU courts got the answers to the norm conflicts posed there 'right' or 'wrong'. These arguments are not unimportant. But they tell us little about how this novel domain of global security law is shaped and sustained in practice. Charting global law through the optic of 'high-profile cases' – like telling world histories through the figures of powerful individuals – obscures more than it reveals. As legal anthropologist Marc Galanter suggests, 'law is to be found in the courtroom no more than health is to be found in the hospital'.[58] When legal texts and courts are privileged as authoritative containers of the law, other crucial sites where legal governance is formed and put into circulation are taken out of view. Even systemically pluralist accounts, which claim to foreground 'the political', have been criticised as too 'court-centric' and 'narrow' for excluding 'transgovernmental networks, private economic actors, non-governmental activists, and legal and other professionals' from global lawmaking processes.[59] It is widely accepted that international law is much more than formal norms.[60] Yet informal norm-making in the global security domain is still dramatically understudied and in need of mapping.[61]

Grasping the Law of the List requires being attentive to the shifting sociolegal terrain in which it is being formed. This means 'following the

---

[57] Koskenniemi, 'Hegemonic regimes', p. 321.

[58] Marc Galanter, 'Justice in many rooms: courts, private ordering and indigenous law' (1981) 13(19) *Journal of Legal Pluralism and Unofficial Law* 1, cited in Desmond Manderson, 'Beyond the provincial: space, aesthetics and modernist legal theory' (1995–6) 20 *Melbourne University Law Review* 1049.

[59] Gregory Shaffer, 'A transnational take on Krisch's pluralist structure of postnational law' (2012) 23(2) *European Journal of International Law* 565, 577.

[60] Joost Pauwelyn, Ramses Wessel and Jan Wouters (eds.), *Informal International Lawmaking* (Oxford: Oxford University Press, 2012).

[61] UN Special Rapporteur on the promotion and protection of human rights and fundamental freedoms while countering terrorism, 'Call for submissions: "soft law" and informal lawmaking in the global counter-terrorism architecture: assessing implications on the promotion and protection of human rights and fundamental freedoms'. Available at: bit.ly/2WYrNTb.

list' beyond the confines of texts and courts and examining *how* it is being materially reproduced through a plurality of governance techniques and knowledge practices. If globalisation is indeed decentring the foundational coordinates of law and putting them into motion, then different conceptual approaches – that are less static and reductionist and more empirical and dynamic – must be developed if we are to chart the emergent architecture of global security law and this listing regime.[62] To that end, this book makes three distinct analytical moves.

1.2   Studying Global Security Law in Motion

1.2.1   Global Legal Assemblage

First, I develop a framework of global legal assemblage to analyse the ISIL and Al-Qaida listing regime and its effects. I do so because conventional macro-accounts of the list – focusing on the interests of the Security Council and the legal reasoning of the courts – only reveal a small part of this preemptive security governance story. The concept of assemblage has been widely used as an analytical frame across the humanities and social sciences to understand complex and dynamic formations.[63] It stems from the philosophy of Gilles Deleuze and Felix Guattari, who use it to describe the symbiotic co-functioning of heterogeneous elements across different domains

---

[62] On globalisation decentring legal foundations, see: Neil Walker, 'Out of place and out of time: law's fading co-ordinates', Working Paper No. 2009/01 (Edinburgh: University of Edinburgh School of Law); and Mireille Delmas-Marty, *Ordering Pluralism: A Conceptual Framework for Understanding the Transnational Legal World* (Oxford: Hart Publishing, 2009). On shifting from static to dynamic analyses, see Mariana Valverde, *Chronotopes of Law: Jurisdiction, Scale and Governance* (London: Routledge, 2015), p. 1.

[63] See: Saskia Sassen, *Territory, Authority, Rights: From Medieval to Global Assemblages* (Princeton NJ: Princeton University Press, 2006); Jane Bennett, *Vibrant Matter: A Political Ecology of Things* (Durham NC: Duke University Press, 2010); Rita Abrahamsen and Michael Williams, *Security beyond the State: Private Security in International Politics* (Cambridge: Cambridge University Press, 2011); Michele Acuto and Simon Curtis (eds.), *Reassembling International Theory: Assemblage Thinking and International Relations* (Basingstoke: Palgrave Pivot, 2013); Marieke de Goede, *Speculative Security: The Politics of Pursuing Terrorist Monies* (Minneapolis MN: University of Minnesota Press, 2012); Heather McKeen-Edwards and Tony Porter, *Transnational Financial Associations and the Governance of Global Finance: Assembling Wealth and Power* (London: Routledge, 2013); Aihwa Ong and Stephen J. Collier (eds.), *Global Assemblages: Technology, Politics, and Ethics as Anthropological Problems* (Oxford: Wiley-Blackwell, 2004); Christian Bueger, 'Territory, authority, expertise: global governance and the counter-piracy assemblage' (2018) 24(3) *European Journal of International Relations* 614.

'linked together to form a whole'.[64] For Deleuze, 'the essential thing, from the point of view of empiricism, is the noun *multiplicity*, which designates ... lines or dimensions which are irreducible to each other. Every "thing" is made up in this way ... Things are never unities or totalities, but *multiplicities*.'[65] Assemblages are ensembles of multiple, emergent relations clustered to produce effects. They are held together through the alignment of 'heterogeneous elements including material substances, technologies, discourses and practices', and they give rise to distinct social and political formations and forms of ordering.[66]

This idea of assemblage, as the forging of connections between heterogeneous elements, is closely related to what Science and Technology Studies (STS) scholars call an 'actor-network' – that is, the sociotechnical chains of material-semiotic relations and agents that are aligned and stabilised to produce particular forms of organisation and knowledge across different fields of practice. For Bruno Latour, for example, the social 'is not a homogeneous thing ... [but] a trail of associations between heterogeneous elements' and is 'visible only by the traces it leaves ... when a new association is being produced between elements which themselves are in no way "social"' – that is, the social sphere is organised as assemblages of relations.[67] It is the forging of these associations and scale-producing practices that determines whether actors can become relatively powerful and that produces political formations: 'no actor is bigger than any other except by means of a transaction (a translation) which must be [empirically] examined'.[68] Reframed through this lens, the key research task becomes one of 'following the actors' and

---

[64] Gilles Deleuze and Felix Guattari, *A Thousand Plateaus: Capitalism and Schizophrenia* (Minneapolis MN: University of Minnesota Press, 1987), p. 406. Martin Müller, 'Assemblages and actor-networks: rethinking socio-material power, politics and space' (2015) 9(1) *Geography Compass* 27, 28.

[65] Gilles Deleuze and Claire Parnet, *Dialogues* (London: The Athlone Press, 1987), p. vii (original emphasis).

[66] Tania Murray Li, 'What is land? Assembling a resource for global investment' (2014) 39(4) *Transactions of the Institute of British Geographers* 589; John Law, *Ordering and Obduracy* (Lancaster: Lancaster University Centre for Science Studies, 2001).

[67] Bruno Latour, *Reassembling the Social: An Introduction to Actor-Network Theory* (Oxford: Oxford University Press, 2005), pp. 5, 8.

[68] Michel Callon and Bruno Latour, 'Unscrewing the big Leviathan: how actors macrostructure reality and how sociologists help them to do so' in Aaron Victor Cicourel and Karin Knorr-Cetina (eds.), *Advances in Social Theory and Methodology: Toward an Integration of Micro and Macro-Sociologies* (London: Routledge & Kegan Paul, 1981) pp. 277, 280–281.

performing a 'sociology of associations'.[69] As John Law explains: 'realities, objects, subjects, materials, and meanings, whatever form they take, these are all explored as an effect of the relations that are assembling and doing them'.[70]

Both of these approaches to the assemblage are deployed interchangeably throughout this book. But because I am primarily concerned with understanding the dynamics of global security law and governance – rather than with philosophy or the conditions of scientific knowledge production – I take the concept in a more explicitly sociolegal direction. I deploy the framework *strategically* – cherry-picking from different assemblage approaches and plugging them into the problems I am examining to generate ideas about the conditions of global legal production. My aim is to carve out a space, beyond the four walls of mainstream scholarship discussed above, to chart how this novel form of global preemptive security governance is created, configured and stretched through practice.

The concept of assemblage brings three analytical advantages to that task, and to the study of global legal problems more generally. First, it decentres the law and prompts 'an expansion of the dimensions of legality'.[71] It does not perpetuate the positivist fiction that law is a bounded system of abstract norms that one knows through legal doctrine and application of legal theory. Nor does it start from the idea of a coherent body of law and ask how it is applied in different social contexts or accommodated by courts to expose the gap between 'law in the books' and 'law in action'.[72] The concept of legal assemblage starts from the more far-reaching claim that global law exists as 'a practical and a contingent achievement'.[73] And it reorientates analyses towards the diverse array of techniques, knowledge practices, forms of expertise, rationalities, authority claims and dynamics that conflict and cohere to make that achievement possible. As Nikolas Rose and Mariana Valverde

---

[69] Bruno Latour, *Science in Action: How to Follow Scientists and Engineers through Society* (Cambridge MA: Harvard University Press, 1987).

[70] John Law, 'Collateral realities' in Fernando Dominguez Rubio and Patrick Baert (eds.), *The Politics of Knowledge* (London: Routledge, 2012), p. 157.

[71] Sally Engle Merry, 'New legal realism and the ethnography of transnational law' (2006) 31(4) *Law and Social Inquiry* 976.

[72] This division has long been the mainstay of law and society research. On the need to rethink this approach in the light of globalisation, see: Eve Darian-Smith, *Laws and Societies in Global Contexts: Contemporary Approaches* (Cambridge: Cambridge University Press, 2013), pp. 1–21.

[73] Andrew Barry, *Material Politics: Disputes Along the Pipeline* (Oxford: Blackwell Publishing, 2013), p. 183.

point out, 'there is no such thing as "The Law". Law as a unified phenomenon governed by certain general principles is a fiction.'[74] Instead what we have are various 'legal complexes – ill-defined, un-coordinated and often decentralized sets of networks, institutions . . . texts and relations of power and of knowledge'.[75] Law, in other words, can be better understood as the relational effect of legal assemblages. This analytical shift transforms global legal research into a more empirical inquiry: one less concerned with grand theorisations of what global law is or transfixed with the 'solid authority' of international organisations[76] and more engaged with novel 'projects of governance' and particular arrangements of legal techniques and practices that are emergent and historically situated.[77]

Second, the concept of assemblage is valuable because it foregrounds *practices* of assemblage. It animates a conception of legal agency as a distributed capacity rather than a powerful thing that powerful actors hold and wield. Most listing literature posits the UN Security Council as the primary institutional actor perched on top of the international legal order, pulling the strings of this global regime. An assemblage approach doesn't deny the power of the collective security system so much as analyse the material conditions of its production, highlighting 'the hard work required to draw heterogeneous elements together, forge connections between them and sustain these connections in the face of tension'.[78] Anthropologist Tania Murray Li grounds this conceptual approach around six crucial assemblage practices that, she argues, usually go unnoticed in studies of governance:

> 1) *Forging alignments*: the work of linking together the objectives of the various parties to an assemblage . . . 2) *Rendering technical*: extracting

---

[74] Nikolas Rose and Mariana Valverde, 'Governed by law?' (1998) 7(4) *Social and Legal Studies* 541, 545.

[75] Mariana Valverde, *Law's Dream of a Common Knowledge* (Princeton NJ: Princeton University Press, 2003), p. 10.

[76] Nico Krisch, 'The structure of postnational authority' (SSRN 2564579, 2015).

[77] Mariana Valverde, '"Despotism" and Ethical Liberal Governance' (1996) 25(3) *Economy and Society* 357, 358. For a fascinating account of assemblage thinking and international organisations, see: Guy Fiti Sinclair, *To Reform the World: International Organisations and the Making of Modern States* (Oxford: Oxford University Press, 2017). For an excellent review of this text, see: Dimitri Van Den Meerssche, 'Scholars in self-estrangement (again): rethinking the law of international organisations' (2017) 5(3) *London Review of International Law* 455.

[78] Tania Murray Li, 'Practices of assemblage and community forest management' (2007) 36(2) *Economy and Society* 263, 264.

from the messiness of the social world ... a set of relations that can be formulated as a diagram in which problem (a) plus intervention (b) will produce (c), a beneficial result. 3) *Authorizing knowledge*: specifying the requisite body of knowledge; confirming enabling assumptions; containing critiques. 4) *Managing failures and contradictions*: presenting failure as the outcome of rectifiable deficiencies; smoothing out contradictions so that they seem superficial rather than fundamental; devising compromises. 5) *Anti-politics*: reposing political questions as matters of technique; closing down debate about how and what to govern ... by reference to expertise ... 6) *Reassembling*: grafting on new elements and reworking old ones [and] deploying existing discourses to new ends.[79]

These practices may seem peripheral to the more important task of understanding international counterterrorism law. But, as this book shows, it is precisely through such seemingly mundane practices, associations and forms of expertise that global security law is being made operative, powerful and global. I argue that it is these kinds of assemblage practices that provide the glue that holds the Law of the List together. This is what it means to analytically repose global law as a contingent achievement and permanent work-in-progress: what pragmatic techniques and governance devices are being crafted and used to resolve practical problems of list administration? And how do these practices and devices shape the listing assemblage in turn? How are the preemptive security logics animating the Law of the List reconciled (or not) with rule of law principles at different sites across the assemblage, and with what effects? What new discursive claims, knowledge practices and deferrals to the authority of expertise are being forged through good faith efforts to ameliorate or smooth over the legal or political conflicts that are stimulated by this list?

As shown throughout this book, global security law and governance is assembled through such practices of problematisation and the forms of problem management and intervention they give rise to.[80] By highlighting 'the situated subjects who do the work of pulling together disparate elements without attributing to them a master-mind or a totalizing plan',

---

[79] Ibid. 265.

[80] The causal link drawn here between problematisation and governmentality is from Michel Foucault and will be discussed in more detail in Chapter 2. See also: Tania Murray Li, *The Will to Improve: Governmentality, Development and the Practice of Politics* (Durham NC: Duke University Press, 2007), p. 7; Nikolas Rose, *Powers of Freedom: Reframing Political Thought* (Cambridge: Cambridge University Press, 1999), p. 20; Rose and Valverde, 'Governed by law?', 546; Kennedy, *A World of Struggle*, pp. 98–100.

the assemblage allows for a more diffuse conception of legal agency to be deployed.[81] This helps us understand how diverse practices – operating under the radar of formal law in response to particular problems of the list – can translate into new forms of global security law on the ground. And by eschewing *a priori* assumptions about what can or cannot be associated together (humans, texts, institutions, objects, technologies) to 'act' in any given actor-network, an assemblage framework allows us to examine what role the list itself plays in configuring the domain of global terrorism it purports to merely represent or target.[82]

Finally, the concept of assemblage enables us to approach questions of scale in more dynamic and nuanced ways. Most legal literature on the list assumes as given that domestic, regional (EU) and international law governance scales are arranged into a formal hierarchy of nested jurisdictions. That is, they implicitly spatialise global law as something big and 'up above', using what James Ferguson and Akhil Gupta refer to as logics of 'verticality' and 'encompassment'.[83] Because each scale is thought to absorb the other as one ascends up the international normative pyramid, domestic, regional and global jurisdictions end up locked in a zero-sum game – where more of one is usually taken to mean less of the other. The key problem with such accounts is that they miss how these supposedly stable structures are themselves undergoing change as they are interconnected in novel ways through the emergence of global security regimes like the ISIL and Al-Qaida list – that is, they take governance scales for granted. As shown in Chapter 3, for example, when the Security Council starts directly targeting specific individuals through targeted sanctions, international and national scales of governance become 'enmeshed' giving rise to a plethora of new problems and conflicts. And as Chapter 2 shows, when subnational security experts are enrolled through the list into new preemptive security networks that enable them to effectively

---

[81] Murray Li, 'Practices of assemblage', 265.

[82] According to the principle of 'generalised symmetry' proposed in ANT, anything that produces effects within an actor-network is deemed an actor or, as it termed, an 'actant'. See, for example: Bruno Latour, *The Making of Law: An Ethnography of the Conseil d'État* (Bristol: Polity Press, 2010); John Law, 'Notes on the theory of the actor-network: ordering, strategy, and heterogeneity' (1992) 5(4) *Systems Practice* 379; Michel Callon, 'Some elements of a sociology of translation: domestication of the scallops and the fisherman of St-Brieuc Bay' in John Law (ed.), *Power, Action and Belief: A New Sociology of Knowledge?* (London: Routledge & Kegan Paul, 1986). The idea of the list as actant is explored in Chapter 2.

[83] James Ferguson and Akhil Gupta, 'Spatializing states: toward an ethnography of neoliberal governmentality' (2002) 29(4) *American Ethnologist* 981.

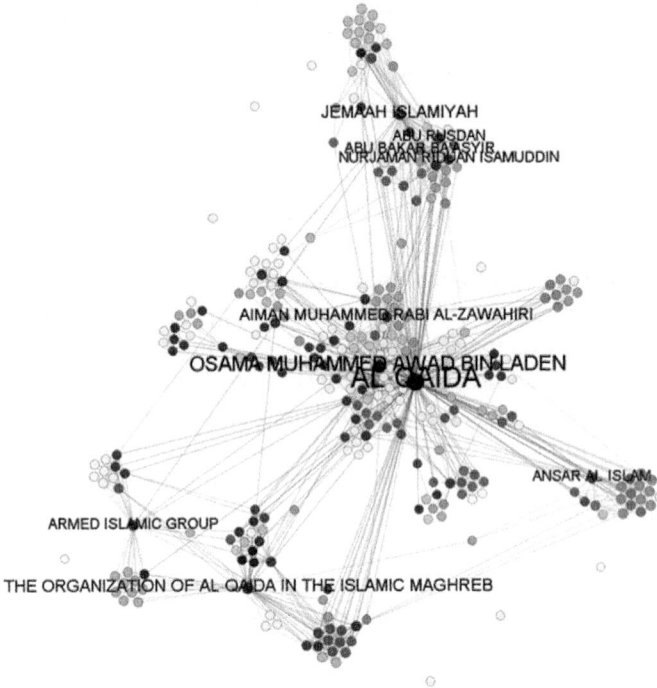

Figure 1.2   Social Network Map of Al-Qaida according to the UN1267 list entries, from:Eric Stollenwerk, Thomas Dörfler and Julian Schibberges, 'Taking a new perspective: mapping the Al Qaeda network through the eyes of the UN Security Council' (2016) 28(5) *Terrorism and Political Violence* 950. Reprinted with permission from Taylor and Francis Ltd. (www.tandfonline.com).

produce global law, we start moving into terrain that is difficult to explain using the conventional toolkit and discourse of international law.

An assemblage framework can help us make sense of these emergent topologies of governance because it is more dynamic in scope and better attuned to problems of scalar complexity. Rather than presupposing an international hierarchy that is immaterial and exists in the aether of abstract norms, it starts from the position that global processes are generating spatiotemporal dynamics and jurisdictional practices that are rearranging how governance works and making legal ordering more porous and heterogeneous. In Saskia Sassen's account, for example, globalisation is marked by the emergence of novel assemblages composed of bits of territory, authority and rights previously part of the nation-state form that have been 'reassembled' into new transboundary domains.[84] Whilst these assemblages 'continue to inhabit national institutional and territorial settings', they 'are no longer part of the national as historically constructed'.[85] They also sit uneasily with the international system of multilateral treaties and governance by supranational organisations. Instead, for Sassen assemblages are best thought of as 'inchoate geographies [for] a new type of ordering, a reality in the making'. Diverse elements from different scales are rearranged together in new ways to produce global effects. The assemblage lens allows us to be especially attentive to these novel reorderings.

In an assemblage framework, therefore, scales are not something preordained but are produced through particular scale-producing practices. As I discuss in detail below, a key insight that I draw from assemblage thinking is that powerful global structures are produced from local structure-making sites, often through relatively fragile alignments of knowledge practices, infrastructures, techniques and relations.[86] This transforms the creation of governance scales into an empirical problem to be examined 'through tracing connections and breaks'.[87] This is one area where this book on global security law departs from most other global law texts. Because lawyers divide the world in jurisdictional terms, nested scales of governance tend to be taken for granted. But when 'the global' is no longer an a priori assumption but a research problem demanding site-specific investigation, we can get a much more textured, relational and dynamic account of global security law in motion.

1.2.2   Preemptive Security As Governmentality

The second analytical move this book makes is to study risk and preemption as practices of governmentality. As discussed above, the ISIL and Al-Qaida list is a preemptive security device – listed individuals are not targeted for acts they have done, but for things that they might do in the future. Preemptive security measures intervening to counter potential future threats have been at the forefront of the global war against

---

[84] Saskia Sassen, 'Neither global nor national: novel assemblages of territory, authority and rights' (2008) 1(1–2) *Ethics and Global Politics* 61; Sassen, *Territory, Authority, Rights*.

[85] Sassen, 'Neither global nor national', 61.

[86] The key reference here is Bruno Latour, including his earlier collaborative work with Michel Callon. See: Latour, *Reassembling the Social*; Callon and Latour, 'Unscrewing the big Leviathan'. See also: Saskia Sassen, *The Global City: New York, London, Tokyo* (Princeton NJ: Princeton University Press, 2001); Sassen, *Territory, Authority, Rights*.

[87] Müller, 'Assemblages and actor-networks', 35.

terrorism and have stimulated considerable debate amongst scholars and jurists.[88] From targeted killing and preventative detention to control orders and mass surveillance, since 9/11 the focus of states and IOs has been on risk-based techniques of 'disruption, restriction and incapacitation'.[89] With counterterrorism, the assumption is that 'if we wait for threats to fully materialize we will have waited too long'.[90] Early intervention on the basis of uncertain knowledge is now the new norm.

This turn towards risk and preemption – and the challenges it poses to the functioning of liberal democracies and the rule of law – is often portrayed in grandiose and epoch-defining terms across different academic disciplines. According to sociologist Ulrich Beck, the low probability–high consequence risks that we currently face (such as terrorism, nuclear contamination and climate change) are so unpredictable and incalculable that they exceed the logics of control and claims to scientific certainty that defined risk management in earlier times.[91] For Beck, 'the hidden central issue in world risk society is how to feign control over the uncontrollable – in politics, law, science, technology, economy and everyday life'.[92] Law thus becomes an ideological construct concealing

---

[88] See, for example: International Commission of Jurists, *Assessing the Damage, Urging Action: Report of the Eminent Jurists Panel on Terrorism, Counter-Terrorism and Human Rights* (Geneva: ICJ, 2009) 91; Bruce Ackerman, *Before the Next Attack: Preserving Civil Liberties in an Age of Terrorism* (New Haven CT: Yale University Press, 2006); David Cole and Jules Lobel, *Less Safe, Less Free: Why America Is Losing the War on Terror* (New York: New Press, 2007); David Dyzenhaus, *The Constitution of Law: Legality in a Time of Emergency* (Cambridge: Cambridge University Press, 2006); Benjamin J. Goold and Liora Lazarus (eds.), *Security and Human rights* (London: Bloomsbury Publishing, 2007); Oliver Kessler and Wouter Werner, 'Extrajudicial killing as risk management' (2008) 39(2–3) *Security Dialogue* 289; Marieke de Goede, 'The politics of preemption and the war on terror in Europe' (2008) 14(1) *European Journal of International Relations* 161; Louise Amoore, 'Risk before justice: when law contests its own suspension' (2008) 21(4) *Leiden Journal of International Law* 847; Didier Bigo, Sergio Carrera, Elspeth Guild and Rob Walker, 'The changing landscape of European liberty and security: the mid-term report of the CHALLENGE project' (2008) 59(192) *International Social Science Journal* 283; Valsamis Mitsilegas, 'The value of privacy in an era of security: embedding constitutional limits on preemptive surveillance' (2014) 8(1) *International Political Sociology* 104.

[89] Jude McCulloch and Sharon Pickering, 'Pre-crime and counter-terrorism: imagining future crime in the "war on terror"' (2009) 49(5) *British Journal of Criminology* 628, 629.

[90] George W. Bush, 'Graduation speech at West Point Military Academy' (1 June 2002). Available at: nyti.ms/2akwrsh.

[91] Ulrich Beck, *Risk Society. Towards a New Modernity* (London: Sage Publications, 1992); Ulrich Beck, *World Risk Society* (Bristol: Polity Press, 1999).

[92] Ulrich Beck, 'The terrorist threat: world risk society revisited' (2002) 19(4) *Theory, Culture and Society* 39, 41.

the painful truth that we are now interminably threatened by cata-
strophes of our own making.

Whilst legal scholar Alan Dershowitz rejects the claim that current risks
are 'unprecedented' in this way, he argues there is currently a 'desperate
need in the world for a coherent and widely accepted jurisprudence of
preemption' that can quantify and 'clarify the balancing judgments that
must be made' by 'rational decision maker[s] responsible for taking preemptive actions'.[93] In Dershowitz's sweeping argument, existing legal
categories and institutional mechanisms are represented as being simply
ill-equipped to deal with the particular problems that anticipatory governance presents. Only the creation of a specifically preemptive jurisprudence
can enable us to properly deal with the threat of global terrorism and
provide 'a check on impulsive ad hoc decision-making during crises'.[94]

And whilst criminologist Lucia Zedner criticises preemptive security
for the way it erodes human rights and 'risks sweeping away the criminal
justice system', like Dershowitz she argues that 'we need to evolve new
normative structures, or perhaps an entire preventative jurisprudence' to
deal with the problems that the inexorable rise of the 'pre-crime society'
poses.[95] For Zedner, 'existing legal categories are dissolving' through the
proliferation of 'Future Law' mechanisms, thus warranting 'an entirely
new conceptual and procedural framework'.[96] This requires transforming criminology from a discipline of 'dissociated critique' into a discipline
of constructive normative theory development capable of defending
liberal values from encroachment by security.[97]

In each of these accounts preemptive security effectively supplants the law.
The key problem with these epochal approaches to risk is that things are
rather less sweeping and more complicated than that in practice. As shown
throughout this book, when preemptive security logics and rule of law
principles inevitably come into conflict, one does not replace the other. It is
not a zero-sum game. Rather, preemptive security dynamics modulate and
rearrange conventional legal practices into novel amalgams and

---

[93] Alan M. Dershowitz, *Preemption: A Knife that Cuts Both Ways* (London: W.W. Norton &
Company, 2006), pp. 27, 241, 13.

[94] Ibid. p. 237.

[95] Lucia Zedner, 'Seeking security by eroding rights: the side-stepping of due process' in
Goold and Lazarus, *Security and Human Rights*, pp. 257, 268; Lucia Zedner, 'Preventive
justice or pre-punishment? The case of control orders' (2007) 60(1) *Current Legal
Problems* 174, 203.

[96] Zedner, 'Preventive justice or pre-punishment', 188, 187.

[97] Lucia Zedner, 'Pre-crime and post-criminology' (2007) 11(2) *Theoretical Criminology*
261, 270.

recombinations that demand empirical attention. Moreover, against Beck I show how the purportedly 'incalculable' threats of global terrorism are indeed being calculated and countered in new ways – this is what the global security law is all about. Incalculability is not a source of interminable doubt. It is the catalyst for new techniques of governing on the basis of uncertainty.

This book therefore relies on the work of Foucault and the diverse body of interdisciplinary scholarship that analyses risk and preemption in counterterrorism as practices of governmentality.[98] For Foucault, governmentality is an 'ensemble formed by the institutions, procedures, analyses and reflections, the calculations and tactics, that allow the exercise of this very specific albeit complex form of power'.[99] Here government is not about political parties and institutions but the 'diversity of powers and knowledges entailed in rendering fields practicable and amenable to intervention'.[100] In governmental analyses risk is not 'a unitary and monolithic technology' or the effect of 'an inescapable "logic" of modernity', but rather a 'product of 'contingency and invention' and a 'complex category made up of many ways of governing problems'.[101] Understanding how preemptive security plays out as a practice of governmentality requires attention to its diverse effects in specific settings.

This governmental approach to preemption has important consequences for how we study and understand processes of global legal change. Much of the legal literature on this issue, for example, defines preemptive security *negatively* in terms of what it is not. It violates due process and breaches fundamental rights. It is represented as something opposite to the liberal order. A governmental approach allows us to grasp the *productive*

---

[98] See, for example: Claudia Aradau and Rens van Munster, 'Governing terrorism through risk: taking precautions, (un)knowing the future' (2007) 13(1) *European Journal of International Relations* 89; Louise Amoore and Marieke de Goede (eds.), *Risk and the War on Terror* (London: Routledge, 2008); Susanne Krasmann, 'Law's knowledge: on the susceptibility and resistance of legal practices to security matters' (2012) 16(4) *Theoretical Criminology* 379; Francesco Ragazzi, 'Suspect community or suspect category? The impact of counter-terrorism as "policed multiculturalism"' (2016) 42(5) *Journal of Ethnic and Migration Studies* 724; Wendy Larner and William Walters (eds.), *Global Governmentality: Governing International Spaces* (London: Routledge, 2004); Yee-Kuang Heng and Ken McDonagh, *Risk, Global Governance and Security: The Other War on Terror* (London: Routledge, 2009).

[99] Michel Foucault, 'Governmentality' in Graham Burchell, Colin Gordon and Peter Miller (eds.), *The Foucault Effect: Studies in Governmentality* (Chicago IL: University of Chicago Press, 1991), pp. 87, 102.

[100] Peter Miller and Nikolas Rose, 'Governing economic life' (1990) 19(1) *Economy and Society* 1, 3.

[101] Pat O'Malley, *Risk, Uncertainty and Government* (London: Glasshouse Press, 2004), p. 7.

dimensions of this form of power in terms of the concrete rearrangements it effects.[102] Furthermore, because of the centrality of knowledge production, 'government is intrinsically linked to the activities of expertise'.[103] As such, each chapter of this book analyses how different forms of expertise – including from UN listing experts, national security officials, judges, diplomats, the UN1267 Ombudsperson, academics and so on – embed and extend global security law and governance in far-reaching ways through practical and technical means. The governmental frame therefore helps me to address the understudied nexus between global law and expertise and bring something new to the debate. My analysis of the list suggests that the politics of expertise is where the real global lawmaking action is taking place here: connecting problems and technologies of global governance with the creation of new forms of preemptive security intervention, often in the background of where we usually think that the law is or ought to be.[104]

1.2.3   Rethinking the Global Exception

In his 2012 General Assembly report the former UN Special Rapporteur on Countering Terrorism and Human Rights noted that the Law of the List 'provides a ready means by which individual States can make executive decisions with far-reaching consequences, apparently unconstrained by domestic judicial review, or the international human rights treaties by which they are bound'.[105] The following year, the ECJ dismissed the Security Council's latest attempts at procedural reform (through the

---

[102]   As Foucault argues:

> We must cease once and for all to describe the effects of power in negative terms: it 'excludes,' it 'represses,' it 'censors,' it 'abstracts,' it 'masks,' it 'conceals.' In fact, power produces; it produces reality; it produces domains of objects and rituals of truth. The individual and the knowledge that may be gained of him belong to this production.

> Michel Foucault, *Discipline and Punish: The Birth of the Prison* (London: Allen Lane, 1977), p. 194. For an analysis of productive power in the domain of terrorism financing, see: de Goede, *Speculative Security*, p. 47.

[103]   Nikolas Rose and Peter Miller, 'Political power beyond the state: problematics of government' (1992) 43(2) *British Journal of Sociology* 173, 175.

[104]   The notion of functional expertise operating in the background and driving global lawmaking comes from David Kennedy and is discussed in more detail in Chapter 2. See, for example: David Kennedy, 'Challenging expert rule: the politics of global governance' (2005) 27 *Sydney Law Review* 5; Kennedy, *A World of Struggle*.

[105]   Ben Emmerson QC, Report of the Special Rapporteur on the Promotion of Human Rights and Fundamental Freedoms while Countering Terrorism, UN Doc. A/67/396 (26 September 2012), p. 5.

Office of the Ombudsperson) as inadequate, confirming that the list still operates in violation of human rights.[106] Finally, in 2016 scholar-experts from Brown University's Watson Institute – who have long been some of the strongest advocates of UN-targeted sanctions policy – came to acknowledge that the 'Al-Qaida sanctions regime . . . has evolved into the realm of the permanent exception'.[107]

But if the list has evolved into a state of exception, what kind of exception is it? There is no formal derogation by any actor involved on grounds of 'public emergency'. There is no national sovereign figurehead deciding to institute this exception, or any state of 'normalcy' that the Security Council might return to. Nor is there any pretence that the listing regime is a temporary measure to be rescinded once the global war on terror is finally won. Indeed, as the threat from Al-Qaida receded, the list was transformed to fight new enemies of the world: ISIL and foreign terrorist fighters (FTFs).

The third analytical move that this book makes is to rethink the problem of the exception in assemblage terms through my empirical study of the list. This exception has been the subject of heated debate since the 9/11 attacks, as scholars have struggled to theoretically reconcile liberal values of government with illiberal practices of executive rule and become engaged in moral conundrums about 'ticking time bombs' dilemmas and the like.[108] Most scholarship on the issue draws on the work of Carl Schmitt or Giorgio Agamben. For these authors it is the *decision* of the sovereign to suspend the normal legal order that is of paramount importance – as Schmitt famously declared in *Political Theology*: 'the Sovereign is he who decides on the exception'.[109] States of exception are also routinely characterised as 'legal black holes' defined by their absence of law.[110]

---

[106]　Court of Justice of the European Union, Joined Cases C-584/10 P, C-593/10 P, C-595/10 P, *United Kingdom of Great Britain and Northern Ireland, and Council of the European Union* v. *Yassin Abdullah Kadi*, Judgment of 18 July 2013.

[107]　Thomas Biersteker, Sue Eckert and Marcos Tourinho (eds.), *Targeted Sanctions: The Impact and Effectiveness of United Nations Action* (Cambridge: Cambridge University Press, 2016), p. 273.

[108]　See, for example: Bruce Ackerman, 'The Emergency Constitution' (2004) 113(5) *Yale Law Journal* 1029; Oren Gross, 'The normless and exceptionless exception: Carl Schmitt's theory of emergency powers and the "norm-exception" dichotomy' (2000) 21 *Cardoza Law Review* 1825; Victor V. Ramraj (ed.), *Emergencies and the Limits of Legality* (Cambridge: Cambridge University Press, 2008).

[109]　Carl Schmitt, *Political Theology: Four Chapters on the Concept of Sovereignty* (Cambridge MA: MIT Press, 1985), pp. 5–6.

[110]　See, for example: Giorgio Agamben, *State of Exception* (Chicago IL: University of Chicago Press, 2005). Agamben argues that the exception creates 'a space devoid of law, a zone of anomie in which all legal determinations . . . are deactivated' (at p. 51).

This 'decisionism' and 'lawlessness' has important analytical and political consequences. In most scholarship, for example, emergencies have become synonymous with the unrestrained exercise of sovereign will. And so, focus is placed on decrees by political figureheads (like George W. Bush), reproducing the idea that emergency power is something held by powerful heads of state and exercised in times of crises. This is not entirely inaccurate, but it also functions as an analytical alibi. It allows the broader field of emergency governance (composed of actors, agents, techniques and practices operating beyond the state) to pass by wholly unnoticed. Or as Jacques Rancière puts it, this approach 'depopulat[es] the political stage by sweeping aside its always ambiguous actors', leaving only 'the sheer relation of state power and individual life'.[111] Because of the emphasis placed on national sovereign decision, conventional approaches are also poorly equipped to grapple with how the exception is reconfigured in global terrain. As Kim Lane Scheppele argues, 'we cannot understand what has happened since September 11 until we can see both international and domestic law together in thinking about the slide into emergency powers'.[112] Moreover, the 'lawless exception' idea can only be sustained if we disregard empirical reality and confine ourselves to the realm of normative theory. As soon as we start examining how things unfold in practice, we quickly see that laws and regulations permeate and condition exceptional security practices. In his analysis of Guantanamo Bay, for example, Nasser Hussain observes that:

> the difficulty in using the theoretical paradigm of the state of exception is that its specific substantive and connotative associations are ones of decision and declaration, abeyance and suspension, and an emptying out of set rules from governance. But this is all at odds with the proliferation of regulations and administrative procedures that mark the daily management of contemporary crises . . . It is empirically the case that what one witnesses in contemporary emergency is a proliferation of new laws and regulations passed in an ad hoc or tactical manner, administrative procedures, and the use of older laws and cases tweaked and transformed for newer purposes.[113]

This book addresses these deficiencies and pushes the problem of exception in a different direction. In my analysis, the exception is not so much a 'state' standing opposed to normal affairs, something formally declared by an all-powerful sovereign or the hidden matrix of power. It is the effect

---

[111] Jacques Rancière, 'Who is the subject of the Rights of Man?' (2004) 103(2–3) *South Atlantic Quarterly* 297, 302.

[112] Scheppele, 'The international state of emergency', 6.

[113] Nasser Hussain, 'Beyond norm and exception: Guantanamo' (2007) 33(4) *Critical Inquiry* 734, 740–1.

of diverse governance techniques, legal interventions, knowledges practices and mundane forms of functional expertise aligned through particular security problems. Exceptional governance, in other words, is
something assembled through a plethora of relatively banal programmes
and techniques and 'little security nothings':[114] humanitarians working
on 'smart sanctions' and deflecting political critique of the regime
(Chapter 3); EU court officials developing procedures for judges to
handle secret intelligence as evidence (Chapter 4); security experts creating new techniques for translating 'global terrorism' into novel fields of
intervention and global aviation officials trying to implement the list by
forging new techniques for preemptively targeting 'risky passengers'
(Chapter 2). On their own, each of these examples may not amount to
much. But when sutured together as an assemblage of co-functioning
elements, I argue, we see a variegated topology of global exceptional
governance emerging. One that is provisional and diffuse yet dense,
jurisgenerative and powerful.

   This analytical move builds on a rich tradition of sociolegal research
and critical security scholarship on this issue.[115] It is an attempt to
rethink problems of exceptional governance in empirical terms outside
of the discourse of sovereignty.[116] As Claudia Aradau argues, 'what is
important is not the distinction between exception and law, but what
practices are deployed and how'.[117] By studying the 'novel
recombination[s] of already existing ... mechanisms and modalities of
power' as practices of assemblage I argue that we can better grasp how
exceptional rule is embedded and stretched through time.[118]

---

[114] On banality, see: Louise Amoore and Marieke de Goede, 'Transactions after 9/11: the
    banal face of the preemptive strike' (2008) 33(2) *Transactions of the Institute of British
    Geographers* 173. On 'little security nothings', see: Jef Huysmans, 'What's in an act? On
    security speech acts and little security nothings' (2011) 42(4–5) *Security Dialogue* 371.

[115] Johns, *Non-Legality in International Law*; Nasser Hussain, *The Jurisprudence of
    Emergency: Colonialism and the Rule of Law* (Ann Arbor MI: University of Michigan
    Press, 2009); Kim Lane Scheppele, 'International Standardization of National Security
    Law' (2010) 4 *Journal of National Security Law and Policy* 437; Aradau and van Munster,
    'Governing terrorism'.

[116] See also: Adi Ophir, 'The politics of catastrophization: emergency and exception' in
    Didier Fassin and Mariella Pandolfi (eds.), *Contemporary States of Emergency: The
    Politics of Military and Humanitarian Interventions* (New York: Zone Books, 2010),
    p. 59.

[117] Claudia Aradau, 'Law Transformed: Guantanamo and the "other" exception' (2007) 28
    (3) *Third World Quarterly* 489, 491.

[118] Andrew Neal, Exceptionalism and the Politics of Counter-Terrorism: Liberty, Security
    and the War on Terror (London: Routledge, 2009), p. 124.

1.3   Notes on the Method Assemblage

1.3.1   Performativity of Method and Situated Knowledges

In mainstream legal research, methodology is ordinarily disavowed as something that lawyers don't particularly need. Law is imbued with an abstract normative quality and particular 'pedigree' that jurists can come to decipher through knowledge of legal doctrine. Reflecting on his own experiences in legal education, for example, Martti Koskenniemi remarked: 'Either "method" equalled discussion about formal sources or it referred simply to techniques of finding the collections of documents from which authoritative statements about the law could be found.'[119] Methodology, in other words, is shorthand for the techniques used by lawyers to 'find the law'. When international law is studied empirically it is usually done so either to confirm the validity of a given legal theory or fine-tune policymaking in a particular functional domain. If methods are reflected on at all, they tend to be assessed instrumentally in terms of their 'usefulness ... to the practising lawyer ... as opposed to the academic analyst' and reduced to a rather inert, vocational service-delivery role.[120]

Conventional social science does not so much disavow the methodological as project 'the social' as a distinct realm discoverable by the researcher through the application of methodological tools. The job of the social scientist in the traditional idiom is to extract generalisable truths from empirical reality so as to ground universal claims. This approach to research assumes, as John Law and John Urry point out, that 'there is a real world with real attributes, and that it is the job of social science to discover those of social and political significance'.[121] In the social-scientific tradition, therefore, methods are like 'free-floating tools in conceptual space'.[122] Different methodological techniques may

---

[119] Martti Koskenniemi, 'Letter to the editors of the symposium' (1999) 93 *American Journal of International Law* 351, 354.

[120] Stephen R. Ratner and Anne Marie Slaughter, 'Appraising the methods of international law: a prospectus for readers' (1999) 93 *American Journal of International Law* 291, 299.

[121] John Law and John Urry, 'Enacting the social' (2004) 33(3) *Economy and Society* 390, 393.

[122] Dvora Yanow, 'Thinking interpretively: philosophical Presuppositions and the human sciences' in Dvora Yanow and Peregrine Schwartz-Shea (eds.), *Interpretation and Method: Empirical Research Methods and the Interpretive Turn* (London: Routledge, 2006), p. 8; cited in: Claudia Aradau and Jef Huysmans, 'Critical methods in international relations: the politics of techniques, devices and acts' (2014) 20(3) *European Journal of International Relations* 596, 597.

produce different results and perspectives on reality. But they leave that reality fundamentally undisturbed.

The approach to methods deployed in this book departs from these positivist accounts in two crucial ways. First, following recent scholarship in critical security studies,[123] sociology[124] and STS,[125] I argue that methods are inherently performative: 'they have effects, they make differences, they enact realities and they help to bring into being what they also discover'.[126] Methods, in other words, are not only *epistemological* tools that enable researchers to know their research problems from different perspectives. They also operate in an *ontological* register to enact the different knowledge objects or realities that they describe. It is beyond the scope of this introduction to explore the implications of this reorientation in depth and, in any event, it is something we will be revisiting in later chapters. Suffice to say, this shift comes with far-reaching consequences for how and why research is done. As John Law and John Urry explain:

> If method is interactively performative, and helps to make realities, then the differences between research findings produced by different methods . . . have an alternative significance. No longer different *perspectives* on a single reality, they become instead the enactment of different *realities* . . . It is a shift that moves us from a single world to the idea that the world is multiply produced in diverse and contested social and material relations. The implication is that there is no single 'world'.[127]

This shift from single to multiple worlds fundamentally shifts the focus of sociolegal research and takes us into more uncertain philosophical terrain. Rather than seeking to extract generalisable truths, methods need to be redone in ways that 'no longer seek the definite, the repeatable, the more or less stable'.[128] So this book focuses on what Foucault called the

---

[123] Aradau and Huysmans, 'Critical methods'; Mark Salter and Can E. Mutlu (eds.), *Research Methods in Critical Security Studies: An Introduction* (London: Routledge, 2013); Anthony Amicelle, Claudia Aradau and Julien Jeandesboz, 'Questioning security devices: performativity, resistance, politics' (2015) 46(4) *Security Dialogue* 293.

[124] John Law, *After Method: Mess in Social Science Research* (London: Routledge, 2004); John Law and Evelyn Ruppert, 'The social life of methods: devices' (2013) 6(3) *Journal of Cultural Economy* 229; John Law, Evelyn Ruppert and Mike Savage, 'Reassembling social science methods: the challenge of digital devices' (2013) 30(4) *Theory, Culture and Society* 22.

[125] Latour, *Reassembling the Social*; Annemarie Mol, *The Body Multiple: Ontology in Medical Practice* (Durham NC: Duke University Press, 2002).

[126] Law and Urry, 'Enacting the social', 393.

[127] Ibid. 397.

[128] Law, *After Method*, p. 6.

'flat and empirical little question' of *how* rather than the usual *what* or *ought* questions that ground legal and political texts.[129] As John Law argues, 'if we want to understand how realities are done or to explore their politics, then we have to attend carefully to practices and ask how they work ... [and] get assembled in particular locations'.[130] Or, as I discuss below, we need to study the local sites that produce the conditions for global security law and analyse listing practices as 'assemblages of relations'.[131] But this shift also means that when I am describing elements of the global listing assemblage throughout this book, my findings are both *real* and *an effect* of my frame and method. Once we move from a singular world to multiple and conflicting worlds, there is no getting around this. There is no 'nowhere' where I can analyse the workings of this list to extract generalisable truths for the reader. To pretend there *is* such a privileged space would be to try and pull what Donna Haraway called the 'god trick'.[132] This is not to say that the findings of this book are arbitrary or fictional. Instead, the knowledge generated here is necessarily *situated*. As Rebecca Coleman and Jessica Ringrose point out: 'taking seriously the idea that methodology is a way of relating to multiply assembled worlds suggests that social scientists are themselves entangled within the assemblages they seek to study'.[133]

The second related point is that if methods are performative practices that help enact the knowledge objects that come about through their use, then they are also intensely political. The way we *do* research partakes in what Annemarie Mol calls 'ontological politics' because it enacts certain realities, and obstructs others.[134] Our methods *interfere* with the world, rather than merely describe it.[135] As discussed earlier in this introduction, I first came to this project as a practising lawyer representing individuals targeted by this global

---

[129] Michel Foucault, 'The Subject and the Power' in James D. Faubian (ed.), *Essential Works of Foucault 1954–1984, vol. 3: Power* (New York: The New Press, 2000), pp. 326, 337.

[130] Law, *After Method*, p. 157.

[131] Ibid.

[132] Donna Haraway, *Simians, Cyborgs, and Women: The Reinvention of Nature* (London: Routledge, 1991), pp. 193.

[133] Rebecca Coleman and Jessica Ringrose, 'Introduction: Deleuze and research methodologies' in Rebecca Coleman and Jessica Ringrose (eds.), *Deleuze and Research Methodologies* (Edinburgh: Edinburgh University Press, 2013), p. 6.

[134] Annemarie Mol, 'Ontological politics: a word and some questions' in John Law and John Hassard (eds.), *Actor Network Theory and After* (Oxford: Blackwell Publishers, 1999), p. 74. See also: Law and Urry, 'Enacting the social', 396.

[135] Haraway, *Simians*; Mol, 'Ontological politics'.

security list. So, I have an intimate knowledge of the violence and injustices of this security regime because I know the experiences of my clients and just how little justification is needed to destroy their lives and the lives of their families. These were people targeted not for acts they have done but for what others think they might potentially do in the future. It was my knowledge of this violence, and of the real limits of human rights claims to speak to it, that first led me to question how the list works as a novel form of global exceptional governance. This positioning and sense of injustice doesn't disappear as soon as I put on my professional or academic hat. It is what motivates my legal work in this area and shapes how I have conducted this research.

This situatedness also had a dramatic effect on how the research for this book was conducted. As a lawyer working in this field, for example, I was granted access to a range of interviewees that non-practitioners would have difficulty reaching. I could easily talk with legal professionals in this domain because I am a legal professional in this domain myself. Trying to grapple with the complexities of using intelligence-as-evidence (as discussed in Chapter 4) emerged from my own difficulties in doing so as lawyer trying to represent the interests of my clients. I could forensically study the inner workings of the UN1267 Ombudsperson delisting process (as discussed in Chapter 3) because I have been through it numerous times myself. And I was able to analyse the political effects of the UN Special Rapporteur's interventions in the General Assembly on this issue because I was directly involved in helping to draft their report (as discussed in Chapter 3). This involvement ended up facilitating numerous contacts in New York and elsewhere that led to more interviews and insights about the ISIL and Al-Qaida listing regime that inform the observations now presented in this book.

My point in making these networks visible is not to lay claim to some special authenticity. Rather, it is to acknowledge my partial positioning and complicity in this knowledge production process, whilst at the same time claiming that this does not detract from its empirical veracity as a faithful 'real world' account. When the research process is reflexively reframed in this way, the operative logic becomes one of sustained engagement rather than dispassionate detachment. That's how this research was conducted. As Haraway argues: 'We do not seek partiality for its own sake, but for the sake of the connections and unexpected openings situated knowledges make possible. The only way to find a larger vision is to be somewhere in particular ... living within limits and contradictions.'[136]

1.3.2 Sites

If this global security list is a multiple, fragmented and unevenly distributed governance technology, how can it best be studied as a research object? How might global security law be understood not merely as a series of all-encompassing UN Charter Chapter VII decrees but productively reposed as something heterogeneous, informal and very much under construction? What methodological tools can be used to analyse emergent forms of exceptional governance in motion? And how can we empirically study something so seemingly expansive and global as the UN ISIL and Al-Qaida listing regime?

This book responds to these problems by studying global security law ethnographically as something produced and sustained from multiple localised sites. Studying 'the global' in this way may seem counterintuitive to those who assume that the global is a much larger research object, operating at an altogether grander scale. However, drawing from recent scholarship in anthropology, sociology, actor-network theory and international relations, the approach adopted in this book is that global processes and things are always made in local 'structure-making' sites or 'legal complexes' whose effects can be studied empirically.[137] Breaking 'the global' down in this way, as Latour points out, has the effect of modifying 'the entire topography of the social world' by performing what he calls a 'flattening of the landscape': wherein the 'macro no longer describes a *wider* or *larger* site in which the micro would be embedded ... but another equally local, equally micro place, which is connected to many others through some medium transporting specific types of traces'.[138] Or as anthropologist George E. Marcus puts it: 'The global is an

---

[136] Haraway, *Simians*, p. 196. It should go without saying that I am not claiming the embodied feminist positioning advocated by Haraway here, but rather drawing on her insights concerning situated knowledge production and partial objectivity to make a point about my reflexivity in this research.

[137] Latour, *Reassembling the Social*, pp. 175–6; Rose and Valverde, 'Governed by law?', 541. The term 'legal complex' is used instead of 'law' to refer to 'the assemblage of legal practices, legal institutions, statutes, legal codes, authorities, discourses, texts, norms and forms of judgment' (at 542).

[138] Latour, *Reassembling the Social*, p. 176.

emergent dimension of arguing about the connection among sites';[139] not a pre-given governance scale securely positioned at the apex of the international order, as lawyers and globalisation theorists often suggest, but a contingent achievement, an effect of legal and political practices or an empirical problem that needs investigation.

Ethnographers conventionally embed themselves in the cultural habits of a particular locale. But when the object of study is mobile and multiply situated, researchers and their methods must become mobile and multiply situated as well. This means using what Marcus has termed 'multisited ethnography', to follow the flows of people and things across local sites to map how relations are made and stabilised and the global is produced in practice. In Nancy Scheper-Hughes' fascinating study, for example, the global market in human organs is studied from a multiplicity of different sites and scales – including interviews with 'kidney patients in their homes' and transplant specialists in their surgeries, to meetings with organ brokers 'in suburban shopping malls' and local kidney sellers 'in squatter camps in Manila'.[140] Multisited methods are deployed to grasp how the human-organs market functions in relation to organised crime and the illicit transplant economy. According to Scheper-Hughes, this project prompted 'odd juxtapositions of ethnography, documentation, surveillance and human rights work' that required her to deviate 'from standard fieldwork practice and ethics', go undercover and approach her research problems with a certain degree of experimentalism and militancy.[141] The assumption underpinning multisited methodological approaches is that we live in a world 'fundamentally characterized by objects in motion', but these flows 'are not coeval, convergent, isomorphic or spatially consistent'.[142] They are heterogeneous, disjunctive and generative of conflict and 'regulatory fractures'.[143] The methodological task, according to Arjun Appadurai, 'is to name and

[139] George E. Marcus, 'Ethnography in/of the world system: the emergence of multi-sited ethnography' (1995) 24 *Annual Review of Anthropology* 95, 99.

[140] Nancy Scheper-Hughes, 'The last commodity: post-human ethics and the global traffic in "fresh" Organs' in Ong and Collier, *Global Assemblages*, pp. 145, 147.

[141] Ibid. p. 148. For example: 'In Turkey in February 2002 I posed as a potential buyer desperately seeking a kidney in order to meet with kidney sellers at a "Russian suitcase market" in . . . Istanbul' (at p. 148).

[142] Arjun Appadurai, 'Grassroots globalization and the research imagination' in Arjun Appadurai (ed.), *Globalization* (Durham NC: Duke University Press, 2001), pp. 1, 5.

[143] Saskia Sassen, 'Spatialities and temporalities of the global: elements for a theorization', in Appadurai, *Globalization*, p. 266.

analyse these mobile . . . forms and to rethink the meaning of research styles and networks appropriate to this mobility'.[144] Multisited ethnographies aim to address these dynamics by 'following connections, associations and putative relationships'.[145]

This book follows this methodological shift and analyses the list as a multisited research object. Multisited ethnographic methods are ideally suited to this project because the list is mobile and composed by a multiplicity of actors from different domains operating at different governance scales. To capture how the global listing assemblage works, each chapter travels to different empirical sites to examine how problems of the list are being negotiated and novel legal and political relations forged. We 'follow the list' to meetings of UN experts and North-African security agencies, for example, and governance projects with the global aviation industry to enhance implementation (Chapter 2). We revisit debates amongst scholars pushing for sanctions to be targeted for global humanitarian reform and trace how their revalorisation as counter-terrorism experts has altered the list in significant ways (Chapter 3). We hone in on the UN1267 Office of the Ombudsperson and the novel governance techniques, discourses and knowledge practices it is crafting to make the listing process 'fair and clear' (Chapter 3). And we go inside the EU courts to explore how judges are dealing with the complexities of reviewing a security list founded on the use of intelligence-as-evidence (Chapter 4). There is no unifying methodology programmatically 'applied' in each chapter. Instead, different methods and theoretical lenses are used across the different sites depending on the particular problems under investigation. So, whilst Chapter 2 explores the politics of listing expertise using actor-network theory (ANT) techniques, Chapter 3 uses genealogical critique to present a counter-history of the Ombudsperson. My aim is to build a text that is generative and 'engages intensively with the kinds of materials that it produces'.[146] 'What is needed', says Marcus, commenting on graduate dissertations, are not documentaries of the global that purport to be seamless, but rather 'practices of composition somewhere between fieldnotes and

---

[144] Appadurai, *Globalization*, p. 7.

[145] Marcus, 'Ethnography', 97.

[146] George E. Marcus, 'Multi-sited ethnography: notes and queries' in Mark-Anthony Falzon (ed.), *Multi-Sited Ethnography: Theory, Praxis and Locality in Contemporary Research* (Farnham: Ashgate, 2009), p. 194.

finished texts'.[147] Analyses, in other words, that open up new ways of studying how global ordering is being constituted in practice.

Each foray to a particular site uses semi-structured interviews with key actors in the assemblage to map the effects of the list as a technology of preemptive security governance. Around forty interviews were conducted in total, between 2012 and 2019, with a diverse array of participants – including UN diplomats and members of the Secretariat, security and intelligence experts, academics working on targeted sanctions, members of the ISIL and Al-Qaida Monitoring Team, judges reviewing listing cases and lawyers representing listed individuals, sanctions officials in national states and EU institutions, members of the UN1267 Sanctions Committee, and experts from other international organisations (like Interpol, the International Civil Aviation Organization (ICAO) and the International Air Transport Association (IATA)) drawn into the listing assemblage. Some interviews were one-off encounters. Others were repeat affairs. My aim was to examine how conflicts of the list were being negotiated and, in so doing, understand 'how particular knowledge claims acquire the functions of expertise' and forms of global ordering emerge,[148] not simply by describing 'what is done', but rather by studying '*how* it is done' and providing an ant's-eye view of the problems.[149] All interviews took (at least in part) a critical approach and used dissenting questions to avoid the common problem of being drip-fed public-relations talking points by political professionals. All interviews except three were undertaken on a confidential basis.[150] Interview dates and locational details have been kept to a bare minimum, or omitted in some cases, throughout the text to preserve the anonymity of the speakers.

The 'field site' of this book is therefore more fragmented and diffuse than those of IR scholars asking whether UN sanctions are meeting their policy objectives,[151] or lawyers asking whether the EU courts were legally

---

[147] Ibid.

[148] Merje Kuus, 'Foreign policy and ethnography: a sceptical intervention' (2013) 18(1) *Geopolitics* 115, 122.

[149] Ibid.

[150] These were the interviews with the former UN1267 Ombudsperson (Ms Kimberly Prost), elaborated upon in Chapter 3. As there is only one Ombudsperson in this area it is impossible to interview them on condition of anonymity.

[151] See, for example: Francesco Giumelli, *Coercing, Constraining and Signalling: Explaining UN and EU Sanctions after the Cold War* (Colchester: ECPR Press, 2011); Biersteker et al., *Targeted Sanctions*.

justified in acting the way they did in the *Kadi* case.[152] 'The difficulty', as Boaventura de Sousa Santos notes, is that 'socio-legal life is constituted by different legal spaces operating simultaneously on different scales and from different interpretive standpoints'.[153] Doing multisited ethnographic fieldwork seeks to methodologically grapple with this complexity. But, as the following chapters show, this produces an account of the list more akin to a Dziga Vertov constructivist montage than a classical 'talking-heads' documentary on the topic.[154]

Yet it would be wrong to assume that a multisited approach to studying global law is more superficial than doctrinal accounts. Or that due to fragmentation, 'everything is simply messy and featureless ... and that no generalisations are possible'.[155] As this book shows, this method enables a more situated and textured account – what Clifford Geertz would call a 'thick description'[156] – of the heterogeneous relations, technical artefacts and knowledge practices being assembled to *produce* this form of law as something powerful and global. Deploying methods more attentive to complexity undoubtedly mutes the immediate 'policy relevance' of this study and frustrates those seeking a comprehensive overview of what global security law is. But, when we move beyond such instrumental concerns, the analytical gains are considerable. It is precisely 'through the complexity of the empirical', as Andrew Barry argues, 'that one gets the sense of the irreducibility and contestability of the social, the disjunctures between the programmatic statement of policy and the messiness of actuality, the contingency of history and intersections of diverse historical and geographical movements'.[157]

Studying the Law of the List as a multisited project also resonates with calls to bring empirical sociolegal methods to bear on contemporary problems of international law and transnational governance. In

---

[152] See the debates between global constitutionalists and global legal pluralists discussed above.

[153] Boaventura de Sousa Santos, 'Law: a map of misreading: toward a postmodern conception of law' (1987) 14(3) *Journal of Law and Society* 279, 288.

[154] The Vertov analogy is from George E. Marcus, see: Marcus, 'Ethnography', 106.

[155] Andrew Barry, *Political Machines: Governing a Technological Society* (London: The Athlone Press, 2001), p. 21.

[156] Clifford Geertz, 'Thick description: toward an interpretive theory of culture' in Michael Martin and Lee C. McIntyre (eds.), *Readings in the Philosophy of Social Science* (Cambridge MA: MIT Press, 1994), p. 213.

[157] Barry, *Political Machines*, p. 24.

a recent *European Journal of International Law* article, for example, Joost Pauwelyn, Ramses Wessel and Jan Wouters made the point that formal international lawmaking was rapidly being supplanted by informal and heterogeneous arrangements of 'new actors, new processes and new outputs'.[158] Given this complexity, the authors conclude that 'the conceptual boundaries of how international law may look in the future are [currently] wide open'.[159] Understanding this complexity, according to Eve Darian-Smith, demands a 'global sociolegal perspective' that 'destabilizes our modern and linear understandings of what law is, where law appears and how law works'.[160] Only approaches that help show how the 'lines of demarcation ... between and within local, regional, international, transnational and global legal arenas' are 'dynamic and porous' are fit for the task of grappling with the dynamics of contemporary global legal ordering.[161] Similarly, Sally Engle Merry calls for a 'deterritorialized ethnography' to 'understand the space of law in the current transnational era'.[162] For Merry, this means scaling sociolegal methods up to track 'the flows of people, ideas, laws and institutions across national boundaries', ethnographically examining 'particular nodes ... within this field of transnational circulation' and mapping how 'emerging legal technologies ... construct and sediment forms of legal knowledge and practice'.[163] In studying the ISIL and Al-Qaida list ethnographically as a multisited research object this book speaks to this shared concern for more dynamic, global sociolegal analysis. It is an experiment that has not been tried before with respect to global security law. The idea is to allow readers to experience the Law of the List as something emergent and very much in motion.

---

[158] Joost Pauwelyn, Ramses A. Wessel and Jan Wouters 'When structures become shackles: stagnation and dynamics in international lawmaking' (2014) 25(3) *European Journal of International Law* 733, 734. See also Peer Zumbansen's work on transnational legal pluralism and argument for 'a shift in perspective ... [and] focus on *actors*, *norms* and *processes* as the building blocks of a methodology of transnational law' – Peer Zumbansen, 'Defining the space for transnational law: legal theory, global governance and legal pluralism' (2012) 21 *Transnational Law and Contemporary Problems* 305, 308 (original emphasis).

[159] Pauwelyn et al., 'When structures become shackles'.

[160] Darian-Smith, *Laws and Societies*, pp. 12, 13.

[161] Ibid. p. 8. On the limits of social science methods vis-à-vis the global, see: Law and Urry, 'Enacting the social', 390.

[162] Engle Merry, 'New legal realism', 993.

[163] Ibid. 976.

1.3.3 Practices

This emphasis on multiple sites also resonates with recent scholarship reappraising the important role of epistemic techniques and practices in law and governance. Here, I draw insights from diverse literatures – including governmentality and STS, assemblage research in the social sciences, the 'practice turn' in international relations and critical security studies and sociolegal studies – to study the UN ISIL and Al-Qaida list from the vantage points of how it is practised. The basic idea I take from each of these approaches is straightforward: that governance unfolds through the techniques, materials and practices used to render particular problems knowable, stable and governable. But the implications of this approach for the study of international law and organisations can be profound. Instead of only seeing the world structured through powerful institutions and agency in the hands of powerful actors, things are ontologically reversed. Institutional formations and agency in legal governance are recast as effects of practice. Consider the question and shift in perspective posed by Foucault in his genealogical study of the modern European state:

> What if the state were nothing more than a way of governing . . . What if all these relations of power that gradually take shape *on the basis of multiple and very diverse processes which gradually coagulate and form an effect*, what if these practices of government were precisely the basis on which the state was constituted?[164]

This book seeks to perform a similar reversal in the area of global security law, examining processes of legal coagulation. What if, instead of looking towards the binding authority and high politics of the Security Council to explain the origins and effects of the list, we shift focus to the domain of technical expertise and examine how things are being materially rearranged in novel and far-reaching ways? What if new forms of legal ordering are emerging from the techniques used to 'know' global terrorism, not just contained in Chapter VII decrees and their implementation by Member States?

Such a reorientation toward practice might enable us to see 'inchoate geographies [for] a new type of ordering, a reality in the making', as Sassen suggests.[165] It might also reveal contradictions and flaws in this

---

[164] Michel Foucault, *Security, Territory, Population: Lectures at the Collège de France 1977–78* (Basingstoke: Palgrave Macmillan, 2007), p. 248 (emphasis added).
[165] Sassen, 'Neither global nor national', 64.

global security project and show how efforts to ameliorate these problems are productive of novel governance effects. 'Government', as Peter Miller and Nikolas Rose have pointed out, 'is a congenitally failing operation'.[166] Attending to how failures are 'smoothed out' to 'seem superficial rather than fundamental' or recombined with existing legal techniques to become something new is a key element of this kind of global sociolegal research.[167] Assemblage, in other words, is both a noun and a verb.[168] We come to know assemblages by studying assemblage practices – or tracing the 'hard work required to draw heterogeneous elements together, forge connections between them and sustain these connections in the face of tension'.[169] When methods for studying global governance are recalibrated towards 'bundles of ideas and practices as realized in particular times and places', as Anna Tsing suggests, they can produce fresh and surprising results.[170]

In her ethnography of global financial governance, for example, Annelise Riles shows how seemingly mundane legal techniques and marginal market practices – what she calls 'collateral knowledge' – enable 'thin but nevertheless robust sociotechnical relations among individuals and machines in different institutions cities and countries' that make global financial governance possible.[171] Legal governance, argues Riles, 'is ultimately not so much a matter of grand designs as it is a set of lived practices and techniques ... that are often disparaged or ignored'.[172] Understanding it requires a revalorisation of 'legal technicalities' to examine how legal knowledges are actually formed.[173] Anne Orford's genealogy of the Responsibility to Protect (R2P) doctrine performs a similar methodological shift. Most accounts situate the emergence of

---

[166] Miller and Rose, 'Governing economic life', 10–11.

[167] Murray Li, 'Practices of assemblage', 265.

[168] Law, *After Method*, p. 42. As Tania Murray Li notes: 'assemblage links directly to a practice, to assemble' – Murray Li, 'Practices of assemblage', 264.

[169] Murray Li, 'Practices of assemblage', 264.

[170] Anna Tsing, 'The global situation' (2000) 15(3) *Cultural Anthropology* 327, 347.

[171] Annelise Riles, *Collateral Knowledge: Legal Reasoning in the Global Financial Markets* (Chicago IL: University of Chicago Press, 2011), p. 230.

[172] Ibid. p. 246. See also: Mariana Valverde, 'Authorizing the production of urban moral order: appellate courts and their knowledge games' (2005) 39(2) *Law and Society Review* 419, 427 – who argues that 'highlighting the dynamics of knowledge processes while backgrounding the content and the politics' in sociolegal research 'can lead to new insights about the taken-for-granted machinery of law' that critical legal scholars routinely dismiss as 'technical'.

[173] Riles, *Collateral Knowledge*, pp. 64–70. This revalorisation of the technical in law is discussed in more detail in the following chapter.

R2P in the humanitarian global governance of the 1990s. But Orford shows how the doctrine was forged through the incremental consolidation of governmental practices aiming at '"the maintenance of order" and "the protection of life" in the decolonised world'.[174] These practices had been developed by the UN since the late 1950s and 'transmitted through operationally orientated documents such as Security Council mandates, rules of engagement, instruction manuals, [and] reports and studies outlining lessons learned'.[175] 'International executive rule', in Orford's fascinating account, 'developed through the systematisation of practice rather than through the development of detailed doctrines or norms'.[176]

This book seeks to build on these efforts to understand global law and governance through practice. In so doing it aims to contribute to methodological debates in sociolegal studies, international law, international relations and critical security studies. The chapters that follow provide a granular empirical account of how the UN ISIL and Al-Qaida listing regime is sustained through knowledge practices and governance technologies aimed at preemptively countering the threats of global terrorism. Chapter 2 analyses the list itself as a key governance actor conditioning this form of global security law in crucially important ways. Chapter 3 pushes the practice focus in a more explicitly ontological direction. Drawing on the 'praxiography' of Mol, I analyse how divergent practices across the assemblage enact the list as a multiple object and posits the Ombudsperson as a key figure holding this multiplicity together through recombinant legal practices and techniques.[177] Chapter 4 examines how the temporal complexities, spatial dynamics and mosaic epistemology of this list are negotiated by judges seeking to perform judicial review and uphold the rule of law. My goal in studying this list through its practices is both forensic and political. Showing how small shifts in relatively mundane knowledge practices at a micro-level can provide important sources of legal change within powerful macro-organisations like the Security Council transforms our understanding of

---

[174] Anne Orford, *International Authority and the Responsibility to Protect* (Cambridge: Cambridge University Press, 2011), p. 1.

[175] Ibid. p. 5.

[176] Ibid. p. 6. See also, Fiti Sinclair, *To Reform the World*. For methodological parallels between Orford's project and Foucault's genealogy of the modern state, see: Anne Orford, 'In praise of description' (2012) 25(3) *Leiden Journal of International Law* 609, 616–18.

[177] Mol, *The Body Multiple*.

global security law into something more partial, contingent and situated. It is a critical analytic tactic that Michel Callon and Latour evocatively refer to as 'unscrewing the Big Leviathan'.[178]

1.3.4   Secrecy and Leaks: Assembling Actor-Networks in Global Security

This listing regime is a more difficult object to empirically study than many others. Because it targets people 'associated with' ISIL and Al-Qaida using closed intelligence material, the inner workings of the list are opaque and shrouded in secrecy. Getting people to talk can be difficult and finding people to talk with, even harder. This presents a methodological dilemma: how can we empirically study a domain of law from a global sociolegal perspective, map a particular research field or 'follow the actors' in a legal assemblage when it is obscured by secrecy justified on security grounds?[179]

This secrecy problem has forced academic researchers to become methodologically inventive. Some file Freedom of Information Act 2000 (FOIA) requests to find the empirical material needed to analyse particular assemblages.[180] Others exploit the eroding public/private divide by interviewing programmers working for firms who build the algorithms that both help companies to identify potential new customers and states to target potentially risky travellers at the border.[181] Swathes of seemingly mundane flight log data have been gathered and analysed to map networks of global rendition and torture.[182] Others

---

[178]   Callon and Latour, 'Unscrewing the big Leviathan', 277.

[179]   Latour, *Reassembling the Social*, pp. 11–12.

[180]   David H. Price, 'Anthropological research and the Freedom of Information Act' (1997) 9(1) *Field Methods* 12; Oliver Belcher and Lauren L. Martin, 'Ethnographies of closed doors: conceptualising openness and closure in US immigration and military institutions' (2013) 45(4) *Area* 403. See also: Roberto J. González, 'Anthropology and the covert: methodological notes on researching military and intelligence programmes' (2012) 28(2) *Anthropology Today* 21.

[181]   See, for example, Louise Amoore's analyses of the UK 'e-border' program, which was studied in these terms: Louise Amoore, 'Data derivatives: On the emergence of a security risk calculus for our times' (2011) 28(6) *Theory, Culture and Society* 24. According to Trevor Paglen state secrecy 'can only be characterized by contradiction' because 'secret relations, programs, sites, and events have to be made out of the same "stuff" that everything else (ie the nonsecret world) is made of' – see: Trevor Paglen, 'Goatsucker: toward a spatial theory of state secrecy' (2010) 28(5) *Environment and Planning D: Society and Space* 759, 760.

[182]   Sam Raphael, Crofton Black, Ruth Blakeley and Steve Kostas, 'Tracking rendition aircraft as a way to understand CIA secret detention and torture in Europe' (2016) 20(1)

use high-powered telescopic photography to document secret military bases or forensic techniques to digitally reconstruct the human effects of drone strikes.[183]

One technique used in this book to address this problem is reliance on leaked classified documents. In November 2010 Wikileaks publicly released more than 250,000 confidential US Embassy cables. Diplomatic cables have long been the preferred format of communication for sending messages between state departments (or foreign ministries) and their diplomatic posts around the world. They were historically transmitted via undersea telegraph cables (hence the name), but since the 1960s have been sent electronically through computer networks and archived in digital repositories.[184] In May 2010, a disaffected US soldier and intelligence analyst (Chelsea Manning) copied cables from a US Department of Defense database and passed them to Wikileaks for publication. Cablegate, as this leak was called, involved 'the largest set of confidential documents ever to be released into the public domain'.[185] Select cables were published by leading newspapers around the globe, leading to embarrassing stories for world leaders to explain. They were also released online as a searchable database for journalists and academics.[186] And this database was used extensively to write this book.

These leaked cables are a veritable treasure trove for researchers investigating secret governance. In this book I have used them in three ways. First, the cables helped me map what would otherwise have been a secret research field to find out who and where the key nodes in the assemblage are. They helped me understand that the key actors in this regime are not necessarily diplomats in UN missions in New York or the

---

International Journal of Human Rights 78. See also The Rendition Project, coordinated by Ruth Blakely and Sam Raphael. Available at: bit.ly/2ao8T10.

[183] Trevor Paglen and Rebecca Solnit, Invisible: Covert Operations and Classified Landscapes (New York: Aperture, 2010). For an overview of the Forensic Architecture project digitally reconstructing drone strikes, see: bit.ly/2a8EOmZ.

[184] For a succinct history, see: Tobias Wille, 'The diplomatic cable' in Mark Salter (ed.), Making Things International II: Catalysts and Reactions (Minneapolis MN: University of Minnesota Press, 2015).For an innovative use of the Wikileaks cables in sociological research, see: Grégoire Mallard, 'Antagonistic recursivities and successive cover-ups: the case of private nuclear proliferation' (2018) 69(4) British Journal of Sociology 1007.

[185] Wikileaks Press Release, Secret US Embassy Cables (28 November 2010). Available at: bit.ly/29H84Du.

[186] Originally, the cables were made available in a searchable database (Cablesearch) built by the European Center for Computer Assisted Reporting. But the site was taken down. The cables are now accessible online as the Wikileaks Public Library of US Diplomacy. Available at: bit.ly/29HT18S.

heads of government counterterrorism departments. Through the cables one can see that functional experts, in-house lawyers, low-level security officials and otherwise faceless bureaucrats play a critical important role in assembling and sustaining this form of global law.

In Chapter 2, for example, I investigate a series of consultation meetings between the UN1267 Monitoring Team and the security agencies of key states in the global war against terror. Through the cables I was able to observe that certain intelligence officials were in conflict with the Security Council because they wanted greater access to US intelligence material and technical assistance (for example, to surveil their populations) in exchange for their cooperation in implementing the list. The cables enabled me to identify who the key interlocutors in this conflict were, including one particular official in a North-African state of key strategic interest. After further internet research, I tracked this official down to an embassy in central Europe. And following a few emails and phone calls, I was able to set up a meeting and travel there for an interview. This three-hour discussion not only provided crucial empirical material for understanding the problems in Chapter 2. It also facilitated research access to other important actors in the listing assemblage who would otherwise have been invisible.

Earlier in this introduction I argued that methods are entangled in enacting the objects that they discover, and the above example neatly underscores this point. Following the associations drawn by the cables allowed me to *produce* the very listing assemblage that my framework and method sought to help me know. As Evelyn Ruppert, John Law and Mike Savage argue, methods are 'simultaneously embedded in and shaped by social worlds, and can in turn become agents that act in and shape those worlds' – a process that they describe as the 'social life of methods'.[187] Leaked documents, in other words, don't just help make the invisible world of global security law visible. They are not just about transparency and representation. In this study, the cables leaked by Wikileaks are also performative.

Second, these leaked cables also helped me identify and better understand what the critical issues with the listing regime are for the key actors within it and to modify my research design accordingly. Whilst legal scholars were preoccupied debating the significance of the *Kadi* case, for example, the cables allowed me to see that powerful states had already got on with the task of trying to undercut the power of the courts by

---

[187] Ruppert et al., 'Reassembling social science methods', 31.

introducing new procedures empowering EU judges to use intelligence as evidence. This had the effect of reorientating my listing research in an entirely different direction. Whilst others were arguing about whether global constitutionalism or global legal pluralism offered the most appropriate frame for understanding the *Kadi* case, the cables helped me to organise interviews inside various institutions to explore how macroproblems of the listing regime were being quietly negotiated outside of formal processes (like court judgments and Security Council debates) through seemingly mundane micro-procedural reforms about rules of evidence. Insights gleaned from these interviews structures the analysis and arguments presented throughout Chapter 4.

In my original research plan for this book I had hypothesised that executive access to intelligence might be a critically important catalyst for conflict in this domain because it allowed the executive to participate in accelerated global networks of information exchange. Globalisation, in other words, is about speed and affording executives relative temporal advantage vis-à-vis legislatures and courts, as advocated in a diverse body of academic scholarship.[188] But the cables quickly allowed me to see the problems of this approach in relation to this particular area of governance. Actors who should have had access to the material supposedly underlying the list were complaining that they had nothing and were effectively being kept out of the decision-making loop. What I had thought might be a relatively seamless world of accelerated global security networks, appeared as something far messier and more shaped by the geopolitics of the Cold War and the 'Five Eyes' intelligence relationship.[189] This cable-induced insight allowed me to revise my original plan and take the project in a different direction. Instead of a body of global security law driven by the transnational intelligence exchange and access to accelerated networks, a different problem

---

[188] See, for example: William E. Scheuerman, *Liberal Democracy and the Social Acceleration of Time* (Baltimore MD: John Hopkins University Press, 2004); Hartmut Rosa and William E. Scheuerman (eds.), *High Speed Society: Social Acceleration, Power and Modernity* (Penn State Park PA: Pennsylvania State University Press, 2009). Saskia Sassen also argues that global assemblages facilitate a redistribution of power within the nation-state towards those elements and agencies that are more directly connected with global structures (for example, in international finance), thus consolidating the power of the executive branch and weakening its overall accountability – Sassen, *Territory, Authority, Rights*, p. 384.

[189] For a succinct introduction to the politics of Five-Eyes intelligence co-operation, see: Privacy International, *Eyes Wide Open: Special Report* (2013). Available at: bit.ly /2NCffBo.

emerged: how can this global security regime persist when listing authorities are taking 'decisions' with such little consideration as to why and
the information supposedly underneath the list is so 'patchy' and
unevenly distributed? This shift prompted a rather different research
agenda and set of findings, as Chapter 4 plainly demonstrates.

Finally, I used the cables as a kind of analytical crowbar during my
interviews to prise open greater access to confidential empirical material.
When researching the political background to the introduction of new
procedural rules at the European General Court (EGC) (as analysed in
Chapter 4), the cables gave me access to the minutes of key meetings
between US and EU officials on this issue. And these minutes gave me
both the names of the bureaucrats who were key players in the negotiations and a very frank account of what they had already said and done on
the issue. After analysing the cables, I emailed and set up various
appointments for interviews. And as the interviews went on, I was able
to quietly introduce the material from the cables into my questions. This
meant that, instead of starting from a relatively uninformed position, my
interview questions could be orientated towards the key conflicts in the
listing assemblage and closely calibrated with my interviewees' positions.
This facilitated rapport-building, which in turn allowed me to elicit more
meaningful, higher-quality data and encourage participants to elaborate
on the confidential material.[190] This crowbar technique worked so well
that one interviewee contacted me afterwards to insist that I could not use
what we had discussed unless I agreed to hand my research over to his
country's security services for vetting.

According to Callon and Latour, actors become powerful by placing
practices 'in a hierarchy in such a way that some become stable and no
longer need be considered ... An actor grows with the number of
relations he or she can put ... in black boxes' where black boxes contain
'that which no longer needs to be reconsidered'.[191] The task of the
researcher is then to open up the particular black box of enquiry and
trace the associations, practices and relations it contains. This is how one
undertakes a 'sociology of associations' and studies an assemblage in the
actor-network tradition.[192] But when 'the blackbox is a locked box',
suggest William Walters and Jacqueline Best, the situation is dramatically

---

[190] On rapport and research quality see, for example: Paul Ryan and Tony Dundan, 'Case
      research Interviews: Eliciting Superior Quality Data' (2008) *International Journal of Case
      Method Research and Application* 443.
[191] Callon and Latour, 'Unscrewing the big Leviathan', 284–5.
[192] Latour, *Reassembling the Social*, p. 9.

altered.[193] In such situations, they argue that 'the researcher must now follow the trail of those mediators who have made it their task to name and open up worlds of secrecy'.[194] When the field is covert, in other words, the differences between hackers, whistle-blowers, investigative journalists and academic researchers are narrowed. Undertaking empirical research on secret governance requires a commitment to openness and methodological disobedience.

1.4   Structure of the Book

The book is built around three empirical chapters examining the listing assemblage from different sites. Each chapter engages with a particular problem and traces how it is negotiated by different actors to help me address the key research questions. There is no overarching narrative linking the different parts into a coherent whole, but key concepts run transversally across the text and are iterated at the different sites under study. This isn't a book where the concepts are set out up-front in the 'theoretical chapter' and then briefly revisited again at the end to tie everything together, with the empirical material sandwiched in between. Rather, the theoretical development takes place throughout the chapters as the empirical material is analysed. This is an approach prompted by the assemblage lens itself and the philosophy of what Deleuze calls 'pragmatics'. According to Deleuze, in rationalist approaches 'the abstract is given the task of explaining and it is the abstract that is realized in the concrete'.[195] But with multiplicities or assemblages, empiricism 'starts with a completely different evaluation: analyzing the states of things in such a way that non-pre-existent concepts can be extracted from them' to 'find the conditions under which something new is produced'.[196]

   The aim of this book then is to open up novel ways of thinking about global security law and governance by providing a detailed sociolegal account of the listing assemblage in motion. Because of the way the book is structured, the chapters don't need to be read in any particular order. Readers are instead encouraged to approach this text generatively, as

---

[193] William Walters and Jacqueline Best, 'Translating the sociology of translation' (2013) 7(3) *International Political Sociology* 345, 346. See also: William Walters, 'Secrecy, publicity and the milieu of security' (2015) 5(3) *Dialogues in Human Geography* 287.
[194] Walters and Best, 'Translating'.
[195] Deleuze and Parnet, Dialogues, p. vii.
[196] Ibid.

a 'box of tools', appropriating the different ideas presented in ways that resonate with their own particular research interests and problems.[197] The book is primarily written as a global law text with an explicit focus on the politics of counterterrorism governance. But it aspires to have broader interdisciplinary appeal, so other readers shouldn't tune out just yet. As suggested in this introductory chapter, different parts of the book will be of interest to those interested in sociolegal studies, global governance and human rights, STS and sociology of knowledge, the 'practice turn' in international relations, ethnographies of globalisation, humanitarian governance, international and transnational law and critical security studies. If you don't find something that resonates straight away, keep reading on through the detail until you do.

Chapter 2 focuses on the UN1267 ISIL and Al-Qaida Analytical Support and Sanctions Monitoring Team – an expert group supporting the Sanctions Committee (made up of the P5 states) to administer the list. This chapter engages with the practical problem of how to target 'global terrorism' – an issue that has eluded earlier attempts at definition and that is shrouded in political and legal uncertainty. Drawing from ANT and governmentality scholarship, I show how the technology of the list itself plays a crucial role in rendering this elusive problem governable – by building a 'global optic' for seeing dispersed terrorist networks and ordering an otherwise diffuse global threat.

I analyse the practice of UN listing experts engaged at two specific sites – in 'consultation meetings' with national security and intelligence officials directed at populating the list with potential targets and in collaboration with experts from other international organisations to make the list interoperable with global policing data (Interpol) and the passenger data held by the global aviation industry (ICAO and IATA). These seemingly innocuous technical practices aiming at better implementing the list have thus far escaped academic attention. Yet this chapter shows how analysing expert knowledge practices can reveal important insights into how global security law is being made powerful, durable and global. If we are interested in understanding how new forms

---

[197] In conversation with Foucault, Gilles Deleuze said that, 'a theory is exactly like a box of tools ... It must be useful ... it is an instrument for multiplication'. Foucault argued that 'theory does not express, translate or serve to apply practice. It is practice.' See: Michel Foucault and Gilles Deleuze, 'Intellectuals and power' in Donald Bouchard (ed.), *Language, Counter-Memory, Practice: Selected Essays and Interviews by Michel Foucault* (Ithaca NY: Cornell University Press, 1977), pp. 205, 208. This idea is discussed by Brian Massumi in his foreword to Deleuze and Guattari's *A Thousand Plateaus*, p. xv.

of global administrative violence are being forged in the shadows of international law and decision-making, then empirically studying the techniques and practices of listing expertise is critically important.

Chapter 3 shifts focus to the enduring problem of accountability in global governance and follows what happens when UN sanctioning powers originally designed to discipline recalcitrant states deemed threats to international peace are recalibrated to directly target individuals suspected of being nodes in global terrorist networks. It provides a detailed genealogical account of the emergence of the UN1267 Office of the Ombudsperson – a novel procedural mechanism created by the Security Council in 2009 to provide redress to listed individuals who believe that they have been wrongly targeted. This conflict about 'fair and clear procedures' in Security Council sanctions has animated the ISIL and Al-Qaida listing regime since its inception and has been the object of considerable debate. Whilst there is still disagreement as to whether the Ombudsperson goes far enough to protect due process rights, most agree that this mechanism is an important step in the right direction towards greater human rights compliance.

My analysis challenges this narrative of global legal progress and complicates the claim that the Ombudsperson provides 'fair and clear' procedures. I show how the Ombudsperson is a composite figure of expertise born out of diverse institutional struggles under conditions of legal fragmentation. My key argument is that different actors in the listing assemblage enact fundamentally different versions of the list through their practice – that is, that the ISIL and Al-Qaida list is best thought of as what STS scholars call a 'multiple object'. When the accountability problems of the list are reposed in this way, we can see that Ombudsperson functions as a kind of institutional glue or 'boundary object' that helps to align the different actors, mute underlying political tensions and hold the different versions of the list together in an uneasy yet stable relation. Drawing from interviews with the Ombudsperson and my own experiences representing individuals in UN delisting proceedings, I critique the claim that this procedural innovation offers 'de facto judicial review'. In my account, these unique delisting practices and techniques embed new forms of preemptive security and render the list durable as a global exceptional governance device. The Ombudsperson mechanism is much more than a global administrative law mechanism and incremental procedural improvement.

Chapter 4 follows the list into the EU courts and the practices of judicial review. It explores what happens when the preemptive security logics of the list and its governance of radical uncertainty meet the principles of judicial proof and evidence long used and protected by the courts. The chapter empirically follows the reform of the procedural rules of the EGC to allow judges to rely on intelligence material without disclosure to litigants for the first time. These reforms were an attempt to resolve the complexities associated with judicially reviewing a list grounded in the use of intelligence-as-evidence and eliminate the kinds of norm conflicts seen in the *Kadi* case.

Most global law scholarship disregards issues of time and space, even though they are widely regarded as key vectors of globalisation across academic disciplines. Chapter 4 speaks to this problem by highlighting the spatiotemporal dynamics and epistemic qualities of the Law of the List. I argue that the listing assemblage is driven by dynamics of 'non-synchrony' and 'dis-location' and animated by a mosaic epistemology where seemingly insignificant details are associated together to infer potential correlations and future threats. In my account, non-synchronous law is legality 'out of sync', composed of divergent temporal logics. By using intelligence-as-evidence, the list brings retrospective and preemptive logics together into productive relation, and this relation is generating legal conflict. The procedural reforms examined in this chapter aim to give judges tools to manage this problem, but I show how they end up engendering further complexity. Judicial review is usually orientated towards a 'decision' that has taken place in the past. But my analysis shows how using intelligence-as-evidence defers this space of decision and confounds this judicial process because the decision that is supposed to be under review is not there. I use the term 'dis-located law' to capture this dynamic process of fracture and deferral and suggest that it is critical to how the Law of the List governs.

The conclusion of the book draws together my key findings and maps out global security problems that require further investigation and research. In my analysis, preemptive security is not supplanting existing legal practices, but reorganising them in novel ways that demand empirical attention if we want to understand how global security law governs the uncertain threats of terrorism in the present. Global security law is not the seamlessly brave new world that many lawyers claim it to be. It is far more heterogeneous, fragmented and complex. Securing the world from transboundary terrorist threats is transforming domestic and international legal ordering in far-reaching ways and consolidating new forms of exceptional governance. This book maps these transformations and provides a detailed account of global security law in motion. It doesn't end by prescribing a corrective programme of legal or political reform. But showing how security problems are governed and global law assembled through the ordering device of the list is an important critical project in its own right. It reveals how international executive rule is extended through new governance techniques, knowledge practices and functional expertise, often tenuously sutured together. And it brings the technologies of power and conditions of possibility of the list to the analytical surface, revealing them as something historically situated and contingent and offering insights into how things might be made otherwise. It is an approach that aims to offer what Foucault calls a 'historical ontology of ourselves' – where 'the critique of what we are is at one and the same time the historical analysis of the limits that are imposed on us and an experiment with the possibility of going beyond them'.[198]

---

[198] Michel Foucault, 'What is enlightenment?' in Paul Rabinow (ed.), *The Foucault Reader* (New York: Pantheon Books, 1984), p. 50.

Global Listing Technologies and the Politics of Expertise[*]

Global counterterrorism emerged as a distinctive policy domain after the 9/11 attacks in 2001. New UN Security Council measures were adopted that were general in nature and that prescribed binding norms that all states must implement, leading the Council to be described as a 'global legislator'.[1] New UN counterterrorism institutions were created to assist the Council in its work.[2] Domestic and regional laws and security strategies were reorientated towards preemptively countering global terrorism.[3] And these elements were brought into novel relation as part of a new discourse aimed at countering the dangers of transnational threats. Global security law is now considered mainstream, yet little has been written about the practices, techniques and struggles that allowed such a profound shift to unfold over such a relatively short space of time. How was something that had long been the subject of heated conflict by states and IOs ('terrorism') not only rendered knowable, but so rapidly turned into an object of preemptive intervention on a global scale?

This chapter addresses this question by analysing UN counterterrorism listing as a novel form of global security law and governance. It

---

[*] Parts of this chapter were previously published in: Marieke de Goede and Gavin Sullivan, 'The politics of security lists' (2016) 34(1) *Environment and Planning D: Society and Space* 67.

[1] Including S/RES/1267 (1999), S/RES/1333 (2000), S/RES/1373 (2001), S/RES/1390 (2002) and S/RES/1540 (2004). See: Paul Szasz, 'The Security Council starts legislating' (2002) 96 (4) *American Journal of International Law* 901; Stefan Talmon, 'The Security Council as world legislature' (2005) 99(1) *American Journal of International Law* 175.

[2] S/RES/1373 (2001), for example, set up the UN CTC. S/RES/1535 (2004) later set up the CTED to assist the CTC in its work.

[3] S/RES/1373 (2001) required Member States to report within ninety days on compliance (para. 6). See: CTC, *Country Reports: Reports by Member States pursuant to Security Council Resolution 1373 (2001)*. On the reorganisation of national law to comply with post-9/11 global security law, see: Kim Lane Scheppele, 'The empire of security and the security of empire' (2013) 27 *Temple International and Comparative Law Journal* 241.

focuses on the crucial assemblage work performed by the UN1267 Analytical Support and Sanctions Monitoring Team – a small group of technical experts responsible for advising the UN1267 Sanctions Committee and keeping the list effectively calibrated. There are no existing empirical studies of this Monitoring Team. The little material that exists is drawn almost entirely from its own published reports and suggests that it is unduly constrained by Security Council politics and disconnected from the evolving ISIL and Al-Qaida threat picture. This chapter challenges this narrative by 'following the list' to two different sites where the team has negotiated seemingly mundane problems of list implementation. First, I examine 'consultation meetings' that have been held between the UN team and national intelligence agencies. Second, I analyse a collaborative governance project between the team and the global aviation industry to enhance enforcement of the list's travel ban. My argument is that the work of these global listing experts is far more wide-ranging, legally productive and politically significant than existing material suggests. But these effects go unnoticed because they tend to be discounted by legal scholars as technical background work and enabled through the simple ordering technology of a list.

The chapter builds on currents of academic literature introduced in Chapter 1 – such as scholarship on international governance practices and global sociolegal research. My aim is to open up novel ways of approaching global security law by reframing the list as a global govern-ance technology and inscription device. I argue that this analytical move allows for more dynamic conceptions of power and agency to be used in the study of global security law and helps show how critical the work of listing expertise is in this domain. Drawing from diverse strands of governmentality scholarship, STS and postnational legal theory, I show how the list (as device) and its expertise (or knowledge practices) are co-productively entangled in ways that make the uncertain threats of global terrorism calculable and amenable to preemptive legal intervention.[4]

Lists have long been deployed as technologies of power and adminis-trative rule. According to Cornelia Vismann, the imperial registries of thirteenth-century Europe 'were more than nifty administrative techni-ques designed to economize on reading and writing; they were nothing less than the media technology for a state as a permanent entity'.[5]

---

[4] Peter Miller and Nikolas Rose, 'Governing economic life' (1990) 19(1) *Economy and Society* 1.

[5] Cornelia Vismann, *Files: Law and Media Technology* (Stanford CA: Stanford University Press, 2008) pp. 81–2.

Registration lists played a crucial role delineating 'healthy' and 'diseased' elements of the population in Nazi Germany, enabling the deportation of the latter to death camps as part of the Third Reich's 'Final Solution'.[6] Listing was a key bureaucratic technique used for the administration of violence by the Khmer Rouge in Cambodia and for the control of 'subversive organizations' in the United States throughout the twentieth century.[7] The list remains a critically important technology of security governance today – from drone warfare to the use of no-fly lists for targeting 'risky' travellers.[8] Listing is an *operational* form of writing that often prefigures new forms of political organisation, regimes of administrative violence and ways of seeing and acting on the world. So, it is unsurprising that this simple ordering technique is a key component of the Security Council's global 'anti-terrorism campaign' and performing crucial assemblage work.[9]

When the list is analytically reframed as a technology or device, the question of listing expertise becomes especially important. If global security law is a project of knowing and countering 'global terrorism' before it materialises, then mapping its assemblage requires close analysis of the expert-object relations it puts into effect.[10] But the relation between global law, expertise and governance remains markedly understudied. Existing scholarship provides powerful normative critiques of international law's deferral to 'the politics of expertise'.[11] Yet it is insufficiently

---

[6] See, for example: Götz Aly, Karl Roth, Edwin Black and Assenka Oksiloff, *The Nazi Census: Identification and Control in the Third Reich* (Philadelphia PA: Temple University Press, 2004); Edwin Black and Bill Wallace, *IBM and the Holocaust: The Strategic Alliance between Nazi Germany and America's Most Powerful Corporation* (New York: Crown Publishers, 2001).

[7] James Tyner, *The Politics of Lists: Bureaucracy and Genocide under the Khmer Rouge* (Morgantown WV: West Virginia University Press, 2018); Robert Justin Goldstein, *American Blacklist: The Attorney General's List of Subversive Organizations* (Lawrence KA: University Press of Kansas, 2008).

[8] de Goede and Sullivan, 'The politics of security lists'; Jutta Weber, 'Keep adding. On kill lists, drone warfare and the politics of databases' (2016) 34(1) *Environment and Planning D: Society and Space* 107.

[9] On global security law as anti-terrorism campaign, see: Kim Lane Scheppele, 'The international state of emergency: challenges to constitutionalism after September 11', Yale Legal Theory Workshop, 21 September 2006 (unpublished manuscript) 3.

[10] Karin Knorr-Cetina, 'Objectual practice' in Theodore R. Schatzki, Karin Knorr Cetina and Eike von Savigny (eds.), *The Practice Turn in Contemporary Theory* (London: Routledge, 2001), p. 196.

[11] Martti Koskenniemi, *The Politics of International Law* (Oxford: Hart Publishing, 2011), p. 340; David Kennedy, *A World of Struggle: How Power, Law and Expertise Shape Global Political Economy* (Princeton NJ: Princeton University Press, 2016).

attentive to how techniques and practices of expertise actually assemble global relations and tends to be empirically disinterested in understanding the specific sites where such global legal-ordering is taking place.

Studying the list as a technology advances this discussion by opening up a much broader set of research questions than those usually pursued by counterterrorism and international legal scholars: how does this list, and the expert knowledge its administration demands, link 'calculations of rule at one place with action at another' to allow 'government at a distance'?[12] What kinds of calculative practices do listing experts produce under the mandate of effective monitoring and implementation? How do problems of the list enrol different actors into new security networks? How does listing enable the uncertainties of 'global terrorism' to be rendered knowable and amenable to preemptive intervention by the Security Council? In sum, how are knowledge practices, technical artefacts, norm processes and forms of expertise assembled together to enable and shape global security law?

This chapter addresses these questions by analysing the list and the Monitoring Team's listing expertise as a production site of global law, using the framework of assemblage and method of multisited ethnography outlined in the Chapter 1.[13] My main argument is that the list formats and conditions this domain of law in discrete yet crucially important ways. Analysing the technicalities of listing practice is integral to the core concern of this book – that is, to understand *how* this form of global security law and exceptional governance is created, sustained and stretched. My aim is to show that the ISIL and Al-Qaida list is much more than mere legal instrument. It is a performative technology or 'actant'[14] that helps constitute the very problems of 'global terrorism' it seeks to target.

To develop these arguments, the chapter is divided into four sections. The first section critically engages with the relevant literature, frames global security listing as a technology of governance and inscription and elaborates on some of the advantages of this approach. The second

---

[12] Miller and Rose, 'Governing economic life', 9.

[13] Bruno Latour, *Reassembling the Social: An Introduction to Actor-Network Theory* (Oxford: Oxford University Press, 2005), pp. 176–7. See also: Sally Engle Merry, 'New legal realism and the ethnography of transnational law' (2006) 31(4) *Law & Social Inquiry* 975. Merry argues that socio-legal research should undertake 'ethnographic analysis of global sites of legal production' (980).

[14] Bruno Latour, *The Politics of Nature: How to Bring the Sciences into Democracy* (Cambridge MA: Harvard University Press, 2004), pp. 70–7. On the list as actant, see: de Goede and Sullivan, 'The politics of security lists'.

section examines the origins of the ISIL and Al-Qaida listing regime in detail, building on the introductory discussion of Chapter 1. My main focus here is tracing the radical repurposing of the list after 9/11 and providing an overview of its changing relation with various forms of UN counterterrorism expertise.

The chapter then provides detailed site-specific analyses of the Monitoring Team's global listing practices. The third section focuses on 'consultation meetings' that bring security and intelligence officials from around the world together with the Monitoring Team to build a comprehensive ISIL and Al-Qaida threat picture. The initiative is publicly justified as a means of keeping the list calibrated and up-to-date. But its aims are far more ambitious and its effects are more far-reaching. I argue that these meetings bring security experts and the technology of the list together to construct a global optic for seeing global terrorism. The list is not an inert object here, but an active agent performing important assemblage work. It helps bypass the problem of defining terrorism; it renders disparate localised threats commensurable; it enrols diverse actors into new preemptive security networks and quantifies potential future threats into something governable in the present. For Ulrich Beck, expertise is confounded in the 'world risk society' when faced with the catastrophic and purportedly incalculable threat of terrorism.[15] Yet here the ISIL and Al-Qaida list and its expertise work together to form what I call a Global Optic or 'centre of calculation',[16] precisely aimed at seeing and governing the uncertain threats of global terrorism before they materialise. Security expertise doesn't retreat in the face of uncertainty, as Beck suggests. It governs through it.[17] Understanding how global security law is made expansively 'global' demands analysis of such techniques and knowledge practices.

The fourth section further develops these claims by analysing recent efforts to make the list interoperable with Interpol biometric databases and Advance Passenger Information (API) and Passenger Name Record (PNR) data used by the global airline industry (IATA). This initiative is part of a broader attempt to reorientate the list from its post-9/11 focus

---

[15] Ulrich Beck, *World Risk Society* (Bristol: Polity Press, 2009)

[16] Bruno Latour, *Science in Action: How to Follow Scientists and Engineers through Society* (Cambridge MA: Harvard University Press, 1987).

[17] Claudia Aradau and Rens Van Munster, 'Governing terrorism through risk: taking precautions, (un)knowing the future' (2007) 13(1) *European Journal of International Relations* 89.

on Al-Qaida towards the threat of ISIL and 'foreign terrorist fighters'. This project tends to be overlooked by outsiders for turning on seemingly mundane questions of reformatting and data management. Yet I argue that it is precisely through such technical, infrastructural problems and standard-setting practices that the scope and power of the list is being stretched and transformed. Data infrastructures and formatting, in other words, are crucially important elements that configure global security law. Expertise is neither merely 'implementing' the list here nor operating ancillary to the international law and politics of the Council. It is forging new forms of global legal-ordering and exceptional governance in its own right.

2.1 The List As a Technology of Governance

In Chapter 1 we observed how most literature on the UN ISIL and Al-Qaida sanctions regime is overwhelmingly positivist in focus. Legal scholars tend to posit an international norm pyramid – with the Security Council on top (as primary agents), regional bodies and national states in the middle (as implementing intermediaries) and sanctioned parties on the bottom – as the implicit framework of analysis.[18] Sanctions scholars tends to use theoretical models of 'senders' (principal authors) and 'receivers' (targets) to assess whether these measures achieve their intended political objectives.[19] Both approaches conceptualise power as a unidirectional application of force moving from point of origin to point of destination. If the list features at all in this material, it is relegated to the status of legal tool, akin to a statutory instrument or executive order, inertly placed in the background.

As Nico Krisch points out, thinking about global authority as 'solid' in this way is problematic because it obscures the more 'liquid' forms of authority shaping global regulatory space. Global indicators, for example, produce powerful effects even though they 'do not operate through formal legal tools' or conform with conventional accounts of how

---

[18] Whilst global constitutionalists might complicate this model – by arguing for the primacy of *jus cogens* norms and the placement of rights-bearing individuals at the top and not the bottom of the pyramid – they nonetheless remain wedded to structures of normative hierarchy in international law. See, for example, Erika de Wet and Jure Vidmar (eds.), *Hierarchy in International Law: The Place of Human Rights* (Oxford: Oxford University Press, 2012).

[19] Francesco Giumelli, *Coercing, Constraining and Signalling: Explaining UN and EU Sanctions after the Cold War* (Colchester: ECPR Press, 2011).

international decision-making is done.[20] By creating commensurable relations between heterogeneous elements and simplifying complex phenomena through quantification, such technologies create 'novel epistemic objects of regulation, domination, experimentation and critique' – they do much more than present 'taken-for-granted facts'.[21] But these effects go unnoticed if we assume international authority rests in the hands of powerful states and IOs and that governance technologies (like indicators or lists) are merely conduits for their power.

The ISIL and Al-Qaida list is much more than the intergovernmental deliberations of the Council and the Chapter VII UN Charter Resolutions that they formally authorise. It is a diffuse global norm and novel legal format that exceeds the 'shackles' of the formal international law from which it was created.[22] Yet to grasp the more generative dimensions of this regime we have to actually examine what the list and its expertise *does*, using analytical tactics fit for the task of global sociolegal enquiry.

To that end, this chapter analyses the ISIL and Al-Qaida list as a technology of government and inscription. My key point of departure from the positivists is that legal technologies (such as lists) are not neutral *instruments* or inert regulatory tools, but creative processes that *do* important things in the world. Technologies emerge 'to overcome the political and epistemological limits of existing knowledge' and, in so doing, they remain intimately entangled within the knowledge objects that come into being through their use.[23] The microbe, for example, is not simply discovered by the microscope but in important ways is constituted by it.[24] Statistics are not just an effect of the modern state, but a means by which the state and the populations it governs came to be

---

[20] Nico Krisch, 'Authority, solid and liquid, in postnational governance' in Roger Cotterrell and Maksymilian Del Mar (eds.), *Authority in Transnational Legal Theory: Theorising across Disciplines* (Cheltenham: Edward Elgar Publishing, 2016), p. 33.

[21] Richard Rottenburg and Sally Engle Merry, 'A world of indicators: the making of governmental knowledge through quantification' in Richard Rottenburg, Sally Engle Merry, Sung-Joon Park and Johanna Mugler (eds.), *The World of Indicators: The Making of Governmental Knowledge through Quantification* (Cambridge: Cambridge University Press, 2015), p. 5.

[22] Joost Pauwelyn, Ramses A. Wessel and Jan Wouters, 'When structures become shackles: stagnation and dynamics in international lawmaking' (2014) 25(3) *European Journal of International Law* 733.

[23] Annelise Riles, 'New agenda for the cultural study of law: taking on the technicalities' (2005) 53 *Buffalo Law Review* 973, 986.

[24] Bruno Latour, *The Pasteurization of France* (Cambridge MA: Harvard University Press, 1993).

created.[25] Economics 'performs, shapes and formats the economy, rather than observing how it functions'.[26] In the same way, objects of political rule and legal governance are effects of the techniques and knowledge practices that calculate, classify and target them. As David Kennedy puts it, in global governance 'the identification of the problem and the selection of tools arise together' – that is, they are co-constitutive in practice.[27] Studying global law through the artefacts, knowledge practices and performative effects of expert rule prompts a different set of questions than those usually asked by international lawyers: 'what productive work do they do as they circulate? What forms of social action are they able to mobilize, and how? What subjects, objects and situations are produced in the manner of their circulation and deployment, and how?'.[28] My point here is not to claim that acts of terrorist violence do not exist outside the law – they obviously do. But rather that empirically following how 'global terrorism' is made actionable through the technology of the list allows us to better understand how this domain of global security law is being assembled and made powerful.

This approach to listing builds on a rich tradition of sociolegal and ethnographic research reappraising the instrumentality of legal instruments.[29] The key value of this work is that it brings the material

---

[25] Michel Foucault, The *Birth of Biopolitics: Lectures at the College de France 1978–1979* (London: Picador, 2008); Ian Hacking, *The Emergence of Probability: A Philosophical Study of Early Ideas about Probability, Induction and Statistical Inference* (Cambridge: Cambridge University Press, 1975); Alain Desrosières, *The Politics of Large Numbers: A History of Statistical Reasoning* (Cambridge MA: Harvard University Press, 1998); Theodore M. Porter, *The Rise of Statistical Thinking: 1820–1900* (Princeton NJ: Princeton University Press, 1986).

[26] Michel Callon (ed.), *The Laws of the Markets* (Oxford: Blackwell Publishing, 1998), p. 2.

[27] Kennedy, *A World of Struggle*, p. 96.

[28] Andrew Lang, 'International lawyers and the study of expertise: representationalism and performativity' in Mosche Hirsch and Andrew Lang (eds.), *Research Handbook on the Sociology of International Law* (Cheltenham: Edward Elgar Publishing, 2018), p. 149.

[29] Mariana Valverde, *Law's Dream of a Common Knowledge* (Princeton NJ: Princeton University Press, 2003); Mariana Valverde, 'Jurisdiction and Scale: "Legal Technicalities" as Resources for Theory' (2009) 18(2) *Social and Legal Studies* 139; Annelise Riles, *Collateral Knowledge: Legal Reasoning in the Global Financial Markets* (Chicago IL: University of Chicago Press, 2011); Annelise Riles, *The Network Inside Out* (Ann Arbor MI: University of Michigan Press, 2001); Bruno Latour, *The Making of Law: An Ethnography of the Conseil d'État* (Bristol: Polity Press, 2010); Emilie Cloatre, *Pills for the Poorest: An Exploration of TRIPS and Access to Medication in Sub-Saharan Africa* (Basingstoke: Palgrave Macmillan, 2013); Fleur Johns, *Non-Legality in International Law: Unruly Law* (Cambridge: Cambridge University Press, 2013); Martha Mundy and Alain Pottage (eds.), *Law, Anthropology, and the Constitution of the Social: Making Persons and Things* (Cambridge: Cambridge University Press, 2004).

and technical aspects of legal governance into view, 'not as ... a by-product [or] a tool of more important agents and forces, but as the protagonist of its own account'.[30] My approach aims to speak to debates on the power of quantification technologies and epistemic practices in international law and global governance.[31] And by using ideas of government and inscription together in my analysis, I aim to bring two strands of academic literature into productive relation – the 'governmentality' scholarship of Michel Foucault and those who have developed his work and the STS literature on 'inscription' devices developed by Bruno Latour and other ANT-inspired scholars.[32]

---

[30] Riles, 'New agenda', 985.

[31] On governance through quantification see, for example: Wendy N. Espeland and Mitchell L. Stevens, 'A sociology of quantification' (2008) 49(3) *European Journal of Sociology* 401; Rottenburg et al., *The World of Indicators*; Kevin E. Davis, Angelina Fisher, Benedict Kingsbury and Sally Engle Merry (eds.), *Governance by Indicators: Global Power through Classification and Rankings* (Cambridge: Cambridge University Press, 2012); Kevin E. Davis, Benedict Kingsbury and Sally Engle Merry, 'Indicators as a technology of global governance' (2012) 46(1) *Law and Society Review* 71; Sally Engle Merry, 'Measuring the World' (2011) 52(S3) *Current Anthropology* S83; Sally Engle Merry and Susan Bibler Coutin, 'Technologies of truth in the anthropology of conflict: AES/ APLA Presidential Address, 2013' (2014) 41(1) *American Ethnologist* 1; Oded Löwenheim, 'Examining the state: a Foucauldian perspective on international "governance indicators"' (2008) 29(2) *Third World Quarterly* 255; Wendy Larner and William Walters (eds.), *Global Governmentality: Governing International Spaces* (London: Routledge, 2004). On global governance practices, see: Knorr-Cetina et al., *The Practice Turn*; Emanuel Adler and Vincent Pouliot (eds.), *International Practices* (Cambridge: Cambridge University Press, 2011); Christian Bueger, 'Pathways to practice: praxiography and international politics' (2014) 6(3) *European Political Science Review* 383; Christian Bueger and Frank Gadinger, *International Practice Theory: New Perspectives* (Basingstoke: Palgrave Macmillan, 2014). There is little material on lists as technologies of governance. Notable exceptions include: Irus Braverman, 'The regulatory life of threatened species lists' in Irus Braverman (ed.), *Animals, Biopolitics, Law: Lively Legalities* (London: Routledge, 2016); Marieke de Goede, Anna Leander and Gavin Sullivan (eds.), 'The politics of the list: Law, security, technology' [Special Issue] (2016) 34(1) *Environment and Planning D: Society and Space* 3.

[32] Despite their different connotations and literatures, I use 'technology' and 'device' interchangeably in this chapter when talking about the list. 'Technologies' is the preferred term in Foucauldian scholarship, 'device' in STS and ANT scholarship. But both highlight the same effect – namely, the performativity of instruments and governance techniques. For a good example combining these approaches this way, see: Miller and Rose, 'Governing economic life'. For recent scholarship on the device as an analytical frame, see: John Law and Evelyn Ruppert, 'The social life of methods: devices' (2013) 6(3) *Journal of Cultural Economy* 229; Anthony Amicelle, Claudia Aradau and Julien Jeandesboz, 'Questioning security devices: performativity, resistance, politics' (2015) 46(4) *Security Dialogue* 293.

For Foucault, modern politics is grounded in a particular rationality of 'governmentality' – that is to say, an 'ensemble formed by the institutions, procedures, analyses and reflections, the calculations and tactics, that allow the exercise of [a] very specific albeit complex form of power', aimed at diffusing modes of economic administration into political practice.[33] Government is not merely made possible through norms and sovereign relations, but is enabled through heterogeneous practices and 'apparatuses' – that is, the 'actual instruments that form and accumulate knowledge, the observational methods, the recording techniques, the investigative research procedures, the verification mechanisms' that are 'formed, organized and put into circulation'.[34] Put differently, 'government is ... a function of technology',[35] because 'it is through technologies that political rationalities and the programs of government they articulate become capable of deployment'.[36]

Understanding global governance problems in technological terms requires sovereignty and law to be analytically repositioned. Because 'with government it is a question not of imposing law on men but ... of employing tactics ... [– or] using laws themselves as tactics – to arrange things in such a way that, through a certain number of means, such and such ends may be achieved'.[37] Studying governmental technologies also prompts a shift in *where* we look to find power unfolding. As Foucault's work shows, governmental power must be analysed at the points where 'it is in immediate relationship with ... its object, its target, its field of application' because it is there that new 'methods of subjugation' and 'tactics of domination' are formed before being 'invested or annexed by global phenomena'.[38]

The ability of macro-actors to 'dominate on a large scale'[39] or effect 'action at a distance',[40] according to Latour, is only possible through what

---

[33] Michel Foucault, 'Governmentality' in Graham Burchell and Peter Miller (eds.), *The Foucault Effect: Studies in Governmentality* (Chicago IL: University of Chicago Press, 1981), p. 102.

[34] Michel Foucault, *Society Must be Defended: Lectures at the Collège de France, 1975–1976* (London: Picador, 2003), p. 33.

[35] Michel Foucault, 'Space, knowledge and power' in Paul Rabinow (ed.), *The Foucault Reader* (New York: Pantheon, 1984), p. 256.

[36] Miller and Rose, 'Governing economic life', 8; Pat O'Malley, 'Risk, power and crime prevention' (1992) 21(3) *Economy and Society* 252.

[37] Foucault, 'Governmentality', p. 95.

[38] Foucault, *Society Must be Defended*, p. 31.

[39] Bruno Latour, 'Visualization and cognition: drawing things together' (1986) 6 *Knowledge and Society* 1, 12, 26.

[40] Latour, *Science in Action*, p. 223.

he terms devices of 'inscription' – that is 'item[s] of apparatus or particular configuration of such items which can transform a material substance into a figure or diagram which is directly usable'.[41] In his study of the interrelation between visualisation and cognition, for example, Latour presents us with a puzzle: why do important figures in the history of scientific innovation always 'work on two-dimensional inscriptions instead of the sky, the air, health, or the brain? What can they do with the first, that you cannot do with the second?'[42] The answer lies in the fact that inscription technologies provide advantage to those who use them and create asymmetries with those who do not. Inscriptions are characteristically mobile, immutable, flat, reproducible, multi-scalar, readily recombinable and geometrically measurable.[43] By allowing heterogeneous items to be rendered 'optically consistent', commensurability can be established: 'Realms of reality that seem far apart . . . are inches apart, once flattened out on the same surface.'[44]

In another example, Latour examines eighteenth-century French navigation in the East Pacific and asks: 'How is it possible to act on events, places and people that are unfamiliar and a long way away?' The answer, he suggests, is by '*somehow* bringing home these events, places and people' to 'centres of calculation' through the use of inscription techniques – that '(a) render them mobile . . . (b) keep them stable . . ., and (c) are combinable so that whatever stuff they are made of, they can be cumulated, aggregated, or shuffled like a pack of cards'.[45] In this way economies of equivalence, 'cycles of accumulation' and commensurable relations can emerge that enable 'a point to become a centre by acting at a distance on many other points'.[46] For Latour, centres of calculation are thus sites 'where information is being created, collected, assembled, transcribed, transported to, simplified and juxtaposed in a single location . . . where everything that is relevant can be seen'.[47]

These scientific innovation examples might seem tangential to the more urgent problems of global terrorism and security governance. But I argue there is something valuable in these accounts for the purposes of

---

[41] Bruno Latour and Steve Woolgar, *Laboratory Life: The Construction of Scientific Facts* (Princeton NJ: Princeton University Press, 1986), p. 51.

[42] Latour, 'Visualization and cognition', 18.

[43] Ibid. 18–20.

[44] Ibid. 25.

[45] Latour, *Science in Action*, pp. 222–3 (emphasis in original).

[46] Ibid. pp. 219, 222.

[47] John Law, *Ordering and Obduracy* (Lancaster: Lancaster University Centre for Science Studies, 2001) 8.

our present enquiry. For Latour, the scale of an actor and their ability to govern is not given a priori. It is contingent upon the inscription technologies at their disposal at any given moment and 'varies with the[ir] ability to produce, capture, sum up and interpret information about other places and times'.[48] This approach opens 'a new topographical relationship' between macro and micro with far-reaching implications for the ways that processes of global ordering are framed:

> The 'macro' no longer describes a wider or larger site in which the micro would be embedded ... but another equally local, equally micro place, which is *connected* to many others through some medium transporting specific types of traces. No place can be said to be bigger than any other place, but some can be said to benefit from far safer connections with many *more* places than others.[49]

The advantages of an assemblage lens have already been discussed, so here I highlight three features of the 'list as technology' approach to show how it can provide greater analytical purchase on the problems explored in this chapter. First, bringing Foucault and Latour together in this way helps us to think about law dynamically and materially, rather than merely as a normative phenomenon. Governance technologies and inscription devices draw empirical attention to the practices and sites that enable global legal processes to unfold and that are *constitutive* of global law. So, instead of asking 'what is law' within relatively bounded contexts like courts, this approach enables us to ask: '*how* is global security law' produced within complex and shifting transnational environments?[50]

Second, framing the list as a technology provides a useful conceptual lens for reappraising the understudied nexus between global law and expertise.[51] There is little research that sheds empirical light on how

---

[48] Latour, 'Visualization and cognition', 26.

[49] Latour, *Reassembling the Social*, p. 176 (original emphasis). Here Latour largely restates an argument made much earlier with Michel Callon. See: Michel Callon and Bruno Latour, 'Unscrewing the big Leviathan: how actors macro-structure reality and how sociologists help them to do so' in Aaron V. Cicourel and Karin Knorr-Cetina (eds.), *Advances in Social Theory and Methodology: Toward an Integration of Micro and Macro-sociologies* (London: Routledge & Kegan Paul, 1981), p. 277.

[50] For discussion of this reorientation from 'what' to 'how', see: Valverde, *Law's Dream*, p. 11.

[51] Monika Ambrus, Karin Arts, Ellen Hey and Helena Raulus (eds.), *The Role of 'Experts' in International and European Decision-Making Processes: Advisors, Decision Makers or Irrelevant Actors?* (Cambridge: Cambridge University Press, 2014) – who note (at p. 1): 'there is only scant analysis of how experts relate to decision-making processes at the

functional expertise assembles and sustains global legal relations.[52] This chapter shows how expert knowledge practices and the technical devices sustaining them are centrally important to the production of global security law, and so need to be made visible and subjected to scrutiny.[53]

Finally, analysing the ISIL and Al-Qaida list as a technology helps 'flatten the landscape' of global security law, enabling more granular analysis of problems of scale.[54] The key insight of Latour's work here is that 'global' actors are not necessarily 'bigger' than any others, but are made more powerful by their relative connectedness and the inscription technologies they use. Instead of assuming a priori the supranational power of this listing regime by reference to its legal foundations (Chapter VII of the UN Charter, UN Security Council Resolutions) or its position

international and European levels'. See, however, the insightful sociolegal analyses of Bryant Garth and Yves Dezalay: Yves Dezalay and Bryant G. Garth, *Dealing in Virtue: International Commercial Arbitration and the Construction of a Transnational Legal Order* (Chicago IL: University of Chicago Press, 1998); Yves Dezalay and Bryant Garth, *The Internationalization of Palace Wars: Lawyers, Economists, and the Contest to Transform Latin American States* (Chicago IL: University of Chicago Press, 2002). See also: Anna Leander and Tanja Aalberts (eds.), 'International Legal Theory: Symposium: Expertise, Uncertainty, and International Law' (2013) 26(4) *Leiden Journal of International Law* 783.

[52] Koskenniemi and Kennedy offer powerful normative critiques of international law's reliance on expertise in an era of fragmentation, but little detailed empirical analysis. For Koskenniemi, international law fragments and 'defers to the politics of expertise' as it is made technical through the creation of functionally differentiated regimes for the management of global problems. This instrumentalises international law in a technical idiom, thereby blunting its normative potential as a 'placeholder for the vocabularies of justice and goodness'. It is also depoliticises by reframing 'problems of politics as problems of expert knowledge', thus 'obscur[ing] the contingent nature of the choices made [and] the fact that at issue is structural bias and not the application of some neutral . . . reason' – see: Koskenniemi, *The Politics*, pp. 340, 361, 35, 68. For Kennedy expertise is problematic because it works from the 'background' behind the spaces where politics is usually thought to take place. As it comes to provide 'the frame for political debates and decisions', the foreground becomes 'a mere spectacle' or residual effect of more opaque background expert practices. Expertise is also problematic because underneath its representation of objective neutrality it works to shrink 'the range of the politically contestable'. See David Kennedy, 'Challenging expert rule: the politics of global governance' (2005) 27 *Sydney Law Review* 5, 11–12; David Kennedy, 'The forgotten politics of international governance' (2001) *European Human Rights Law Review* 117, 120. As Fleur Johns argues, Kennedy's work 'speaks at too great a remove from the rather dense, self-referential practices of international legal technique' – Johns, *Non-Legality in International Law*, p. 18. For a more detailed effort to empirically map expertise in global law, see: Kennedy, *A World of Struggle*.

[53] 'When background work has been most successful, it is very difficult to see' – see: Kennedy, *A World of Struggle*, p. 116.

[54] Latour, *Reassembling the Social*, p. 182.

in the international normative hierarchy, this approach helps problematise the 'global' in global security law by reframing it as an emergent process of ordering. As discussed above, global security law is produced through ordering practices emanating 'from local sites that manufacture global structures'.[55] This approach opens an important space for empirically investigating how listing works as a 'structure-making site'[56] and understanding how small shifts in knowledge production practices can provide important sources of legal and political change within large IOs capable of generating powerful global effects.

2.2 Global Counterterrorism and the Politics of Rendering Technical

'Terrorism' has long defied international attempts to transform it into a stable and knowable object.[57] Despite the increasing array of global security laws, there is still no international agreement on what constitutes 'terrorism'. The problem has been an incessant source of international conflict between states for almost eighty years. More than sixty proposed definitions were put forward for agreement between 1936 and 1981 without success.[58] An ad hoc committee convened by the UN General Assembly in 1972 to draft a convention on international terrorism failed to agree on the core issues to be prohibited. Another committee was convened in 1996 to try and build an international convention on terrorism and resolve the vexing definitional issue. Yet, despite decades of debate, this committee also failed to reach agreement on what 'terrorism' is. International conventions prohibiting particular aspects of 'terrorism' all bypass this definitional issue by adopting an act-specific focus. The Security Council has previously adopted resolutions in response to

---

[55] Ibid. p. 176. I am indebted here to Christian Bueger's innovative work on global maritime security. See, for example: Christian Bueger, 'Making things known: epistemic infrastructures, the United Nations and the translation of piracy' (2015) 9 *International Political Sociology* 1; Bueger, 'Pathways to practice'.

[56] Latour, *Reassembling the Social*. For Latour: 'If you cut some underlying structure from its local application, nothing happens ... if you cut a structure-making site from its connections, it simply stops being able to structure anything' (p. 176).

[57] Lisa Stampnitzky, *Disciplining Terror: How Experts Invented Terrorism* (Cambridge: Cambridge University Press, 2013).

[58] Mark Muller, 'Terrorism, proscription and the right to resist in the age of conflict' (2008) 20 *Denning Law Journal* 111, 113.

specific acts of terrorism,[59] but, due to 'cold war deadlock' in the Council it preferred to defer this issue to the General Assembly.[60]

Three elements underpin this unruliness. Until recently terrorism was framed in both law and politics as something that unfolded within a local or regional, rather than global, terrain of conflict.[61] There are also deep and persistent disagreements on the appropriate status to be accorded to 'state terrorism' or violence by state-sponsored forces. And there is still no consensus on whether the use of violence by national liberation and self-determination movements should be considered as terrorism or lawful resistance. The distinctions between friends and enemies that animate global politics ultimately remain arbitrary.[62] The problem with trying to reach international agreement on what terrorism is, according to Martti Koskenniemi, is that 'everybody participates ... with two concerns in mind: to agree on nothing that might prejudice the future interests of my country, but to try as hard as possible to attain a definition that will strike at every conceivable future adversary'.[63] When the definitional debate transpires in this way, 'the result can only be inconclusive'.[64]

Yet these conflicts on the nature of 'terrorism' that characterised late twentieth-century world politics have now been effectively eclipsed by the technology of the ISIL and Al-Qaida list. Most scholars point towards changing Security Council dynamics or the emergence of transnational threats by non-state actors to explain the proliferation of global security governance after the Cold War. But, as this chapter shows, it is the legal technologies and expert practices translating threats into new forms of preemptive security intervention that must be examined if we are to account for the astonishing rise of global security law. The Law of the List is critical in the 'knowing' and governing of global terrorism.

---

[59] Sanctions were adopted against Libya in 1992, for example, following the bombing of Pan Am flight 103 over Lockerbie, Scotland (S/RES/731).

[60] Eric Rosand, 'The UN-led multilateral institutional response to jihadist terrorism: is a global counterterrorism body needed?' (2006) 11(3) *Journal of Conflict and Security Law* 399, 408.

[61] Ibid.; Roslyn Higgins cited in Ben Saul, 'Terrorism and international criminal law: questions of (in)coherence and (il)legitimacy' in Gideon Boas, William Schabas and Michael P. Scharf (eds.), *International Criminal Justice: Legitimacy and Coherence* (Cheltenham: Edward Elgar Publishing, 2012), p. 193.

[62] Carl Schmitt, *Political Theology: Four Chapters on the Concept of Sovereignty* (Chicago IL: MIT Press, 1985).

[63] Koskenniemi, *The Politics*, p. 340.

[64] Ibid.

In the ISIL and Al-Qaida listing regime, 'law defers to the politics of expertise' because UN sanctions are administered by committees of diplomats from Security Council states 'who have neither the interest, time or resources to do the job properly'.[65] The UN1267 Sanctions Committee is composed of mid-level P5 diplomats of First Secretary or Counsellor level who generally have no prior experience of working on counterterrorism issues domestically, let alone on a global scale. As such, it has 'tended to become unnecessarily consumed in negotiating process-orientated papers and focusing on the political rather than technical aspects' of the issue.[66] Because these diplomats regularly move onto other assignments in different areas, the Committee suffers from high turnover of staff and a lack of accumulated organisational knowledge. Like other functional regimes managing global problems, the list is crucially dependent upon the technical knowledge-work and ongoing administration of experts. As one former US sanctions official and independent UN monitor put it:

> While the UN Security Council is well placed to design and impose sanctions, and can draw on necessary expertise for this purpose, it is not well placed to verse and monitor actual implementation and enforcement of the sanctions. That function must be assigned to an independent group, which, in turn, can make its findings known to the Security Council.[67]

When the scope of the listing regime was first extended to include Osama Bin Laden and Al-Qaida in 2000, the Security Council called for an expert committee to be set up to advise them on how the arms embargo and closing down of terrorist training camps could best be monitored. In July 2001, following a recommendation made by this Committee of Experts on Afghanistan, the Council called for a new Monitoring Group to be created consisting of five independent experts based in New York. The group was initially tasked with monitoring implementation of measures that were, at that time, limited to the Taliban-controlled areas of Afghanistan. But, when the regime was radically modified following 9/11 to target potential terrorist threats worldwide, the mandate of the Monitoring Group was dramatically altered to suit. These experts now had to monitor a unique set of sanctions targeting 'an

---

[65] Ibid. pp. 340, 86.
[66] Rosand, 'The UN-led multilateral institutional response', 423.
[67] Victor D. Comras, *Flawed Diplomacy: The United Nations and the War on Terrorism* (Lincoln NE: Potomac, 2010), p. 132.

amorphous, highly mobile, and expanding global terrorist network with no fixed address'.[68]

Independent expert teams had long been valued in the UN for their ability to criticise or legitimise the acts and omissions of states in ways that diplomats and UN Secretariat staff could not. Because Security Council politics is consensus-based, it is difficult for the Council 'to identify non-performers ("name and shame") or even agree on a set of standards against which to measure performance'.[69] The UN1267 Monitoring Group took this non-compliance aspect of its mandate very seriously. It issued six robust reports identifying non-compliance by states and criticising the ineffectiveness of the list before it was disbanded by the Council in 2004 for politically overstepping the mark.

Rather than relying on formal government reports made through diplomatic channels, the group made (sometimes unannounced) country visits to assess the actual extent of sanctions compliance. Because of the sensitive nature of information in this area, the group relied on 'private contact with counter-terrorism investigators and researchers, former intelligence officers, ... experts in universities and ... the private sector ... [and] former government colleagues' to undertake its enquiries.[70] Numerous states were identified as acting in ways that undermined the sanctions effort. Russia and China were criticised for allowing the flow of arms to the Taliban. Saudi Arabia was singled out for allowing suspected terrorist financiers to continue operating in its territory. Italy, Liechtenstein and Switzerland were also criticised for allowing targeted individuals to travel and operate businesses in their countries. The Group's reports found that the Al-Qaida travel ban and arms embargo were largely symbolic in nature and that the asset freeze was poorly and partially implemented. Unless 'a much tougher and more comprehensive resolution' was introduced, the group concluded, 'little or no progress will be achieved'.[71] Because it used unorthodox methods, asserted an unusually high degree of political independence and made frank assessments of non-compliance by states, the Group was heavily criticised for exceeding the scope of its mandate. After publicly stating that it had 'never had information presented ... which would indicate ... a direct link'[72] between Saddam Hussein and Al-Qaida – in direct

---

[68] Ibid. p. 115.
[69] Rosand, 'The UN-led multilateral institutional response', 423.
[70] Comras, *Flawed Diplomacy*, p. 118.
[71] Ibid. p. 125
[72] Rosand, 'The UN-led multilateral institutional response'.

contradiction with the arguments being made at that time to justify the Iraq war – the USA finally withdrew its political support and let the group's time-limited mandate expire.

It was from this political drama that the UN1267 Analytical Support and Sanctions Monitoring Team (hereafter, the 'Monitoring Team') was born. The team consisted of eight counterterrorism experts, with administrative support from the Security Council Affairs Division (SCAD) of the UN Secretariat. From the outset the Security Council strictly curtailed the Monitoring Team's independence. It was required 'to operate under the direction of the Committee' and 'submit a comprehensive programme of work to the Committee for its approval and review'.[73] All proposed travel was to be disclosed to the Committee and relevant states in advance.[74] Draft reports were to be presented to states for review prior to publication and their comments taken into account before circulation to the Committee.[75] The previous Monitoring Group had been granted relative autonomy to perform its 'naming and shaming'. But this freedom was withdrawn from the Monitoring Team, with non-compliance and implementation assessment effectively brought back under direct Sanctions Committee control.[76]

These changes – and the shift from Monitoring Group to Monitoring Team – have been variously criticised in the academic literature for diminishing the independence of the Monitoring Team's expertise; reducing its ability to cultivate and rely on closed material and so provide frank assessments of the mismatch between list and threat; subjecting its work and findings to excessive political scrutiny and control; and undermining the Council's ability to hold recalcitrant states to account, thus eroding its newly asserted Chapter VII authority in this area.[77] Whilst these critiques correctly highlight the political conditions in which the Monitoring Team was formed, they miss the most important effect of this reorganisation process. Rather than issuing high-profile public reports, criticising states for their intransigence and engaging with the high politics of the Council, the Monitoring Team developed a focus on

[73] S/RES/1526 (2004), Annex.
[74] Ibid.
[75] Ibid.
[76] Comras, *Flawed Diplomacy*, p. 126.
[77] See principally: Rosand, 'The UN-led multilateral institutional response'; Comras, *Flawed Diplomacy*; Barak Mendelsohn, 'Threat analysis and the UN's 1267 Sanctions Committee' (2015) 27(4) *Terrorism and Political Violence* 609; Barak Mendelsohn, *Combating Jihadism: American Hegemony and Interstate Cooperation in the War on Terrorism* (Chicago IL: University of Chicago Press, 2009).

technical issues and deficiencies of process perceived as less politically contentious.

This technical and procedural turn of UN counterterrorism expertise is crucially important to the assemblage of the listing regime for two reasons. First, it enables the expert knowledge work of the Monitoring Team to unfold as something unseen and inconsequential, composed of relatively mundane technical processes or 'little security nothings'.[78] The literature frames the shift from Monitoring Group to Monitoring Team negatively – as a diminutive retreat of expertise from its compliance function as an intergovernmental appendage in a forum of UN high politics to the politically safe and marginal terrain of internal processes and technicalities. But I argue that this shift also needs to be grasped positively in terms of what it enables – namely, banal processes of 'associating, assembling and dispersing security practices' that operate at a more granular level, underneath the radar of legal and political visibility.[79] The power of listing expertise in this domain was reorganised, not diminished, by retreating from the more confrontational 'solid authority' of Council and its intergovernmental politics. As a result of this retreat, it could develop with 'greater liquidity'[80] across a diverse array of capillary points and more effectively 'invest ... itself in institutions, become ... embodied in techniques, and equip ... itself with instruments'.[81] As analyses of the Counter Terrorism Committee (CTC) and Global Counterterrorism Forum (GCTF) show, the movement towards mundane sites and the use of

---

[78] Jef Huysmans, 'What's in an act? On security speech acts and little security nothings' (2011) 42(4–5) *Security Dialogue* 371. See also: Louise Amoore and Marieke de Goede, 'Transactions after 9/11: the banal face of the preemptive strike' (2008) 33(2) *Transactions of the Institute of British Geographers* 173. Such issues included 'loopholes in the sanctions measures; procedural requirements for listing and delisting; ... underuse of the Committee's Consolidated list [and] the need to ... strengthen contacts with ... international and regional law enforcement' bodies – Comras, *Flawed Diplomacy*, p. 129. By 'unseen' I do not mean 'concealed' – even though much of the Monitoring Team's listing work is opaque. Following Annelise Riles, I mean that it allows counterterrorism expertise to exist 'on the surface, in plain view, and yet precisely for this reason [remain] unseen': Annelise Riles, cited in Nigel Thrift, 'Movement-space: the changing domain of thinking resulting from the development of new kinds of spatial awareness' (2004) 33(4) *Economy and Society* 582, 585.

[79] Huysmans, 'What's in an act?', 379.

[80] Krisch, 'Authority, solid and liquid', p. 43.

[81] Michel Foucault, *Power/Knowledge: Selected Interviews and Other Writings, 1972–1977* (New York: Pantheon, 1980), p. 96.

informal governance techniques by the Council are far from inconsequential and need to be analytically reappraised[82] because it is from there that new security practices and powers are created and put into global circulation.

The redefinition of global security problems in technical terms also allows counterterrorism experts to exert greater control over them and bolster their authority, relative to others in the field. The greater the focus on technical questions of list administration and implementation, the more preempting global terrorism comes to rely on relevant security expertise. As Foucault and many others have noted, 'problematisation' and 'rendering technical' are co-constitutive processes. On the one hand, this produces depoliticising effects as complex political problems are reposed in technical terms. 'Questions that are rendered technical', writes Tania Murray Li, 'are simultaneously rendered nonpolitical'.[83] Yet, on the other hand, it opens up new terrains where the 'politics of redefinition' unfolds – that is, 'the strategic definition of a situation or problem by reference to a technical idiom so as to open the door for applying the expertise related to that idiom, together with the attendant structural bias'.[84] For Koskenniemi, the process of rendering technical is the main driving force behind the fragmentation of international law. With specialisation, 'legal vocabular[ies] of rules and principles, precedents or institutions' increasingly have little purchase. Instead, 'relevant calculations always seem to require technical expertise' couched in 'technical vocabularies of ad hoc accommodation, coordination and optimal effect'.[85] Yet there is little empirical research on how the politics of expertise is shaping global security law. As Kennedy notes, 'we need better maps of expertise' but 'mapping the knowledge of experts is complex and technical work'.[86]

---

[82] See, for example: Isobel Roele, 'Disciplinary power and the UN Security Council Counter Terrorism Committee' (2014) 19(1) *Journal of Conflict and Security Law* 49; Alejandro Rodiles, *Coalitions of the Willing and International Law: the Interplay between Formality and Informality* (Cambridge: Cambridge University Press, 2018); Nathanael Tilahun Ali, *Regulatory Counter-Terrorism: A Critical Appraisal of Proactive Global Governance* (London: Routledge, 2018); Alejandro Rodiles and Gavin Sullivan, 'Global security assemblages: international counterterrorism law in motion' (forthcoming, draft on file with author).

[83] Tania Murray Li, *The Will to Improve*, p. 7.

[84] Koskenniemi, *The Politics*, p. 67.

[85] Ibid. pp. 340, 359.

[86] Kennedy, 'Challenging expert rule', 14.

The following section of this chapter takes this mapping project seriously by analysing two specific sites where global security listing expertise is unfolding in response to seemingly mundane problems of list implementation. These sites and problems concern technical projects developed by the Monitoring Team that have received no academic attention and are only marginally discussed in the team's public reports to the Council. Yet I argue that both highlight crucial elements of the politics of security expertise and suggest novel ways of understanding how global security law and governance is made expansive and powerful. Foregrounding the technology of the list allows us to see how the Council governs complex global problems through knowledge production practices as much as through Chapter VII resolutions and the global legislative programmes they put into play. Following the socio-technicalities of expertise helps show the 'epistemic infrastructures' of global law and politics.[87]

2.3   Security Listing and the Construction of the Global Optic

My first site of enquiry involves a series of regional meetings undertaken between the Monitoring Team and national security and intelligence officials. In 2006, to ensure effective implementation of the list, the Monitoring Team was granted additional powers to 'consult with Member States' intelligence and security services, including through regional fora, in order to facilitate the sharing of information and to strengthen enforcement of the measures'.[88] These consultation meetings actually began shortly after the team's formation in 2004[89] and have continued each year, every four months, since that time.[90] Other than occasional updates in the Monitoring Team's biannual reports to the Security Council, nothing has been written to date about either their purpose or results.

The Security Council is made up of states with the most powerful and best-resourced intelligence services in the world. What added-value could a small team of UN counterterrorism experts possibly bring that

---

[87] The idea of 'epistemic infrastructure' is drawn from Karin Knorr-Cetina, as discussed in Bueger, 'Making things known'.

[88] S/RES/1735 (2006), Annex.

[89] Interview with former member of the 1267 Monitoring Team, New York, November 2012 (Interview A).

[90] Interview with former member of the 1267 Monitoring Team, New York, June 2014 (Interview B).

is not already available to their own national security services? And the use of intelligence within the Security Council has long been controversial. Doesn't intelligence-sharing facilitated by experts with delegated authority from the Council take the UN back into such contested territory? What other purposes, effects and forms of global security governance could these meetings enable?

In my analysis, these expert meetings have three interrelated aims: constructing a 'global optic' for seeing global terrorism; enabling uncertain future threats to be countered before they emerge; and enlisting actors into new preemptive security networks with the potential for intelligence exchange. Each of these aims is concerned with producing and stabilising global terrorism as an object of political and legal intervention through the list. They reveal, in other words, how the list works as a performative technology to constitute and condition the very problem that it aims to target.

This account supports my claim that the ISIL and Al-Qaida list is not an inert object, but an active agent that undertakes crucially important legal assemblage work. It quantifies and orders an otherwise diffuse threat, it bypasses definitional problems ('what is terrorism?') and political conflicts about self-determination that constrained counterterrorism in the twentieth century, and it aligns diverse actors so they can 'see the threat in the same way'.[91] As I argue in this book, understanding how global security law works means grappling with its conditions of possibility. Empirically analysing how the list and listing expertise are entangled and co-produced through problems of list administration shows us these conditions as they emerge and are put into global circulation.

2.3.1 A Global Optic for Seeing Global Terrorism

The first and primary objective of these meetings, according to one former member of the Monitoring Team, is to build a new 'global perspective' for seeing and countering 'global terrorism'. Because officials from national states are largely concerned with issues of national security, the transnational threats posed by global terrorist networks often fall outside the scope of their analysis:

> The analysis that [Member States] have domestically is really based on a domestic assessment and may not see lots of other things in the world.

[91] Interview A.

> And they will see everything through the optic of that, that country – you know, . . . the security services, law enforcement agencies are considering *national* security. So, Member State A will assess its security in isolation to a certain extent from Member States B, C, D and E . . . They [may say] . . . 'Our national security is affected by member state B, because people may come from there to commit attacks' . . . . But that's still seeing it from that optic of Member State A.[92]

But because the ISIL and Al-Qaida list preemptively targets the uncertain threats of 'global terrorism' rather than reacts to localised 'terrorist acts', it requires a 'global' analytical perspective or optic:

> What we do is say: 'This is how Member State A sees it; this is how Member State B sees it; this is how Member State A sees Member State B and Member State B sees Member State A'. Now you are seeing everything on a broad, analytical and objective approach, rather than on the very subjective approach the Member State might have. And that's because that's their job. And that's our job. And that's where we bring considerable added-value.[93]

Constructing a new lens to see the problem of global terrorism is not merely an effect of expert know-how. It is something that the technology of the list enables. First, it is the everyday task of list administration that brings disparate actors together with UN counterterrorism experts and gives them the reason to try to work together in the first place. As one team member explained, the list 'gives you the mandate to collect information . . . You need to be on the list to devote travel time, hotel costs and the time of the officials of the other country to justify working on this intensively.'[94] In this sense, and as discussed in more detail later in this chapter at section 2.3.3 – the list works as a translation device, helping align a diverse range of different security actors into a common preemptive security project.

The format of the list also allows a new kind of 'optical consistency' to emerge in relation to problems of global terrorism.[95] As discussed above, defining terrorism and turning it into an object of international prohibition was the source of protracted debate for much of the twentieth century. But the ISIL and Al-Qaida list bypasses this definitional problem and pushes the epistemological question of terrorism to one side, by providing a legal technology for knowing and countering global

---

[92] Ibid.
[93] Ibid.
[94] Ibid.
[95] Latour, 'Visualization and cognition', 7.

terrorism (listing) without ever having the need to define it. As one Monitoring Team member put it:

> The 1267 regime covers specific individuals and groups who are consid-ered terrorist by their actions, but not because they conform to a definition. And that lack of definition is very important, of course. Insofar as the General Assembly is prepared to allow the Security Council to take over the issue of counterterrorism, they do so on the basis that the definition issue remains with the General Assembly and the six committees ... let's be clear about that.[96]

Global security law is often criticised on the grounds that it fails to define its object, but this criticism overlooks two crucially important points. As suggested above, the failure to define terrorism is a fundamental condi-tion of possibility for global security law and not a source of lack. Leaving the definitional problem open is a political prerequisite for Security Council action in this domain. Moreover, for most counterterrorism experts interviewed for this book, the vexing definitional issue ('what is terrorism?') is beside the point because these sanctions operationalise 'global terrorism' as a technical problem of effective list administration and preemptive security practice that require ongoing expert calibration. In the current global legal landscape, in other words, terrorism is some-thing that is listed rather than defined. Or more accurately, it is a global security problem rendered visible and actionable through the legal tech-nology of the list. As one Monitoring Team member explained, Security Council efforts to counter terrorism through listing grew out of its practical inability to take any other form of tangible intervention against Al-Qaida after 9/11:

> Al-Qaida was this *threat that no one could easily quantify* ... And *the only international* tool that the Security Council could grasp was really the sanctions regime ... There is nothing else they could do. Make statements about the horrors of terrorism? ... But [that] doesn't actually do much more than offer political support, does it? [The Council] is not opera-tional, obviously. And they couldn't authorise force, because who are you going to fight? So really the sanctions regime was the only option.[97]

The list's capacity to quantify 'global terrorism' and translate it into a specific object of intervention provides the key to explaining its remark-able uptake and success as a security governance technology. As scholars like Jack Goody have shown, the power of the list as an inscription device

---

[96] Interview A.
[97] Ibid. (emphasis added).

lies precisely in its ability to decontextualise and order diverse pieces of information into newly simplified and 'overgeneralised' semantic fields, where they can be made 'subject to possible rearrangement'.[98] Lists are simple yet *powerful* technologies because they contain significant 'generative possibilities'.[99] As with other governance technologies like global indicators, lists work by *producing* commensurable relations between remote things that were not equivalent before.[100] With the ISIL and Al-Qaida list this jurisgenerative power starts with its exceptionally broad criteria for list inclusion, namely:

(a) Participating in the financing, planning, facilitating, preparing, or perpetrating of acts or activities by, in conjunction with, under the name of, on behalf of, or in support of;
(b) Supplying, selling or transferring arms and related material to;
(c) Recruiting for; or otherwise supporting acts or activities of Al-Qaida, ISIL or any cell, affiliate, splinter group or derivative thereof...[101]

In 2012, these criteria were stretched even further to include 'association with' anyone already on the list – effectively making the targeting threshold one of being 'associated with anyone associated with' Al-Qaida or any cell, affiliate, splinter group or derivative.[102] The rationale for broadening the list's targeting standard, according to one former team member, was 'the changing nature of the threat':

> If you need to show ... that Boko Haram is closely associated with Ayman al-Zawahiri in Pakistan or Afghanistan, you've got a very tall order on your hands. So, the changing nature of the threat that diversifies Al-Qaida made it necessary to say 'Not every buddy of Zawahiri is only Al-Qaida'. There are also people who have never met Zawahiri, never will meet Zawahiri and who will never talk to Zawahiri, who nevertheless sign on to Al-Qaida as a branch, franchise, idea, ideology or whatever you want to call it and therefore constitute a threat to international peace and security.[103]

Given its breadth and scope, the list provides a unique legal mechanism for disparate individuals and groups around the world to be collated,

---

[98] Jack Goody, *The Domestication of the Savage Mind* (Cambridge: Cambridge University Press, 1977), pp. 74–111, 104.
[99] Ibid.
[100] Goody notes that lists can be used 'to develop a generalised system of equivalences even in the absence of a generalised medium of exchange': Ibid., 88.
[101] S/RES/2368 (2017), para. 2a–c (emphasis added).
[102] S/RES/2083 (2012).
[103] Interview B.

connected together and preemptively targeted in new ways. Diverse forms of political Islam are conflated together – from Palestine, Somalia, Russia, Tunisia, the Philippines, China and Nigeria – as nodes of the same global terrorist network, even though they may have no actual association outside of the list. ISIL and Al-Nusrah Front, for example, are both listed as affiliates or splinter groups of Al-Qaida, even though they were actively in armed conflict with each other for control of Syria and Iraq.[104] As one Monitoring Team member explained: 'What is on the list is not necessarily . . . an academic definition of Al-Qaida.' It is rather 'what a varying composition of Security Council memberships since 1999 have perceived as the main threats'. According to this expert, one of the key functions of the list is that it 'clarifies for the expert team what Al-Qaida is'.[105]

When 'association with' ISIL and Al-Qaida is reduced to a legal common denominator so low, the actual connections between different list entries become difficult to sustain outside of the economy of the list. As one former team member explained, with the dissipation of the 'Al-Qaida central' threat and its replacement with much more localised episodes of political violence, what gets listed for being 'associated with' Al-Qaida has become an unending question of ideological affinity:

> Al-Qaida is no longer the sort of threat that it was – if it ever was, but it's certainly no longer. It's regional bits that *maybe* share something with Al-Qaida in an *overarching philosophy*. But in practice, in their activities, it's something *completely* different.
>
> So, you say we've done our job. This worked. Al-Qaida is beaten. It's no longer the threat that it was. But we still have these little remnants

---

[104] The contentiousness of the claim that ISIL and Al-Nusrah Front are affiliated subgroups of Al-Qaida is reflected in US domestic constitutional debates about whether the Authorization to Use Military Force Act (AUMF), passed in the aftermath of the 9/11 attacks, justifies US Presidential authorisation for airstrikes against ISIL in Syria without additional approval by Congress. See, for example: Shoon Kathleen Murray, 'The contemporary presidency: stretching the 2001 AUMF: a history of two presidencies' (2015) 45(1) *Presidential Studies Quarterly* 175; Ryan J. Vogel, 'Ending the "drone war" or expanding it? Assessing the legal authority for continued US operations against Al-Qa'ida after Afghanistan' (2015) *Albany Government Law Review* 8; Harold Koh, *The Trump Administration and International Law* (Oxford: Oxford University Press, 2019), pp. 91–126; Greg Miller and Karen de Young, 'In Syria, Obama stretches legal and policy constraints he created for counterterrorism' *Washington Post* (Washington, 23 September 2014). Available at: wapo.st/2bbx32h; Spencer Ackerman, 'Obama maintains Al-Qaida and Isis are "one and the same" despite evidence of schism' *The Guardian* (London, 2 October 2014). Available at: bit.ly/2aYW39l.

[105] Interview B.

around the place, which have *some sort* of association and now represent
a different sort of threat which requires national or local action.

... So as this one [i.e. the Al-Qaida regime] comes down, these ones [i.e.
more local and regionally focused regimes] can come up. That's really the
model. Because otherwise, ... when are you going to stop? When can you say
Al-Qaida is defeated? It's not. You can't defeat an idea. [So] when can you say
therefore it's no longer a threat to international peace and security?[106]

As scholars in the sociology of quantification have shown, 'the act of
measurement can produce ... the supposedly pre-existing phenomena
being measured'.[107] Here, the list similarly works as an inscription device
to create and sustain the very object of 'global terrorism' that it purports
to represent and seeks to target.[108] Effective list calibration first requires
UN listing expertise to extract 'global' threat information from a diverse
array of national and bilaterally filtered localised intelligence material:

Let's [take] the United States as an example ... If we provide a report on
what's happening in Algeria ... that will be very different from the reports
they're getting from the field. Because when they deal with the Algerian
services or the Algerian Government all that analysis is, and their presentation is, coloured by bilateral issues – there's a hundred and one bilateral
issues which come into that. When *we* talk to Algeria or Yemen or whatever, *it's just about this – the international dimensions of the local threat.*[109]

---

[106] Interview A (emphasis added). In 2012 the Monitoring Team noted that the threat posed
by 'Al-Qaida central' had declined following the death of bin Laden and drone warfare in
Pakistan and Afghanistan. Whilst other groups like Boko Haram professed nominal
support for 'global terrorism', these groups 'focus primarily on local or regional targets'.
And whilst individuals or small cells 'may keep the idea of Al-Qaida alive ... the
sanctions regime is not well suited to deal with that threat'. Accordingly, the team
recommended 'revising the narrative' of the listing regime and narrowing its global
scope by adopting a regional, risk-based approach. But this suggestion was firmly
rejected by the Sanctions Committee and the team was tacitly rebuked. In response,
the Committee 'emphasize[d] its mandate as a global sanctions regime aimed at countering the threat posed by Al-Qaida and associated individuals and entities' and that 'the
Monitoring Team's mandate is global ... [and] should focus on all areas where the threat
exists and where the Committee might consider focusing future designations'. See,
respectively: UN Doc. S/2012/729, paras. 3–29; and UN Doc. S/2012/730, paras. 4–5.

[107] Merry and Coutin, 'Technologies of truth', 1. On the performativity of calculative
practices see: Porter, *The Rise of Statistical Thinking*; Callon, *The Laws of the Markets*;
Desrosières, *The Politics of Large Numbers*; Nikolas Rose, *Powers of Freedom: Reframing
Political Thought* (Cambridge: Cambridge University Press, 1999); Wendy Espeland and
Mitchell Stevens, 'Commensuration as a social process' (1998) 24 *Annual Review of
Sociology* 313; Geoffrey Bowker and Susan Leigh Star, *Sorting Things Out: Classification
and its Consequences* (Cambridge MA: MIT Press, 1999).

[108] On enacting terrorism as a governance object through the technology of the list, see also:
de Goede and Sullivan, 'The politics of security lists'.

[109] Interview A (emphasis added).

Once the 'global' dimension of local threat information has been identified and extracted by UN counterterrorism experts, it is invariably listed – either by updating existing list entries with additional derogatory information or indirectly generating possibilities for new list entries via state nomination. Listing expertise allows diverse localised threats to be identified, stripped of their specificity and globally rescaled without modifying their internal properties. National security agencies still retain their ability to disrupt the lives of terrorist suspects in their jurisdictions using whatever national tools are at their disposal. If there are domestic judicial proceedings against suspects, these are left undisturbed because the list is 'preventative in nature and ... not reliant upon criminal standards set out under national law'.[110] And as one team member explained: 'If someone gets off our list, no Member State is required to cease any of the measures they have put in place – watching [them], restricting their movements inside the country – just because they got off the sanctions list. *The domestic threat is different from what the Security Council thinks.*'[111] As Figure 2.1 shows, what counts is the 'global' threat information – that is, potential 'association with' ISIL and Al-Qaida or any cell, affiliate, splinter group or anyone 'associated with' them in turn – and how this material can be extracted, interconnected and arranged alongside existing entries in the optically consistent and standardised format of the list.

The Monitoring Team does not formally recommend the listing of individuals. That process still takes place via Member State nomination in the Sanctions Committee. But the consultation meetings they convene nonetheless perform an essential and invaluable function in enacting the listing procedure. They bring security and intelligence actors together with UN listing experts to identify and share information about those to be targeted and those who already are. The process of translating local threat traces onto a visually ordered global list is also an editing process of 'uncertainty absorption'[112] that works by removing the contingencies of how listing produces knowledge of global terrorism in the first place. Speculative intelligence or allegations are rescaled and reformatted into

---

[110] UN1267 Sanctions Committee, *Guidelines of the Committee for the Conduct of Its Work* (5 September 2018), para. 6(d).

[111] Interview B (emphasis added).

[112] 'Uncertainty absorption' is a process that 'takes place when inferences are drawn from a body of evidence, and the inferences instead of the evidence itself, are then communicated': James G. March and Herbert A. Simon, *Organizations* (Oxford: Wiley, 1958) 165, cited in Espeland and Stevens, 'A sociology of quantification', 421–2. Latour describes the process as the *cascading effect* of 'ever simplified inscriptions that allow[s] harder facts to be produced at greater cost' – Latour, 'Visualization and cognition', 16.

UNITED NATIONS SECURITY COUNCIL

Search the UN

About the Council | Sanctions | Members | Meetings | Documents | News

Home » SAID BEN ABDELHAKIM BEN OMAR AL-CHERIF

SAID BEN ABDELHAKIM BEN OMAR AL-CHERIF

In accordance with paragraph 36 of resolution 2161 (2014) , the Al-Qaida Sanctions Committee makes accessible a narrative summary of reasons for the listing for individuals, groups, undertakings and entities included in the Al-Qaida Sanctions List.

QDi.138
SAID BEN ABDELHAKIM BEN OMAR AL-CHERIF
Date on which the narrative summary became available on the Committee's website: 28 March 2011
Date(s) on which the narrative summary was updated: 3 February 2015
Reason for listing:
Said ben Abdelhakim ben Omar al-Cherif was listed on **12 November 2003** pursuant to paragraphs 1 and 2 of resolution 1390 (2002) as being associated with Al-Qaida, Usama bin Laden or the Taliban for "participating in the financing, planning, facilitating, preparing or perpetrating of acts or activities by, in conjunction with, under the name of, on behalf or in support of", "recruiting for" or "otherwise supporting acts or activities of" Al-Qaida (QDe.004) and Ansar al-Islam (QDe.098).

Additional information:
Said ben Abdelhakim ben Omar al-Cherif has belonged to a terrorist cell set up in Milan, Italy, with several branches, probably in other European countries. The cell was linked to Al-Qaida (QDe.004) and was focused on obtaining forged documents to send to terrorists in European and Middle Eastern countries and on recruiting individuals for terrorist training, mainly in Iraq, organized by Ansar al-Islam (QDe.098).

Al-Cherif provided the terrorist cell with use of his property and all his activities were directed towards supporting it. He was able to support the cell's activities financially probably through the proceeds of crime.

Al-Cherif cooperated with other individuals linked with terrorism, maintaining direct communications with other leaders, recruiting individuals to undertake military operations and ensuring the network's security. He also provided Al-Qaida members in Malaysia with forged documents.

On 7 February 2008, Al-Cherif was sentenced to eight years and ten months imprisonment for membership in a terrorist association and other related crimes by a court in Italy.

On 9 January 2009, Al-Cherif was sentenced in Italy to eight years imprisonment followed by expulsion to Tunisia for sending individuals to Iraq and Afghanistan to carry out terrorist acts, including suicide attacks, aiding would-be terrorists to enter Iraq, helping illegal immigrants to enter European countries, and aiding suspected terrorists to leave Italy.

Related listed individuals and entities:
Al-Qaida (QDe.004), listed on 6 October 2001

Ansar al-Islam (QDe.098), listed on 24 February 2003

Imed ben Mekki Zarkaoui (QDi.139), listed on 12 November 2003

Kamal ben Maoeldi ben Hassan al-Hamraoui (QDi.140), listed on 12 November 2003

Maxamed Cabdullaah Ciise (QDi.141), listed on 12 November 2003

Radi Abd el Samie Abou el Yazid el Ayashi (QDi.142), listed on 12 November 2003

Hamadi ben Abdul Aziz ben Ali Bouyehia (QDi.143), listed on 12 November 2003

Mohammad Tahir Hammid (QDi.144), listed on 12 November 2003

Mohamed Amin Mostafa (QDi.147), listed on 12 November 2003

Nessim ben Mohamed al-Cherif ben Mohamed Saleh al-Saadi (QDi.148), listed on 12 November 2003

Noureddine ben Ali ben Belkassem al-Drissi (QDi.149), listed on 12 November 2003

Al-Azhar ben Khalifa ben Ahmed Rouine (QDi.150), listed on 12 November 2003

Mourad ben Ali ben al-Basheer al-Trabelsi (QDi.151), listed on 12 November 2003

Jamal Housni (QDi.221), listed on 2 August 2006

Nessim ben Romdhane Sahraoui (QDi.222), listed on 2 August 2006

Merai Zoghbai (QDi.223), listed on 2 August 2006

Figure 2.1 Narrative Summary of Reasons, showing 'associations' with other listed individuals. Available at: bit.ly/2xMMnvp. © (2019) United Nations. Reprinted with permission from the United Nations.

a more stable knowledge form that purportedly carries a higher degree of objectivity, authority and certainty.

One of my clients, for example, was tried and acquitted in court of the charge of membership of an international terrorist organisation – the Salafist Group for Call and Combat. He was then listed as an individual who 'has belonged to a terrorist organization . . . . that has been involved in criminal activity on behalf of the Salafist Group for Call and Combat, listed as the Organization of al-Qaida in the Islamic Maghreb (QE.

T.14.01), and other Al-Qaida-related (QE.A.4.01) terrorist groups'.[113]
The legal proceedings that had tested and refuted this allegation (albeit
to the criminal standards of the court rather than the speculative standards of the list) were simply edited out of his list entry. Reformatting
diverse entries together on an optically consistent list absorbs uncertainty
by presenting inferences as more factually solid forms of evidence, discarding potentially exculpatory material in the process.[114]

For the Security Council to counter global terrorism it must first come to
know it. But, in this context, knowledge is not a sudden revelation of truth
or an effect of the wisdom of experts. It is created through knowledge
practices and the 'whole cycle of accumulations' involved in gathering
traces from dispersed sites and bringing them back to 'centres of calculation', where they can be 'cumulated, aggregated, or shuffled'.[115] As Latour
points out, it is such processes that enable a centre to become 'familiar with
things, peoples and events which are distant' and so able to act as a centre
on many distant places at the same time.[116] It is this asymmetry that is key
to understanding how 'the global' is enacted in this example of global
security law in action. Here, knowledge of global terrorism is not so much
discovered as constructed. And power is made powerful through techniques of visual mastery and scale production that catalyse shifts 'in what
counts as centre and what counts as periphery'.[117]

I argue that this is precisely what these consultation meetings, UN
listing expertise and the list co-produce. They create a 'structure making
site' for identifying, calculating and stabilising 'global terrorism' as
a novel field of intervention by the Security Council, whilst avoiding
the critical problem of having to actually define in law what terrorism
is.[118] The ISIL and Al-Qaida list is the inscription technology that makes
this global security governance move possible. It transforms complex,
diffuse and localised threats into a simplified, optically consistent and
commensurable set of individual list entries that can be readily manipulated by the Council and implemented with worldwide effect.

---

[113] Excerpt from client's Narrative Summary of Reasons for Listing, issued by the UN1267
Sanctions Committee. This summary was taken out of the public domain after his
delisting.
[114] On the problems of exculpatory material here, see: UN Doc. A/67/396
(26 September 2012), paras. 26 and 45.
[115] Latour, *Science in Action*, pp. 222–3.
[116] Ibid. p. 220.
[117] Ibid. p. 226.
[118] Latour, *Reassembling the Social*, p. 176.

2.3.2   Equilibrium of Possibilities: Countering Potential Threats before They Emerge

Rendering global terrorism amenable to intervention is not only a question of extracting, decontextualising and spatially reordering diverse elements onto a list. It is also a temporal problem: how can radically uncertain potential threats be made knowable and countered before they materialise? The second aim of these meetings, explored below, engages with this temporal problem of preemption: how can the 'horizon of possible futures [be] arrayed in such a way as to govern, to decide, or to act in the present'?[119] How can the Monitoring Team experts, in collaboration with national security actors, work together through these meetings to preempt global terrorist threats?

The listing regime is equipped with a number of features that enable it to intervene early and tame uncertain futures. Sanction Committee Guidelines expressly state that the list is intended to be 'preventative in nature' – which means that individuals and groups are targeted not because of what they have done but rather because of what they might *potentially do* at some point in the future.[120] As one former team member put it: 'Our Security Council list . . . is only [about] what is in the future, not what was in the past.'[121] Designation is not based upon evidence of wrongdoing, but on secret material that purportedly allows inferences to be drawn suggesting that the target is either 'associated with' ISIL, Al-Qaida or affiliated groups or someone 'associated with' them.

Yet, whilst this targeting criterion broadens the scope of the net that can be cast and the range of people who can be listed, the list's potential for preemptive *intervention* can only be realised if states have the political will and legal capacity to implement and use it. 'The sanctions regime', as one former team member explained, 'is of course an obligation on Member States, not on the people under sanction – an obvious point but [one that's] worth making'.[122] And many states where global terrorism is considered most threatening by the Council lack the necessary experience of using intelligence-based administrative asset-freezing devices as preemptive security technologies. As one former team member put it: 'This is not an issue of people having, or lacking, a political commitment to apply the

---

[119] Louise Amoore, *The Politics of Possibility: Risk and Security Beyond Probability* (Duke University Press, 2013), p. 5.
[120] UN1267 Sanctions Committee, *Guidelines*.
[121] Interview B.
[122] Interview A.

sanctions. But ... an issue of Member States not understanding what they should do to apply the sanctions, ... lacking the capacity to do so and also, not really understanding why they should bother.'[123] The key problem to overcome, according to one former Committee member, is a lack of understanding about the differences between preemptive and criminal justice-based techniques for countering terrorism:

> I've just been involved in discussions with West African states about implementation. Last year, I was in discussions in Dar El Salaam with East African states. And my colleague ... was just recently in Tunis to discuss with the North African states. Their implementation problems stem from a fundamental misunderstanding about what sanctions are versus what anti-money laundering asset restraining measures are. And it's that basic misunderstanding that we need to overcome to make the sanctions regime more effective.[124]

If 'effective implementation' of the list is about remedying these 'fundamental misunderstandings', then the Monitoring Team's technical work at these consultation meetings is aimed at fostering conditions conducive to an environment of preemptive security to develop. New security mechanisms, as Foucault reminds us, don't simply emerge by replacing earlier forms with new ones. They emerge by changing the 'dominant characteristic, or more exactly, the system of correlation between juridico-legal mechanisms, disciplinary mechanisms and mechanisms of security'.[125] How then do these meetings between national counterterrorism officials and UN listing experts allow new 'systems of correlation' to be drawn for potential global threats to be countered before they emerge? In the following pages I explore this problem by analysing a hand-drawn diagram (Figure 2.2) provided by one former team member when asked in interview what purpose these list consultation meetings served:

> *Interviewee:* I once made a very nice graph on how you become an Al-Qaida terrorist and what the possibilities of the state are and the risks of the state to counter it. Have you got a pen? ... It's basically a pyramid with revolving circles and inverted possibilities of states (so it needs to be in a box).

---

[123] Ibid.

[124] Interview with former member of the UN1267 Sanctions Committee, New York, June 2014 (Interview C).

[125] Michel Foucault, *Security, Territory, Population: Lectures at the College de France 1977–1978* (Basingstoke: Palgrave Macmillan, 2007), p. 8.

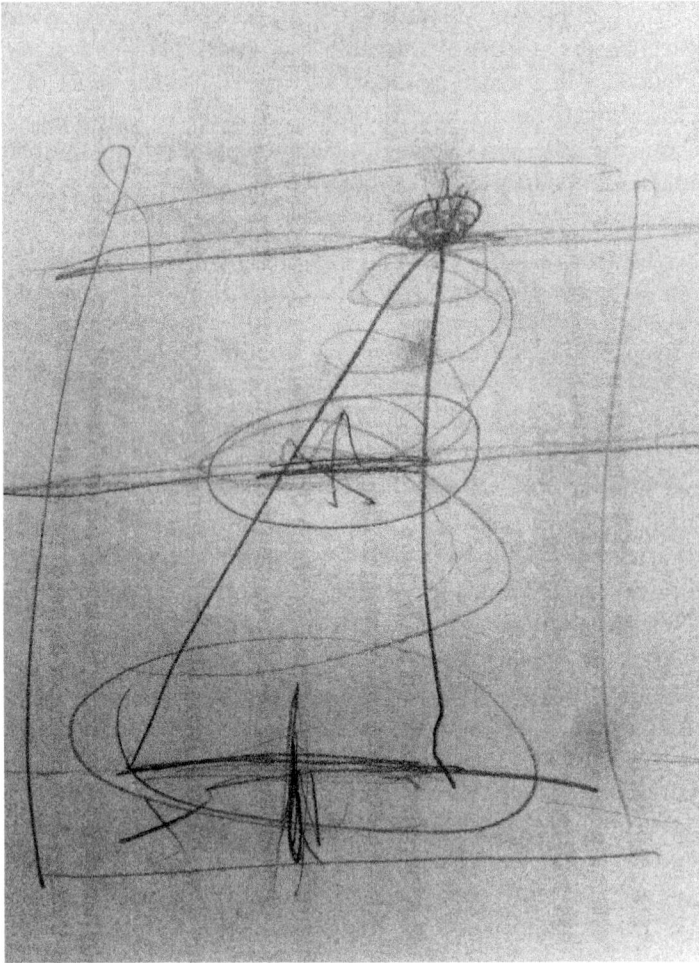

Figure 2.2   'Equilibrium of Possibilities' diagram provided by former Monitoring Team member in interview, June 2014. Reprinted with permission.

Down here, at the base, you have lots of people who are semi-radicalized (as far as terrorism is concerned) and . . . very big issues (like the Palestinian conflict). If you solve the Palestinian conflict, you cut off half of the people.

Up here [at the top], you've got your Al-Qaida terrorist. And he goes through trainings, and madrasas, and radicalisation and joins different groups before he becomes an Al-Qaida terrorist. Up here, you have *absolutely* everything in your statecraft at your disposal. However, you're only reaching *that* particular individual. If you fail, you've got a terror attack.

So, the decreasing possibilities of states to have a large-scale effect is the problem. Because . . . at the time when the guy is already a terrorist you need to be one hundred percent successful. One attack is enough and things are going to politically change in your country. Here [at the top] you have all these instruments, but you have *massive* risk. Here [at the bottom] you have massive issues with political problems, but with potentially massive impact.

So what we are doing is we're cutting the threat *here*, in the middle. Where you have an *equilibrium of possibilities* of what you can do and political difficulties connected with this. And you're already achieving a much more selective group of individuals than you would down here [at the bottom], because most of them are never going to go here [at the top]. Most of these [in the middle] *are* going to end up here [at the top], eventually.

GS: So [the aim is] to target that middle area?

Interviewee: This is what the meetings are doing. Not the Security Council. The Security Council is part of the instrumentarium up here [at the top]. What these meetings and [our] analytical capability is doing is to raise the recognition of *threat* – and the possibility of countering it and of the information that is necessary to counter it – at this middle level. Where you don't wait until the guy is at your airport and you need to prevent him from entering your country because he wants to blow up your building. But [where] already, *much further ahead*, you are aware of what the potential threat is.

GS: So it's about seeing threats as they emerge . . . . and becoming more dynamic in identifying them?

Interviewee: Yes.[126]

What are we to make of this model of the 'equilibrium of possibilities' and the explanation provided? What can it tell us about how UN listing expertise enacts political rationalities of preemption and makes the threats of global terrorism knowable and legally targetable – that is, the relation between expertise and global security law? If it is a map, what kind of topography or threat environment does it help us navigate? Rather than look *behind* the diagram to elucidate some hidden explanation, it is more productive to start from the surface of the drawing by highlighting two of its salient features.

The first notable thing about this model is its simplicity. It sees radically uncertain future threats posed by transnational terrorism in terms of a simple geometric form shaped by a relatively stable set of variables and

---

[126] Interview B (emphasis added).

forces. This pyramid is radically reductionist. Yet that is the source of its power.[127] It works by stripping back and discarding the complexities of political violence and recasting unknowable futures as stable epistemic objects with an identifiable trajectory or pathway. We are told that most people at the middle of this pyramid will eventually move to the apex. In this model, individuals are inexorably pulled from political grievance towards terrorist violence. But how can listing experts operate with such certainty when their knowledge-practices are grounded in the speculative inferences of intelligence material?[128] We are also told that the pyramid 'needs to be in a box', but are not told why. The 'box' works here as a border that frames the target population of the list. It distinguishes 'semi-radicalised' Muslims (who are politically concerned about issues 'like the Palestinian conflict' yet harbour potential Al-Qaida terrorists) from other populations (who are not).

This diagram of listing expertise in action is an analogue of the 'staircase to terrorism' that is widely deployed as an analytical model for countering terrorist radicalisation (see Figure 2.3). According to Fathali Moghaddam, the US psychologist who popularised the 'staircase' approach, terrorism is best conceptualised as a multi-storey building. The ground floor represents broader populations where perceptions of justice and injustice are important. The top floor represents an individual who is trained to overcome their psychological inhibitions and is ready to carry out acts of terrorist violence. The middle floors are the domains where potential terrorists 'become disengaged from morality as it defined by governmental authorities (and often by the majority in society) and morally engaged in the way[s] .... constructed by the terrorist organization'. The middle floors are a tipping point, where potential terrorists begin to see 'terrorism as a justified strategy'.[129] The movement from disaffected individual to terrorist is shown as a narrowing staircase. As an individual moves up, 'they see fewer and fewer choices, until the only possible outcome is the destruction of others, or oneself, or both'.[130]

---

[127] The power of inscriptions lies in their simplicity and capacity to make diverse phenomena commensurable. See: Latour, *Science in Action* and 'Visualization and cognition'; Timothy Mitchell, *Rule of Experts: Egypt, Techno-Politics, Modernity* (Berkeley CA: University of California Press, 2002).

[128] See Chapter 4 for a more detailed discussion of the use of intelligence-as-evidence in the listing assemblage.

[129] Fathali M. Moghaddam, 'The staircase to terrorism: a psychological exploration' (2005) 60(2) *American Psychologist* 161, 165.

[130] Ibid. 161.

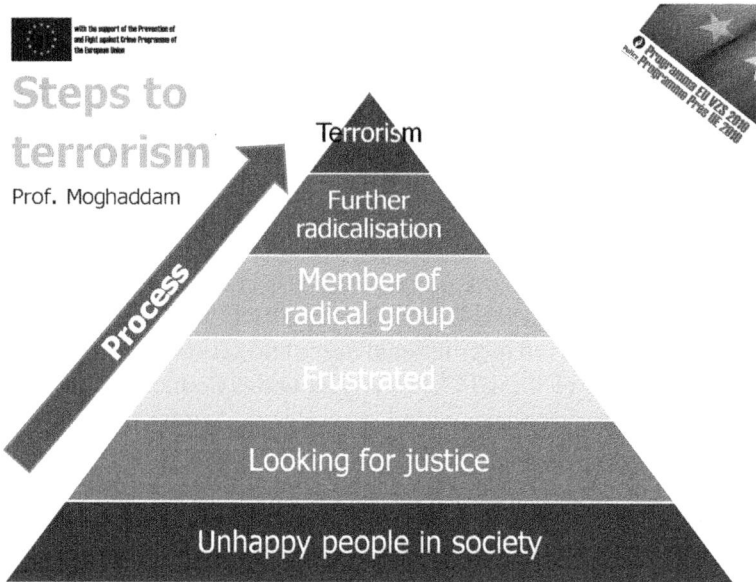

Figure 2.3   The 'Staircase to Terrorism' model used in the Belgian Community Policing Preventing Radicalisation and Terrorism (CoPPRa) Initiative and Trainers Manual 2010. Reprinted with permission.[131]

Such counter-radicalisation models stretch notions of terrorist risk and threat and broaden the field of anticipatory governance. Placing those considered 'risky' and 'at risk of becoming risky' together on a common terrorist trajectory extends the scope of the threat used to justify preemptive security action. As Charlotte Heath-Kelly notes in her study of the UK government's PREVENT strategy, 'the at-risk subject of radicalisation is vulnerable to developing a propensity of dangerousness – meaning that they are *always already rendered as dangerous*'.[132] By fusing a 'relationship of equivalence between particular indicators of social dislocation and the potential for violence', Marieke De Goede and Stephanie Simon argue that such models work by reframing individual events otherwise considered unproblematic as something 'potentially

---

[131] For analysis of this 'staircase model' in counter-radicalisation, see: Marieke de Goede and Stephanie Simon, 'Governing future radicals in Europe' (2013) 45(2) *Antipode* 315, 321–3. This picture of the staircase is taken from that article.

[132] Charlotte Heath-Kelly, 'Counter-terrorism and the counterfactual: producing the "radicalisation" discourse and the UK PREVENT strategy' (2013) 15(3) *British Journal of Politics and International Relations* 394 (emphasis added).

worthy of pre-emptive intervention'.[133] That counter-radicalisation models like the 'staircase to terrorism' inform global security listing practices shows the mobility of anticipatory governance techniques across fields. Such movement is unsurprising, given the extremely broad scope of the list's targeting criteria. The individual potentially 'at risk of becoming risky' and the individual potentially 'associated with someone associated with' ISIL or Al-Qaida are similarly elastic categories.

But this convergence shows just how far removed we are here from conventional understandings of what the Security Council is authorised to do to counter threats to international peace and security. As discussed earlier, Chapter VII of the UN Charter grants the Council exceptional powers 'to take measures deemed indispensable to countering a specific concrete situation that is posing a threat to international peace and security'.[134] For most scholars, Chapter VII action requires threats to have a certain degree of particularity and concreteness before the Security Council can counter them. Yet, as this diagram shows, the ISIL and Al-Qaida list is aimed at governing and averting uncertain potential dangers well in advance of any concrete manifestation of threat – where 'already, much further ahead, you are aware of what the potential threat is'.[135] Here, global listing expertise is not only implementing the list or 'recasting problems of politics as problems of expert knowledge'.[136] It is significantly stretching the scope of potential threats that the Security Council can govern in practice.

The second key feature of this diagram (Figure 2.2) is the way listing is said to be aimed at cutting the threat of global terrorism 'in the middle' and establishing an 'equilibrium of possibilities'. What might this equilibrium possibly mean? And how can a threat as diffuse as global terrorism ever be governed in an equilibrium state? To address such questions, it is helpful to revisit the work of Foucault. From the second half of the eighteenth century, Foucault observed the emergence of a new technology of power that was not disciplinary but something he termed 'biopolitical'. Whilst disciplinary power 'concentrates, focuses and encloses' the bodies of individuals to exert control over them and produce 'individualizing effects', biopolitics is directed at the *population* as a political problem and:

---

[133] De Goede and Simon, 'Governing future radicals', 322–3.
[134] UN Doc. A/65/258 (6 August 2010), 11.
[135] Interview B.
[136] Koskenniemi, *The Politics*, p. 338.

introduce[s] mechanisms that are very different from the functions of disciplinary mechanisms ... Their purpose is not to modify ... a given individual insofar as he is an individual but essentially, to intervene at the level at which these general phenomena are determined ... Most important of all, regulatory mechanisms must be established to establish an equilibrium, maintain an average, establish a sort of homeostasis, and compensate for variations within this general population and its aleatory field. In a word, security mechanisms have to be installed around the random element inherent in a population of a living beings so as to ... achieve overall states of equilibration or regularity ... [and] protect the security of the whole from internal dangers.[137]

Though discipline and biopolitics are distinct and rely on different instruments, they 'are not mutually exclusive and can be articulated with each other'.[138] One way they are linked, according to Foucault, is through the circulation of mobile norms 'that can be applied to both a body one wishes to discipline and a population one wishes to regularise'.[139] For Foucault, norms 'emerge out of the very nature of that which is governed' in contrast to legal rules which 'are external to that which is being governed'.[140] With security, norms work through 'the plotting of differential curves of normality' and 'differential risks' rather than by trying 'to get people, movements and actions to conform' to the normal as with disciplinary modes of power.[141] The key point is that, with the expansion of biopolitics, 'law operates more and more as a - norm'[142] or 'an interplay of differential normalities'.[143] With biopolitics, law works by 'break[ing] subjects and objects into elemental degrees of risk', sifting the good from the bad and generating homeostasis through the increasing use of security mechanisms.[144]

When this listing expert explains the rationale for these consultation meetings in terms of establishing 'an equilibrium of possibilities' (Figure 2.2), I argue that we can see this mobile norm and interplay of differential

---

[137] Foucault, *Society Must be Defended*, p. 246. It is beyond the scope of this chapter to analyse Foucault's thinking on biopolitics and security in detail. My aim here is limited to introducing these ideas to think through the problems presented by this empirical material.

[138] Ibid. p. 250.

[139] Ibid. p. 253.

[140] Nikolas Rose and Mariana Valverde, 'Governed by law?' (1998) 7(4) *Social and Legal Studies* 541, 544.

[141] Foucault, *Security, Territory, Population*, pp. 63, 61, 57.

[142] Michel Foucault, *The History of Sexuality Vol. 1* (New York: Pantheon, 1978), p. 144.

[143] Foucault, *Security, Territory, Population*, p. 63.

[144] Amoore, *The Politics of Possibility*, p. 65.

normalities being put into global circulation.[145] The main justification provided for the list is that it targets specific individuals deemed threats to international peace and security under Chapter VII of the UN Charter. But there is also an array of governmental techniques and knowledge practices that are giving shape to this regime and pushing the envelope of what global listing can govern in practice. This 'equilibrium of possibilities' example shows how security listing works as a hybrid legal form.[146] It is part Chapter VII sovereign measure, whereby the Security Council effectively legislates for the globe by prescribing what states must do to comply with its Resolutions. It is part disciplinary tool that works by freezing the assets and controlling the movements of listed individuals deemed 'associated with' ISIL or Al-Qaida. And it is part biopolitical norm that targets a suspect population situated in the informal 'middle area' of the terrorist staircase – 'not yet' threatening to carry out terrorist acts and undermining international peace and security, but going to get there eventually, according to the national counterterrorism officials, UN experts and preemptive security logics constructing this list.

The main justification for this list is that it targets specific individuals that threaten international peace and security under Chapter VII of the UN Charter and offers a more precise form of global governance than the comprehensive sanctions which it replaced. But the explanation provided here renders this 'smart sanction' rationale problematic by showing how global listing works by also modulating a much *broader* population and potential threat environment. There is an array of governmental techniques and knowledge practices that are also giving shape to this sanctions regime and pushing the envelope of what listing can govern and secure in practice. Legal challenges in this area highlight the Council's formal UN Charter powers as against the human rights of listed individuals. But the listing process analysed above works by new forms of security expertise disaggregating individuals into 'measurable risk factors'[147] that are then targeted at a far more generic level for purposes of separating the good from the bad and 'maintaining an average'.[148] Listing opens a broad field of intervention stretching from the apex of the international order, where

---

[145] My use of the term 'mobile norm' here is taken from Amoore, ibid. 17–18.

[146] As Rose and Valverde observe, legal mechanisms have long 'played a key role in the authorization of disciplinary and bio-political authority' and thus laws and norms have long been mutually interdependent: Rose and Valverde, 'Governed by law?', 550.

[147] Mariana Valverde and Michael Mopas, 'Insecurity and the dream of targeted governance' in Larner and Walters, *Global Governmentality*, p. 240.

[148] Foucault, *Society Must be Defended*, p. 246.

the Council's formal instrumentarium is situated, to the informal middle area of the staircase or 'heterogeneous transactional zone',[149] where global listing expertise intervenes and performs its work. Reframed in this way, UN counterterrorism listing is less an exercise in targeted governance and more a novel programme of global biopolitical management.[150]

2.3.3 Enlistment: Connecting Networks to Networks

The third aim of the consultation meetings analysed in this chapter is that of *enrolment* or *enlistment*. That is, the assemblage of an array of security actors into new global preemptive security networks built around the administration of this list, the construction of a 'global optic' and the potential for intelligence exchange. As one Monitoring Team expert explained, it is the creation of new multilateral intelligence-exchange networks that is one of the most important effects of these meetings:

> We are the only team in the entire UN [Security] Council sanctions structure [that] have a mandate to convene Intelligence Service conferences. We just had one in Vienna last week where twelve ... heads of Intelligence Services from very diverse countries came to talk about the threat of Al-Qaida in Africa ... That's something that [just] doesn't happen ... [where] you have twelve different intelligence services sharing information with the team, but *also with each other*, and *connecting networks with each other* ...
>
> Multilateral [sharing] is very unique to the 'five eyes' community – so Britain, Canada, Australia, UK and US. Other than that, multilateral intelligence sharing inside the EU is already a big problem. [But] if you talk about multilateral intelligence sharing between a European country, an African country and a central Asian country, it's just not happening except for us.[151]

The idea of UN experts forging new forms of multilateral intelligence-sharing is contentious. When US Secretary of State Colin Powell made his infamous presentation before the Security Council in 2003 seeking authorisation for the use of military force against Iraq, he claimed that his statements were 'backed up by ... solid sources. These are not assertions. What we are giving you are facts and conclusions based on

---

[149] Rose and Valverde, 'Governed by law?', 549.
[150] See also: Hans-Martin Jaeger, 'UN reform, biopolitics, and global governmentality' (2010) 2(1) *International Theory* 50.
[151] Interview B (emphasis added).

solid intelligence.'[152] Yet, ultimately, his claims that Iraq possessed weapons of mass destruction were found to be unsubstantiated and the use of intelligence by the Council has long been fraught with political controversy as a result.[153] In his study on this issue Simon Chesterman notes that, although UN counter proliferation and counterterrorism programmes increasingly rely on intelligence, they are 'forced to draw upon national agencies' for this material. Consequently, inside the UN there 'is not multilateral intelligence per se, but applications of national intelligence to serve national interests that happen to correspond to international security'.[154] Yet multilateral intelligence-sharing is precisely what these consultation meetings are enabling as part of the project of building an optic for seeing 'global terrorism'. This development is novel in the context of the Security Council. But it is consistent with the post-9/11 shifts to better 'connect the dots'[155] and transform intelligence-gathering into an adaptive learning process to better understand transnational threat complexities.[156]

UN counterterrorism expertise is the crucial conduit for these meetings to take place and intelligence-sharing networks to emerge because of its perceived objectivity and political neutrality. As one team member put it, 'we have not met a state that does not talk to us . . . If you think about the world, certain Member States don't talk to each other. We bring analytical expertise with us', which allows the team to, 'have a much better spread in [state X] than any other Member State save the Americans'.[157] It is the purportedly 'apolitical' nature of their expertise that enables the team to gain a deeper rapport with, and 'better spread'

---

[152] Text of Colin Powell's speech to the UN Security Council, *BBC News*, 5 February 2003. Available at bbc.in/1GXm9pF.

[153] For an overview of the UN's historical relation with different forms of intelligence analysis, see: Simon Chesterman, 'Shared secrets: intelligence and collective security', Lowy Institute Paper10 (Double Bay NSW: Lowry Institute, 2006).

[154] Ibid. 69–70. See also: Simon Chesterman, 'Does the UN have intelligence?' (2006) 48(3) *Survival* 149.

[155] Stewart Baker, US Department of Homeland Security, cited in Louise Amoore and Marieke de Goede, 'Introduction: governing by risk in the war on terror' in Louise Amoore and Marieke de Goede (eds.), *Risk and the War on Terror* (London: Routledge, 2008), p. 6.

[156] See, for example: Gregory F. Treverton, *Intelligence for an Age of Terror* (Cambridge: Cambridge University Press, 2009). Treverton, former Director of the RAND Corporation's *Center for Global Risk and Security*, argues that intelligence analysis needs to transform into fluid forms of 'organizational sensemaking' if it is to create effective products in relation to global terrorism.

[157] Interview B.

amongst, intelligence services strategically important in the fight against global terrorism. According to one member, the key is that '*we don't have a political role. We are this neutral convening factor that allows them to come*. It's not a conference of Russia or America. It's not a NATO ally conference ... [We provide] a very neutral territory to convene.'[158]

For this global listing expert, 'politics' is something contained in the intergovernmental forum of the Security Council. The 'technical' and the 'political' are clearly delineated as very different domains. But when we understand the list as a technology of governance and inscription, the terrain of global politics is broadened.[159] Reframed this way, the 'political' precisely lies in the ability of listing expertise to provide 'a neutral territory to convene' because it enables a network to be established for localised threat traces to be collected, rescaled, taken back to a central point (the Security Council) and linked to preemptive security intervention at many other sites around the world. It is security expertise driven by problems of list administration that enables 'government at a distance' to take place.[160] The ability of UN security experts to convene meetings and connect networks with networks through the mediating device of the list is one of the most powerful political processes of all.

The fact that perceived expert neutrality 'allows them to come', as this Monitoring Team member put it, points to another important element of listing expertise in this context – which has little to do with the 'objectivity' of their expert knowledge and more to do with institutional power that authorises it. That these listing experts carry the delegated authority of the UN is also crucial in this environment. One US Embassy cable, for example, recounts confidential discussions held between the team's former co-ordinator (Richard Barrett, ex-head of MI6 counterterrorism) and officials from the US Mission to the UN (USUN) concerning a meeting the team convened 'with heads of intelligence and security services from Algeria, Libya, Morocco, Pakistan, Saudi Arabia, UAE and Yemen on January 23–24 [2008] in Vienna':

> Barrett further emphasized that these officials viewed the 1267 Committee and the Monitoring Team as *a neutral interlocutor that could facilitate US and EU assistance to them under multilateral cover*. Many of these officials

---

[158] Ibid. (emphasis added).

[159] See, for example: Bruce Braun and Sarah J. Whatmore, 'The stuff of politics: an introduction' in Bruce Braun and Sarah J. Whatmore (eds.), *Political Matter: Technoscience, Democracy and Public Life* (Minneapolis MN: University of Minnesota Press, 2010).

[160] Miller and Rose, 'Governing economic life', 9; Latour, *Reassembling the Social*, p. 176.

believe it is easier for their governments to be seen cooperating with the UN than to be accused of responding to the bilateral demands of the US or other western countries.[161]

Here it is the fact that the team's listing expertise is housed within the UN that is critically important, because it provides 'multilateral cover' for national security officials to gain access to US and EU intelligence. 'These officials', the cable continues 'want to be treated as equals by their US and EU counterparts'.[162] They 'see the UN as an actor that could convince the US and Europe to agree to greater operational cooperation with them'.[163] These consultation meetings are thus valued for their potential to bypass established Cold War intelligence ties and create new transnational security and intelligence exchange networks:

> In a separate conversation with USUN, Barrett described the type of assistance sought, which includes: cooperation on intelligence sharing, including on intelligence that supports listing requests; technical help with intercepts; and more action from EU countries in response to the threat posed by persons located in Europe – including those under asylum – who incite terrorism in the region, but whose freedom of speech is nonetheless protected.[164]

According to Kim Lane Scheppele the rapid uptake of global security law by states after 9/11 can be explained by such political motivations. That is, national executive security actors have pushed the implementation of new Security Council measures because they have 'a strong interest in gaining the power that [these] new legal regime[s] gives them relative to the other players in their own domestic space'.[165] This thesis is important, and clearly resonates with the Wikileaks cables discussed above. But it requires qualification in two important ways to help us make sense of this empirical material.

First, the dynamics of global exception are not just a question of formally extending security powers through the promulgation of sweeping legal measures by the Security Council and national states. That is the first legal step. It is necessary, but in itself insufficient, to account for how global security law is built and made powerful. Expert practices and security networks stimulated by the resolution of seemingly mundane

---

[161] US Embassy Cable 08USUNNEWYORK313 (dated 7 April 2008), para. 7 (emphasis added).
[162] Ibid.
[163] Ibid.
[164] Ibid.
[165] Scheppele, 'The international state of emergency', 5.

technical problems enabled by these laws also drive exceptional governance.

Second, there is an implicit assumption in the literature on international states of emergency that the expansion of draconian domestic security powers flows unproblematically from the creation of new UN global security regimes and the convergence of shared executive interests they enable. But when the exception is analysed as a process of global legal assemblage, rather than as a 'state' of emergency, its contingency, heterogeneity and potential failure can more readily be drawn into view and global emergencies become something far more politically messy and complicated as a result.

During an interview with one former Monitoring Team member, for example, I asked about their 'creative work linking together the security and intelligence services in North Africa and the Middle East with the aim of bringing them in closer proximity to the P5 states'. In response, I was told this rationale was 'Bullshit . . . that was not what we were doing. That's what we *said* we were doing to justify to the Council the expenditure of the whole thing.'[166] According to this expert, a central figure involved in organising the first consultation meetings, their original aim was:

> to bring the countries together to be able to give the reviews to the Security Council on intelligence, because the intelligence was not reaching the Council . . . That is why I have suggested this idea and talked to all intelligence services through my national contacts to make it happen . . . *I wanted to make the list . . . more vibrant.* I wanted to make the list reflect the real threat.[167]

But this process failed, according to this listing expert, because the views of regional intelligence services 'were being censored before [they] reached the Council'. On further probing I was told this was due to the Security Council's reluctance to act outside established bilateral relations:

> It was basically the P5. The other member states, not the P5, they would bring the experts on counterterrorism to the table. And they would want to make a deal. The P5 always wanted to have the deal done outside the Council. On bilateral ties . . . 'It's a matter of superpower relations. It's the way it's done' . . . They wanted to have the decisions done in capitals. Not with the UN.[168]

---

[166] Interview with former member of the UN 1267 Monitoring Team, 2013 (Interview D).
[167] Ibid.
[168] Ibid.

Wikileaks cables corroborate the view that this attempt to build an optic for seeing 'global terrorism' was plagued with problems because the P5 failed to take the operational concerns of North-African, Middle-Eastern and South-Asian intelligence services seriously. In one cable – entitled, *'UN/1267 Sanctions: Arab and Pakistani Security Officials Complain Security Council Slow to Sanction Al-Qaida'* – the former Monitoring Team coordinator updates the Sanctions Committee and US officials on a 2008 'consultation meeting' that took place in Vienna: 'These [intelligence] officials are frustrated that their requests to recommend specific individuals affiliated with al-Qaida or the Taliban for sanctions by the Security Council are frequently put on hold, either temporarily or for long periods of time.'[169] The cable discusses how twelve Libyan list nominations and thirty-two Moroccan list nominations had been placed on hold by the USA, UK, France, Russia and Belgium for up to four years and warns the Committee that this 'will discourage [these states] from proposing additional subjects for sanctions in the future'.[170]

So, the three key Monitoring Team experts I interviewed about these consultation meetings provided divergent views about their purposes, merits and effects. For some, the meetings constitute successful experiments in building a new optic for seeing 'global terrorism' and building new multilateral networks of intelligence exchange. For others, the meetings have been a resounding failure that simply reasserted established superpower relations and bilateral ties between P5 states.

Irrespective of the content of these meetings and whether new intelligence flows are being created or established bilateral ties reaffirmed, I argue that the power of this experiment lies in its ongoing capacity for *enrolment* or, more accurately, *enlistment*. Problems of the list, and the opportunities for intelligence exchange that its effective implementation affords, serves to enrol a diverse array of security actors into new global preemptive security networks. This is what it means for UN security experts 'to connect networks with networks' as suggested above. As one former team member explained, implicitly distinguishing the Monitoring Team's approach from the Monitoring Group:

> The Sanctions regime, of course, is an obligation on Member States, not on the people who are under sanction … So, this is [about] *getting Member States to really see the threat in the same way*, co-ordinate their activities and pull together to ensure that the chain had no weak links …

---

[169] US Embassy Cable 08USUNNEWYORK313.
[170] Ibid.

> [Its] a question really of explaining that Member State's *obligations weren't just obligations* they had to conform with but also that there were reasons behind that – [that] these were the reasons why it was important to have a global regime . . . The Monitoring Team of eight experts really took that job on.[171]

Getting people to 'see the threat in the same way' means enrolling diverse security actors to see terrorism through the 'global optic' of the list and to govern it preemptively as the list begets. In this process, the power of expertise does not lie in 'naming and shaming' states or enforcing implementation but rather '[forging] a shared understanding and shared approach' that enables states 'more importantly, to feel that they were part of . . . the international effort':[172]

> This wasn't just some group of . . . five permanent members, ordering the world to do things the[y] . . . might not think were particularly useful . . . But say[ing] to states, you know, 'What is the threat as you see it? What could the international community be doing to help you?' . . . So, we went around to a lot of those countries talking about what they thought, and what the Security Council thought and trying to mix that operational aspect with the political aspects. And then beyond that, grouping countries together so that they would have a joint view – which is obviously much more powerful when expressed to the Security Council than if they've got independent and slightly conflicting views.[173]

The Team's expertise and the 'consultation meetings' they have convened through the list have been crucially important means of establishing new shared relations of equivalence in this domain:

> It was important to [say to] states, 'Ok. What are you doing on counter-terrorism; what are you doing about the Al-Qaida threat? How do you assess that threat and how does this international activity support what you're doing and fit in with what you're doing?' And that allowed Member States to adapt their counterterrorism measures, if you like, in a sort of coherent way globally. And it also allowed us to tell the Security Council, you know, where this regime might work but [also] where it might not work and so where they'd like to sort of maybe amend it a little bit. Whether the people who are subject to sanctions were appropriate, according to some of the key Member States who knew them better than some of the members of the Security Council. And so, we built up a relationship with mainly, you know, Middle Eastern, North African and South Asian countries.[174]

---

[171] Interview A (emphasis added).
[172] Ibid.
[173] Ibid.
[174] Ibid.

It is by convincing national security officials of the benefits of pre-emptive targeting through listing – and showing them what this list can *do* – that UN listing experts build institutional rapport, stimulate a 'shared feeling' and enlist political and operational support for the Security Council's anti-terrorism campaign. One of the benefits highlighted during country visits, according to one former Committee member, is how the list can work to generate intelligence and be used as a source of 'leverage':

> Once an individual . . . is placed on the sanctions list . . . [it] *will yield its own additional flow of information or intelligence* . . . There will be suspicious transaction reports . . . [and] chatter on the wires that wasn't there before. And the hope is that . . . [they] will seek to distance themselves from their previous involvement by coming to cooperate with law enforcement in order to demonstrate that they have severed the relevant ties . . . So, the critical thing about the Al-Qaida sanctions regime . . . [is] the follow up to a listing – what . . . benefit[s] both the Council and the relevant Member State from that listing.[175]

Such cooperation can also be a valuable way of generating potential informants from amongst the broad pool of perceived 'material supporters at the periphery'.[176] Targeting people on the periphery is useful because it can often 'create the leverage [for them] to say: "Get me off this list. I will help you with information. I know about the tiers that are more difficult for you to trace".'[177] The idea of counterterrorism officials using listing for generating informants amongst targeted communities has long been the source of speculation, but has rarely been acknowledged. Litigation ongoing in the USA, for example, alleges that the Federal Bureau of Investigation (FBI) placed people on the US no-fly list as a means of trying either to coerce them into becoming informants in their local communities or punish them for refusing to do so.[178] So it is unsurprising that similar motives might motivate other officials to use the ISIL and Al-Qaida global list to target peripheral persons of interest in their territories and provide a means of 'persuading them that there is a strategic benefit to them of making better use of the list'.[179]

---

[175] Interview C (emphasis added).
[176] Ibid. This argument is examined in Chapter 3 when discussing the team's support for list accountability reform.
[177] Ibid.
[178] For details see: Ramzi Kassem and Baher Azmy, 'Spying or no flying' *Al Jazeera* (7 May 2014). Available at: bit.ly/30DROsP See: *Tanvir* v. *Tanzin* 915 F.3d 898 (2d Cir. 2019). At the time of writing, this had been appealed to the US Supreme Court.
[179] Interview C.

Even listing peripheral individuals, about whom security officials may have very little information to infer association with ISIL or Al-Qaida, can help generate intelligence and transform speculative security allegations into more solid forms of evidence. According to one expert, the critical step is to list individuals first and then 'get that listed person right into making their contrary claims'. Through this process, 'their contrary claims can be followed up, can be discredited, and can actually form further grounds for the listing'. According to this interviewee, this is one 'positive way in which you can move a closed information situation into an open information situation'.[180] Thus listing can be used in conditions of uncertainty to absorb some of the uncertainties involved with the listing itself.

Finally, listing provides a powerful way to stigmatise its targets:

> In Africa we have discovered that there is a genuine fear of being put on a sanctions list. Not because assets will get frozen or travel will be denied but because of social and familial stigma. We think that that could be used significantly more in a context like with Boko Haram ... to [help] tip the balance towards the good guys.[181]

A key impetus for enlisting people into these preemptive security networks is the inability of the Security Council to enforce its own decisions, in spite of the supreme nature of its Chapter VII powers:

> UN Security Council Resolutions are binding decisions under Chapter 7. When they are done under Chapter 7, it's no option ... [But] how many states might have violated the Security Council's [sanctions] in the past ... [and] what is the punishment? What is the punishment for North Korea or someone helping North Korea ... [or] someone helping Iran from the UN Security Council's perspective? You've got the punishment by ... stakeholders who have their own, much harsher, sanction regimes against violators. *But the UN Security Council has no mechanism to enforce its decisions.* It is an intergovernmental organization. That means, theoretically, that everyone is of the same weight ... If you violate [sanctions, the] ... maximum of what happens to you is you get bad press for few days and then no one cares afterwards.[182]

Another former team member described this as part of a process of the Council trying to reinforce its authority under the UN Charter:

---

[180] Ibid.
[181] Ibid.
[182] Interview B (emphasis added).

Some permanent members would say, 'Well, you know, damn it. This is what we want to do and that's what we're going to do ... [and] Member States have to comply because they signed the Charter and they've signed up to be members of the UN so, end of story'. But clearly ... what are you going to do if someone doesn't implement your sanctions? What options have you got? You're not going to impose secondary sanctions on them – very, very unlikely and even if you did who would comply with that? It would be sort of an abuse of power almost ... You're not going to go to war over it ... You're just going to make political statements saying, 'Well we think you should comply'. But ... if nothing changes as a result, [then] you've lost it [i.e. your authority] haven't you?[183]

It is enlistment that provides the answer to this strategic problem, enabling global security laws issued by the Council to exert greater control over the problems of global terrorism they seek to counter. It allows the Monitoring Team to achieve through specialised, technical means what had eluded the more confrontational efforts of the earlier Monitoring Group. And it provides a conduit for translating the direct legal commands of the Council into more indirect mechanisms of rule – creating a 'shared feeling' that enables security officials to feel that international 'obligations weren't just obligations'.

The effects of global listing expertise in this context are similar to the 'soft power' initiatives used by bodies like the UN CTC. In her study of the CTC, Isobel Roele observes how seemingly innocuous technical practices such as 'implementation assessments', 'guiding principles' and UN workshops for 'enhancing dialogue' embed asymmetrical power relations between core and periphery and discipline recalcitrant states into participating in the Security Council's counterterrorism agenda.[184] Roele uses a framework of disciplinary power to account for such effects: 'Global counter-terrorism is only as strong ... as its weakest link. Consequently, the normalization of *all* states is vital to the success of the counter-terrorism project.'[185] For Kim Lane Scheppele the rapid uptake of global security law can be explained through the ways it combines both disciplinary and renewed imperial logics of control. In global security law, as with colonial empires, 'the center gets from the periphery what the center needs [i.e. "terrorists"]. In exchange, the peripheral states, and especially their leaders, get powerful protection and approval from the center.'[186] Here global security law reflects the

---

[183] Interview A.
[184] Roele, 'Disciplinary power'.
[185] Ibid. 50 (emphasis added).
[186] Scheppele, 'The empire of security', 250.

interests of powerful states and their 'strategies of legitimation' – 'leaders in the periphery use their backing from the center to enhance their local power while leaders at the core use the control they exercise over the periphery to shore up their power at the core'.[187]

Both approaches offer valuable insights into how this emerging field of law is developing. Yet I argue that understanding the proliferation of global security law also requires close empirical analysis of the specific governance technologies and forms of security expertise that are being forged and put into global circulation. The 'consultation meetings' examined in this chapter clearly do enable novel relations between periphery and core and reassert imperial relations. But as Geoffrey Bowker and Susan Leigh Star remind us, 'the material culture of ... empire is not found in pomp and circumstance, nor even in the first instance at the point of a gun, *but rather at the point of a list*'.[188] In other words, it is the technology of the list and its expertise that is doing much of the hard work to enrol the different security actors and sustain the knowledge-practices that make this particular form of global law both possible and powerful. Global security law is not only a body of imperial decrees issued by the Security Council legislating for the world. It is also a 'legal complex'[189] of quasi-legal interventions, expert techniques, dispersed forms of authority and preemptive security practices produced through the governance of novel knowledge objects – or, as argued in this book, a global legal assemblage.

2.4 Data Infrastructures and the Politics of Formatting

In the previous section we examined how the technology of the list works to create a new optic for seeing 'global terrorism'. By closely following listing expertise in action we observed how seemingly innocuous technical problems of list administration create the conditions for assembling this domain of global law and stretching what it is capable of doing in practice. In this section we examine another specific site and technical

---

[187] Ibid. 249, 251.

[188] Bowker and Star, *Sorting Things Out*, p. 137 (emphasis added). See also: de Goede and Sullivan, 'The politics of security lists'. On the materiality of empire see: Daniel R. Headrick, *The Tools of Empire: Technology and European Imperialism in the Nineteenth Century* (Oxford: Oxford University Press, 1981).

[189] Rose and Valverde use the idea of the 'legal complex' to refer 'to the assemblage of legal practices, legal institutions, statutes, legal codes, authorities, discourses, texts, norms and forms of judgement' – 'Governed by law?', 542.

problem that the Monitoring Team has been addressing as part of its mandate for effectively implementing the list: the problem of data infrastructures and formatting. That is, creating the technical conditions for making the ISIL and Al-Qaida list interoperable with other data standards and methods of data analysis to extend its global reach and application.

In this section I examine the Monitoring Team's implementation efforts in relation to two interrelated formats – (i) biometric information and (ii) API and PNR data – drawing out its political and legal effects. According to the experts involved, this reformatting of the list is a technically complex but relatively minor issue far removed from the more pressing political concerns of the Security Council. As one team member described it: 'This is basically the list, with the information on the list, in a different format. So, *the substantive information is the same.*'[190] In this formulation, the list is an inert object or instrument first applied in context A and then simply reapplied or extended into context B. It is a question of implementation.

However, as I show in this section, technical reformatting is a creative, jurisgenerative and profoundly political governance move. Reformatting the list performs what is called in ANT a 'translation'.[191] It doesn't simply move the list from context A to context B – it *changes* the list in accordance with the new criteria, ordering practices and spatiotemporal dynamics that condition the different formats. Translation, in other words, is a productive process or 'form of modification' that transforms the list into something else.[192] I argue that focusing on list reformatting is important because it shows how global security law is embedded and stretched through technical listing practice. It generates new global security governance terrain but is obscured through functional expertise as mere background work. As with our earlier discussion of the 'global optic', the ISIL and Al-Qaida list emerges from this analysis of reformatting as a crucial actant in the global security domain. It exerts agency in its own right, performs important legal assemblage work, builds new ensembles of relations and helps to produce global terrorism as an expansive object of political and legal intervention.

---

[190] Interview B (emphasis added).
[191] On translation, see: Callon and Latour, 'Unscrewing the big Leviathan', p. 279. On reformatting as translation, see de Goede and Sullivan, 'The politics of security lists'.
[192] Andrew Barry, 'The translation zone' (2013) 41(3) *Millennium: Journal of International Studies* 413, 414, as cited and discussed in de Goede and Sullivan, 'The politics of security lists', 79.

2.4.1   Reformatting the List and Building the 'Third Hurdle'

Most discussion about the ISIL and Al-Qaida list focuses on its coercive asset-freezing powers. But the asset-freeze is only one component of the sanctions. Those listed are also subjected to a global travel ban. This ban – which requires states to 'prevent the entry into or the transit through their territories' of all individuals on the ISIL and Al-Qaida list – was poorly enforced for many years. The Security Council tried to close the gaps in 2004 by ensuring that amendments to the list were automatically sent 'to all States, regional and subregional organizations for inclusion, to the extent possible, of listed names in their respective electronic databases and relevant border enforcement and entry/exit tracking systems'.[193] Yet this call largely went unnoticed and – as the team candidly acknowledged in its fourth public report: 'Listed persons continue to travel, despite the mandatory language of the travel ban, whether via the use of stolen, lost or fraudulent travel documents or through the inattention/disregard of the sanction by Member States.'[194]

In 2005 the Security Council (through the Monitoring Team) began two initiatives to ameliorate this situation. In collaboration with the International Criminal Police Organization (Interpol), they launched the *Interpol–United Nations Security Council Special Notice* system for locating and preventing the movement of listed persons. Special notices exist in two versions. The public version is available on the Interpol website. Its original format, as shown below in Figure 2.4, was 'in essence, a kind of "wanted" poster',[195] containing photographs, aliases, physical descriptors and known travel documents associated with each Al-Qaida list entry. Its appearance has since been modified to copy the 'Narrative Summary of Reasons for Listing' maintained by the Sanctions Committee.[196]

The restricted version is only available to Interpol licence-holders – including most national police and border agencies around the world but also, anomalously, the SCAD administrators who support the Monitoring Team inside the UN Secretariat.[197] The closed version 'adds value' by containing additional 'law enforcement-confidential

[193] S/RES/1526 (2004), at para. 19.
[194] UN Doc. S/2006/154 (10 March 2006), para. 83.
[195] Ibid. para. 92.
[196] See: Interpol, *United Nations Security Council Special Notices*. Available at: bit.ly /2JGNP9f.
[197] Interview B.

Interpol-United Nations Security Council Special Notice

Subject To UN Sanctions

AL KHALAYLEH (ALIAS AL - ZARQAWI), Ahmad Fadil Nazal

Identity Particulars	
Present family name:	AL KHALAYLEH (ALIAS AL - ZARQAWI)
Forename:	AHMAD FADIL NAZAL
Sex:	MALE
Date of birth:	30 October 1966 (39 years old)
Place of birth:	AL ZARQAA, Jordan
Language spoken:	Arabic
Nationality:	Jordan
Other Names:	ABOU MUSAAB EL ZARQAWI , ABU IBRAHIM , ABU MUSAB AL ZARQAWI , AL KHALAYLEH , AL MUHAGER , AL MUHAJER , AL ZARQAWI , ALKHALAYLEH , AZZARKAOUI , EL KHELAI ALLAH , EL KHELLAI ALLAH , EL ZARQUAWI , GARIB , MUHANNAD , ZARKAOUI
Other Forenames:	ABOU MOUSSAAB , ABOU MOUSSAB , ABOU MUSAAB , ABU MUSA'AB , AHMAD FADIL NAZAL , AHMED , AHMED FAD AL NAZZAR KHALAYLAH SAID , AHMED FAD AL NAZZAR KHALAYLAH SAID ABU MUSAB
Other Dates of Birth:	20 October 1966 , 30 October 1966

Identity Documents			
Type	Nr	Issued on	Place of Issue
PASSPORT	264958	4 April 1999	
IDENTITY CARD	1433035	4 April 1999	ALZARQA

Physical description	
Height:	1.80 meter <-> 71 inches
Colour of eyes:	BROWN
Colour of hair:	CHESTNUT

UN Sanctions

Pursuant to Security Council Resolution 1267 (1999) and successor resolutions including Resolution 1617 (2005) , the Subject is under the following UN Sanctions: Freezing of Assets, Travel Ban and Arms Embargo.

WANTED by Interpol

UN Sanctions

YOUR NATIONAL OR LOCAL POLICE

@ ICPO-INTERPOL General Secretariat, (Command & Coordination Center,
Tel: +33 472 44 76 76 / +33 472 44 79 80 - Email : ccc@interpol.int

©Interpol, 29 January 2006.

Figure 2.4 Interpol–UN Special Notice (Public Version), 2006. Available at: bit.ly /2xXHhwj. © (2019) United Nations. Reprinted with permission from the United Nations.

information, such as fingerprints and details of relevant national investigations and operations under way'.[198] By 2013 Interpol Special Notices
had been created for almost all list entries, with 20 per cent including
photo identifiers.[199] By July 2019, all but one of the 260 individuals on the
list had links to Interpol Special Notices in their UN list entries.

In 2005, Monitoring Team counterterrorism experts also met with
officials from the ICAO and the IATA. ICAO is the UN agency
responsible for setting global aviation standards and IATA is the
trade association representing the global airline industry. These meetings identified 'several areas of convergence', which soon translated
into collaborative working projects in relation to travel documentation standards and passenger-screening practices.[200] To that end, the
Monitoring Team has been working intensively with ICAO, IATA
and Interpol since 2013 with a view to delivering practical results on
improved aviation industry implementation of the travel ban.[201] UN
Security Council resolutions in this area now routinely cite and 'note
with appreciation' their collaborative work with Interpol, ICAO and
IATA.[202]

For UN listing experts, these initiatives with Interpol, ICAO and IATA
are driven by two primary aims – interoperability and preemption. Both
processes aim at 'enhancing' the implementation of the ISIL and Al-Qaida
list by rendering it interoperable – with the biometric platforms increasingly
used by border security agencies, the various watchlists and databases
maintained by Interpol and the API/PNR datasets used in the aviation
industry. The problem, as one ICAO official explained, is that the ISIL
and Al-Qaida list was formatted in a way that makes it effectively unusable
in the global transport environment: 'Although it's available online through
the website, it's not known in any system that automatically checks against
it.'[203] To resolve this issue the Monitoring Team has been reformatting the
list in ways that police, border agencies, the financial sector and the airline
industry are familiar working with. Chapter VII UN Charter measure or
not, making global security law global requires technical interoperability. As

---

[198] UN Doc. S/2006/154, para. 93.
[199] UN Doc. S/2013/467 (2 August 2013), 18.
[200] UN Doc. S/2006/154, para. 97.
[201] Interview B.
[202] See, for example, S/RES/2178 (2014), S/RES/2309 (2016) and S/RES/2396 (2017).
[203] Interview with ICAO official, Montreal (via Skype), March 2014 (Interview E). The
availability of the list in .xml format is specifically designed to facilitate interoperability
with the banking and financial industries, and also API (as discussed below).

one team member put it: 'If [the list] is not interoperable, you simply cannot implement it. Because [what] we are looking at is global implementation.'[204]

These technical initiatives are also directed at transforming the pre-emptive bordering capabilities of the travel ban. The aim is to make the ban better able to intervene in the middle zone of the 'equilibrium of possibilities' shown earlier in Figure 2.2 – where 'you don't wait until the guy is at your airport and you need to prevent him from entering your country ... but [where] already, *much* further ahead, you are aware of what the potential threat is'.[205] The travel ban was historically concerned with preventing listed individuals from *entering into* or *transiting* through a particular territory.[206] In their 2006 report the Monitoring Team raised the question of whether the formal prohibition on transit might also be read as imposing additional obligations on states 'to prevent the departure of listed persons from their territories'. At that time, the team concluded that 'the resolution may not prohibit all "departures from" a territory, because the Council could easily have said so' if that is what it had intended.[207] Yet using the list to target 'much further ahead' in time has been the prime rationale for the Monitoring Team's collaborations with Interpol, ICAO and IATA. The aim has been to reorientate the travel ban from entry and transit towards pre-screening and 'exit control'. As one ICAO expert put it, the travel ban is 'no longer about stopping people at borders. *It's about stopping people before they even think about crossing borders* and that's a little bit different.'[208] One former team member described this process as part of the task of building, what he termed, a new 'third hurdle':

> First of all, you have to get an identity document and/or a visa to travel. Hurdle one. That was addressed years ago – partially with the Interpol databases but [also] with strengthening our relationship with the foreign ... and interior ministries. Hurdle one ... can be overcome by the individual if he simply forges his identity.
>
> The second hurdle usually was the arrival at the border and the entry in the country. Now you have countries without borders. You have border controls that may not be as strict. You may have a legal problem that the

---

[204] Interview B.

[205] Ibid. (emphasis added).

[206] I say 'historically' because the situation has shifted dramatically following the introduction of S/RES/2178 (2014) against 'foreign terrorist fighters'. The significance of the Resolution 2178 and its relation to these technical reform processes is explored later in this chapter and in the conclusion of this book.

[207] UN Doc. S/2006/154, para. 85.

[208] Interview E (emphasis added).

police guy cannot access directly Interpol data [so] ... it also has [its] problems. And that *was* the last hurdle. If the guy could get a visa and a passport and if he could get across the border, then he was in.

But we want to have now a *third hurdle*. Which means: in the electronic process of getting your *means to travel* – your airline ticket and your boarding on the airplane – you have a third hurdle. A third possibility ... where your identity is checked against the United Nations Security Council list.

The more hurdles you erect for listed individuals, the more difficult it is for them to subvert the travel ban.[209]

When framed as a question of implementation the process seems straightforward. The Council creates global law over here and it is then the task of technical experts to ensure that this body of global law is properly applied over there. But when this project of 'the third hurdle' is disaggregated and examined more closely the global lawmaking/global law-implementing distinction becomes more difficult to sustain. When the list is analysed as a technology of governance and form of productive power, we can see that these data infrastructure and interoperability projects do much more than simply implement. They transform the list and help to forge new governance possibilities that alter, at a quite fundamental level, what this form of global law is and how it performs its global security work.

2.4.2   Translation, Scale and the List As a Hybrid Norm

Interoperability is more than a technical move that enhances implementation of the list through convergence of context A into context B. It is a process that makes global security listing more dynamic and heterogeneous. As Annemarie Mol has said, 'objects come into being ... with the practices in which they are manipulated. And since the object of manipulation tends to differ from one practice to another, reality multiplies.'[210] Making the ISIL and Al-Qaida list interoperable with other data formats similarly does more than enhance its application. It renders the list multiple and performs a 'translation'.[211] Biometric, API

---

[209] Interview B (emphasis in original).

[210] Annemarie Mol, *The Body Multiple: Ontology in Medical Practice* (Durham NC: Duke University Press, 2002), p. 5.

[211] As de Goede and Sullivan argue: 'Moving records from one list/database to another ... does not just change the "context" in which the information is used. It changes the information itself: its technical appearance, the meaning it is inscribed with, the elements it is associated with, and the effects is it able to have' – 'The politics of security lists', 79.

and PNR interoperability create other kinds of lists with different spatiotemporal dynamics and governance effects as the one maintained on the Sanctions Committee website and incorporated into the domestic legal orders of Member States.

The technical process of PNR interoperability starts by unbundling targeted individuals on the ISIL and Al-Qaida list into a more diverse array of associated PNR-compatible data packets. One former team member, differentiating the list interoperability process required in the financial and aviation industries, explained this disaggregation process in the following way:

> The PNR packaging is different from the XML packaging so the data is in different format because ICAO assumes rightfully that you are one individual, one name, one passport . . . However, on our list we have multiple names, multiple aka's, multiple passports from different countries. So, we need to package the data in a way that you have a headline, maybe a number and then underneath that number, individual identities. This aka is connected to this birth date is connected to this passport number is connected to this address. This aka is connected to only this address. This aka is connected to this passport.[212]

The rationale for slicing individual targets up into sets of sub-individual identifiers this way is faster and more efficient global circulation. It is anticipated that the travel-banning process can accelerate as a result – by reducing the risk of 'false positives' and better synchronising the list with the transactional speed of the global aviation marketplace:

> With the banking industry . . . we're talking billions of transactions a day. So, everything has to be machines . . . [and] in a data format, that they can feed into their software programs . . . Otherwise, the entire financial system grinds to a halt. Same thing will need to be for air travel. You cannot grind to a halt international air travel because you have ten thousand matching, or partially matching, hits. So, you need to make sure that you provide data in a form that is usable . . . so that airlines can check and reduce the amount of partial or false leads they have . . . to ensure that air travel is no longer interrupted by this.[213]

The technical aim is therefore to reformat the ISIL and Al-Qaida list into 'individual packages that mesh with the way that the airline industry sells tickets'.[214] Once 'the data transfer is engineered – between us, the Security Council, IATA and ICAO – we will then *also have a list* checking when

---

[212] Interview B.
[213] Ibid.
[214] Ibid. (emphasis added).

the data of the individual passengers is created whether these individuals are on the United Nations Security Council list'.[215] This new list, however, is not simply a one-to-one copy of the list on the UN Sanctions Committee's website. Splitting individuals (with 'one name, one passport') into different information packages changes the targets on the list into a much more mobile and dynamic set of associated data elements. Once disaggregated and rendered PNR-interoperable, these packages can then circulate with all passenger data collected from the three main Global Distribution Systems (GDS) used by air carriers and 'pushed' towards databases operated by national agencies for PNR travel-data risk analysis.[216] Meshing listed individuals into data packages formatted to global aviation industry standards significantly alters the spatial and temporal scope of the list, allowing it to circulate at greater velocity and over a far more extensive global terrain.

This meshing of list and travel data together is part of a broader shift from state-centred border control towards new bordering capabilities that are simultaneously subnational and globally scaled. When the travel ban is mediated through travel data 'national borders and bordering capabilities' are 'uncoupled'.[217] Once uncoupled, the ban is no longer reliant on national states for its enforcement – which, as I have shown, is one of the key rationales for the Monitoring Team's work on this issue. The list can then be enacted at subnational local sites (when someone tries to buy an airline ticket) that are interconnected via global electronic networks and databases. So again, we can see the technology of the list deeply imbricated in the production of 'the global' by enacting an accelerated, novel and dynamic form of transnational legal-ordering.[218] This isn't a form of 'global law beyond the state'[219] because national security

---

[215] Ibid.

[216] For an overview of the data workflow process envisaged by the 2011 EU PNR proposal, see: Rocco Bellanova and Denis Duez, 'A different view on the "making" of European security: the EU Passenger Name Record System as a socio-technical assemblage' (2012) 17(2) *European Foreign Affairs Review* 109, 115.

[217] Saskia Sassen, 'Bordering capabilities versus borders: implications for national borders' (2009) 30 *Michigan Journal of International Law* 567. See also: Saskia Sassen, *Territory, Authority, Rights: From Medieval to Global Assemblage* (Princeton NJ: Princeton University Press, 2006), pp. 222–76.

[218] On the list as a technology for producing the global, see: Urs Staeheli, 'Listing the global: dis/connectivity beyond representation?' (2012) 13(3) *Distinktion: Scandinavian Journal of Social Theory* 233.

[219] Gunther Teubner, 'Global Bukowina: legal pluralism in the world society' in Gunther Teubner (ed.), *Global Law without a State* (Aldershot: Ashgate Publishing, 1997).

agencies remain closely involved in the travel data assessment and electronic-bordering process. It is a multi-scalar legal process made possible through a 'list-plus-algorithm' format that creates new forms of global authority and 'alignments of people, places and things – or fragmented approximations of the same – on the global plane'.[220] Reformatting doesn't just better implement the list, as the experts involved have suggested. It translates it into something else.

This process also creates new security mechanisms. Making the list interoperable with travel data significantly broadens its field of application and alters what it can do as a preemptive security device. In the scenario outlined above by the UN listing expert, making the list interoperable with travel data merely enables another list to be created to check 'when the data of the individual passengers is created whether these individuals are on the United Nations Security Council list'.[221] Here the list works in what Foucault calls a disciplinary mode to identify known listed individuals and interdict their travel. But travel data is not only collected and used by states to identify known threats and individuals. It is also analysed algorithmically to identify *unknown* threats, unusual patterns or anomalies and persons who might potentially be of interest to border and security services.[222]

When an ISIL and Al-Qaida list entry is disaggregated into multiple data packages that associate different names, passports, dates of birth, akas and addresses, these elements can be algorithmically analysed to draw inferences and possible links to the travel records, names and addresses, credit card details of new, and as yet unknown, individuals. People who may have lived in the same town, have a similar name to one of the akas, be of the same religion and/or age range or used a credit card with an address proximate to the address of someone listed might now be identified as someone of interest at the border or someone to prevent from travelling. When the list works in this way it is not only performing the *disciplinary* function of banning the travel of known individuals. It is also working as a *security* mechanism for identifying unknown individuals who might pose a potential threat. Just as with the 'equilibrium of possibilities' discussed earlier, we once more see the list working as

---

[220] Fleur Johns, 'The turn to data analytics and international law' (2014) 3(4) *ESIL Reflections* 6. See also: Fleur Johns, 'The list plus algorithm as global law' (2016) 34(1) *Environment and Planning D: Society and Space* 126.

[221] Interview B.

[222] For an excellent analysis of the use of travel data to identify unknown terrorists, see Amoore, *The Politics of Possibility*.

a hybrid legal form – part sovereign ban and part biopolitical norm – and broadening its field of intervention.

Using travel records to implement the list and ban the travel of targeted individuals, however, can only adequately work if the passenger data of *all travellers* can be collected and analysed. The use of travel data for preemptive security purposes has long been hugely controversial.[223] But through a series of far-reaching measures adopted since 2014, the Security Council has been progressively advancing this issue and creating new data collection and analysis obligations for states and airlines.

In 2013, following a recommendation from the Monitoring Team, the Sanctions Committee held that 'not being subject to the Al-Qaida sanctions regime travel ban *is a requirement for individuals seeking entry* into the national territories of Member States' and notified all states to change their guidelines accordingly.[224] In September 2014, following the Monitoring Team's technical work on these matters, Resolution 2178 was adopted by the UN Security Council. This requires states to compel airlines to provide them with API data for detecting the attempted travel of individuals on the ISIL and Al-Qaida list and encourages states to 'employ evidence-based traveller risk assessment and screening procedures including collection and analysis of travel data' to 'prevent the movement of terrorists' – that is, algorithmic data analysis.[225] Resolution 2309 (2016) reaffirmed these obligations for API analysis, highlighted the importance of Chicago Convention standards for aviation security and called upon all states to strengthen their information-sharing for border security purposes.[226] Resolution 2368 (2017) similarly calls upon states to

---

[223] In 2006, for example, the ECJ held that the EU–US PNR sharing agreement violated fundamental rights. A new agreement was agreed and put in place in 2012. In 2013 the European Parliament's Civil Liberties Committee (LIBE) rejected the European Commission's EU PNR proposal on human rights grounds. But a provisional deal was reached between the EU Parliament and Council of Ministers in December 2015 and the EU PNR Directive finally came into effect on 21 April 2016. The global aviation industry has long opposed the increased cost burden associated with capturing, formatting and transmitting travel data for border control and security purposes on the grounds that 'passenger data is a border security requirement. States should not charge airlines (or passengers) in a bid to subsidize their own development costs.' Industry costs for restructuring how PNR data is collected, stored or exchanged have been estimated to be in excess of US$2 billion. See, respectively: Joined Cases C-317/04 and C-318/04, *European Parliament v. Council* [2006] ECR I 4721; European Parliament News, *EU Passenger Name Record (PNR) Directive: An Overview* (1 June 2016). Available at: bit.ly /2xXe2dg. IATA *Passenger Data Exchange: The Basics*. Available at: bit.ly/2M5kC9U.

[224] UN Doc. S/2013/698 (26 November 2013), para. 17 (emphasis added).

[225] S/RES/2178 (2014), para. 2.

[226] S/RES/2309 (2016).

'develop the capability to process Passenger Name Records (PNR) data' and encouraged states to 'require airlines under their jurisdiction [to] provide PNR to their relevant national authorities'.[227] Resolution 2396 (2017) reiterated the obligation to collect and analyse API data and strengthened the requirements for collecting and analysing PNR data. It also broadened the purpose of collection from detecting attempted travel of those on the list to detecting the attempted travel of foreign terrorist fighters as well.[228] And in May 2019 the UN Office of Counter-Terrorism launched the UN Countering Terrorist Travel Programme (CTTP), in partnership with Counter-Terrorism Committee Executive Directorate (CTED), ICAO, the Office of Information and Communications Technology, UN Office on Drugs and Crime (UNODC) and in close cooperation with Interpol to provide capacity-building to states to implement these measures.[229] Within the space of five years, travel data analytics and interoperability has become a central and rapidly expanding component of UN-led global security law and governance programmes.

The Monitoring Team's efforts on biometrics were initially focused on gathering biometric material on listed individuals, reformatting the list via the Special Notice system and encouraging greater use of Interpol databases by border security officials.[230] But they soon began connecting (both technically and discursively) effective list implementation with greater use of biometrics technologies at the border. As one team report from 2013 noted: 'Although biometric data are an effective tool for checking the identity of a listed individual, *many countries have not yet introduced this technology*. Consequently, the use of a combination of false, forged and stolen documents by listed individuals to conceal their identity and/or profile *presents a hurdle to the application of sanctions*.'[231] The following year the Monitoring Team observed that 'the potential disruptive capability of the travel ban ... depends also on adequate implementation through border control mechanisms'.[232] Using biometric data was said to help detect attempted travel by listed individuals,

[227] S/RES/2368 (2017), para. 36.
[228] S/RES/2396 (2017).
[229] See: UN Office of Counter-Terrorism, *UN Countering Terrorist Travel*. Available at: bit .ly/2JKfF4F.
[230] See, for example: UN Doc. S/2014/770 (29 October 2014), para. 60; UN Doc. S/2015/441 (16 June 2015), paras. 60–2; UN Doc. S/2016/629 (19 July 2016), paras. 91–2.
[231] UN Doc. S/2013/467 (2 August 2013), para. 58 (emphasis added).
[232] UN Doc. S/2014/41 (23 January 2014), para. 40. The problem with PNR and API data, according to experts interviewed for this research is that it remains inherently unreliable.

reduce the risk of false positives in applying the travel ban and improve the overall fairness of the listing regime. Following requests by the Monitoring Team, the Sanctions Committee requested that states provide the team with biometric information about listed individuals – including photographs and fingerprint data.[233] In January 2017 the ISIL and Al-Qaida list was modified to include links to the corresponding Interpol Special Notices, to 'enable swifter access to [the] biometric data' that they contained.[234] Because of their interoperability with the list and the way they enhance application of the travel ban, Special Notices have now become 'a "one-stop" document for Member States on listed individuals'.[235] Interpol deploys facial recognition and fingerprint-matching software to compare images and prints of persons of interest with images and prints in its Special Notices and Global Foreign Terrorist Fighter database. But only one-third of all Interpol members currently have connectivity to Interpol databases established at their borders.[236] As a result, the Monitoring Team has recently pushed the Sanctions Committee 'to explore, in cooperation with the Monitoring Team, technical possibilities as to how biometric data, in particular pictures of listed individuals, could be made available via the sanctions list' and to also write to all states, 'stressing the need to ensure access to the [Interpol] databases at all border points to facilitate screening against' the list.[237] Once implemented more fully, these technical changes will effectively render the ISIL and Al-Qaida list interoperable with the biometric databases administered by Interpol.

In December 2017 the Security Council adopted Resolution 2396 under Chapter VII of the UN Charter. This resolution broke new ground by requiring all states to develop and implement systems for collecting biometric data 'to properly identify terrorists, including foreign terrorist fighters' and to 'share this data responsibly' with states, Interpol and other relevant IOs.[238] What 'sharing responsibly' means was quickly set out in a ninety-six-page accompanying compendium of best practices

---

In contrast to biometrics, data entry errors by airline staff can result in incorrect information being used as the basis for security decisions.

[233] UN Doc. S/2014/770 (29 October 2014), para. 60; UN Doc. S/2016/629 (19 July 2016), para. 92.

[234] UN Doc. S/2017/35 (13 January 2017), para. 83.

[235] UN Doc. S/2015/441 (16 June 2015), para. 60.

[236] UN Doc. S/2018/705 (27 July 2018), para. 87.

[237] UN Doc. S/2018/14/Rev.1 (27 February 2018), para. 90; UN Doc. S/2019/50 (15 January 2019), para. 98. See also: S/RES/2396 (2017), para. 16.

[238] S/RES/2396 (2017), para. 15.

drafted by CTED and the UN Office of Counter Terrorism (UNOCT), in close association with the leading biometrics private industry group, the Biometric Institute.[239] Under Resolution 2396, states were also required to develop watch lists and databases 'of known and suspected terrorists' and to share this data broadly, both domestically and internationally, to 'screen travellers and conduct risk assessments'.[240] Legal scholars, UN experts and NGOs have noted the potentially grave human rights implications of this extraordinary Chapter VII measure and criticised the Council for globally legislating on these issues with scant regard for the protection of human rights or risk of abuse by state and non-state actors.[241] This extraordinary Resolution is seen as something akin to a decree of global sovereign power, with the Council deciding upon the exception. But, as my analysis shows, this exception has been built on the reformatting initiatives of UN listing experts and extended in scope by a plethora of guidelines, technical standards and forms of data exchange between states, private actors and IOs that this reformatting has enabled. As one Monitoring Team member described the team's longer-term strategic thinking on this issue:

> The technical development [i.e. for biometric facial recognition] is not yet global. But what is exceptional today is global in ten years. And this is the UN (nothing happens in six months) and this is the UN then dealing with ICAO (an equally big organisation) . . . What is more or less exceptional now – India, UAE, Thailand, Indonesia, America, Europe, face recognition by entry – will be the norm by the time that we get there.[242]

In each of the examples outlined above – API/PNR data exchange, changing entry conditions for all travellers and the use of biometric identifiers – we can see individual restrictive measures against 260 listed individuals being extended in ways that enable new security mechanisms

---

[239] CTED and UNOCT, *United Nations Compendium of Recommended Practices for the Responsible Use and Sharing of Biometrics in Counter-terrorism* (2018). Available at: bit.ly /2ygyeHf.

[240] Ibid. para. 13.

[241] See, for example: Fionnuala Ní Aoláin, 'The UN Security Council, global watch lists, biometrics, and the threat to the rule of law', *Just Security* (17 January 2018). Available at: bit.ly/32YnD1K; Privacy International, *Briefing to the UN Counter-Terrorism Executive Directorate on the responsible use and sharing of biometric data to tackle terrorism* (June 2019). Available at: bit.ly/2YqxIKF; UN Special Rapporteur on the promotion and protection of human rights and fundamental freedoms while countering terrorism, *Submission to the Report of the Office of the United High Commissioner for Human Rights on the Right to Privacy in the Digital Age*. Available at: bit.ly/2JXPebD.

[242] Interview B.

to be applied to the global annual population of 4.6 billion airline passengers.[243] We can also observe some of the interplay between the more mundane technical work of listing expertise and the 'solid authority' of the Security Council's Chapter VII powers. Each example helps to show how relatively minor technical shifts concerning problems of list administration can generate far-reaching global security effects. Here, listing expertise can be seen as something quasi-legal and jurisgenerative: it both stretches what existing global security laws can secure in practice and creates the material foundations for new global security laws to be formally adopted. As one Monitoring Team member described it:

> I think ... where we can be useful is actually advancing an agenda – for example, ... [with] biometrics. Who is actually going to go and talk to airlines to understand what they do on it? Who is going to go to talk to Interpol to figure out how they can *transmit* biometrics? Who is going to say, 'Here is the list, Here is how biometrics can work and here is how it can't? ... It's a bit techy and a bit dull on one level. But it is actually *incredibly* important in advancing the actual efficacy of a regime.[244]

Critical security scholars tend to represent security listing as a relatively simple technology distinct from the more dynamic and processual security techniques grounded in machine learning and algorithmic analysis. According to Louise Amoore, 'so overwhelming is the pursuit of the as yet unknown future risk' in technologies such as biometric and PNR-profiling 'that the sounding alert of the watch list – a disciplinary form of security risk management ... – is rarely heard'.[245] Because listing is said to use 'fixed disciplinary criteria', it is distinguished from algorithmic techniques that deploy 'possibilistic logics' to 'infer possible futures on the basis of underlying fragmented elements of data'.[246] Yet the examples analysed above show a more interdependent and hybridised relation between fixed and dynamic security mechanisms. In my account, listing technology (and the need to effectively implement it against targeted individuals) also functions as an important catalyst for more wide-ranging and 'possibilistic' forms of preemptive security governance to develop – including the algorithmic analysis of travel and biometric data to identify as yet unknown terrorists and foreign terrorist fighters (FTFs).

---

[243] IATA, 'Cautious optimism extends into 2019 – airlines heading for a decade in the black', Press Release No. 72 (12 December 2018). Available at: bit.ly/2MlFj1j.

[244] Interview with former member of the 1267 Monitoring Team, New York (via Skype), June 2014 (Interview F) (emphasis in original).

[245] Amoore, *The Politics of Possibility*, pp. 89–90.

[246] Ibid. p. 61.

This suggests that dynamics of mobility and fixity and discipline and biopower are not mutually exclusive but rather co-present in global security law.[247] How they interrelate is an empirical question that requires practice-orientated and site-specific analysis. In other words, it's a question of assemblage.

2.4.3 Global Standards, Universal Auditing and the Politics of Redefinition

Building a third hurdle for travellers is not only a question of reformatting and realising technical interoperability. It is a project that engages with, and requires modification of, international standards, best practices and regulatory guidelines. Historically, ICAO and IATA have primarily been concerned with transport, rather than border and security functions. When the Monitoring Team first sought to work with IATA to have airlines check passengers against the Al-Qaida list, for example, its efforts were rebuffed on the grounds that 'airlines [did] not see it as their responsibility to go further than checking that a passenger has a valid travel document'.[248] Aviation standards on passenger facilitation have long been geared towards efficient boarding and disembarkation from point of departure. What happened once passengers left the airplane and headed for immigration arrivals has largely been something that airlines have left for national border security agencies to handle.

One anomalous area where the concerns of aviation and border security intersect, however, is in the category of 'inadmissible persons' – defined by the Convention on International Civil Aviation (hereafter, the 'Chicago Convention') as 'a person who is or will be refused admission to a State by its authorities'.[249] Airlines are bound to adhere to the immigration laws of the states that afford them landing rights[250] and are legally

---

[247] According to Saskia Sassen: 'the spatiality/temporality of globalization itself contains dynamics of mobility and fixity. While mobility and fixity may easily be classified as two mutually types of dynamics ... they are not necessarily so ... [and] under some conditions one presupposes the other.' – Sassen, 'Bordering capabilities', 383. On the co-presence of discipline and biopower in security mechanisms, see: Foucault, *Security, Territory, Population*, p. 8.

[248] UN Doc. S/2009/502 (2 October 2009), para. 72.

[249] *Convention on International Civil Aviation* (hereafter, 'Chicago Convention'), Annex 9 (Facilitation).

[250] Chicago Convention, Article 13.

responsible for passengers up until the point they reach the arrivals terminal of the receiving state.[251] If a passenger is found to be inadmissible by immigration authorities, then it is the airline's responsibility to either take them back to the country the flight departed from or to another country that accepts them.[252] If the airline acted negligently or failed to apply due diligence in assessing the relevant travel documentation or entry requirements of the receiving state, it can be fined. In 2010, 80 per cent of airlines worldwide each paid fines of on average US$286,000 for carrying inadmissible passengers, most of whom were asylum seekers turned back by border officials at entry.[253] Historically, inadmissible passengers have fallen into one of three categories: either individuals who are (i) without proper travel documentation for entry and transit; (ii) carrying fraudulent documents or undocumented; or (iii) others who fail to meet entry requirements (for example, because of lack of the requisite funds or for security reasons).[254] Although this legal framework only imposes obligations on airlines to check that their passengers meet the *entry* requirements of the states they are travelling towards, this checking process actually takes place before departure – when passengers either buy their tickets (and create PNR data) or check in (and create API data). As such, the category of 'inadmissible passenger' provides a valuable opportunity to bring the border forward in time and use travel data analytics to create a form of exit control enabled by states but enforced via everyday commercial aviation transactions.

So, it is unsurprising that the Monitoring Team has sought to extend the definition of 'inadmissible persons' to include individuals on UN sanctions lists.[255] As one former team member explained:

> With the term 'Inadmissible Passengers' ICAO has created a legal case where the state now has the right to say, 'This guy – because his passport is no longer valid, he doesn't have the visa, in some countries because he doesn't have the necessary vaccinations – is not getting into my country'. But the 'Inadmissible Passenger' case *addresses only the point of entry in the country* ... We thought there is an opening here – where we now have the technical capabilities of the airlines [and] we have states already demanding such [travel] data from the airlines. We might as well just tell the airlines: 'Look – there are a thousand UN sanctioned

---

[251] Chicago Convention, Chapter 3, Section K, Standard 3.43.
[252] Chicago Convention, Chapter 5, Standard 5.11.
[253] Lisa Angiolelli, *IATA Campaign Results: Passenger Data* (2012).
[254] IATA/Control Authorities Working Group, *Guidelines for the Removal of Inadmissible Passengers* (2002). Available at: bit.ly/1xiMprt.
[255] UN Doc. S/2014/888 (11 December 2014), para. 52.

> individuals . . . These one thousand individuals: *don't even bother trying to transport them* because by law they will be have to be transported back and you will be fined' . . . And that's why we are working with ICAO on changing the rules.[256]

The impetus for trying to change the rules on international air travel are twofold. First, there is the temporal problem. The current rules of global aviation carriage impose duties on airlines in relation to conditions of *entry*. If they are to enhance the implementation of the list and build a third hurdle, then airlines must be able to intervene before passengers depart – either at, or before, time of *exit*. Doing so on the basis of travel data, however, presents all kinds of novel liability risks. So, the second rationale for changing aviation standards is to provide the legal cover to mitigate the liability risks that airlines will face as they become more actively involved in preemptive security and border policing:

> Data protection, false matches. You don't want innocent people not being able to travel. It's litigation potential for airlines. That's why at the end of the day there needs to be some ICAO regulation which *demands* that airlines do that. Because then the airlines can say: 'I'm sorry, I'm not doing this because I don't like you. I'm doing this because the Annex to the Chicago Convention, the highest legal document on air travel, *tells* me to do it'. That's why it's crucial.[257]

In 2013–14 the Monitoring Team met with IATA and ICAO multiple times to explore the possibility of amending the definition of inadmissible persons in the Chicago Convention.[258] On suggestion from the Monitoring Team, the President of the Security Council also wrote to the Secretary-General of the World Customs Organization (WCO) to request the WCO to update its API/PNR recommendations to prevent listed persons from travelling as inadmissible persons in order to effectively implement the travel ban.[259] As a result of this intervention, the issue was taken up by the WCO/IATA/ICAO API/PNR Contact Committee and the WCO Permanent Technical Committee (PTC), leading to two important changes. In 2014, the WCO/IATA/ICAO Guidelines on API were amended to specifically note that API can

---

[256] Interview B (emphasis in original).

[257] Ibid. (emphasis in original).

[258] UN Doc. S/2014/41 (23 January 2014), para. 39; UN Doc. S/2014/888 (11 December 2014), para. 52. However, the definition of inadmissible passengers in Annex 9 of the Chicago Convention had not yet been amended at the time of writing.

[259] Kunio Mikuriya, 'API and PNR: Two key words on the global security agenda', *WCO News* (No. 77, June 2015), 12.

allow border control agencies to prevent listed persons from boarding aircraft and enable carriers to comply with legislation 'implementing travel bans against those on United Nations Security Council sanctions lists'.[260] And in 2015, the PTC and WCO Council endorsed an amendment to WCO recommendations on the use of API/PNR to include 'effective implementation of UN travel bans against sanctioned individuals' as part of the list of actions that all members of the WCO, Customs and Economic Unions must take.[261] Following another recommendation from the Team, the Sanctions Committee asked all states to include the list and travel ban in their guidelines for inadmissible passengers and to inform TIMATIC, a database managed by IATA, of this change.[262]

Global regulatory change in the aviation domain is not something that readily falls within the Security Council's jurisdiction to counter threats to international peace and security. Making API analysis a global norm to enhance the travel ban or changing the definition of 'inadmissible passengers' to include listed individuals requires amendments to the Annexes of the Chicago Convention, which set global aviation standards and recommended practices (SARPs), and only the ICAO Council (or executive branch of thirty-six Member States) can amend these standards on a two-thirds majority vote during a meeting expressly called for that purpose.[263] In April 2016, the Monitoring Team was invited to address the Ninth Meeting of the ICAO Facilitation Panel. In a presentation entitled, 'UN Security Council Travel Ban on Al-Qaida and Associates: Implementation Opportunities and Challenges', the team discussed the interoperability of the list with API data and requested that the Chicago Convention be amended to include Security Council provisions in Resolution 2178 (2014) concerning API and to have individuals on the ISIL and Al-Qaida list deemed inadmissible passengers.[264] As a result of the team's sustained work on this issue, in October 2017 the collection and analysis of API for detecting the movement of listed persons and FTFs became a global standard under Annex 9 of the Chicago

---

[260] *WCO/IATA/ICAO Guidelines on Advance Passenger Information* (2014), para. 3.8. See also: UN Doc. S/2014/770 (27 October 2014), para. 61.

[261] WCO Doc. PC0421E1b, Permanent Technical Committee, 209th/210th Sessions, *Summary Document* (6 October 2015), paras. 13–16.

[262] UN Doc. S/2013/467 (2 August 2013), para. 59; UN Doc. S/2014/41 (23 January 2014), para. 39.

[263] Chicago Convention, Article 90.

[264] ISIL and Al-Qaida Analytical Support and Sanctions Monitoring Team, 'United Nations Security Council travel ban on Al-Qaida and associates: implementation opportunities and challenges' (April 2016). Available at: bit.ly/2ZiJb71.

Convention. All states must now establish API systems consistent with the WCO/IATA/ICAO API guidelines, which effectively exclude listed persons as inadmissible.[265] As the Monitoring Team has observed, this amendment 'is a significant step to ensure that the flow of passenger data can be effectively utilized to implement the travel ban against listed individuals'.[266] Through an array of technical moves, reformatting decisions, data-processing guidelines and global standardisation practices, list interoperability and the third hurdle of travel were finally assembled.

Given the degree of multilateral deliberation involved with ICAO, IATA and the WCO, one former team member described this initiative as 'very much a political issue'.[267] Yet what is political here is not so much bureaucratic wrangling as what Koskenniemi calls 'the politics of redefinition' – that is, 'the strategic definition of a situation or a problem by reference to a technical idiom so as to open the door for applying the expertise related to that idiom together with the attendant structural bias'.[268] The travel ban is a key component of a sanction adopted by the Security Council under its Chapter VII mandate to counter threats to international peace and security. Building a third hurdle by requiring all states to collect and analyse API data and redefining listed individuals as 'inadmissible passengers' provokes a legal-discursive shift from the vocabularies of public international law and collective security to global aviation standards and recommended best practices for airlines. Redefinition of this sort generates 'shifts in the production of types of outcomes within international institutions'.[269] But what *is* novel, according to Koskenniemi, is how such changes are now 'described in the neutral language of expertise', thus 'obscur[ing] the contingent nature of the choices made, [and] the fact that [*what is*] at issue is structural bias and not the application of some neutral … security reason'.[270]

---

[265] ICAO, *Annex 9 to the Convention on International Civil Aviation: Facilitation*, 15th edn. International Standards and Recommended Practices (October 2017), SARP 9.5–9.16. See also: S/RES/2396 (2017), para. 11.

[266] UN Doc. S/2018/14/Rev.1 (27 February 2018), para. 71. See also: UN Doc. S/2018/705 (27 July 2018), paras. 83–6.

[267] Interview B. For an overview of the SARP process, see: ICAO, *Making an ICAO Standard*. Available at: bit.ly/1pmY2sI.

[268] Koskenniemi, *The Politics*, p. 67.

[269] Ibid., p. 68.

[270] Ibid. For Koskenniemi, 'political conflict will often take the form of a conflict of jurisdictions' (p. 335). See also: Mariana Valverde, *Chronotopes of Law: Jurisdiction, Scale and Governance* (London: Routledge, 2015). For Valverde, 'by deciding the 'who governs' question, the game of jurisdiction simultaneously but implicitly determines *how* something is to be governed' (p. 84) (emphasis in original).

The technical project of constructing a third hurdle examined in this chapter is part of a broader initiative to preemptively counter the threat of FTFs. Recent Security Council Resolutions impose obligations on all states to prevent the movement of suspected FTFs and anyone else about whom they have 'credible information that provides reasonable grounds to believe' may be 'associated with' ISIL, Al-Qaida or associated groups.[271] As people come to be stopped from travelling according to such far-reaching speculative criteria, legal challenges will be initiated for violating the fundamental right to freedom of movement, legal scholars will write articles about these cases and there will be broader public debate about the appropriate balance between liberty and security in times of crisis. What might once have been framed as a normative clash between collective security and human rights can now readily be reframed as a foreseeable consequence of global aviation standards applicable to all airline passengers as part of the very condition of their carriage. Technical reframing takes this juridical and political conflict towards a rather different and specialised space with its own functional interests, expert vocabularies, structural biases and patterned institutional practices.[272] What might otherwise have been the main normative frame is rendered contingent and weakened, presented as merely one approach amongst many for resolving such a problem.[273] In this way, international law becomes increasingly fragmented and marginalised, 'pushed aside by a mosaic of particular rules and institutions, each following its embedded preferences'.[274]

These technical processes reveal close relations between listing expertise and global security law. Here we see UN counterterrorism experts with a mandate to implement the list openly pushing forward an international legal change agenda to pursue their strategic aims under technical cover. Just as corporate lawyers engage in regulatory reform to transform the legal system in ways that strategically advance the best interests of their corporate clients, here the Monitoring Team (1) has a clear objective (enhanced list implementation); (2) has identified the key obstacles impeding the realisation of that objective; and (3) has actively engaged in a long-term reform process directed at overcoming those challenges by changing the rules of the game and embedding its particular preferences. This example of listing experts reformatting the

[271] S/RES 2178 (2014), para. 8.
[272] Koskenniemi, *The Politics*.
[273] Ibid. p. 67.
[274] Ibid. p. 339.

list and building the third hurdle clearly highlights, in other words, technical processes of global security lawmaking in motion.

As with the other initiatives analysed in this chapter, we are well beyond the point where technical expertise simply implements the list whilst global security law is properly made elsewhere, through the formal deliberations of the Security Council. Yet, for the experts interviewed for this research, it was precisely this displacement – i.e. that global lawmaking was happening elsewhere – and process of disavowal that allowed them to work on this issue as a technical, rather than a legal, problem.

ICAO rules and standards are technically 'soft law'. They can be disapproved by a majority of states.[275] States have the right to formally notify ICAO of differences between their national practices and international standards. And SARPs do not have the legal force of the Chicago Convention, which is subject to the international law of treaties.[276] But if no 'filing of differences' are submitted within sixty days of amendments being made by the ICAO Council,[277] these standards *do* have binding effect on all states worldwide. For Jose Alvarez, the SARPs issued by ICAO are a clear example of 'IO regulation existing in a netherworld between binding and non-binding'.[278] As Kirchner points out, 'although they do not yet cross the threshold from inter- to supra-national law, the[se] international standards go far beyond the average power enjoyed by the executive body of an international organization'.[279]

But what makes these ICAO standards so powerful a form of global security law is the way they can leverage technologies of audit and the power of the market to discipline states and airlines into compliance and compel them to more extensively securitise their practices. After the 9/11 attacks the ICAO Council adopted the Aviation Security Plan of Action (AVSEC). AVSEC enacted 'a comprehensive programme of regular, mandatory, systematic and harmonized audits to be carried out by ICAO in all Contracting States' and launched a new oversight process – the ICAO Universal Security

---

[275] Chicago Convention, Article 90.
[276] For a discussion of the legal status of ICAO SARPs, see: Michael Milde, *International Air Law and ICAO. Vol. 4* (The Hague: Eleven International Publishing, 2008) 119–206. See also: Jose E. Alvarez, *International Organizations as Law Makers* (Oxford: Oxford University Press, 2005), pp. 223–4.
[277] Chicago Convention, Article 38.
[278] Alvarez, *International Organizations*, p. 223.
[279] Stefan Kirchner, 'Effective law-making in times of global crisis – a role for international organizations' (2010) 2(1) *Goettingen Journal of International Law* 267, 289.

Audit Programme (USAP).[280] In 2007 the ICAO Council determined that USAP should be specifically extended to include the security-related provisions of Annex 9, where the new standards on API data processing are contained. When ICAO auditors identify deficiencies, states must submit a corrective plan within sixty days setting out what steps they will take to rectify the problems. Whilst information about non-compliance is not openly disclosed for security purposes, it is shared securely with ICAO members and subjected to 'a limited level of transparency'.[281]

As listing experts are acutely aware, this new auditing process can be used to generate very powerful effects. It opens up new ways of creating and enforcing global security law outside of the Council and enrolling different actors at different governance scales more fully into the global listing assemblage:

> My argument always is: ... let's not fight the fight of making the world a better place. We, as the Committee or the expert team cannot ensure that Chad – or any other African country, or any other country in the world – has stringent border controls on its land ports. However, airports in Chad ... [and] airports in America are vetted security wise *exactly the same* by ICAO. So, on air travel, we *have already* an agreed minimum standard. If we can implement and influence the minimum standard that *ICAO gives* for security by these changes in the regulations, then *we can* address everyone globally. Because, if you're not up to ICAO standards, ICAO simply sends out a warning to airlines. And no one flies to your airport. And they do an *audit* of your airport every five years. And if there is something lacking there *again* [there's] not only a warning to all member states ... There's also a warning *to all airlines*. And then 99 per cent of airlines will not feel comfortable to fly to [that] airport.[282]

The strength of this preemptive bordering capability therefore lies not only in the technology of the audit and its disciplining effects, but how

---

[280] Ruwantissa Abeyratne, *Aviation Security Law* (New York: Springer, 2010), p. 265. For an overview see: ICAO, *The Universal Security Audit Programme Continuous Monitoring Approach (USAP-CMA) and its Objective.* Available at: bit.ly/1xiMwDl.

[281] ICAO Resolution A36-20, A36-WP/336 and Plenary Action Sheet No. 3. USAP audits implementation of Annex 17 of the Chicago Convention (Security) and the security-related provisions of Annex 9 (Facilitation), including the use of API and PNR discussed throughout this chapter (audited as 'Entry Procedures and Responsibilities'). Priority Action area 3.7 of ICAO's *Global Aviation Security Plan* (GASeP) – which has been strongly reaffirmed by the UN Security Council – is to 'evaluate the use of passenger information to inform and assist aviation security'. See: ICAO Doc. 10118, Global Aviation Security Plan (2017); S/RES/2309 (2016); S/RES/2396 (2017), paras. 9–12, 14.

[282] Interview B (emphasis in original).

this audit process intersects with and harnesses the power of the market to incentivise change, penalise recalcitrance and 'increase the motivation':

> So, you have, like with FATF [Financial Action Task Force], an *outside motivator* for states to do this. Because with FATF, it costs a lot of money [i.e., for non-compliance]. And with ICAO as the auditor of security standards, it would cost *also* a lot of money – because airlines would no longer fly there and because reputation is damaged to [both] your airport [and] to your country ... With these technical instruments one can incentivize and coerce. And increase the motivation ... These motivating factors are *very, very crucial* in implementation. If you don't have them, then it [i.e. implementing the travel ban] is still a choice.[283]

It would be a mistake to read this shift towards technical standardisation by UN listing experts as a move from the 'hard' to the 'soft'. As global governance scholars have argued, the effects of informal mechanisms like indicators and best practice guidelines are often 'unlikely to be weaker than they would be in a coercive frame'.[284] Auditing is a technology of governance that enables a 'control of control'.[285] It produces 'enforced self-regulation',[286] conducting the 'conduct of others in desired directions by acting on their will, their circumstances or their environment' without unduly 'encroaching on their "freedom"'.[287] When list, standard and audit are used together with the threat of financial damage they can be a powerful governmental ensemble. Such technical arrangements 'may well be more effective in "disciplining" and "normalizing" states than the more visible, confrontational exercises of authority' that have long characterised UN Security Council politics.[288]

2.5   What's in a List? Inscription, Translation, Preemption

When the Monitoring Team was created out of the demise of the Monitoring Group, confrontational techniques of 'naming and shaming' states to enforce sanctions fell by the wayside. Global listing expertise

---

[283] Ibid. (emphasis in original).

[284] Krisch, 'Authority, solid and liquid', p. 15.

[285] Michael Power, *The Audit Society: Rituals of Verification* (Oxford: Oxford University Press, 1999), p. 66.

[286] Michael Power, 'Evaluating the audit explosion' (2003) 25(3) *Law and Policy* 185, 189.

[287] Nikolas Rose and Peter Miller, 'Political power beyond the state: problematics of government' (1992) 43(2) *British Journal of Sociology* 173, 175, 187.

[288] Krisch, 'Authority, solid and liquid', p. 15, citing Roele's work on the CTC, 'Disciplinary power'.

thereafter adopted an overtly technical focus and concentrated on list administration issues perceived as less politically contentious. Most literature frames this 'technical turn' as something that led UN counter-terrorism expertise to be weakened. Yet in this chapter I have reread this shift and the technicalities of listing expertise that ensued as something profoundly political and legally productive. Doing so required departing from instrumentalist sanctions scholarship and reframing the list as a novel governance technology and important protagonist in the assemblage of this legal domain. This allowed us to take listing expertise out from the shadows cast by the Security Council's authority and revalorise it as a crucially important conduit for making and shaping the Law of the List in practice.

The first site examined how the list and listing expertise are entangled in the project of knowing and countering 'global terrorism'. I analysed how the administration of the list enables a 'global optic' to be built that helps constitute and condition the very object it seeks to target. The 'consultation meetings' between UN listing experts and national security officials were studied ethnographically as 'structure-making' sites that enact global-ordering through the technology of the list. By using the 'equilibrium of possibilities' diagram as a heuristic device, listing was reappraised as a counter-radicalisation measure directed towards a far broader threat population than the 260 individuals it targets.[289] The list is a powerful device for enrolling a diverse array of actors into new pre-emptive global security networks. It is much more than a mere instrument and the expertise that administers it is far from insignificant. Showing *how* – through granular sociolegal analysis of list assemblage practices – is key to grasping what is novel and powerful about this form of global legal-ordering.

The second site of listing expertise examined in this chapter unpacked the seemingly mundane process of list reformatting and interoperability. This is technical work of the kind that ordinarily goes underneath the radar of global governance and international legal scholarship. Yet, when closely analysed – without a priori conceptions of global scale, how threats to international security may be legitimately countered or what 'law' properly is or ought to be – such processes are revealed as politically significant and legally productive. In the conventional view, list reformatting involves taking information from context A and putting it into context B – 'the substantive

[289] Correct as of 30 July 2019.

information is the same'.[290] But my analysis shows reformatting to be a generative process of translation that helps enable other modes of security-listing with quite different spatiotemporal dynamics and governance effects. Rendering the list interoperable with travel data, for example, significantly broadens its field of circulation and potential intervention. It decouples the travel ban from territorial borders and enables it to circulate electronically as a deterritorialised bordering capability. This process expands and stretches what the travel ban can do and enables new security mechanisms to be introduced – not only for individuals on the list but also for the global travelling population as a whole. Transforming listed individuals into 'inadmissible passengers' was presented as a relatively minor technical tweak. But building a 'third hurdle' is much more than just enhanced list implementation. It is an ambitious and far-reaching global reform project that harnesses technologies of standard setting, best practice guidelines, auditing and market powers to produce novel coercive effects.

Chapter 1 introduced the framework of assemblage. But this chapter has shown some of what the assemblage can do as an analytical tool. Most scholarship on the ISIL and Al-Qaida sanctions takes hierarchical scales of governance for granted – with the global at the top, the regional in the middle and the national and local at the bottom. This chapter unsettles this assumption by analysing how localised expert practices are mediated through the governing technology of the list in ways that generate large-scale effects and help shape new forms of global-ordering. That is, by studying 'the global' in global security law as an emergent property assembled in different sites connected through listing practices a different topology of governance can emerge.[291] This has meant adopting a mobile and multisited methodology, following the list as an ethnographic object to consultation meetings in North Africa and technical discussions on global data standardisation inside ICAO. As Callon and Latour point out: '*There are* of course macro-actors and micro-actors, but the difference between them is brought about by power relations and the constructions of networks that will *elude analysis* if we presume

---

[290] Interview B.

[291] As George E. Marcus notes: 'The global is an emergent dimension of arguing about the connections between sites': George E.. Marcus, 'Ethnography in/of the world system: The emergence of multi-sited ethnography' (1995) *Annual Review of Anthropology* 95, 99.

a priori that macro-actors are bigger than or superior to micro-actors.'[292]

This chapter has argued that listing technology is a 'crucial container of practice',[293] forging connections and assembling relations in ways that make global security law powerful and durable. But showing how the list and listing expertise together create a 'centre of calculation' is not the same as claiming that the Security Council is an all-powerful agent of global control because centres are always multiple and contingent upon the ability of powerful actors 'to successfully enrol and mobilise persons, procedures and artefacts in the pursuit of its goals'.[294] Studying the list as an assemblage helps to reveal the strengths, but also the *weaknesses*, of global security law. As Latour observes: 'If you cut some underlying structure from its local application, nothing happens ... [but] if you cut a structure-making site from its connections, it simply stops being able to structure anything'.[295]

The relation between counterterrorism expertise and global listing analysed in this chapter has been insufficiently studied to date. Whilst scholars like Kennedy and Koskenniemi offer powerful normative critiques of international law's increasing deferral to expertise, there remains very little sociolegal research on how expertise actually works to enact, alter and sustain global legal relations. Whilst this chapter has highlighted some of the powerful effects of the Monitoring Team's technical work, this is not reducible to a story of invisible technocrats seeking to rule the world. As Nikolas Rose and Peter Miller point out, 'government is a congenitally failing operation: the sublime image of a perfect regulatory machine is internal to the mind of the programmers. The world of programmes is heterogeneous and ... complexif[ies] the real, so solutions for one programme tend to be the problems for another.'[296]

Yet the Monitoring Team is only one of the many expert institutions assembling the Law of the List. The following Chapters 3 and 4 continue to explore this theme by examining how diverse forms of expertise are enrolled through problems of the list. And, as we will see, these experts are also enacting novel knowledge-practices, forging connections and

---

[292] Callon and Latour, 'Unscrewing the big Leviathan', p. 280 (emphasis in original).
[293] Bueger, 'Pathways to practice', 397.
[294] Rose and Miller, 'Political power beyond the state', 183, 185.
[295] Latour, *Reassembling the Social*, p. 176.
[296] Ibid. p. 190.

engaging in the hard work of holding this body of global security law stable and developing opportunities to extend it in important, and sometimes unpredictable, ways. Listing expertise is not something that the Monitoring Team retains some monopoly over. Because government is always 'intrinsically linked to the problems around which it circulates', global listing expertise is as multiple as the tensions and conflicts of the list itself.[297]

---

[297] Rose and Miller, 'Political power beyond the state', 181.

The List As Multiple Object: the UN Office of the Ombudsperson*

Chapter 2 followed the practices of UN listing experts to show how global terrorism is governed through the technology of the list. We saw how problematisation and the problem-management it stimulates enables global security law at a granular level. This chapter extends this insight to the problem of accountability in global security governance, analysing the listing assemblage from the vantage point of another crucial site: the UN1267 Office of the Ombudsperson.

The Security Council was originally granted sanctioning powers to avert the threat of inter-state war. But the ISIL and Al-Qaida list aims at individuals suspected of being nodes in global terrorist networks. This radical reorientation in targeting, from states to individuals, generates profound effects. It expands the scope of Council's powers to counter threats to peace and security under Chapter VII of the UN Charter.[1] It shrinks the 'distance between national and international law in this domain', facilitating 'an increasing enmeshment' between these layers of governance.[2] It allows the Council to exercise novel jurisdiction over matters previously thought to be the exclusive pre-serve of states.[3] And by enabling action outside the collective security

---

* Parts of this chapter were previously published in: Gavin Sullivan and Ben Hayes, *Blacklisted: Targeted Sanctions, Preemptive Security and Fundamental Rights* (Berlin: ECCHR, 2011); Gavin Sullivan and Marieke de Goede, 'Between law and the exception: the UN1267 Ombudsperson as a hybrid model of legal expertise' (2013) 26(4) *Leiden Journal of International Law* 833; and Gavin Sullivan, 'Transnational legal assemblages and global security law: topologies and temporalities of the list' (2014) 5(1) *Transnational Legal Theory* 81.

[1] For an overview, see: Vera Gowlland-Debbas, 'The Security Council as enforcer of human rights' in Bardo Fassbender (ed.), *Securing Human Rights? Achievements and Challenges of the UN Security Council* (Oxford: Oxford University Press, 2011), p. 36.

[2] Nico Krisch, *Beyond Constitutionalism: The Pluralist Structure of Postnational Law* (Oxford: Oxford University Press, 2010), p. 157.

[3] See, for example, the discussion on 'stretching the international peace and security envelope' in the Credible List section 3.5 below.

system originally envisaged in the Charter, it opens a vexing account-ability problem: how can the UN Security Council legitimately exer-cise governmental powers over individuals on a worldwide scale without those targeted being able to challenge their decisions or otherwise hold them to account?

This chapter examines the effects of this list accountability problem, culminating in the emergence of the UN1267 Office of the Ombudsperson (hereafter, 'the Ombudsperson'). The Ombudsperson was created by the Council in 2009 to provide listed parties with a procedure for redress.[4] For the first time, targeted individuals could submit 'delisting' applications to an independent legal expert asking to be taken off the list.[5] After gathering information from targeted persons and states, and engaging in 'dialogue meetings' with listed individuals, the Ombudsperson compiles a 'comprehensive report' recommending that the person either stay on or be removed from the list. This report is then sent to the Sanctions Committee to assist it in taking its confidential decision on delisting. In 2011 a 'reverse presumption' procedure was introduced to strengthen the Ombudsperson's powers. Under this presumption, listings automatically terminate sixty days after a delisting recommendation by the Ombudsperson unless the Council decides by consensus that they should remain in place.[6]

This review mechanism has been widely celebrated as a fairness and accountability success story. By mid-2019, seventy-seven delist-ing requests had been made to the Ombudsperson and only nineteen had been subsequently refused by the Security Council.[7] Some com-mentators have concluded that with the Ombudsperson 'the rights of individuals to be informed, have access to, and be heard, appear to have [now] been addressed'.[8] Others are more circumspect and highlight the mechanism's persistent due process problems. Yet almost everyone agrees that the Ombudsperson is a procedural 'improvement' and an important step in the right direction – part of international law's

---

[4] S/RES/1904 (2009).

[5] The post was held by Ms. Kimberly Prost from 2010 to 2015 and Ms. Catherine Marchi-Uhel from 2015 to 2017. Since July 2018, following an eleven-month gap, the post has been held by a former Swiss judge, Mr. Daniel Kipfer Fasciati.

[6] S/RES/1989 (2011), para. 23.

[7] Ombudsperson to the ISIL (Da'esh) and Al-Qaida Sanctions Committee, *Status of Cases*. Available at: bit.ly/2ZgDBSu.

[8] Sue Eckert and Thomas Biersteker, *Due Process and Targeted Sanctions: An Update of the 'Watson Report'* (Geneva: Watson Institute for International Studies, Brown University and the Graduate Institute, 2012), p. 23 – hereafter, the 2012 Watson Report.

progressive movement to regulate the spaces of 'non-legality' that incessantly escape it[9] – and that, with some extra procedural adjustments here and greater institutional learning there, the Ombudsperson could evolve into a leading example of international accountability and 'global administrative law' in action.[10]

This chapter challenges this dominant teleological narrative of global legal progress by providing a critical genealogical account of the Ombudsperson's emergence and practice. Genealogy is a Foucauldian means of 'studying the "how of power"'.[11] Unlike conventional historiography, genealogy 'aims at the construction of intelligible trajectories of events, discourses and practices with neither a determinative source nor an unfolding toward finality'.[12] It is a methodological tool that emphasises contingency and heterogeneity and traces the generative effects of material practices. It prompts an avowedly critical stance that destabilises the present and 'open[s] it to the possibility of . . . being otherwise'.[13] This genealogical approach allows us to analyse the creation of the Ombudsperson as a productive process deeply entangled in questions of power and the 'politics of redefinition', rather than an incremental legal step towards some as-yet-to-be realised better normative end.[14]

---

[9] Fleur Johns, *Non-Legality in International Law: Unruly Law* (Cambridge: Cambridge University Press, 2013).

[10] For an introduction to the GAL approach to postnational accountability, see: Benedict Kingsbury, Nico Krisch and Richard B. Stewart, 'The emergence of global administrative law' (2005) 68(3/4) *Law and Contemporary problems* 15; Nico Krisch and Benedict Kingsbury, 'Introduction: Global Governance and Global Administrative Law in the International Legal Order' (2006) 17(1) *European Journal of International Law* 1; Benedict Kingsbury, 'The concept of "law" in global administrative law' (2009) 20(1) *European Journal of International Law* 23; Benedict Kingsbury and Lorenzo Casini, 'Global administrative law dimensions of international organizations law' (2009) 6(2) *International Organizations Law Review*, 319; Simon Chesterman, 'Globalization rules: accountability, power, and the prospects for global administrative law' (2008) 14(1) *Global Governance* 39.

[11] Michel Foucault, *Society Must Be Defended: Lectures at the Collège de France 1975–1976* (London: Picador, 2003), p. 24. I have described this approach as Foucauldian, but Foucault's use of genealogy derived from Nietzsche: Friedrich Nietzsche, *On the Genealogy of Morals and Ecce Homo* (New York: Vintage, 2010); and Michel Foucault, 'Nietzsche, genealogy, history' in Donald F. Bouchard (ed.), *Language, Counter-Memory, Practice: Selected Essays and Interviews* (Ithaca NY: Cornell University Press, 1977).

[12] Mitchell Dean, 'A genealogy of the government of poverty' (1992) 21(3) *Economy and Society* 215, 217.

[13] Ben Golder, *Foucault and the Politics of Rights* (Stanford CA: Stanford University Press, 2015), p. 35.

[14] As Martti Koskenniemi notes: 'Political intervention is today often a politics of redefinition, that is to say, the strategic definition of a situation or a problem by reference to

I argue that the Ombudsperson is better thought of as a governance effect arising from multiple conflicts between different actors across the listing assemblage: a composite figure of expertise born out of diverse institutional struggles under conditions of international legal fragmentation. This heterogeneity is important because it continues to shape what this experiment is and delimit what it is capable (and not capable) of doing. Existing accounts tend to describe the origins of the Ombudsperson from the UN Security Council's perspective. Different actors may have different perspectives on how to solve list accountability problems, but these perspectives are only valued insofar as they influence the principal agent and are institutionalised as norms or allow forms of accountability to emerge that comply with prevailing procedural fairness and human rights standards.

This chapter departs from these accounts in two important ways. First, I suggest that the divergences between actors here run much deeper than usually suggested. This list accountability conflict is not just about different perspectives being brought to bear on the same problem, all ultimately mediated and resolved through the actions of the Security Council. I argue that different actors across the listing assemblage enact multiple realities of what the list is and how its accountability problems should best be dealt with through their practices. Objects, as Annemarie Mol suggests, are not passive and 'waiting to be seen from the point of view of seemingly endless series of perspectives. Instead, objects come into being ... with the practices in which they are manipulated ... [and] are not the same from one site to another.'[15] Shifting the focus from norms to situated practices allows me to analyse the list as a multiple object and provide a thick descriptive account of its ontological politics.[16] Following Mol I argue that praxiographic accounts, which ethnographically study practices and locate knowledge in 'activities ... instruments and procedures', allow us to better grasp how the varied relations that make up this assemblage are

a technical idiom so as to open the door for applying the expertise related to that idiom, together with the attendant structural bias.' – Martti Koskenniemi, *The Politics of International Law* (Oxford: Hart Publishing, 2011), p. 67.

[15] Annemarie Mol, *The Body Multiple: Ontology in Medical Practice* (Durham NC: Duke University Press, 2002), p. 5.

[16] On the multiple object and ontological politics, see: Mol, *The Body Multiple*, pp. 4–7, viii; and Annemarie Mol, 'Ontological politics. a word and some questions' (1999) 47(S1) *Sociological Review* 74. On ethnography as thick description, see: Clifford Geertz, 'Thick description: toward an interpretive theory of culture' in Michael Martin and Lee C McIntyre (eds.), *Readings in the Philosophy of Social Science* (Cambridge MA: MIT Press, 1994), p. 213.

constructed, sustained and changed.[17] Praxiography allows us to follow how the list works and changes as a global legal assemblage.

Second, my analysis of the Ombudsperson in this chapter is not a story of how human rights norms do or do not come to be institutionally embedded within the UN. I do not try to assess how this redress mechanism complies with existing legal standards, as there are already plenty of journal articles that do just that.[18] Instead, drawing empirical insights from interviews with listing experts (including former Ombudspersons), leaked cables and my own professional experiences as a lawyer in this field, I reframe the Ombudsperson as a contingent achievement or 'miracle', as one cable described it.[19] As this chapter shows (building on Chapter 2), global security law is much more than the Chapter VII UN Charter decrees issued by the UN Security Council. It is enabled and sustained through diverse epistemic and governance practices and novel forms of expertise that demand empirical analysis. So, whilst the Ombudsperson is often advanced as an ideal accountability solution,

---

[17] Mol, *The Body Multiple*. For Mol, praxiography 'does not search for knowledge in subjects who have it in their minds' but rather 'locates knowledge primarily in activities, events … instruments and procedures' (at p. 32). The analytical advantage of praxiography is that it 'takes up the argument that the turn to practice is not primarily about theory, but about the practice of doing research' – Christian Bueger, 'Pathways to practice: praxiography and international politics' (2014) 6(3) *European Political Science Review* 383, 385. On the ontological politics of 'enactment', see: Steve Woolgar and Javier Lezaun, 'The wrong bin bag: a turn to ontology in science and technology studies?' (2013) 43(3) *Social Studies of Science* 321.

[18] Lisa Ginsborg and Martin Scheinin. 'You can't always get what you want: the Kadi II conundrum and the security council 1267 terrorist sanctions regime' (2011) 8(1) *Essex Human Rights Review* 7; Erika de Wet, 'Human rights considerations and the enforcement of targeted sanctions in Europe: the emergence of core standards of judicial protection' in Fassbender, *Securing Human Rights?*; Jared Genser and Kate Barth, 'When due process concerns become dangerous: the Security Council's 1267 regime and the need for reform' (2010) 33(1) *Boston College International and Comparative Law Review* 1; Grant L. Willis, 'Security Council Targeted sanctions, due process and the 1267 Ombudsperson' (2010) 42 *Georgetown Journal of International Law* 673; Erika de Wet, 'From Kadi to Nada: judicial techniques favouring human rights over United Nations Security Council Sanctions' (2013) 12(4) *Chinese Journal of International Law* 787; Stephan Hollenberg, 'The Security Council's 1267/1989 Targeted Sanctions Regime and the Use of Confidential Information: A Proposal for Decentralization of Review' (2015) 28(1) *Leiden Journal of International Law* 49; Devika Hovell, 'Kadi: king-slayer or king-maker? The shifting allocation of decision-making power between the UN Security Council and courts' (2016) 79(1) *Modern Law Review* 147.

[19] US Embassy Cable 10USEUBRUSSELS212 (24 February 2010).

this chapter moves in a different direction, reframing the Ombudsperson as an ongoing political and legal problem.

The chapter is divided into six sections, each focusing on a specific actor in the listing assemblage and highlighting the particular idiom and type of list they enact through their practice. My narrative is polycentric, rather than chronological, to better get at the divergent interests, frames and objectives at stake in these accountability conflicts. National and EU courts, academic experts and think tanks, 'like-minded' reformist states, listing officials, along with UN Special Rapporteurs, the Security Council P5, legal scholars and human rights NGOs, all bring their own discourses, practices and expertise into the accountability problems of the list. This chapter seeks to highlight this heterogeneity in order to provide a detailed account of the Ombudsperson's conditions of emergence and durability.

My account highlights five different versions of the ISIL and Al-Qaida list enacted through this accountability conflict:

- a Legal List, grounded in normative critique by national and regional courts;
- a Humanitarian List enacted by academic-experts committed to targeted sanctions as a humanitarian governance project;
- the dynamic Living List of the Monitoring Team that forever evolves to counter new obstacles and threats;
- the Compliant List of the UN Special Rapporteur on Counter-Terrorism defined by strict adherence to human rights norms; and
- a Credible List of the Security Council P5 aimed at ensuring state compliance with Chapter VII UNSC resolutions.

These different versions of the list are overlapping, yet distinct. They are not different perspectives on the same list, but different enactments of the list in friction with each other. The differences highlighted in this conflict, in other words, are not just epistemological but ontological as well. The Legal List, the Living List, the Humanitarian List, the Compliant List and the Credible List are all vying to resolve an accountability problem framed in their own terms by bringing it within their remit and control.

As outlined in Chapter 2, assemblages are multiplicities made up of heterogeneous elements. These diverse elements may hold together in ways that enable governance to take place, but the assemblage does not subsume them into a coherent whole or expressions of an underlying logic. This irreducibility is a key feature of this approach and it informs the idea of the list as a multiple object developed throughout this chapter. As Allen observes, the assemblage seeks to capture the idea that 'institutional arrangements of power ... can more or less hold together, despite being made up of a co-existence of diverse logics and priorities, often pulling in different directions'.[20] When studying multiplicities, a key empirical question becomes: how are the different elements of the assemblage held together and institutionally sustained in practice?

The final section of the chapter seeks to address this question by analysing the Ombudsperson itself as a unique figure of global legal expertise. It draws from interviews undertaken with the former position-holder (Kimberly Prost) between 2012 and 2019 and my own professional experiences – both as a lawyer representing targeted individuals in Ombudsperson delisting proceedings from 2011 to 2019 and an assistant in the UN Special Rapporteur on Counterterrorism's 2012 report to the UN General Assembly on this issue.[21] As with the Monitoring Team examined in Chapter 2, there is no empirical, sociolegal research on this accountability mechanism. What has been written tends to rely on the Ombudsperson's own published reports about their work and is disconnected from how this delisting procedure actually operates in practice.

My analysis addresses this gap by examining the novel decision-making processes, 'dialogue' meetings and speculative evidential standards the Ombudsperson has crafted to work in this 'special' environment. I argue that these assemblage practices help mute underlying political and legal tensions and glue the ISIL and Al-Qaida list together as a global governance regime, containing the multiplicity set out earlier in the chapter. Observations from my own legal practice are used to show the stark inequities of the delisting procedure and critique claims that this mechanism offers 'in essence, de facto judicial review'[22] and procedural fairness for listed individuals. What emerges from this analysis is a textured account of global emergency law in motion and an empirical map of the listing assemblage in action. My aim is to reposition the Office of the Ombudsperson as a crucial actor in the listing assemblage and to transform the Ombudsperson from an inert institutional end-product of a protracted list accountability debate to a key protagonist and figure of legal expertise – sustaining the list in the face of tensions, managing its

---

[20] John Allen, 'Powerful assemblages' (2011) 43(2) *Area* 154, 155.
[21] My involvement in the production of this report is discussed below, in the 'Compliant List' section of this chapter at 3.4.
[22] 2012 Watson Report, p. 37.

failures and contradictions by smoothing out legal and political conflicts and making the exceptional governance of this preemptive regime durable.

3.1 The Legal List: Asserting Individual Rights and Pursuing Accountability in the Courts[23]

National and regional (EU) courts and international complaint bodies have led the way in pushing for UN procedural reform and placing individual rights and global security law into productive relation. Were it not for litigation and attempts to obtain redress by listed individuals the Office of the Ombudsperson would certainly have never been created. The following section provides a brief overview of the key cases on this issue, highlighting how different courts have responded to the accountability problems of the list. The judicial approach is distinctive insofar as it measures the list against domestic constitutional protections, fundamental rights and international human rights norms. As detailed and argued below, the courts have enacted a Legal List that continues to exert powerful constitutionalising effects that go well beyond their specific jurisdictional borders.

3.1.1   Sayadi and Vinck *(2008)*

One of the earliest legal critiques of the list's accountability flaws came from the UN Human Rights Committee (HRC), the supervisory organ of the International Covenant on Civil and Political Rights (ICCPR). In 1994 two Belgian nationals (Nabil Sayadi and Patricia Vinck, hereafter SV) co-founded an Islamic charity (Fondation Secours Mondial) as a European branch of the US-based Global Relief Fund (GRF). When the GRF was put on the US and UN terrorism lists in 2002, the Belgian authorities started a criminal investigation into SV and recommended their inclusion on the Al-Qaida list. After being listed by the UNSC in 2003 SV asked the Belgian government to help get them taken off. But the Belgian government refused to assist, claiming it was bound to give primacy to international law.[24] So SV brought legal action in the

---

[23] I use the term 'court' to group these cases together, even though the HRC is a UN human rights treaty body.

[24] *Sayadi and Vinck* v. *Belgium* (Communication No. 1472/2006, 29 December 2008), UN Doc. CCPR/C/94/D/1472/2006, para. 2.4. The delisting procedure at that time was entirely diplomatic. A request could be made to the Sanctions Committee, but only by

Belgian courts and obtained an order requiring Belgium 'to urgently initiate a de-listing procedure with the United Nations Sanctions Committee ... under penalty of a daily fine of €250 for delay in performance'.[25] The government then submitted two delisting requests to the Sanctions Committee, without success. As a result, SV filed a complaint with the HRC arguing that Belgium had violated its fundamental rights to fair trial and effective remedy by nominating them for listing by the UNSC without providing any 'relevant information' to explain why.

The HRC found that Belgium had indeed violated SV's rights to freedom of movement and privacy, but not their rights to a fair trial.[26] This omission was criticised as 'a missed opportunity' by scholars for not pressing the issue of human rights compliance.[27] But the decision was important because it affirmed for the first time that the HRC had jurisdiction to hear complaints on listing issues and that states implementing Chapter VII Resolutions must adhere to international human rights protections. Furthermore, Belgium was compelled 'to do all it can to have their names removed from the list as soon as possible'.[28] The decision also sent a clear message to the UNSC: in the absence of a remedy at the UN level, the HRC can hear complaints from listed individuals that will effectively force states to choose between violating their citizens' human rights or breaching their UN Charter obligations.[29]

3.1.2 Abdelrazik v. Canada (2009)

Abfousian Abdelrazik is a Sudanese/Canadian dual national who was placed on the ISIL and Al-Qaida list in 2006 at the request of the US government (see Figure 3.1). He had been visiting family in Sudan at the

---

a listed person's state of residence or citizenship. See UN1267 Sanctions Committee, 'Guidelines for the Committee of the Conduct of its Work' (7 November 2002), para. 7.

25 Ibid. para. 2.5.

26 Ibid. The Committee found a violation of the right to free movement enshrined in Article 12(3) of the ICCPR because the prohibition on leaving the country imposed by the travel ban was 'not necessary to protect national security or public order' (para. 10.8). Because listing was held by the Committee to be preventative in nature it did not constitute a 'criminal charge' required to engage Article 14 of the ICCPR.

27 Marko Milanovic, 'The Human Rights Committee's views in Sayadi v Belgium: a missed opportunity' (2009) 3 Goettingen Journal of International Law 519; de Wet, 'Human rights considerations'.

28 Sayadi and Vinck, para. 12.

29 Helen Keller and Andreas Fischer, 'The UN anti-terror sanctions regime under pressure' (2009) 9(2) Human Rights Law Review 257, 263.

Figure 3.1 Abousfian Abdelrazik at a press conference in Montreal, 15 June 2011. He is in front of an anti-UN blacklisting banner painted by the Project Fly Home group that helped campaign for his return to Canada and eventual delisting. © (2011) Paul Chiasson/Press Association (PA). Reprinted with permission from PA Images.

time of his listing and intermittently detained there without charge at the request of the Canadian Security Intelligence Service (CSIS).[30] After his release, Abdelrazik sought to return to Canada. But Canada refused to issue the necessary travel documents because he was on a US no-fly list as a result of his UNSC listing. Abdelrazik then brought judicial review proceedings in the Canadian Federal Court to challenge 'Canada's conduct allegedly thwarting the applicant's return to Canada from Sudan and consequently breaching his right as a Canadian citizen to enter Canada'.[31] The government argued that the Sanctions Committee was responsible for preventing Abdelrazik's return because it was *its* listing decision that subjected him to a global travel ban and an asset freeze prohibiting the provision of funds for travel and repatriation. The Court disagreed and held that Canada had breached Abdelrazik's fundamental rights. The government was ordered to provide his travel documentation, airfare and an escort to ensure safe return in spite of the travel ban imposed by the Security Council.

The *Abdelrazik* judgment shows how far domestic courts are prepared to go in defying unjust demands by the Security Council. Here, the absence of a UN remedy provoked a constitutional dilemma and pushed Canada towards taking domestic steps that risk 'disobeying' the Security Council.[32] As Antonios Tzanakopoulos notes, one key effect of this decision is that 'the Executive must now either comply with what it believes is the correct interpretation of SCR [Security Council Resolution] 1822 and disobey its own court; or it must comply with its domestic court's decision and risk being found in breach of SCR 1822 and thus Article 25 of the UN Charter'.[33] In arriving at this decision the Court robustly criticised the unfairness of the UN listing and delisting

---

[30] *Abdelrazik* v. *Canada* (Minister of Foreign Affairs) 2009 F.C. 580, paras. 66, 91.

[31] Ibid. 2. The complex processes that caused Abdelrazik's exile from Canada is recounted at paras. 11–41 and 66–131. On the politics of Abdelrazik's repatriation, see: US Embassy Cable 09OTTAWA478 (dated 18 June 2009). A short documentary, *The Long Way Home* (2017, dir. Aisha Jamal and Ariel Nasr) also retells Abdelrazik's story. See: imdb.to /2K7mnlo.

[32] Antonios Tzanakopoulos, *Disobeying the Security Council: Countermeasures against Wrongful Sanctions* (Oxford: Oxford University Press, 2011).

[33] Antonios Tzanakopoulos, 'An effective remedy for Josef K: Canadian judge "Defies" Security Council Sanctions through interpretation', *EJIL Talk* weblog (19 June 2009). Available at: bit.ly/1IaS2HX. See also Antonios Tzanakopoulos, 'United Nations sanctions in Domestic courts from interpretation to defiance in Abdelrazik v. Canada' (2010) 8(1) *Journal of International Criminal Justice* 249; Devika Hovell, 'A dialogue model: the role of the domestic judge in Security Council decision-making' (2013) 26(3) *Leiden Journal of International Law* 579; Craig Forcese and Kent Roach, 'Limping into the future:

process. The presiding judge (Justice Zinn) described the listing regime as *Kafkaesque*[34] and linked the Court's assertive review to the remedial inaction at the UN level.[35] In an oft-cited passage from the judgment Zinn J. stated:

> I add my name to those who view the 1267 Committee regime as a denial of basic legal remedies and as *untenable under the principles of international human rights*. There is nothing in the listing or de-listing procedure that recognizes the principles of natural justice or that provides for basic procedural fairness . . . [T]he 1267 Committee listing and delisting processes do not even include a limited right to a hearing. It can hardly be said that the 1267 Committee process meets the requirement of independence and impartiality when . . . the nation requesting the listing is one of the members of the body that decides whether to list or . . . to delist a person. The accuser is also the judge.[36]

Such criticism is important because it delegitimises the Council's claim to authority and challenges its novel assertion of jurisdiction in this area. And, as detailed below, this case has emboldened other judicial actors to be similarly defiant when faced with legal challenges from listed individuals. Here, the Canadian Court resolved the clash between the national and global legal orders by interpreting the UNSC Resolution in a way 'that allowed Canada to pay the airfare for Mr Abdelrazik's return . . . even though the text of the resolution did not provide for this possibility'.[37] That is, by creatively reading a UNSC Chapter VII measure as authorising something that it prima facie prohibits.

the UN 1267 terrorism listing process at the crossroads' (2010) 42 *George Washington International Law Review* 217, 252–8.

[34] 'The 1267 Committee regime is . . . a situation for a listed person not unlike that of Josef K. in Kafka's *The Trial*, who awakens one morning and, for reasons never revealed to him . . . is arrested and prosecuted for an unspecified crime' – *Abdelrazik*, para. 53. Abdelrazik was finally taken off the list in November 2011: UN Doc. SC/10467, *Security Council Al-Qaida Sanctions Committee Deletes Entry of Abu Sufian al-Salamabi Muhammed Ahmed Abd al-Razziq from Its List* (30 November 2011). Available at: bit.ly /1DrcIyE.

[35] Zinn J. states (at para. 53), 'it is disingenuous . . . [to claim] that if he is wrongly listed the remedy is for Mr. Abdelrazik to apply to the 1267 Committee for de-listing and not to engage this Court'.

[36] *Abdelrazik*, para. 51 (emphasis added). At the time of writing, Mr Abdelrazik was engaged in civil litigation against the Canadian government for an apology and compensation for the alleged complicity of the CSIS in his torture whilst in Sudan.

[37] de Wet, 'Human rights considerations', p. 164. It excluded 'airspace' from the 'territory' the travel ban regulates – *Abdelrazik*, para. 127.

3.1.3 Ahmed and Others *(2010)*

In January 2010 the UK Supreme Court delivered its leading judgment on the conflict between the UN ISIL and Al-Qaida list and the UK constitutional order. *HM Treasury* v. *Ahmed and Others* involved five people listed by the UK government further to Security Council Resolutions 1267 and 1373.[38] The case challenged the measures automatically implementing these resolutions into UK law – the Al Qaida and Taliban (UN Measures) Order 2006 (AQO) and the Terrorism (UN Measures) Order 2006 (TO). Orders giving effect in the UK to UNSC Resolutions must be deemed 'necessary and expedient'. The litigants argued that the AQO and TO failed to meet that criteria because they interfered with their fundamental rights and denied them an effective remedy. When those on the list sought to challenge their listing before the UK courts, for example, it became clear that the UK listing decision could not be contested because it had been taken automatically following their designation at the UN level. Once again, targeted individuals were effectively told that their listing was something out of their government's hands that could not be subjected to meaningful judicial review at the domestic level.

The Supreme Court unanimously held that these implementing orders were unlawful. Under the common law legality principle, serious interferences with fundamental rights need a clear foundation in statute and must be no greater than required.[39] Yet these listing measures were found to be particularly severe – they 'strike at the heart of an individual's basic right to live his [sic] own life as he chooses' – and without proper parliamentary authorisation.[40] So the Court used the English common law to address the accountability problems of the list and quash the implementing orders. For

---

[38] *HM Treasury* v. *Ahmed and Others* [2010] UKSC 2. G (Mohamed al-Ghabra) and Hay (Hani El Sayed Sabaei Youssef) had been placed on the UN1267 list in 2006 and 2005 respectively. A (Mohamed Jabar Ahmed), K (Mohamed Azmir Khan), M (Michael Marteen) had been placed on the UK's domestic terrorism list implementing S/RES/ 1373 (2001) in 2007. All of their challenges were rolled into one joint appeal for the UK Supreme Court.

[39] It is a principle of UK constitutional law that parliament can pass laws breaching human rights, but only if they do so unambiguously. See Lord Hoffmann in *R* v. *Secretary of State for the Home Department, Ex p Simms* [2000] 2 AC 115: 'Parliament can, if it chooses, legislate contrary to fundamental principles of human rights ... But the principle of legality means that ... [it] must squarely confront what it is doing and accept the political cost. Fundamental rights cannot be overridden by general or ambiguous words.' (para. 131).

[40] *Ahmed*, para. 60. Such a severe interference with fundamental rights would require unambiguous statutory language. It could not be implied from the general wording of the authorising Act in this case.

Nico Krisch this decision 'largely avoids the difficult issues at the intersection of the different layers of law' and cautiously offers 'little more than a warning shot' to the Security Council.[41] And to comply with the judgment, the UK government introduced new primary legislation that 'merely re-enact[ed] the orders quashed by the court', muting the decision's potential political impact.[42]

But determining whether listed individuals had access to any mechanism of review required the Court to indirectly review the remedial possibilities (or lack thereof) at the UN level. Here, the Court openly dismissed the procedural reforms the Security Council had introduced up until that time as irrelevant, declaring that 'there was not when the designations were made, and still is not, any effective judicial remedy' available for listed individuals to properly exercise their defence rights.[43] This case also made the exceptional politics of global listing especially visible. 'It is no exaggeration to say', said Lord Hope, 'that designated persons are effectively prisoners of the state'.[44] One of the litigants (Mohamed al-Ghabra), for example, was informed by the UK authorities that his assets were frozen because he had been included on the UN Al-Qaida list that the government was duly bound to implement. But he was not told that it was the UK government which had secretly nominated him for inclusion on the list, thereby effectively shutting down the possibility of judicial review by relying on UN (rather than UK measures) to target him. As Elspeth Guild notes in her commentary: 'There appears here a transparent use of the Security Council as a venue through which to wash national executive decisions which otherwise would be subject to judicial control of their vulnerability to court supervision in the interests of the individual.'[45] The case also highlighted the disparities between the legislative and executive branches of government in global security law, by showing how a list with 'devastating' coercive effects can be given direct effect in the UK through executive regulations without any parliamentary oversight.[46]

---

[41] Krisch, *Beyond Constitutionalism*, p. 164.
[42] Ibid.
[43] *Ahmed*, para. 78.
[44] Ibid. para. 60.
[45] Elspeth Guild, *EU Counter-Terrorism Action: A Fault Line between Law and Politics?* (Brussels: CEPS Liberty and Security in Europe Series 2010), p. 7.
[46] *Ahmed*, para. 60. The process of automatically implementing the UN ISIL and Al-Qaida list through executive orders made pursuant to the United Nations Act 1946 that was challenged in this case highlights how global security law allows domestic executives to expand their own power 'relative to everyone else in their domestic political space': Kim Lane Scheppele, 'The international state of emergency: challenges to constitutionalism

3.1.4   Nada v. Switzerland (2012)

In October 2001 Youssef Nada and his associated business entities were placed on the UN1267 list by the US government, which believed he was a key financier for the Al-Qaida network. Nada was an Egyptian/Italian national resident in a tiny Italian tax enclave (Campione d'Italia) wholly circumscribed by Swiss territory.[47] As a result of the global travel ban flowing from his listing, Nada was prevented from leaving this enclave and so effectively placed under house arrest. In 2005 he brought legal proceedings in the Swiss courts against the measure implementing the ISIL and Al-Qaida list into Swiss law, arguing that because Switzerland had previously found the allegations of his alleged terrorist association to be unfounded there were no legitimate grounds for keeping him under sanction.

In November 2007 the Swiss Federal Tribunal dismissed the case. The court acknowledged that the UN delisting procedures were patently inadequate and left Nada unable to exercise his fair trial rights,[48] but it denied having the jurisdiction to review whether national measures implementing the UN1267 list were lawful because doing so would place Switzerland in breach of its UN obligations. Put differently: states have no discretion when it comes to implementing Chapter VII UN Security Council Resolutions, unless they violate peremptory (jus cogens) norms of international law.

Following this decision, Nada filed a complaint to the European Court of Human Rights (ECtHR) alleging that Switzerland had violated his rights to effective remedy and private and family life. He also submitted applications to the UN Focal Point enacted by Resolution 1730 (2006) asking to be removed from the list. His first UN request was refused due to US opposition, but his second request was granted thanks to US support[49] and, as a result, Nada and his companies were delisted in 2009.[50]

---

after September 11', Yale Legal Theory Workshop (21 September 2006) (unpublished manuscript), p. 5.

[47] Campione is 1.6 square kilometres in area.

[48] As protected by Article 6(1) of the European Convention on Human Rights and Article 14(1) of the ICCPR. *Youssef Mustapha Nada v. SECO*, Staatssekretariat fur Wirtschaft (Schweizer Bundesgericht) (14 November 2007), 1A.45/2007/daa, para. 8(3).

[49] US Embassy Cable 08STATE4740 (dated 15 January 2008) para. 8. US opposition to delisting followed concerns from Italy that it was being pressured by its courts to support his delisting before the Committee. See: US Embassy Cables 07ROME2515 (dated 28 December 2007) and 08ROME190 (dated 11 February 2008).

[50] Egypt (then under the rule of Hosni Mubarak) vociferously opposed the delisting of Nada because he was seen as 'the most important financier' of the Muslim Brotherhood. See: US

In 2012 the Strasbourg Court finally delivered its judgment upholding Nada's complaint. Switzerland had argued that it should 'not be held responsible internationally for the implementation of the measures in issue' because it was compelled to act as it had due to its UN Charter obligations.[51] But the Court asserted jurisdiction to hear the claim[52] and firmly rejected this argument, finding that 'Switzerland enjoyed some latitude ... in implementing the relevant binding resolutions of the United Nations Security Council.'[53] In a decision that draws from the *Sayadi and Vinck, Abdelrazik, Ahmed and Others* and *Kadi* cases, the Court found that Switzerland violated Nada's fundamental rights – for example, by delaying for more than four years in informing the UN1267 Sanctions Committee that Swiss investigations had found the allegations against him to be unfounded[54] and failing to substantively examine Nada's complaints and provide him with 'any effective means of obtaining the removal of his name from the list'.[55]

The *Nada* decision is a scathing indictment of the UN ISIL and Al-Qaida listing regime by Europe's leading human rights court. In arriving at the decision, the Court indirectly assessed and criticised the inadequacies of UN delisting procedures.[56] The Court defied the UN Security Council's authority by demanding EU Member States exercise discretion when implementing the list to ensure compliance with human rights standards – that is, by requiring states to 'enforce domestic human rights guarantees even if this would lead to their non-compliance with UNSC resolutions'.[57] Just as other critics (like the UN Special Rapporteur on Counterterrorism) had suggested, this decision suggests that 'if there is

---

Embassy Cables 09CAIRO1363 (dated 15 July 2009) and 09CAIRO1976 (dated 19 October 2009).

[51] *Nada v. Switzerland* App. No. 10593/ 08 (ECtHR, 12 September 2012), paras. 102–3.

[52] Ibid. paras. 121–3.

[53] Ibid. para. 180.

[54] Ibid. paras. 188–200.

[55] Ibid. para. 213.

[56] Ibid. paras. 211–12. More explicit criticism of the Ombudsperson mechanism was delivered by the ECtHR in the subsequent Iraqi sanctions case of *Al Dulimi* in which the Court drew heavily on the 2012 report by the UN Special Rapporteur on Counterterrorism (discussed in the 'Compliant List' section at 3.4 below) to find that the Ombudsperson falls short of international human rights standards. See: *Al-Dulimi and Montana Management Inc. v. Switzerland* App. No. 5809/08 (ECtHR, 26 November 2013), paras. 118–22.

[57] Marko Milanovic, 'European Court decides Nada v Switzerland', *EJIL Talk* weblog (14 September 2012). Available at: bit.ly/1MLJGvL.

no proper or adequate international review available, national review procedures – even for international lists – are necessary'.[58] In adopting such a pluralist approach, the ECtHR opened the possibility for EU states to defy the Security Council by not implementing the list nationally even though individuals may remain listed as ISIL or Al-Qaida associates globally.[59]

3.1.5   The Kadi cases (2005–13)

The most powerful judicial rebuke of the UN listing regime and its accountability flaws was delivered by the EU courts in a series of cases brought by Yassin Abdullah Kadi – a Saudi national and founder of the Al Barakaat International Foundation, formerly one of the key hawala banking operators used for the transfer of remittances by the Somali diaspora.[60] The *Kadi* cases feature in each chapter of this book because of their influence in shaping the listing assemblage. The following section examines the legal issues driving this litigation and justifying the various decisions taken by the EU courts.

Kadi and Al Barakaat were placed on the UN1267 list by the US government in the aftermath of the 9/11 attacks. In late 2001 Kadi commenced legal proceedings in the EU courts challenging the European Commission Regulation that implemented the UN list into the EU legal order for violating his fundamental rights – including the right to be heard, the right to respect for property and right to an effective remedy. In 2005 the European General Court (EGC, formerly known as the Court of First Instance) rejected the case, on the grounds that it lacked jurisdiction to review the implementing measure. The disputed regulation implements a Chapter VII Resolution of the Security Council. As such, the Court held that the European Commission and Council exercised 'circumscribed powers' and 'had no autonomous discretion' in

---

[58] UN Doc. A/65/258, Report of the Special Rapporteur on the Promotion and Protection of Human Rights and Fundamental Freedoms while Countering Terrorism (6 August 2010), para. 39. See also: Dick Marty, Council of Europe Parliamentary Assembly Report *United Nations Security Council and European Union Blacklists* Doc. 11454 (16 November 2007), para. 84.

[59] de Wet, 'From Kadi to Nada', 805.

[60] For analyses of the securitisation of hawala in the post-9/11 period see: Marieke de Goede, 'Hawala discourses and the war on terrorist finance' (2003) 21(5) *Environment and Planning D: Society and Space* 513; Mona Atia, 'In whose interest? Financial surveillance and the circuits of exception in the war on terror' (2007) 25 *Environment and Planning D: Society and Space* 447.

this matter.[61] The EGC held that it could only indirectly review UNSC Resolutions if they violated *jus cogens* norms.[62] Because no such violations were found here, the case was dismissed.[63]

Kadi appealed to the ECJ arguing that the EGC had erred by finding that the EU institutions were bound to implement Security Council listing decisions without providing targeted individuals the opportunity for redress. The appeal was bolstered by the Opinion of Advocate General (AG) Poiares Maduro, who argued that the EGC had misconstrued the proper relation between the EU courts and the UNSC. Crucially, for Maduro, it is 'the Community Courts [that] determine the effects of international obligations within the Community legal order by reference to conditions set by Community law'.[64] The contested regulation in this case clearly violated Kadi's rights. For Maduro: '[H]ad there been a genuine and effective mechanism of judicial control by an independent tribunal at the level of the United Nations, then this might have released the Community from the obligation to provide for judicial control of [the] implementing measures.'[65] But because no such UN mechanism existed, the EU courts must review the implementing regulation and find it unlawful for breaching EU constitutional principles.

In 2008 the ECJ delivered its groundbreaking judgment overturning the EGC's decision. Closely following the opinion of AG Poiares Maduro, the Court held that EU institutions must respect fundamental rights when implementing UNSC Resolutions: 'the obligations imposed by an international agreement cannot have the effect of prejudicing the constitutional principles of the EC Treaty, which include the principle that all Community acts must respect fundamental rights'.[66] Listed individuals must be properly informed of the reasons for listing and be able to contest those reasons before an independent body. Yet, in this case – because no review mechanism existed at the UN level and the reasons for listing were not available for review at the EU level – 'the rights of the defence . . . were patently not respected'.[67] The Court thus asserted the authority to 'ensure

---

[61] Case T-315/01 *Kadi v. Council and Commission* [2005] ECR II 3649, para. 214. See also: Case T-306/01 *Yusuf and Al Barakaat International Foundation* v. *Council and Commission* [2005] ECR II 3533, para. 265.

[62] *Kadi* ibid. para. 226.

[63] Ibid. para 261–90.

[64] Joined Cases C-402/05 P and C-415/05 P, *Kadi and Al Barakaat* v. *Council and Commission* [2008] ECR I 6351, Opinion of AG Poiares Maduro, para. 23.

[65] Ibid. para. 54.

[66] *Kadi and Al Barakaat*, para. 285.

[67] Ibid. para. 334.

the review, in principle the full review' of EU measures implementing the UN1267 list.[68] But it tried to limit the scope of this potentially far-reaching power by claiming that it is wholly EU focused and does 'not entail any challenge to the primacy of [Chapter VII Security Council resolutions] in international law'.[69]

Following this decision, EU authorities sent Kadi a 'Narrative Summary of Reasons' prepared by the UN1267 Sanctions Committee and gave him the opportunity to comment. They then relisted him, arguing that with this summary they had discharged their duty to respect his fundamental rights by informing him of the case against him. Kadi promptly filed another legal complaint and in 2010 the EGC found his renewed listing unlawful. The Court held that the 'in principle, full review' envisaged by the ECJ in 2008 extended to 'the substantive assessments of the Sanctions Committee itself and the evidence underlying' its decisions.[70] As Cuyvers observes, 'this means that EU courts should have full access to all evidence relied on and that listings may not be based on evidence not communicated to the Court'.[71] But in this case EU authorities had performed a wholly inadequate review in which 'the applicant's rights of defence [were] observed only in the most formal and superficial sense, as the Commission in actual fact considered itself strictly bound by the Sanctions Committee's findings'.[72] Furthermore, they had failed to provide 'even the most minimal access to the evidence against [Kadi] . . . despite his express request'.[73] And, whilst the UN1267 Office of the Ombudsperson created in 2009 was acknowledged, it was ultimately dismissed as irrelevant: 'the Office of the Ombudsperson cannot be equated with the provision of an effective judicial procedure for review of decisions of the Sanctions Committee'.[74] Accordingly, the EGC held that Kadi was left unable to 'launch an effective challenge to the allegations against him' and properly exercise his right to judicial review.

---

[68] Ibid. para. 326.

[69] Ibid. para. 288.

[70] Case T-85/09, *Kadi* v. *Commission* [2010] ECR II 5177, para. 129.

[71] Armin Cuyvers, '"Give me one good reason": The unified standard of review for sanctions after Kadi II' (2014) 51(6) *Common Market Law Review* 1759, 1763.

[72] *Kadi* v. *Commission,* para. 171.

[73] Ibid. para. 173.

[74] Ibid. para. 128: 'the Security Council has still not deemed it appropriate to establish an independent and impartial body responsible for hearing and determining, as regards matters of law and fact, actions against individual decisions taken by the Sanctions Committee'.

The EU authorities appealed once more to the ECJ and, whilst awaiting judgment, the UN Sanctions Committee removed Kadi from the UN1267 list.[75] In July 2013 the ECJ finally delivered its decision. This case is multifaceted and discussed in more detail elsewhere in this book.[76] The key issue concerned the scope, standard and intensity of judicial review that the EU courts must apply to measures implementing UNSC Resolutions. The EU and UK (with twelve other Member States intervening) argued that the applicable standard of review ought to be tempered by the special 'international context' of the UNSC.[77] The EGC had thus erred by failing to 'take into account the many material obstacles that exist to the communication of [underlying] information and evidence to the European Union institutions'[78] and by forgetting that the EU has no discretion when implementing Chapter VII measures. For EU listing authorities, the EGC's call to review 'the substantive assessments of the Sanctions Committee itself' was therefore 'excessively interventionist'.[79]

Yet the ECJ held that the EU courts must indeed review the substance of listing decisions, but limited the scope of 'full review' by declaring that only one sufficiently detailed reason (and not all of the underlying evidence, as previously suggested by the EGC) needed to be provided.[80] In this case the ECJ reviewed the substance of the listing decision itself for the first time, finding that the allegations in the Narrative Summary were sufficiently precise to allow for a proper defence but inadequately substantiated by supporting evidence.[81] According to the Court, its substantive review was 'all the more essential' because existing delisting procedures at the UN level fail to provide 'effective judicial protection'.[82] In other words, despite the international profile the Office of the Ombudsperson had generated, it remains wholly inadequate as a judicial review mechanism.

---

[75] UN Doc. SC/10785, *Security Council Al-Qaida Sanctions Committee Deletes Entry of Yasin Abdullah Ezzedine Qadi from Its List* (5 October 2012). Available at: bit.ly/1SInck4.
[76] See the discussion in Chapter 1 and detailed analysis in Chapter 4.
[77] Joined Cases C-584/10P, C-593/10P and C-595/10P, *Commission, Council and United Kingdom v. Kadi* (18 July 2013), para. 72.
[78] Ibid. para. 79.
[79] Ibid. para. 74.
[80] Ibid. paras. 138–9.
[81] Ibid. paras. 153–63.
[82] Ibid. para. 133.

3.1.6   The Legal List, Judicial Critique and the Primacy of Fundamental Rights

This overview of judicial resistance is far from comprehensive, but it nonetheless shows how different courts and complaint bodies around the world (UK, Canada, EU and the UN) have responded to the accountability problems of the ISIL and Al-Qaida list in markedly similar ways. Despite their obvious divergences on points of law, four common effects tie these disparate decisions together and give the Legal List coherence and the ability to act as a catalyst for list accountability reform.

First, each case exerts pressure on national states and/or regional organisations (i.e. the EU) to effectively choose between upholding their constitutional principles or adhering to the mandatory Chapter VII demands of the UN Security Council. The argument that the hands of states are tied by their international obligations is firmly rejected here by courts finding room (however limited) for the exercise of discretion and state responsibility. If UN terrorist listing has 'enmeshed' international and national legal orders more closely together, then these cases have sought to disentangle this enmeshment and 're-establish greater distance between the layers' of legal-ordering.[83]

Second, in so doing, the courts have provided a robust challenge to the supreme authority of the UNSC by indirectly reviewing its global listing decisions. The UN Security Council is, of course, not bound by the decisions of subsidiary courts. But it is reliant on states to implement its Chapter VII decisions and, in the event of normative conflicts arising, the Security Council has the UN Charter to compel states to do so. These judicial challenges render this national imperative to implement UNSC Resolutions conditional and uncertain, threatening to undermine the Council's powers and weakening its force by requiring compliance with domestic constitutional protections. So, despite the formal legal architecture and international hierarchy of norms, there are powerful incentives for the Council to comply with these decisions by inferior courts.

Third, each decision examined above linked domestic defiance of international obligations with the lack of rights protection available at the UN level.[84] This is a powerful nexus that has helped enable human rights compliance to become central in the discourse of global security

---

[83] Krisch, *Beyond Constitutionalism*, pp. 187–8.

[84] Dan Sarooshi and Antonios Tzanakopoulos, 'United Kingdom' in August Reinisch (ed.), *The Privileges and Immunities of International Organizations in Domestic Courts* (Oxford: Oxford University Press, 2013), p. 302.

law. This nexus has been forged even though the UN 'is not a party to any of the universal or regional treaties and conventions for the protection of human rights and fundamental freedoms' and so is 'not directly bound by the respective provisions guaranteeing standards of due process'.[85] According to Bardo Fassbender, when Chapter VII measures of the UNSC directly impact on individuals rights and freedoms – as these cases make plain – 'there is a legitimate expectation that the UN ... observes standards of due process, or "fair and clear procedures", on which the person concerned can rely'.[86]

Finally, these legal challenges show the particularity of contemporary 'collective' security measures and reveal just how deeply post-9/11 global security law has penetrated the constitutional orders of national states and regional bodies.[87] They show how executive actors have 'use[d] the cover of international law to undermine domestic constitutions' and 'loosen [the] constraints' of rights protections in the global war on terror, expanding their power 'relative to everyone else in their domestic political space' and significantly altering 'the legal bases of state action' in the security field.[88] The Law of the List is not a traditional form of international law with pretensions of universal values, but a far-reaching pre-emptive legal weapon and inchoate mechanism of world government.[89]

The courts have been crucial actors in creating and shaping the Office of the Ombudsperson. Yet the Legal List they have enacted to measure the Council's listing regime and render it accountable is only one part of the assemblage. Another key network of actors, moral discourse and version of the list has provided a vitally important vector for change in

[85] Bardo Fassbender, 'Targeted sanctions imposed by the UN Security Council and due process rights' (2006) 3 *International Organizations Law Review* 437, 445.

[86] Ibid. 468.

[87] For Neil Walker, these conflicts reveal how global security law 'struggles to justify itself in universal terms. The object may be unlimited – all who can pose a threat to stability, but it is universal neither in its justification nor in its manifest source.': Neil Walker, 'Out of Place and out of time: law's fading co-ordinates', Working Paper No 2009/01 Edinburgh: University of Edinburgh School of Law, 2009), 42.

[88] Scheppele, 'The international state of emergency', 1, 5.

[89] Walker, 'Out of Place'. As José Alvarez notes with regard to 'hegemonic international law': 'This is Council-generated "universal international law" very different from most international lawyers' original conception. This is *ostensibly* multilateral law that is unilateral in many of its effects.' – José E. Alvarez, *International Organizations as Law-Makers* (Oxford: Oxford University Press, 2005), p. 644 (original emphasis). See also: Nico Krisch, 'The rise and fall of collective security: terrorism, US hegemony, and the plight of the Security Council' in Christian Walter, Silja Vöneky, Volker Röben and Frank Schorkopf (eds.), *Terrorism as a Challenge for National and International Law: Security versus Liberty?* (New York: Springer, 2004), p. 891.

this area. But to understand its effects, we need to start by revisiting the ethical beginnings of the 'targeted' sanctions instrument.

3.2 The Humanitarian List: Academic Expertise and the Moral Economy of Targeted Sanctions

As discussed in Chapter 1, the use of UN sanctions against Iraq in the 1990s precipitated a humanitarian crisis. Measures directed against the Saddam Hussein regime ended up inflicting severe harm on the civilian population they ultimately aimed to protect.[90] Following widespread critique of the 'blunt instrument'[91] of comprehensive sanctions, the UN supported a multinational reform process led by Switzerland, Germany and Sweden to redesign sanctions and counter what became known as their 'unintended consequences'.[92] The result was 'smart' or 'targeted' sanctions, which have since become the Council's most common tool for responding to perceived threats. The UN1267 regime adopted in 1999 was not the first UN smart sanctions experiment, but, given its unique focus on global networks, the profound due process conflicts it has created and the enhanced political importance of counterterrorism in the post-9/11 era, it is the listing regime that has defined the UN targeted sanctions experiment from inception to the present.

Targeted sanctions were thus created as a mechanism of 'humanitarian government' during the fertile post-Cold War period when 'human

---

[90] As Mueller and Mueller observed, 'economic sanctions may well have been a necessary cause of the deaths of more people in Iraq that have been slain by all so-called weapons of mass destruction throughout history': John Mueller and Karl Mueller, 'Sanctions of mass destruction' (1999) 78 *Foreign Affairs* 43.

[91] The term comes from the former UN Secretary General Boutros Boutros-Ghali: 'Sanctions . . . are a blunt instrument. They raise the ethical question of whether suffering inflicted on vulnerable groups in the target country is a legitimate means of exerting pressure on political leaders whose behaviour is unlikely to be affected by the plight of their subjects. Sanctions also always have unintended or unwanted effects.' See: UN Doc. A/50/60-S/1995/1, *Supplement to an Agenda for Peace* (3 January 1995), para. 70. See also: UN Doc. SG/SM/7360, Secretary General Reviews Lessons Learned during Sanctions Decade in Remarks to International Peace Academy Seminar (17 April 2000).

[92] The literature on the 'unintended consequences' of sanctions is vast. See, for example, Drew Christiansen and Gerard F. Powers, 'Unintended consequences' (1993) 49 *Bulletin of the Atomic Sciences* 41, and Mikael Eriksson, 'Unintended consequences of targeted sanctions' in Christopher Daase and Cornelius Friesendorf (eds.), *Rethinking Security Governance: The Problem of Unintended Consequences* (London: Routledge, 2010). For a critique in relation to terrorist listing, see: Louise Boon-Kuo, Ben Hayes, Vicki Sentas and Gavin Sullivan, *Building Peace in Permanent War: Terrorist Listing and Conflict Transformation* (Amsterdam: Transnational Institute, 2015).

security' discourse and intervention practices like the R2P doctrine were taking shape.[93] It was an instrument formed through the concerted reform efforts of a transnational policy network of scholars, think tanks, regulators, UN officials and security experts brought together by a common desire to reduce civilian suffering. Prominent academics from international relations, political science and peace studies have from the outset been critically important nodes in this governance network.[94] Many went on to later advise the Security Council, guide reform efforts and shape political debates on the problems of the list. Despite ostensible humanitarian objections to war, after 9/11 these humanitarian scholars were elevated and revalorised as global counterterrorism experts. The following section of this chapter analyses their crucial list assemblage work. It shows how these academics played leading roles both in creating the Office of the Ombudsperson and then later defending this unique institutional experiment from political and legal attack. In my analysis the humanitarian impulse that stimulated targeted sanctions did not end with the 1990s. It continues to animate the Humanitarian List that these scholar-experts have enacted and exert residual effects on how the Law of the List is configured, shaped and justified.

3.2.1   Targeted Governance: Recalibrating the Civilian Pain–Political Gain Nexus

How can UN intervention to counter international threats be reorganised in the post-Cold war era to minimise 'life threatening suffering' and realise a New Humanitarian Order?[95] What role

---

[93] Daniel W. Drezner, 'Sanctions sometimes smart: targeted sanctions in theory and practice' (2011) 13(1) *International Studies Review* 96, 98. See also Jean Cohen, *Globalization and Sovereignty: Rethinking Legality, Legitimacy, and Constitutionalism* (Cambridge: Cambridge University Press, 2012), pp. 266–72. Despite their common discursive origins, and in contrast to the wealth of academic literature critically analysing R2P and human security as novel forms of global biopolitics and humanitarian war, there is a dearth of analysis engaging with targeted sanctions in similar ways. Didier Fassin uses the term 'humanitarian government' to refer to the 'deployment of moral sentiments in contemporary politics' and the political shift towards the alleviation of 'suffering and misfortune'. Didier Fassin, *Humanitarian Reason: Moral History of the Present* (Berkeley CA: University of California Press, 2012) 1, 7.

[94] Including, for example, Thomas Weiss, George A. Lopez, Thomas Biersteker, John Ruggie, Barnett Rubin, David Cortright, Vera Gowlland-Debbas, Margaret Doxey, Larry Minear and Peter Wallenstein.

[95] Larry Minear and Thomas G. Weiss, 'Groping and coping in the Gulf crises: discerning the shape of a new humanitarian order' (1992) 9(4) *World Policy Journal* 755.

might UN sanctions play in 'expand[ing] the legitimate area of international action' and realising this ambitious global humanitarian reform project?[96] During the 'sanctions decade' of the 1990s such questions animated debates in global governance and sanctions scholarship.[97] At that time, US scholars Thomas Weiss and Larry Minear worked together on the Humanitarianism and War Project at Brown University's Watson Institute for International Studies. Together with David Cortright and George A. Lopez of Notre Dame University's Kroc Institute for International Peace Studies, they co-edited the influential 1997 book *Political Gain and Civilian Pain: Humanitarian Impacts of Economic Sanctions.*[98] This book was significant because it brought two hitherto distinct policy areas into productive relation – namely, 'the wider use of multilateral economic sanctions and … [the] more assertive humanitarianism' characterising UN intervention at that time. It also brought together two academic institutions (the Watson Institute and Kroc Institute) that have dominated scholarly policy debates on targeted sanctions ever since.

UN sanctions have long been embraced as a more humane and ethical alternative to the use of military force.[99] Civilian populations may indeed suffer through sanctions, but not as much as if their country was embroiled in war. The book problematised this assumption by demonstrating that 'the short-term humanitarian consequences and the long-term structural effects of economic sanctions are often themselves as harmful as war itself'.[100] Sanctions, it was argued, needed to break the 'political gain–civilian pain' nexus – that is, the idea that civilians should suffer to exacerbate political unrest and enhance the prospects of regime

---

[96] Thomas G. Weiss, David Cortright, George A. Lopez and Larry Minear (eds.), *Political Gain and Civilian Pain: The Humanitarian Impacts of Economic Sanctions* (Lanham MD: Rowman & Littlefield, 1997), p. 4.

[97] David Cortright and George A. Lopez (eds.), *The Sanctions Decade: Assessing UN Strategies in the 1990s* (Boulder CO: Lynne Rienner, 2000).

[98] Weiss et al., *Political Gain.* I use this book here as a device for representing the emergence of targeted sanctions, and not to suggest that it somehow created this policy field in itself. Parallel research and reform projects were also being undertaken in the UK at the time. See, for example: Koenraad van Brabant, 'Can sanctions be smarter? The current debate: report of a conference held in London, 16–17 December 1998' (London: ODI, 1999). Available at: bit.ly/2Or1g1t.

[99] There is a huge body of literature on economic sanctions as a form of just war. For a summary see George A. Lopez, 'More ethical than not: sanctions as surgical tools' (1999) 13 *International Affairs* 143.

[100] Weiss et al., *Political Gain,* p. xv.

change in targeted states.[101] Only a 'smart sanctions strategy of targeted constraints on the financial assets and capital vulnerabilities of elites' has the potential to 'apply ... economic coercion with the requisite finesse and precision' and realise 'a more humane and a more effective sanctions policy'.[102]

When this book was first presented to the Watson Institute board in 1998 an important synergy was forged and a research project put into motion.[103] Following the meeting, the former Chair of the Institute approached the Director and said:

> 'Well you said at the beginning that financial [sanctions] are more effective than trade ... and now we have heard that comprehensive sanctions have all these negative consequences. *So why not target financial sanctions?*' And of course, there was a lot of people from finance in the room and they were nodding their heads. And he said, 'I think the Watson Institute should start a project on this' ... [And] so that's how we started.[104]

Under the direction of Thomas Biersteker (a leading US international relations scholar) working closely with Sue Eckert (a former US government official who worked on expert control in the Clinton Administration), the Watson Institute soon became an important repository of academic expertise on UN targeted sanctions policy. Along with Nico Schrijver and Larissa van den Herik (both legal scholars from the University of Leiden) this Institute has long defined the boundaries of political and legal debate on this issue – building consensus on how best to resolve some problems of the list whilst deemphasising and 'blackboxing' others.[105] These scholars have been critically important actors

---

[101] See, for example, Patrick Clawson, 'Sanctions as punishment, enforcement and prelude to further action' (1993) 7 *Ethics and International Affairs* 20.

[102] Weiss et al., *Political Gain.* p. 240.

[103] The Watson Institute board of the time was composed of eminently powerful figures, including John Birkelund (former US intelligence officer and President of Dillon Read bank), Leslie Gelb (then President of the Council on Foreign Relations), William Rhodes (Vice Chair of Citibank), John Whitehead (former Chairman of Goldman Sachs and Director of the New York Stock Exchange) and Thomas Pickering (former US career Ambassador).

[104] Interview with Watson Institute scholar, Toronto, March 2014 (Interview G) (original emphasis). All subsequent quotes in this Chapter attributed to Watson Institute scholars derive from this interview, unless indicated otherwise.

[105] 'An actor grows with the number of relations he or she ... can put in black boxes. A black box contains that which no longer needs to be reconsidered, those things whose contents have become matters of indifference.': Michel Callon and Bruno Latour, 'Unscrewing the big Leviathan: how actors macro-structure reality and how sociologists help them to do

'bringing disparate elements together and forging connections between them' to sustain the Ombudsperson mechanism in the face of challenge.[106] Understanding their power first requires analysis of how their academic expertise on counterterrorism sanctions was constructed, valorised and accepted as authoritative.

3.2.2   Constituting Expertise and UN–Academic Symbiosis (1998–2004)

In 1998 the Watson Institute, along with the Council on Foreign Relations, organised a series of workshops in New York with UN officials, diplomats, academics and prominent bankers and lawyers to lay the groundwork for their targeted sanctions research and reform agenda. Here, Institute scholars forged close relations with two critically important 'translators' or 'policy entrepreneurs' – Joseph Stephanides (former head of Security Council Sanctions Unit in the UN Secretariat Department of Political Affairs) and Jenö Staehelin (then Swiss Ambassador to the UN).[107] Both were key organisers of the 'Expert Seminar on Targeting UN Financial Sanctions' (or Interlaken Process) in which the Institute was later invited to participate.[108] After the 1999 Interlaken meeting, Stephanides asked scholars from the Watson Institute to share their thoughts on this sanctions policy reform process and then, without consultation, sent their memo to Staehelin inside the Swiss UN mission:

---

so' in Karin Knorr Cetina and Aaron V. Cicourel (eds.), *Advances in Social Theory and Methodology* (London: Routledge, 1981), pp. 284–5. See also: Bruno Latour, *Science in Action: How to Follow Scientists and Engineers through Society* (Cambridge MA: Harvard University Press, 1987): 'The assembly of disorderly and unreliable allies is thus slowly turned into something that closely resembles an organised whole. When such cohesion is obtained we at last have *a black box*.' (p. 131, original emphasis).

[106] Tania Murray Li, 'Practices of assemblage and community forest management' (2007) 36 (2) *Economy and Society* 263.

[107] On policy entrepreneurs see: Michael Mintrom, 'Policy entrepreneurs and the diffusion of innovation' (1997) *American Journal of Political Science* 738; and Martha Finnemore and Kathryn Sikkink, 'International norm dynamics and political change' (1998) 52(4) *International Organization* 887. In this chapter I prefer to analyse such activity as 'translation'.

[108] Other scholars in attendance at the Second Interlaken meeting included George A. Lopez (Kroc Institute, University of Notre Dame, USA), Claude Bruderlein (Harvard University, USA), Vera Gowlland-Debbas (Graduate Institute of International Studies, Switzerland) and John Ruggie (Harvard University, and former advisor to UN Secretary-General Kofi Annan).

> And that's when the Swiss approached us . . . The policy entrepreneur from
> the Secretariat said 'OK. Get the Swiss to give you money to do this report to
> carry the process forward'. And that's actually how this unfolded . . . [and]
> where the connection between the Swiss Government and the work the
> Watson Institute has been doing really started.[109]

The ensuing report (the Interlaken Manual 'for design and implementation') was important for three key reasons. First, it was a 'ready to use'
research instrument to assist officials drafting UNSC Resolutions on
targeted sanctions, providing 'a menu of different language modules of
text to include in future resolutions from which policymakers can
choose'.[110] As such it functioned as a vehicle of 'methods standardisation', cohering the objectives of different actors through common legal
language and facilitating their collaborative involvement in the task of
building targeted sanctions policy together.[111] Second, the Manual – and
the UN sanctions reform process it spearheaded – also operated as an
enrolment device that expanded the possibilities for consensus and
collective security action by the Security Council P5. The Manual's
depoliticised and technical formatting, as one former UN Secretariat
official observed, had important and unforeseen political effects:

> UN SECRETARIAT: I can tell you, I felt very, very happy – and I never said this officially
> of course – that I saw repeatedly the Chinese delegation come into the [Security]
> Council. And visible in their briefs, they had the Interlaken (Manual). Simply because
> the formulations were highly technical and professional, done by experts (not by us
> generalists) they were extremely important to them. So, they were transformed from
> being totally ignorant and nihilistic [on this issue] . . . and hence we saw additional
> [collective security] measures pass since then.
> GS: And not just sanctions-related, presumably?
> UN SECRETARIAT: Exactly, yes.[112]

Third, and most importantly for my argument in this chapter, the
Manual was a key resource for bolstering the expertise and authority of

---

[109] Interview G.
[110] Watson Institute, *Targeted Financial Sanctions: A Manual for Design and
Implementation – Contributions from the Interlaken Process* (Geneva: Watson Institute,
2001), pp. vi, 1.
[111] Susan Leigh Star and James R. Griesemer, 'Institutional ecology, translations' and
boundary objects: amateurs and professionals in Berkeley's Museum of Vertebrate
Zoology 1907–39' (1989) 19(3) *Social Studies of Science* 387.
[112] Interview with former UN Secretariat official, New York, June 2014 (Interview H). The
value of targeted counterterrorism sanctions as a mechanism of consensus building in
the Council was a recurrent theme in my interviews with UN officials.

the Watson Institute scholars, and creating the foundations of their counterterrorism list assemblage work to follow:

> [Its] a rather powerful transgovernmental network that operates in this domain ... You have a certain ... shared community, a certain knowledge. It's linguistic ... [and] expertise defined. You need to know a certain amount of technical expertise to enter into the conversation. And once you're at that level and credible at it, then people use each other ... Because we authored the Interlaken Manual ... that gave us a certain expertise. That was our credibility.[113]

Actors in this network did indeed go on to use each other in diverse and mutually beneficial ways.[114] And with each new collaboration, the possibilities for academic experts to exert influence over this emergent global policy domain expanded. UN Secretariat officials, for example, worked with Watson Institute and Kroc Institute scholars to advance global humanitarian reform in ways they would not otherwise have been able, building networks of expertise and reframing political problems as technical ones that academics were best placed to resolve.[115] As one former Secretariat official put it:

> The Security Council members were beleaguered with ... an onslaught of daily work ... And the [sanctions] system had never been implemented due to the ... Cold War ... Due to lack of time, and also this divide, the Council could not do strategic planning. And so therefore we did it for them. But we tried to always let them claim paternity for what we engineered.[116]

Taking advantage of the fact that the UN diplomats responsible for designing and administering sanctions lacked the time, experience and

---

[113] Interview G.

[114] See, for example: Thomas Biersteker, 'Scholarly participation in transnational policy networks: the case of targeted sanctions' in Mariano E. Bertucci and Abraham Lowenthal (eds.), *Narrowing the Gap: Scholars, Policy-Makers and International Affairs* (Baltimore MD: John Hopkins University Press, 2012).

[115] See, for example, David Cortright and George A. Lopez (eds.), *Smart Sanctions: Targeting Economic Statecraft* (Lanham MD: Rowman & Littlefield, 2002) – where Stephanides thanks both Cortright and Lopez 'for their leadership in dissecting the issue of targeted sanctions and helping to place it on the international agenda' (p. viii).

[116] Interview H. This process supports both Koskenniemi's argument about international law's fragmentation and shift towards the 'politics of expertise' and the claims of constructivist IR scholars on the autonomy of IOs. See, for example: Koskenniemi, *The Politics*, p. 331; Michael Barnett and Martha Finnemore, *Rules for the World: International Organizations in Global Politics* (Ithaca NY: Cornell University Press, 2004).

resources to do so, Secretariat officials strategically forged relationships with scholars to help reform sanctions policy, bypass the intergovernmental deadlocks of the Council and create new possibilities for post-Cold War political cooperation. For the scholars this offered valuable opportunities to influence global security policy, procure research funding, carve out targeted sanctions as a distinct field of scholarship and humanitarian governance and build their expertise. For the Secretariat officials, involving 'unassuming academic experts' to produce policy-directed targeted sanctions research helped them advance far-reaching global humanitarian reform in discrete and cost-effective ways that are 'better ... for us, otherwise, we might be accused of being partisan' and operating outside the legitimate bounds of bureaucratic neutrality.[117] For the UN Secretariat, therefore, scholars are an integral part of the formula for global political change:

> Those behind this must be transient, following all and be the person who will be weaving and synthesising ... And the strategy is, first, to be incremental and not to be a full surprise. Once you have come to some level of accomplishment, you issue a crisp, very non-controversial factual report. And then the countries that have been sponsoring the process have the honour to write a letter to the President of the Security Council and say, 'Your Excellency. My government – along with the government of so and so and the NGOs and whoever were motivated to assist in the process of ... [working] towards more improved measures – organised a round table or whatever and the attached is the initial report ... We would be grateful if you could circulate [it] to all Member States ... for their information and consideration.' ... When you have done the whole exercise, you [then] organize a more theatrical conference. We invited everybody. And then it adopts something. And then you send it to them [i.e. the Security Council]. And that becomes the bible. So that's the strategy.

GS: And that is how the Interlaken Manual was created?
SECRETARIAT: Yes. Trust me: it works! It's a very cost-effective way of doing business with a trivial commitment of money, instead of the frontal, egotistic ... [approach].[118]

Scholar-experts were also engaged to advance global sanctions reform through education initiatives. In 2002–4 the Watson Institute was

---

[117] Ibid. As Barnett and Finnemore point out, IO bureaucracies exercise significant political power yet they 'need to be seen as impartial servants' and are 'legitimated by a myth of depoliticization' (ibid. 21).
[118] Interview H. See, for example: UN Doc. A/60/887-S/2006/331 (14 June 2006).

commissioned to provide targeted sanctions simulations and training workshops with the UNSC, Member States and Secretariat officials at the US Naval War College and Watson Institute facilities in Rhode Island (see Figure 3.2). These weekend retreats were important ways to informally build networks of actors in this field, allowing the Watson Institute and UN officials to work together 'symbiotically' and as part of 'a community that shared information' on this issue:

> We would get people in the Secretariat Sanctions Unit saying ... 'When you do your scenario, could you put something in that tries out this idea?' ... So, we would actually be a vehicle for what the Secretariat could never do on its own ... It [was] a kind of experiment, where we were co-creating possibilities. And ... some of the stuff we did ended up in [global] policy.[119]

Such workshops gave Institute scholars the opportunity to connect new diplomats from the elected ten (E10) Member States with key targeted sanctions interlocutors inside the UN bureaucracy 'who you can get [information from] if you've got a technical question [and] you don't want to raise it in a formal meeting'.[120] Because E10 officials only have two-year terms and generally arrive untrained, this practical connection-building work was highly valued. It helped scholars embed themselves as crucial nodes in this network and indispensable conveyors of historical knowledge on this issue.

Enacting scenarios within a university setting also allowed Security Council officials to feel 'like students again', levelling out (however fleetingly) their entrenched political divisions.[121] But most importantly, this symbiosis created the conditions for new academic–UN policy networks to emerge based on shared technical knowledge rather than Member State or institutional affiliation:

> There was a certain kind of informal sense of community and taking people out of New York was the key to that. Because in New York they're in 'I need to consult Capital' [mode]. But ... [here] you're meeting socially, you're having dinner ... [and] creating different kinds of networks that ... cut across functional roles. It's not like 'I'm in this Unit or in that Unit'. No. And what do we share? We share expertise and knowledge about the sanctions.[122]

---

[119] Interview G.
[120] Ibid.
[121] Ibid.
[122] Ibid.

Figure 3.2 Participants in Watson Institute Workshop on UN Sanctions Reform, Brown University, 16–17 July 2004, including Thomas Biersteker (LHS), Joseph Stephanides (middle) and Sue Eckert (RHS). The workshop was hosted by the Watson Institute in conjunction with the UN Secretariat, sponsored by the Swiss, German and Swedish governments and attended by members of the UNSC and senior diplomats. It ran targeted sanction simulations in an informal 'retreat' environment, three hours by train from New York. Source: *Report of the Workshop on UN Sanctions 2004*. © Reprinted with permission from the Watson Institute for International and Public Affairs.

According to Weiss, Tatiana Carayannis and Richard Jolly, most IO literature analyses Member States or the UN Secretariat to account for changes within the UN. But there is a markedly understudied 'third UN' – composed of 'outsider–insider' clusters of 'NGOs, academics, consultants, experts [and] independent commissions' – that increasingly determines UN action.[123] The first phase of the Watson Institute's activity on this issue clearly shows this 'third UN' in action, building important knowledge practices, discursive relations and expert networks and putting them into motion. These scholar-experts were more than external advisors or agents with delegated authority from their UN principals. They had already started positioning themselves as authoritative experts on targeted sanctions. In the aftermath of 9/11 they went on to become a key part of the 'epistemic infrastructure' through which problems of global terrorism came to be known and countered.[124]

3.2.3   From Humanitarian Concern to Global Security Expertise (2005–9)

The original impulse motivating the targeting of sanctions was global humanitarian reform. But, with the 9/11 attacks in 2001, the political focus and rationale for UN targeted sanctions dramatically changed. What had been initially embraced as an instrument of humanitarian governance was now rapidly recalibrated as a weapon of global preemptive warfare. And the humanitarian and International Relations (IR) scholars who were involved from the outset were revalorised as global security experts. Cortright and Lopez's edited collection *Uniting Against Terror: Co-operative Nonmilitary Responses to the Global Terrorist Threat,* succinctly captures this strategic recomposition unfolding:

> The research for this volume began soon after the United Nations Security Council passed Resolution 1373 on 28 September 2001. That resolution

---

[123] Thomas G. Weiss, Tatiana Carayannis and Richard Jolly. 'The "Third" United Nations' (2009) 15(1) *Global Governance: A Review of Multilateralism and International Organizations* 123, 123, 127.

[124] Christian Bueger, 'Making things known: epistemic practices, the United Nations, and the translation of piracy' (2015) 9 *International Political Sociology* 1; Karin Knorr Cetina, *Epistemic Cultures: How the Sciences Make Knowledge* (Cambridge MA: Harvard University Press, 1999); Karin Knorr Cetina, 'Objectual practice' in Theodore Schatzi, Karin Knorr Cetina and Eike von Savigny (eds.), *The Practice Turn in Contemporary Theory* (London: Routledge, 2001).

created the Counter-Terrorism Committee (CTC) and called on all states to ... lock down the financial assets of individuals and organizations associated with terrorism ... [by using] the tools of targeted sanctions we had researched in previous years ... As the CTC began its work ... we were able to carry on our roles of scholars/analysts and practical inter-locutors with UN officials, focused now on countering terrorism. Thus began our expanded research agenda.[125]

This transformation – from targeted sanctions scholar to figure of global security expertise – was experienced by the academics involved as some-thing arbitrary and circumstantial:

[It was] right after September 11. When people literally said ... 'You're an expert on [the countering of financing of terrorism]. And I said, 'What constitutes expertise? How did I become an expert'? ... And it was only because of the fact that I was working on the instrument of targeted financial measures – and, of course, that 1267 was already up and running. And then suddenly that forced us into this sort of role of experts on the subject.[126]

But this rearrangement was not merely an effect of political circum-stance. It was sought after and fostered by the scholar-experts them-selves. 'We were', as Interviewee A reflected, 'probably, in part, opportunistic. We took advantage of the now great interest in the subject and that our work was now relevant and important and useful in some way.'[127] These academics found that they could attract more funding and political capital for their targeted sanctions research as counterterrorism experts. Valorisation had the circular effect of 'skew[ing] the work in that direction'.[128] Reorientating sanctions research towards the dismantling of Al-Qaida meant that 'we were not looking at other applications [of sanctions] any longer with as much attention or scrutiny'.[129] The humanitarian reason that had allowed targeted sanctions to evolve as a global policy instrument was

---

[125] David Cortright, and George A. Lopez (eds.), *Uniting Against Terror: Cooperative Nonmilitary Responses to the Global Terrorist Threat* (Cambridge MA: MIT Press, 2007), p. xi.

[126] Interview G.

[127] Ibid.

[128] Ibid.

[129] Ibid. On expert knowledge defining 'reference point[s] for interaction' that make 'some 'strategies of action' available and closes off others, see: Ole Jacob Sending and Iver B. Neumann, 'Banking on power: how some practices in an international organization anchor others' in Emanuel Adler and Vincent Pouliot (eds.), *International Practices* (Cambridge: Cambridge University Press, 2011), p. 232.

supplanted in the post-9/11 environment by the shared imperative of helping 'starve the terrorists of funding'.[130]

But the unfairness of the list had started to become an issue of political concern, largely as a result of domestic legal challenges and protracted attempts by Member States to secure the delisting of their nationals.[131] In September 2005 the UN General Assembly 'call[ed] upon the Security Council ... to ensure that fair and clear procedures for placing individuals and entities on sanctions lists and removing them' were implemented.[132] The UN Office of Legal Affairs (OLA) also commissioned the legal scholar, Bardo Fassbender, to prepare a report clarifying whether (and how) the Security Council was obliged to provide due process rights to those targeted by sanctions.[133] It was from this political

---

[130] President, Secretary of the Treasury O'Neill and Secretary of State Powell on Executive Order, 'President Freezes Terrorists' Assets' (Washington: US Department of State, 24 September 2001). Available at: bit.ly/31DjUoC.

[131] In November 2001, for example, three Somali Swedes were placed on the 1267 list by the USA for alleged association with the Al Barakaat financial network. All three denied the allegations, complained they had no opportunity for redress and asked the Swedish government to intervene. Sweden asked the USA to provide proof of wrongdoing, but all they were sent was generic news material and background documents about Al-Qaida and the Al Barakaat network. Sweden thus sought to secure their delisting at the UN level, but were initially rebuffed. Twelve members of the Council supported the petition, but the USA, UK and Russia objected. In August 2002, the individuals were finally delisted after the Swedish government provided the US OFAC with evidence showing that there were no connections between these individuals and Al-Qaida, as well as written assurances from the individuals themselves that they would not associate with Al Barakaat. This process emboldened Sweden to critique the inequities of the listing regime and advocate for due-process reforms to be adopted by the Council. See, for example: Bruce Zagaris, 'Somali Swedes challenge terrorism freeze' (2002) 18(7) *International Enforcement Law Reporter* 277; Eric Rosand, 'The Security Council's efforts to monitor the implementation of Al Qaeda/Taliban sanctions' (2004) 98(4) *American Journal of International Law* 745; Juan Zarate, *Treasury's War: The Unleashing of a New Era of Financial Warfare* (New York: Public Affairs, 2013), pp. 38–9; Iain Cameron, 'UN Targeted Sanctions, Legal Safeguards and the European Convention on Human Rights' (2003) 72 *Nordic Journal of International Law* 159; and Iain Cameron, *Targeted Sanctions and Legal Safeguards*, Report to the Swedish Foreign Office (October 2002). For German and EU support for reform, see: UN Doc. S/PV.4892 (12 January 2014).

[132] UN Doc. A/Res/60/1, *World Summit Outcome* (24 October 2005), para. 109.

[133] Bardo Fassbender, 'Targeted sanctions and due process. The responsibility of the UN Security Council to ensure that fair and clear procedures are made available to individuals and entities targeted with sanctions under Chapter VII of the UN Charter' Study Commissioned by the United Nations Office for Legal Affairs (New York: Office of the Legal Counsel 2006). The Fassbender report concluded that because UN targeted sanctions have 'a direct impact on the rights and freedoms of the individual' they create 'a legitimate expectation that the UN will observe standards of due process' (p. 7). See

context that the Watson Institute produced its two most influential policy reports on the ISIL and Al-Qaida list: *Strengthening Targeted Sanctions through Fair and Clear Procedures* (2006) and *Addressing Challenges to Targeted Sanctions – An Update of the 'Watson Report'* (2009).[134]

The 2006 report, commissioned by Germany, Sweden and Switzerland, aimed to 'clarify the issues and advance common objectives of fair and clear procedures in the application of targeted sanctions'.[135] It recommended that an 'administrative focal point' be created in the Secretariat to receive delisting requests and ensure that individuals were notified of their listing – a suggestion later adopted by the Council in Resolution 1730 (2006).[136] It also suggested listings be reviewed biannually to ensure their accuracy and relevance – a proposal later introduced in Resolution 1822 (2008).[137]

Yet the key value of this document lies in its presentation of the effective remedy problem. It outlined five possible procedural review mechanisms that the Security Council could adopt to 'prevent potentially damaging legal challenges to targeted sanctions' and 'enhance the[ir] perception . . . as being responsive and transparent'.[138] These included: (i) expanding the Monitoring Team's remit to allow it advise on delisting matters; (ii) creating an Ombudsperson mechanism within the UN Secretariat; and/or (iii) assembling a Panel of Experts akin to the UN Human Rights Committee. Because each review mechanism would be established under UNSC authority, its recommendations would be non-binding. Two other review mechanisms with actual decision-making powers were also suggested – an independent arbitral panel and a UN tribunal with the competence to judicially review Sanctions Committee decisions.[139]

---

also: Bardo Fassbender, 'Targeted sanctions imposed by the UN Security Council and due process rights' (2006) 3 *International Organizations Law Review* 437.

[134] Watson Institute, *Strengthening Targeted Sanctions through Fair and Clear Procedures: White Paper* (Geneva: Watson Institute for International Studies, 2006), hereafter the 2006 Watson Report; Thomas Biersteker and Sue Eckert, *Addressing Challenges to Targeted Sanctions: An Update to the 'Watson Report'* (Geneva: Graduate Institute Watson Institute for International Studies, 2009), hereafter, the 2009 Watson Report.

[135] 2006 Watson Report, p. 50.

[136] S/RES/1730 (2006), para. 1 and Annex. The Focal Point idea was first advanced in a diplomatic 'non-paper' by the French government.

[137] S/RES/1822 (2008).

[138] 2006 Watson Report, pp. 8, 43.

[139] These reform options with real decision-making powers were only included in the report due to pressure from the governments who commissioned the research. According to leaked US Embassy cables, one of the co-authors met privately with officials from the US mission to the UN during the report's public launch in New York. In private, they

The report carefully avoided endorsing one particular reform option over any other. Instead, according to Biersteker, 'what we provided was an organized, analytical framework for policy comparison, an independently and theoretically derived set of evaluation criteria, and an assessment of the degree to which different options met those criteria'.[140] Each option was subjected to a cost–benefit analysis and presented as part of a 'range of choices from which member states could choose' to optimally realise fair and clear procedures.[141] The accountability problems of the ISIL and Al-Qaida list were thus reposed in technical, apolitical terms. For these scholars, the key issue was managerial: 'to determine what institutional mechanism and combination of elements [best] meet the test of an effective remedy'.[142]

Yet as Martti Koskenniemi reminds us, in the fragmented global legal landscape of the present 'there is no "innocent" or impartial neutral terrain from the perspective of which regime interaction could be managed'.[143] Instead, 'all management involves deciding in favour of some and against other interests, [and] the setting up of a hierarchy ... that prefers some outlooks at the costs of others'.[144] Functional expertise incessantly seeks to embed its own structural bias as the norm against which regime conflicts – for example, between security and human rights – are assessed. 'Everybody enters' the world of regimes 'from the perspective of one's own preferences that are always already partial ... but striving toward universal recognition'.[145] In this way, the fragmentation of international law facilitates hegemonic struggle by experts and the conditions for its own interminable reproduction.[146]

And so it is with the Watson Institute's 2006 report. Critically analysing this study through the lens of Koskenniemi's work allows us to better

---

'assured us [i.e. the US government] that the Institute did not endorse the "more extreme options" in the paper, such as an independent arbitral panel to consider delisting proposals or judicial review of UNSC decisions'. Thus, despite the report's technocratic presentation of the different options, from early on the Watson Institute supported ad hoc political, rather than judicial, solutions to this accountability problem. See: US Embassy Cable 06USUNNEWYORK714 (dated 4 April 2006).

[140] Biersteker, 'Scholarly participation', 143.

[141] Ibid.

[142] 2006 Watson Report, p. 44.

[143] Martti Koskenniemi, 'Hegemonic regimes' in Margaret A. Young (ed.), *Regime Interaction in International Law: Facing Fragmentation* (Cambridge: Cambridge University Press, 2012), p. 320.

[144] Ibid.

[145] Ibid.

[146] Koskenniemi, *The Politics*, p. 338.

see how it embeds important contingent assumptions as given. As discussed earlier, UN targeted sanctions shrink the space between the global and national domains. By reorientating collective security action towards individuals, the ISIL and Al-Qaida list directly interferes with human rights, creating novel constitutional conflicts and legal problems. Yet, for the Watson Institute scholars, this entanglement with individual rights claims is of secondary concern because, in their view, 'it is important to remember', at the end of the day, 'that the imposition of sanctions is more of a political and administrative process than a legal one'.[147] Terrorist-listing may indeed violate human rights but only as the 'unintended consequence' of a Security Council targeted sanctions policy that is implicitly assumed to be primary and altogether more important.

This jurisdictional move and prioritisation of the Security Council's Chapter VII authority has important effects on how accountability problems of the list are framed and made amenable to improvement.[148] Like proponents of emergency powers who contend that fundamental rights must be modified during periods of exceptional governance, the Watson Institute scholars quickly move from the primacy of 'the political' to argue that, because of the 'extraordinary nature of the Security Council's role in promoting international peace and security, some margin of appreciation or flexibility in interpretation as to what constitutes effective remedy is appropriate'.[149] They note that the right to effective remedy ordinarily requires 'that a review mechanism [must] have binding authority or the power to decide a case'.[150] Yet 'it is possible', they insist, 'that ultimate decision-making responsibility remains [vested] in the

---

[147] 2006 Watson Report, p. 7. When UN listing decisions target individuals and interfere with their fundamental rights one could just as easily argue that they are indeed legal measures.

[148] For Koskenniemi, 'In a world of plural regimes, political conflict is waged on the description and redescription of aspects of the world so as to make them fall under the jurisdiction of particular institutions.' – Koskenniemi, *The Politics*, pp. 337–8. See also: Mariana Valverde, 'Jurisdiction and scale: legal "technicalities" as resources for theory' (2009) 18(2) *Social and Legal Studies* 139.

[149] The argument is similar to the one advanced by scholars of the exception that in times of emergency constitutional rights need to be restricted or redefined if they are to have any relevance. See, for example: Bruce Ackerman, 'The emergency constitution' (2004) 133 (5) *Yale Law Journal* 1029; Oren Gross, 'Chaos and rules: should responses to violent crises always be constitutional?' (2003) 122 (5) *Yale Law Journal* 101; Alan Dershowitz, *Why Terrorism Works: Understanding the Threat, Responding to the Challenge* (New Haven CT: Yale University Press, 2002).

[150] 2006 Watson Report, p. 55.

sanctions committee or Security Council'.[151] What needs to be created, in other words, is a diluted form of 'judicial review-lite' that resembles conventional review but lacks any of its core features. As shown below, this would eventually lead to a decision-maker without the power of decision and a list review mechanism that is incapable of reviewing listing decisions.[152]

It would be three years before this possibility would come to be institutionally realised. The piecemeal reforms adopted by the Council up until 2009 did little to quell judicial criticisms of the ISIL and Al-Qaida listing regime. The Focal Point mechanism set up by Resolution 1730 (2006) was promptly dismissed by the courts as nothing more than an administrative mailbox for the Security Council. A 'Group of Like-Minded States' was then assembled to pressure the Council to create a review mechanism that was compliant with international human rights norms.[153] But it was the ECJ's 2008 *Kadi* decision that dramatically amplified this critique and made speedy resolution of the list's accountability flaws much more politically urgent. 'Bold action is needed', declared US Ambassador to the UN Susan Rice in 2009, 'to salvage the UN1267 al-Qaeda/Taliban targeted sanctions regime' and stop it from being 'seriously undermined by criticisms – and adverse European court rulings – asserting that procedures for listing and delisting names are not adequately fair and clear'.[154] An eighteen-month UN review of the UN1267 listing regime scheduled for December 2009 provided the catalyst for the next round of reforms and proposed solutions to this problem to be advanced.

---

[151] Ibid (emphasis added).

[152] For Dyzenhaus such institutional experiments are 'legal grey holes' because they contain 'the facade or form of the rule of Law rather than any substantive protections'. Yet as I argue in this chapter they are legally embedded forms of global exception and these humanitarian scholar-experts have played a crucial role in their assemblage: David Dyzenhaus, *The Constitution of Law: Legality in a Time of Emergency* (Cambridge: Cambridge University Press, 2006), p. 3.

[153] The Like-Minded Group was set up in 2008 and initially included Denmark, Germany, Liechtenstein, the Netherlands, Sweden and Switzerland. Belgium, Costa Rica and Finland joined in 2009. See, for example: UN Doc. A/62/891 – S/2008/428 (2 July 2008). Here the group recommended an independent UN expert panel be created to review listing decisions, loosely modelled on the World Bank Inspections Panels. For an overview of the activities of the Like-Minded states on this issue, see: Katalin Tünde Huber and Alejandro Rodiles, 'An Ombudsperson in the United Nations Security Council: a paradigm shift' (2012) *Anuario Mexicano de Derecho Internacional: Décimo Anniversario* 107.

[154] US Embassy Cable 09USUNNEWYORK818 (dated 4 September 2009).

The scholar-experts who had helped create UN targeted sanctions policy were amongst those most prominently advocating for procedural reforms to 'save' the ISIL and Al-Qaida listing regime from further judicial attack. Lopez and Cortright of the Kroc Institute released two public reports during this period – *Overdue Process: Protecting Human Rights while Sanctioning Alleged Terrorists* (April 2009) and *Human Rights and Targeted Sanctions: An Action Agenda for Strengthening Due Process Procedures* (November 2009).[155] Biersteker and Eckert of the Watson Institute prepared an influential policy document entitled *Addressing Challenges to Targeted Sanctions: An Update of the 'Watson Report'* (October 2009). These reports were launched at public events in New York and European capitals just prior to the new Security Council listing resolution being adopted in December 2009.

The Kroc Institute's approach was tempered by a pragmatic assessment of 'the political climate in which any of the proposals will be considered'.[156] The 'crux of the dilemma', in its view, is that reforms complying with international human rights are 'politically infeasible', due to P5 opposition, and reforms potentially supportable by the Security Council 'contain shortcomings' vis-à-vis accepted international human rights standards.[157] Breaking this 'impasse', suggest the Kroc Institute scholars, requires adopting a strategy of 'pursuing incremental change'. Following the Watson Institute, they advocate shifting the terms of the accountability debate to 'focus on developing mechanisms that . . . provide *quasi-judicial review procedures* while preserving the prerogatives of the Security Council'.[158] In the counterterrorism domain, such experiments often end up embedding states of exception and undermining fundamental rights. But there is little risk of legal violence occurring here because, in the optimistic vision of the Kroc Institute

---

[155] George A Lopez, David Cortright, Alistair Millar and Linda Gerber Stellingwerf, *Overdue Process: Protecting Human Rights while Sanctioning Alleged Terrorists*, Report to Cordaid from the Fourth Freedom Forum and Kroc Institute for International Peace Studies (Notre Dame NI: University of Notre Dame, April 2009); David Cortright, George A. Lopez, Gerber Stellingwerf, Eliot Fackler and Persinger Joshua Weaver, *Human Rights and Targeted Sanctions: An Action Agenda for Strengthening Due Process Procedures* (Sanctions and Security Research Program, November 2009). Available at: bit.ly/2MuNtVf.

[156] Lopez at al., *Overdue Process*, p. 7.

[157] Ibid.

[158] Cortright et al., *Human Rights and Targeted Sanctions*, p. 10 (emphasis added). For these Kroc Institute scholars, expanding the Monitoring Team's role to assist in delisting applications and setting up an independent review panel of experts to make non-binding recommendations was the preferable reform option.

scholars, the Security Council is evolving into a more human-rights sensitive institution and 'the tide is gradually turning' on this issue:

> the Security Council listing system is on an evolutionary path toward modestly improved due process procedures ... [and] the Council has entered a period of system response and adjustment. After an initial period in which listing decisions were made hastily and with little regard for human rights, the Security Council has adopted an approach of greater responsibility and sensitivity to due process rights. Under these circumstances ... the most effective strategy may be to apply continuous pressure for the system to adapt further and ... move the reform process forward.[159]

Leaked cables show how key political actors sought to harness and shape the Kroc Institute's mode of 'pragmatic' engagement. In March 2009 the Canadian Mission to the UN convened a meeting of diplomats, UN Secretariat officials and academics (including Lopez, Cortright and Biersteker) to discuss 'challenges facing targeted sanctions' and provide a platform for these scholars to launch a 'new process' of learning and reform modelled on the earlier Interlaken meetings.[160] 'This "process"', stressed Cortright, 'would not be an official UN-mandated endeavour, but rather a loose collection of academics, experts and diplomats who seek to harmonize their collective efforts'.[161] It would be organised through informal working groups and aimed at 'develop[ing] recommendations that were relevant to policymakers' on issues such as fair and clear procedures.[162]

Although incipient, the USA quickly recognised this initiative's potential importance and noted that 'similar informal initiatives in the past have been influential in developing the sanctions tools that the Security Council uses to respond to threats to peace'.[163] Yet it was critical for the US government that such initiatives stayed sensible: 'USUN will continue to urge leading participants to ensure their recommendations are relevant and grounded in political reality. *To this end* USUN has recommended that the US academics involved in this initiative meet with Washington policymakers at an early stage.'[164] Engaging scholar-

---

[159] Ibid. p. 9.
[160] US Embassy Cable 09USUNNEWYORK301 (dated 23 March 2009).
[161] Ibid. Note: this quote is hearsay – it is from a US official who wrote the cable recounting what Cortright said.
[162] Ibid.
[163] Ibid. (emphasis added).
[164] Ibid. (emphasis added).

experts to ensure 'policy relevance', in other words, provided a vehicle for de-politicisation and a means of 'heading off more radical and dangerous proposals' for list reform.[165]

The Watson Institute's 2009 'update' marked a turning point in its engagement with the list accountability problem. Like the earlier study, it laid out a range of reform options on a 'balance sheet' and assessed the pros and cons of each – including various review mechanisms with an advisory role under UNSC authority (expanded Monitoring Team, Advisory Panel and Ombudsperson) and an independent judicial body capable of taking binding decisions. The key point of departure, however, lies in the report's recommendations. Here the Institute put its managerial approach to one side and laid its political preferences on the table, advocating for the creation of a UN Ombudsperson to 'meet [the] contemporary challenges of global governance in this issue domain'.[166]

Within two months this recommendation would be given the force of global law as a Chapter VII Resolution of the Security Council. US government support and 'ownership' of this reform process was a critical element underpinning this Resolution's adoption. Yet this support did not simply organically emerge from the Obama administration's more 'enlightened' approach to global counterterrorism governance. It was a complex negotiation which the Watson Institute scholars played a key role in proactively facilitating. As interviewee G explained, in 2009 'we crossed the line . . . for the first time, we went from analysis to advocacy'.[167] Drawing on the political resources and contacts opened up by their sustained policy engagement and accumulated technical expertise on this issue, these scholar-experts engaged in a multipronged and ultimately successful lobbying offensive to secure their preferred form of UN procedural reform. The Watson Institute's academic expertise networks were fully engaged to push the Ombudsperson forward within the White House:

> We used even more ties . . . I mentioned earlier Harold Koh and Anne-Marie Slaughter. Well Harold was in the Obama administration . . . – a key position as International Legal Advisor to the Secretary [of State]. So, Harold was coming to [my city]. I said, 'Harold, I'm going to come to your lecture. Let me just send you this draft report that we've written'. He

---

read it on the plane. We talked about it [my city]. So, I got straight to the Secretary of State's Legal Advisor. Anne-Marie is an old friend. So, I made sure that we got a meeting in Policy Planning. And I talked with Anne-Marie and her staff about the issue. So, we *lobbied* – because we had friends [in the US government] – . . . and we became advocates because we did have a position now.[168]

The State Department has traditionally represented the US government in UN affairs. But terrorism listing has long been the preserve of the Office of Foreign Assets Control (OFAC) within the Treasury Department, which has the added advantage of its own in-house intelligence agency to facilitate the global preemptive targeting and asset-freezing process.[169] Changing US government thinking on the UN1267 list thus required these scholars (now counterterrorism experts) to engage this powerful institution of 'financial warfare',[170] responsible for hastily populating the UN list with most of its 'toxic designations'[171] in the aftermath of 9/11. As one scholar noted: 'US policy is not made by the State Department. State is entirely secondary to Treasury [on this issue]. Treasury is what drives the policy in the US. And that's why we went there.' The interviewee continued:

INTERVIEWEE: We went into OFAC and . . . [found] we could gain their confidence. We went into an OFAC secure room . . . where they decide . . . whom to designate. It's a scary place, because there were all these electronics around us and it was in this kind of bunker within the Treasury Department. And we sat down with *the people who make the designations* from OFAC. And they had *no idea* that this had any implications beyond the US. They were like: 'Really? Oh, and this would

---

[168] Ibid (original emphasis). Harold Koh (Professor of International Law at Yale University) was an International Legal Advisor to the US State Department from 2009 to 2013. Anne-Marie Slaughter (currently president and CEO of the New America Foundation) was Director of Policy Planning at the US State Department from 2009 to 2011. The locational details of the meeting with Koh have been made generic here to preserve anonymity.

[169] OFAC has its own dedicated, in-house intelligence agency – the Office of Terrorism and Financial Intelligence.

[170] Zarate, *Treasury's War*. Zarate was formerly the Assistant Secretary of the Treasury for Terrorist Financing during the Bush administration. He argues that after 9/11: '[*Treasury*] began to devise means of using money as a weapon against terrorists . . . As a result, we are now living in a new era of financial warfare. The ability to undercut and disrupt the financial flows and networks of our enemies gave the United States a different kind of leverage' (p. 2).

[171] 2009 Watson Report, p. 24. See also: US Embassy Cable 09USUNNEWYORK301 – which cites Biersteker and defines 'toxic designations' as 'UN designations made in the immediate wake of the 9/11 attacks that were based on weak information and have since undermined the integrity of the 1267 sanctions regime'.

potentially have an impact on the instrument of targeted sanctions? 'Yes. This is why we're [here]' . . . Some of them were quite resistant to the idea that anyone would look into their [decisions] . . . But we actually sat down and talked with them and tried to expand their knowledge of this.

GS: Specifically, about the problem of effective remedy at the UN?

INTERVIEWEE: Yes . . . that there *has* to be a review mechanism at the UN level.[172]

The Watson Institute also pressed the Ombudsperson issue in personal meetings with the OFAC Director, who was arguably *the key figure* able to shift the US position on this from firm opposition to reluctant support: '[We] sat down with Adam Szubin for an hour . . . and basically lobbied Adam saying, "Look, you need to lighten up, just let up". Now that's when *we* crossed the line, when we became advocates for a policy'.[173] The aim of this meeting, according to Biersteker, was simple: to use 'our research as the basis for arguing that Treasury should drop its resistance to UN level reforms'.[174]

This carefully focused and politically astute lobbying campaign evidently worked.[175] The USA soon began taking the lead in the drafting process for the upcoming Security Council Resolution on this issue. The USUN finally acknowledged there was 'room to improve' and confirmed it would soon 'take additional steps to ensure that the process for listing and delisting individuals is as fair and transparent as possible'.[176] And in December 2009 Security Council Resolution 1904 was unanimously adopted, establishing the UN1267 Office of the Ombudsperson.[177]

---

[172] Interview G (original emphasis)).

[173] Ibid (original emphasis). On the shift from US opposition to support, compare US Embassy Cable 06USUNNEWYORK714 and US Embassy Cable 09USUNNEWYORK818.

[174] Biersteker, 'Scholarly participation', 144.

[175] The Watson Institute was not solely responsible for this shift. For an excellent account of the politics of this process, see Carlotta Minnella, 'Human rights in the counter-terrorist sanctions regime' in *Imperfect Socializers: International Institutions in Multilateral Counter-Terrorist Cooperation* (DPhil thesis, University of Oxford) copy on file with author.

[176] Alejandro Wolff, 'Statement by Ambassador Alejandro Wolff, US Deputy Permanent Representative, in the Security Council, on the 1267, 1373 and 1540 Committee Briefings' (13 November 2009).

[177] The creation of the Ombudsperson did not bring the activities of these scholar experts to an end. Rather, it prompted a new phase of work defending the Ombudsperson from political attack, arguing it should be extended to other sanctions regimes and undertaking further assessments of the effectiveness of sanctions through the Targeted Sanctions Initiative (bit.ly/2OApLcS) and the High Level Review of UN Sanctions (www.hlr-unsanctions.org/). This third phase of activity is analysed later in this chapter.

3.2.4   Academic Expertise, Targeted Sanctions and the Global Listing Assemblage

The emergence of the UN Office of the Ombudsperson is usually explained as the result of dialogue between the UN Security Council and the EU courts. But this section has highlighted the critical role that engaged scholars have played in creating this experimental review mechanism. At one level, it is a story about the power of specialised academic expertise and the importance of micro-political knowledge practices in enabling and shaping global law. At another level, it shows how humanitarian logics and technologies of preemptive warfare have become enmeshed and symbiotic in global security and how humanitarians 'increasingly provide the terms in which global power is exercised'.[178]

In Chapter 2 we observed how the jurisgenerative work of the Monitoring Team was obscured in technicalities and how listing experts considered their work as mere implementation, with the politics of global listing taking place elsewhere, in the Council and Sanctions Committee. The scholars here disavow the political effects of their work and expertise in similar ways. As one Watson Institute scholar put it, 'we are part of the network up to a certain point. But when governments decide, "OK, we are crafting a new Resolution", . . . when it actually comes to the design, the doors are closed.'[179]

Yet the formal intergovernmental domain is only one privileged site where the Law of the List is produced. As Michel Foucault reminds us, power is not a thing that can be held, but rather a relation that 'functions in the form of a chain'[180] and 'something that has to be *made*'.[181] Or as

---

[178] David Kennedy, 'Reassessing international humanitarianism: the dark sides', The Allen Hope Southey Memorial Lecture (University of Melbourne Law School, 8 June 2004), 2. This security-humanitarianism nexus is important because when legal violence is made humane, it becomes more widely accepted and frequently deployed. See, for example: David Kennedy, *The Dark Sides of Virtue: Reassessing International Humanitarianism* (Princeton NJ: Princeton University Press, 2005); Eyal Weizman, *The Least of All Possible Evils: Humanitarian Violence from Arendt to Gaza* (New York: Verso, 2012); Matt Craven, 'Humanitarianism and the Quest for Smarter Sanctions' (2002) 13(1) *European Journal of International Law* 43.

[179] Interview G. As Kennedy notes: 'Experts sustain their self-image as "background" by locating the "political" elsewhere': David Kennedy 'Challenging expert rule: the politics of global governance' (2005) 27 *Sydney Law Review* 5, 15.

[180] Foucault, *Society Must Be Defended*, p. 29.

[181] Bruno Latour, 'The powers of association' in John Law (ed.), *Power, Action and Belief: A New Sociology of Knowledge* (London: Routledge, 1986), p. 274 (emphasis added).

Bruno Latour puts it: 'those who are powerful are not those who "hold" power in principle, but those who practically define or redefine what "holds" everyone together'.[182] Using an assemblage framework allows us to conceptualise legal governance as 'the consequence of an intense activity of enrolling, convincing and enlisting' and an effect of diverse practices of *translation*, not just an external force and the cause of social behaviour.[183] When we analyse these scholar-experts in terms of their capacity to hold the diverse relations of the list together (i.e. their assemblage practices) their power comes into view. It allows us to reappraise scholarly expertise on targeted sanctions as a key element in this area of global lawmaking:

> I would say that we weren't that original or creative – because the Ombudsperson idea was a Danish non-paper and the Focal Point was a French non-paper. So, these things were already in circulation. What we did was: *we assembled them* . . . We created this frame, this structure, a way of thinking about the arguments . . . that [*was*] accessible, non-threatening and familiar to the policy world. We didn't invent or solve it on our own. *We simply assembled.*[184]

Yet as we have seen, there is nothing especially simple about practices of assemblage. They can involve 'the hard and ongoing work of legitimation', the forging of new epistemic objects and infrastructures, the privileging of some expert knowledge claims with their attendant structural biases and the active disregard of others as external and irrelevant.[185] Through their technical expertise, policy-orientated research, managerial framing, network building and important boundary-policing work, these scholar-experts effectively established themselves as an 'obligatory passage point'[186] through which all positions and debates on 'fair and clear procedures' for UN terrorism listing were filtered and shaped. The

---

[182] Ibid. p. 273.

[183] Ibid.

[184] Interview G (emphasis added).

[185] Tania Murray Li, 'What is land? Assembling a resource for global investment' (2014) 39 (4) *Transactions of the Institute of British Geographers* 589, 592.

[186] The term 'obligatory passage point' (OPP) is used in ANT to refer to a point that all actors are made to pass through in knowledge-production chains. It describes the processes that particular actors use to render themselves indispensable in any given network. As Latour puts it, once an actor has inserted themselves as an OPP, 'whatever you do and wherever you go, you have to pass through the[ir] . . . position and . . . help them further their interests – Latour, *Science in Action*, p. 120. See also: John Law and Michel Callon, 'Engineering and sociology in a military aircraft project: a network analysis of technological change' (1998) 35(3) *Social Problems* 284; and Star and Griesemer, 'Institutional ecology'.

Watson Institute scholar whom I interviewed for this project sum-marised their assemblage work on this issue in the following terms:

INTERVIEWEE: Well we collated, we put it [i.e. listing accountability debates] into a structure ... We don't say this is what should be done. We lay out the options ...

GS: But you structured the debate and that's perhaps more powerful?

INTERVIEWEE: Exactly. That's what we did ... [And so, officials have] credited the Watson Report with defining the issue in New York ... Now we have put ourselves in a more general position of expertise ... [and] are sort of corner-ing the market because everybody who works on UN targeted sanctions as a subject is part of our [Targeted Sanctions] Consortium ... We've actually heard that both the UK Foreign Office and even the State Department are starting to use our categories ... If we can get *that* level of policy to start using *our language* then, wow, we are actually having some impact now. Whether that makes the Institute worse or abused, that's a different kind of challenge to think about.[187]

Discursive programmes, as Foucault observed, are much more than inert background frames and 'induce a whole series of effects in the real ... . They crystallize into institutions, they inform individual behaviour, they act as grids for the perception and evaluation of things.'[188] Without the dedicated assemblage and discursive work of these scholar-experts the UN Office of the Ombudsperson would never have emerged, and other responses to the list accountability problem may have been developed instead. Driven by a desire to reduce civilian suffering and achieve global policy relevance, these academics have shaped this body of law in profound ways and become revalorised as security experts in the process. As Biersteker has argued: 'When we scholars participate in TPNs [transnational policy networks] ... it is not as neutral outsiders. We participate in ways that should be self-reflectively and critically examined.'[189] This section has sought to address this question by examining academic engagement with the problems of the list as a powerful and generative source of global security law.

---

[187] Interview G (original emphasis).

[188] Michel Foucault, 'Questions of method' in Graham Burchell, Colin Gordon and Peter Miller (eds.), *The Foucault Effect: Studies in Governmentality* (Chicago IL: University of Chicago Press, 1991) 81; cited in Murray Li, 'What is land?'. According to Li, the power of discursive technologies and devices to perform 'extraordinary feats of assembly work ... should not be underestimated' (593).

[189] Biersteker, 'Scholarly participation', 148.

3.3   The Living List: the ISIL and Al-Qaida Monitoring Team As Accountability Advocates

In Chapter 2, we observed how the formation of the Monitoring Team in 2004 precipitated a markedly 'technical turn' in UN terrorism listing expertise. Instead of naming and shaming states for inadequate implementation of the list, the team focused its attention on technical issues thought to be less politically contentious. As part of this shift, under the direction of former MI6 counterterrorism lead Richard Barrett (2004–12), list accountability problems became key matters of concern for the team. Many of the procedural reforms it proposed during this period ended up being adopted by the Council in some form. Yet the team's motivations for changing the list were not the same as those of the courts, critics and academics analysed in team reports. The version of the list enacted through the team's interventions in this accountability conflict were something distinct.

In the following section I suggest five reasons why intelligence, defence and government analysts from a small UN expert team with strategic 'fusion capabilities'[190] came to champion due process for those 'associated with' ISIL and Al-Qaida and create the conditions for the Ombudsperson to emerge. I highlight the crucially important assemblage work of the Monitoring Team that has sustained the Ombudsperson experiment in the face of political and legal tension. I argue that the team's engagement on this issue is animated by a Living List, dynamically evolving to meet new threats and exploit strategic opportunities. The Living List grapples with accountability concerns instrumentally and strategically – as a means of forging new security mechanisms, bolstering the power of functional expertise in this area and embedding the global political authority of the Council.

3.3.1   *Accountability As Opportunity: the List As 'Test Bed and Standard Setter'*

The Monitoring Team is acutely aware that the ISIL and Al-Qaida list is a unique instrument of global security law and that 'it is very unlikely we're going to get another thing like this – a global regime', targeting an amorphous threat with enough plasticity that all Security Council members can agree because global terrorism is not defined and 'no-one

---

[190] Interview with former member of the 1267 Monitoring Team, New York (via Skype), June 2014 (Interview F).

supports Al-Qaida'.[191] Making sure the ISIL and Al-Qaida list endures is seen as a key way to maintain this political consensus and ensure that 'we won't go back to a Council which is fundamentally divided on issues among the permanent members'.[192] As one former team member explained: 'there's great international interest in keeping the Council together as an expression of international resolve. We don't want this regime upsetting that international resolve. We want it to be *reinforcing* that international resolve' and sustaining the Council's assertion of Chapter VII authority to police global terrorism, and other threats to peace and security, into the future.[193] Resolving the accountability problems of the list in the present is thus seen as important by the team because it opens up further global governance opportunities down the line:

> Security Council resolutions get adopted, [but] they don't often get rescinded. So, if you're setting up a regime – and particularly this sanctions regime, the 1267 regime – you're setting up something which is going to provide precedents for sanctions regimes *way* down the road. If this works – and *particularly in the legal aspects of due process aspects, if it works*, if it becomes better and more effective, if it's implemented more thoroughly as a result of the measures that are introduced and procedures which are changed – then you can be *absolutely sure* this will set the pattern for other regimes.[194]

Earlier Monitoring Team reports cautioned the Council against considering any review mechanisms that might 'erode its absolute authority to take action on matters affecting international peace and security, as enshrined in the Charter'.[195] But by 2009 the team was taking the longer view and recommending that the Council take the initiative away from its critics. It argued that the Council should 'get ahead of the law in this area' by establishing 'some form of independent review', suggesting that an Ombudsperson mechanism would be the most preferable reform option.[196]

---

[191] Interview with former member of the 1267 Monitoring Team, New York, November 2012 (Interview A).

[192] Ibid.

[193] Ibid. (original emphasis).

[194] Ibid. (emphasis added).

[195] UNSC, Eighth Report of the Analytical Support and Sanctions Monitoring Team established pursuant to Security Council Resolution 1526 (2004) (2008) S/2008/324, para. 41.

[196] UNSC, Tenth Report of the Analytical Support and Sanctions Implementation Monitoring Team established pursuant to Security Council Resolution 1526 (2004) (2009) S/2009/502, paras. 42, 46.

It is important to underscore that the team's advocacy for 'fair and clear procedures' has little to do with protecting human rights or bolstering functional expertise. It is more concerned with nurturing a powerful, yet fragile, political resource that 'is proving to be a very good test bed and *standard setter*' for new forms of collective security action to be developed in the future.[197]

3.3.2   Tackling Due Process to Undermine the Threat of Judicial Review

At the same time, due process problems are presented by the Monitoring Team as a potential source of danger and 'legal risk' that must be mitigated.[198] The lack of effective remedy at the UN level and the rise in judicial review by listed individuals before national and regional courts is repeatedly advanced by the team as a potential threat to the legitimacy and 'legal authority of the Security Council in all matters, not just in the imposition of sanctions'.[199] This argument is primarily informed by analyses of the political implications of EU listing cases such as *Kadi*: 'If States cannot implement decisions taken by the Council under Chapter VII of the Charter of the United Nations without contravening their own laws, the global community will lose the power to take coordinated action against threats to international peace and security.'[200]

For the Monitoring Team, these listing cases are like canaries in the proverbial coal mine. They are early warnings that show what might happen if the Security Council remained intransigently opposed to the introduction of procedural reforms with capacity to satisfy national and regional courts. Although it has not happened, the ECJ – representing a community of twenty-eight of the most powerful states in the world, including two members of the Security Council P5[201] – *could* issue a decision that effectively prevents Member States from applying UN Chapter VII measures in their

---

[197] Interview A (emphasis added).
[198] Interview F.
[199] UNSC, Eleventh Report of the Analytical Support and Sanctions Implementation Monitoring Team established pursuant to Security Council Resolution 1526 (2004) (2011) S/2011/245, para. 30.
[200] UNSC S/2009/502, p. 5.
[201] At the time of writing, the UK remains a Member State of the EU, but that may change as of 31 October 2019.

jurisdiction. 'And if the EU isn't going to implement, no-one's going to implement', thus introducing a massive chink in the chain. Security against transnational terrorism has been characterised as a 'weakest link' global public good because it 'can be rendered futile if only a small group of governments does not cooperate'.[202] 'So these court decisions', as one former team member stressed, 'are *incredibly* important, they're *fundamental* to survival of the sanctions regime'.[203] From this viewpoint, managing due process problems through some kind of review mechanism 'that leaves the fundamental Security Council structures intact' but 'makes some minor modifications to the Committee's procedures' provides an important way of neutering an embryonic threat to the Council's political authority.[204] Simply put: 'the more effective the de-listing procedures' offered at the UN level are, 'the less likely that listed individuals and entities will choose to launch challenges in national courts'.[205]

In fact, after the Office of the Ombudsperson was created in 2009 the Monitoring Team quickly determined that it 'appears to meet the standard of effective review'[206] and in practice takes decisions 'that are just as binding as those of a national or regional judicial body'.[207] And now that the persistent due process problems of the list had apparently been resolved, listed persons ought to be made – through an innovative twist of the 'exhaustion of domestic remedies' rule – to first 'exhaust the process available at the United Nations before seeking relief in their

---

[202] Nico Krisch, 'The decay of consent: international law in an age of global public goods' (2014) 108(1) *American Journal of International Law* 1, 20 (original emphasis). As Richard Barrett has argued in his academic work on counterterrorism financing: 'The global nature of financial markets ... suggest the need for a universal regime. A hole in the defences, wherever it might be, could allow money to enter the system and flow to a recipient planning or supporting terrorism. Regulation should apply universally so as to close all possible gaps, and to ensure uniformity of effort': Richard Barrett, 'Time to reexamine regulation designed to counter the financing of terrorism' (2009) 41(7) *Case Western Reserve Journal of International Law* 7, 11.

[203] Interview A (original emphasis).

[204] UNSC, Third Report of the Analytical Support and Sanctions Monitoring Team established pursuant to Security Council Resolution 1526 (2004) (2005) S/2005/572, para. 53.

[205] UNSC, Ninth Report of the Analytical Support and Sanctions Monitoring Team established pursuant to Security Council Resolution 1526 (2004) (2009) S/2009/245, para. 31.

[206] UNSC, Twelfth Report of the Analytical Support and Sanctions Implementation Monitoring Team established pursuant to Security Council Resolution 1526 (2004) (2012) S/2012/729, para. 16.

[207] UNSC, Thirteenth Report of the Analytical Support and Sanctions Implementation Monitoring Team established pursuant to Security Council Resolution 1526 (2004) (2012) S/2012/968, p. 6.

national and regional systems'.[208] Although this 'exhaustion of international remedies' idea was never implemented,[209] it highlights how eager
the team was to push UN reforms forward to undermine EU judicial
review.

The Monitoring Team was also at pains to stress that this threat must
be dealt with *preemptively*. Even though 'the law is not clear in this area',
the team argued that the Council 'would be ill-advised to do nothing'.[210]
Instead, it should take the upper hand 'and exercise their authority in this
matter' by establishing 'the desired standard of review, rather than
effectively cede this role to others' – that is, by leaving the accountability
flaws and remedies to be determined by the courts below.[211] As one
former team member put it, 'the Council should not be a body playing
catch-up. It should be getting ahead of problems and dealing with'
them.[212] If the Council fails to *set* the reform agenda and instead
responds to Court decisions as they arise then 'the optics are absolutely

---

[208] UNSC S/2009/502, para. 43. The Monitoring Team was the first to make this far-
reaching argument. Thereafter, the former Special Rapporteur on countering terrorism
(Martin Scheinin) entered the fray by supporting the idea, but only if the Council could
ensure that (1) 'any listing proposal requires the submission of the full set of information
that is used as the substantive basis for the listing proposal;' (2) 'the person . . . subjected
to the listing proposal has the right and practical means to effectively challenge [it]'; (3)
'the Delisting Ombudsperson has access to the full set of information used for the listing;'
and (4) 'the delisting recommendations by the Ombudsperson or delisting proposals by
the designating State are in practice respected, so that they are not overturned through
a consensus decision by the 1267 Committee or referred to the full Security Council'.
This argument was then stripped of its procedural protections and elaborately extended
by Juliane Kokott (an Advocate General of the ECJ) and her legal secretary, Christoph
Sobotta in an article published in the lead up to the 2013 ECJ *Kadi* decision. Their text –
which is based on what I suggest are unfounded assumptions about the Ombudsperson
delisting process – draws 'inspiration' from case law on 'cooperation between EU
institutions and Member States' and procedural rules of international human rights
law to argue that an exhaustion of international remedies rule of this kind could be used
'to reduce significantly the risk of conflict between UN sanctions and EU judicial
protection' in listing cases. See, respectively: UNOHCHR, Human Rights/Counter
Terrorism: The New UN Listing Regimes for the Taliban and Al-Qaida, Statement by
the Special Rapporteur on Human Rights and Counter Terrorism, Martin Scheinin
(29 June 2011); Juliane Kokott and Christoph Sobotta, 'The Kadi case – constitutional
core values and international law – finding the balance?' (2012) 23(4) *European Journal
of International Law* 1015, 1022–4.

[209] The Council did ultimately endorse the idea, but it did not seek to make it mandatory.
See: S/RES/2083 (17 December 2012) para. 24 – which requests states to 'encourage'
those seeking delisting to first seek relief via the Ombudsperson.

[210] UNSC S/2009/502, para. 42.

[211] Ibid.

[212] Interview A.

terrible'.[213] Because then 'it looks as though you're acting in fear' and being compelled to act by less powerful institutions, rather than exercising your absolute authority, 'and some permanent members take that very seriously'.[214]

3.3.3   Accountability As an Obstacle: Due Process As a Time Waster

A third rationale advanced by the Team in support of procedural reform frames due process as an obstacle that needs to be overcome so the Security Council can free up resources to get on with the business of fighting the global war against ISIL and Al-Qaida. In this zero-sum approach, procedural fairness is valued only for its utility in enabling better *implementation* of global security governance:

> GS: So ... in terms of the cases, despite what some of the states might be suggesting, they really are concerned about ... the legitimacy question?
>
> INTERVIEWEE: ... It's not [legitimacy]. Legitimacy is more of an argument up there. It's implementation. *We want these things to be implemented and this is going to get in the way of the implementation.* It's not just the EU either. Turkey have had cases. In Pakistan, you've got cases. And you can guarantee that there'll be cases all over the place if there was a chink [in the chain].[215]

This fairness–implementation nexus began being drawn by the Monitoring Team shortly after its inception. This discourse has been extremely productive because, as shown later in this chapter, it taps directly into the Security Council's prime concern with the obedience of UN Member States. By 2005 the team was reporting to the Council that legal challenges 'pose a serious impediment to the success of the sanctions regime, not least by discouraging States to add names to the List'.[216] Accountability concerns were preventing States from 'applying sanctions with the required rigour, thereby undermining the[ir] credibility and effectiveness'.[217] This nexus became a continual refrain in the team reports leading up to the creation of the Ombudsperson. One reason

---

[213] Ibid.

[214] Ibid.

[215] Ibid. (original emphasis).

[216] UNSC, Second Report of the Analytical Support and Sanctions Monitoring Team established pursuant to Security Council Resolution 1526 (2004) (2005) S/2005/83, para. 50.

[217] Ibid. para. 54.

advanced in 2007 to explain why so few states were proposing names to be listed 'has to do with the Committee's procedures, which some States believe are insufficiently in tune with human rights concerns'.[218] Another report from this period notes in a rather circumspect and defeated tone that 'the regime carries on, but with mixed support', observing with some frustration how the 'persistent call' for improving UN delisting procedures has been largely ignored to date by the Security Council P5:

> The procedures and processes behind the regime are slow to change and the Committee and the Team need to find ways to manage the expectations of States . . . [But] the Committee . . . *must* seek better ways to show that it is examining their comments and suggestions in depth, and with a will to make changes as a result.[219]

This idea of due process as governance obstacle becomes most apparent after the Office of the Ombudsperson was created. The Monitoring Team's hasty conclusions about the Ombudsperson working as well as a court and providing those targeted with a de facto effective remedy were part of a much broader strategic effort to 'refocus the narrative' about the list towards issues of implementation and away from persistent problems of accountability and unfairness.[220] In a 2011 report, for example, the Team stated that it would not be recommending further procedural reforms 'because the challenge now lies far more with Member State implementation than with refinements of the Committee procedures' and that 'the aim of the Security Council must now be to reassure the courts that the sanctions regime established pursuant to Security Council resolution 1267 is fair'.[221] Team reports, as one former member explained, 'are reports to the Committee although we write them very

---

[218] UNSC, Sixth Report of the Analytical Support and Sanctions Monitoring Team established pursuant to Security Council Resolution 1526 (2004) (2007) S/2007/132, para. 16.

[219] UNSC, Seventh Report of the Analytical Support and Sanctions Monitoring Team established pursuant to Security Council Resolution 1526 (2004) (2007) S/2007/677, para. 9 (emphasis added).

[220] I describe this shift as a 'broader' effort because the Security Council P5 states, academic experts and the Monitoring Team all change the way they represent this issue in markedly convergent ways in response to the 2012 report by the UN Special Rapporteur on Countering Terrorism (as discussed in the Compliant List section at 3.4 below). For a recent example that partakes in this pragmatic refocusing, see: Larissa van den Herik, 'Peripheral hegemony in the quest to ensure Security Council accountability for its individualized UN sanctions regimes' (2014) 19(3) *Journal of Conflict and Security Law* 427. As noted in Humanitarian List section of this chapter at 3.2, van den Herik is a one of the leading scholar-experts working with the Watson Institute on targeted sanctions.

[221] UNSC S/2011/245, p. 6

much with the public in mind'.[222] So, as part of this broader messaging effort to assuage the concerns of courts and critics in the lead up to the 2013 ECJ *Kadi* II decision, the team changed how it framed the account-ability problems of the list, de-emphasising their political importance.

Due process flaws, for example, were now recast merely as the 'perception that listed persons continue to lack an effective remedy'.[223] In the Monitoring Team's view, the ISIL and Al-Qaida list had finally reached 'a stable, if temporary, equilibrium with respect to due process issues'[224] as a result of the Ombudsperson, so now 'Member States have little justification for incomplete compliance with the sanc-tions measures on the grounds that the regime lacks fairness'.[225] Only two remaining issues – the ongoing *Kadi* litigation (discussed in Section 3.1.5) and the critical report of the UN Special Rapporteur on Countering Terrorism (discussed below) – carry the potential to 'upset this balance'[226] and 'distract' the Security Council 'from looking forward'[227] and realising its broader 'implementation agenda'.[228]

In a fragmented legal area exemplifying what Walker calls 'the global disorder of normative orders',[229] this discursive refocusing towards list implementation and effectiveness is not a neutral move. It helps bring an overtly 'managerial approach'[230] to bear on resolving the problems of the list that precludes any serious consideration of its accountability flaws. Assuming that accountability issues have now been resolved serves to ring-fence and marginalise critics, listed persons and courts – who are contesting the fairness of the list – as misguided for looking back towards 'abstract' and 'structural due process issues'.[231] In other words,

---

[222] Interview A.
[223] UNSC S/2011/245, para. 36.
[224] UNSC S/2012/968, para. 17.
[225] UNSC S/2012/729, para. 23.
[226] UNSC S/2012/968, para. 17.
[227] UNSC S/2012/729, para. 33.
[228] Interview F. According to this expert, who joined the team after the creation of the Ombudsperson: 'I am very clear that my mandate coming into this job was not to neglect due process or fairness ... but to really focus a bit more on implementation and growing ... the strategic communications of regime ... To my mind the ultimate metric is: are these sanctions respected and are they implemented?'
[229] Neil Walker, 'Beyond boundary disputes and basic grids: Mapping the global disorder of normative orders' (2008) 6(3–4) *International Journal of Constitutional Law* 373.
[230] Koskenniemi, 'Hegemonic regimes'.
[231] UNSC S/2012/968, para. 21. In an excellent article Alejandro Rodiles argues that the key problem with managerialism is that it 'tends to fade out certain issues in favour of the effectiveness it pursues' – which, in this context, means side-lining human rights concerns. See: Alejandro Rodiles, 'The design of UN sanctions through the interplay

the discourse of effectiveness was used by the Monitoring Team to forge tighter alignments amongst actors in the listing assemblage about what is important and what is not, whilst deflecting critique and smoothing over deep-seated fractures as something irrelevant. In this way, the Ombudsperson mechanism and due process challenges it contains are put to work as an 'anti-politics machine ' – that is, a device that 'depoliticiz[es] everything it touches, everywhere whisking political realities out of sight, all the while performing, almost unnoticed, its own pre-eminently political operation of expanding . . . power'.[232] When the ECJ finally issued its decision in the 2013 *Kadi* case, which effectively contradicted its claims of procedural fairness, the Monitoring Team simply remarked that 'the Court was not persuaded by arguments that improvements to delisting procedures since 2008 diminished the need for such searching review by European courts'.[233]

3.3.4   Relevance: Pruning the List of Low-Hanging Fruit to Keep it Calibrated

A fourth rationale advanced by the Monitoring Team for addressing list accountability problems concerns the question of relevance. That is, the need to maintain a credible list that reflects the threat posed by ISIL and Al Qaida and that is operationally relevant for security services to use.[234]

As discussed in Chapter 1, the years immediately following 9/11 saw scores of people hastily nominated for inclusion on the list – mostly by the USA, but often in co-sponsored decisions with the UK and other states, such as Italy – with little to no consideration as to how they were allegedly linked to Al-Qaida. According to insider accounts, US Treasury officials were under considerable pressure to show demonstrable

---

with informal arrangements' in Larissa van den Herik (ed.), *Research Handbook on International Law and United Nations Sanctions* (Cheltenham: Edward Elgar Publishing, 2017). Van den Herik's claim – 'Peripheral hegemony', 427, 443, 439 – that the ECJ's 'non-negotiable commitment to high standards of judicial review' and 'dismissive appraisal of the UN system' by refusing to recognise the 'revolutionary reform' of the Ombudsperson in its 2013 *Kadi* decision is an assertion of 'peripheral hegemony', performs in academic discourse what the Monitoring Team seeks to do here in its reports to the Council.

[232] James Ferguson, *The Anti-Politics Machine: Development, Depoliticization, and Bureaucratic Power in Lesotho* (Cambridge: Cambridge University Press, 1990), p. xv.

[233] UNSC, Fifteenth Report of the Analytical Support and Sanctions Implementation Monitoring Team established pursuant to Security Council Resolution 1526 (2004) (2014) S/2014/41, para. 28.

[234] On the list being operationally irrelevant see, for example: UNSC S/2007/132, para. 17.

progress in the financial war against Al-Qaida and adding names to the UN1267 list 'was one of the best indicators' of success in this regard.[235] 'It was almost comical', as former US Treasury General Counsel David Aufhauser later remarked, 'we just listed out as many of the usual suspects as we could and said, Let's go freeze some of their assets'.[236] The extraordinarily loose targeting criteria of 'associated with' was only elaborated by the Council in 2005, by which time more than 400 people and groups had been designated, most of whom remain listed today.[237] As a result, the ISIL and Al-Qaida list remains stacked with what one former team member called 'low-hanging fruit', individuals about whom most states, including P5 states, may know little, if anything at all.[238]

Picking low-hanging fruit off the list and pruning it, however, has proven more difficult than one might think. Taking someone off the list requires the consent of the states that nominated them for inclusion, as well as input from states where listed people were born or have resided. Where multiple states are responsible for the listing, consensus must be achieved.[239] But states are reluctant to delist because of the political risk that whoever they take off might turn out to be terrorists. As one former team member put it:

> It's always going to be more difficult to get people off than get people on ... Would you as a Home Secretary in the UK be willing to sign a document that says you support the delisting of such and such? Where they might say, 'Well, this is historic'. But they're not necessarily convinced that there is no threat. Would you sign that?[240]

The other related obstacle to getting rid of unfounded or out-of-date listings has to do with the fact that removal requires the active involvement of states. And, as is clear from the Ombudsperson's reports and my own observations of the delisting procedure discussed later in this chapter, when asked to provide supporting information states have tended to

---

[235] Thomas Biersteker, 'Targeted sanctions and individual human rights' (2010) 65(1) *International Journal: Canada's Journal of Global Policy Analysis* 99, 102.

[236] Cited in Ron Suskind, *The Price of Loyalty: George W Bush, the White House, and the Education of Paul O'Neill* (New York: Simon & Schuster, 2004), p. 193.

[237] S/RES/1617 (2005), para. 2.

[238] Leaked US Embassy Cables associated with the comprehensive review of the list in 2009 – 2010 pursuant to S/RES/1822 (2008), para. 25, show a plethora of cases where there were insufficient grounds for listing in the US government's view. Yet many of those flagged as being listed without sufficient supporting evidence in 2009 remain on the list today.

[239] S/RES/1989 (2011), para. 28.

[240] Interview F.

either provide nothing at all or rely on generic assertions of threat.[241] It is difficult for states to support delisting if they do not know why people were listed in the first place, even if they were the country that put them on.[242] To work around this collective inertia problem, and get rid of the 'low-hanging fruit', in 2012 the Monitoring Team proposed a new procedure for the triennial UN1267 list review process: unless states could explain why someone should remain on the list, the default position should be that they are taken off.[243] But the Council rejected the proposal[244] and so the 'low-hanging fruit' dilemma persists.

So long as it is considered safer to have people indefinitely listed on a preventative UN list, there will be scores of people who may pose little or no threat to international peace and security, but who cannot be delisted. Yet the need to get them delisted becomes more pressing with time because each person left there who should probably be removed is another potential *Kadi* case waiting to happen.

So, the Monitoring Team has pushed for review mechanisms like the Ombudsperson because they help perform an essential list-pruning function. Such procedures can short circuit the complexities of national

---

[241] See, for example: UNSC, Fifth Report of the Office of the Ombudsperson, pursuant to Security Council Resolution 2083 (2012) (2013) S/2013/71, para. 34. Here the Ombudsperson observed that:

   One of the most pressing challenges to the effectiveness of the whole process, remains the lack of specificity in the material submitted by States with respect to individual cases. Of particular concern are States' responses that provide only broad assertions as to purported support activity on the part of petitioners and limited, and in some instances, no substantiating information or detail ... In the absence of specific information, it is very difficult and in some instances impossible to properly assess the sufficiency, reasonableness and credibility of the underlying information or to have a meaningful dialogue with and receive a specific response from the petitioner.

[242] See, for example: US Embassy Cable 09ROME652 (dated 9 June 2009) which discusses how 'on behalf of the US, Italy had proposed numerous candidates for designation' on the list 'about which they knew little' and that Italy will have difficulty justifying these listings 'unless they get ... [supporting] information' from the US government.

[243] UNSC S/2012/968, para. 24: 'Unless the designating State argues for continued listing, and provides its detailed reasons for doing so, the Committee should act as if the designating State had recommended delisting'. This proposal was also strongly supported by the Ombudsperson and builds on an earlier 'attention-grabbing proposal' by the US government to make listing decisions time-limited by making 'the default outcome of the [review] process ... the expiration of a designation instead of its retention'. See, UNSC, Seventh Report of the Office of the Ombudsperson, pursuant to Security Council Resolution 2083 (2012) (2014) S/2014/73, paras. 65–8; and US Embassy Cable 09USUNNEWYORK818, para. 10.

[244] UNSC, Fourteenth Report of the Analytical Support and Sanctions Implementation Monitoring Team established pursuant to Security Council Resolution 1526 (2004), (2013) S/2013/467, para. 24.

security politics and intergovernmental negotiation, helping to get rid of unfounded listings and undermining potential litigation challenges without the risk of setting dangerous legal precedent.

Dealing with the list's accountability flaws thus provides a means to an end – and 'the end game is having an effective regime against this amorphous and very hard to define threat'.[245] As one former team member explained, the ISIL and Al-Qaida list 'is always going to be backward looking. But you've got to make it as forward looking as you possibly can.'[246] Maintaining a list 'that reflects ... and adapts to the current threat' is important, according to another former team member, because that 'also allows you to then address all the cases where there may be questions about relevance'.[247] Having a list that is accurate is a laudable enough aim. What interests me here though is how the discourse of relevance comes to subsume and transform persistent problems of unfairness. Here, due process is not so much about accountability or providing individual redress. It is something tied to the realisation of a much more ambitious global governance project: the creation of 'the living list'.[248]

This term was first coined by former US Ambassador to the UN, Susan Rice, when justifying the US government's support for creation of the Ombudsperson mechanism. It dovetails with the Monitoring Team's strategic 'refocusing of the narrative' about the list post-2011. 'The whole purpose here', said Rice, 'is to make the 1267 regime and the list a living process ... that [is] refreshed and renewed with additional listings when appropriate and delistings when individuals no longer merit being on' it.[249] It's a goal that the Monitoring Team has long pushed for in its reports to the Security Council, but which until recently received little political support from the P5 states.[250] In the imaginary of the living list, the ISIL and Al-Qaida sanctions regime is an agile, dynamic and flexible global security governance tool – not clunky, steeped in international bureaucratic wrangling, resistant to structural change and stacked with out-of-date targets once thought by someone to

---

[245] Interview A.
[246] Ibid.
[247] Interview with former member of the Monitoring Team, New York (via Skype), August 2014 (Interview I).
[248] USUN, 'Remarks by Ambassador Susan E. Rice, U.S. Permanent Representative to the United Nations, on Security Council Resolution 1904, Sudan, and the Middle East, at the Security Council Stakeout', Press Release (17 December 2009).
[249] Ibid.
[250] See, for example: UNSC S/2012/729, paras. 9–29.

pose a potential threat. The discourse of relevance and the idea of the living list has certainly helped to smooth the way for reforms such as the Ombudsperson. But linking the protection of due process to the realisation of an almost impossible governance project also produces a subtle displacement. It helps defer into the indefinite future calls for list accountability reform that are more meaningful and robust than the Ombudsperson.

3.3.5   Ensuring Accountability to Preserve the List As a Potential Intelligence Resource

The fifth rationale provided by the Monitoring Team for institutionalising a form of list review is that it can help yield valuable intelligence – not only about people who are on the list and trying to get off it, but anyone else associated with them. In the months before the Office of the Ombudsperson was created, when there was a great deal of debate about what specific procedural reforms to introduce, the Monitoring Team recommended 'that the Committee consider ways to gather the maximum information possible about the activities of individuals and entities that apply for de-listing'.[251]

When the Ombudsperson mechanism was created by Resolution 1904 (2009), new processes for information-gathering and exchange were incorporated into its architecture – including a two-month 'dialogue phase' during the delisting process. Legal scholars and critics warmly welcomed this move as a step towards greater fairness and giving listed people a right to be heard. Global administrative lawyers were particularly effusive in their praise. As discussed later in this chapter at Section 3.6.3, however, when I share some of my own advocacy experiences of this dialogue phase, it is important to remember that this 'dialogue' procedure is not simply about giving the accused their long-awaited day in court.

The list targets people speculatively on the basis of what *they might do* in the future using an extraordinarily broad standard designed more for 'the sandy foundations of diplomatic negotiation' than legal challenge, as its ordinarily understood.[252] Dialogue with the Ombudsperson 'gives petitioners the occasion to express themselves' and so has been firmly

---

[251] UNSC S/2009/245, para. 32.

[252] Ben Emmerson, 'Statement by Ben Emmerson QC, Special Rapporteur on Countering Terrorism' (UN General Assembly, 21 November 2012), transcript with author.

encouraged by the Council.[253] But it also provides an important opportunity for generating new intelligence about potential terrorist 'associations' – for example, by requiring those listed to explain in what ways they have ever known or been associated with people on the list or anyone else deemed associated with them in turn. These associations can then be used to either *broaden* the scope of the preemptive security net that the ISIL and Al-Qaida list casts (by identifying new potential targets or persons of suspicion), *deepen* it (by providing some kind of derogatory information where none existed previously) or *translate* it for use in other fora (by moving from 'a closed material situation into an open information situation' that 'can then be used to form judicial proceedings' as well as 'by the committee to defend the listing before the Ombudsperson').[254]

All information that listed persons provide during dialogue is shared with 'relevant States, the Committee and the Monitoring Team', who can then ask any further 'follow up' questions of the petitioner in the event of 'incomplete responses'.[255] The team then stores this information indefinitely in its files (which for each listed person 'can be up to a few thousand pages'),[256] using it to help the Ombudsperson draft the report to the Security Council recommending either continued listing or delisting, as well as updating their narrative summaries of terrorist association (as discussed in Chapter 2).[257] Procedures of list review, like the Ombudsperson's 'dialogue phase', thus carry their own strategic benefits. They are a potential intelligence resource that can help expand the scope of preemptive security governance mechanisms, as well as keeping them well pruned and in check. In any event, as one former team member explained, any listed person prepared to go through the rigmarole of the Ombudsperson delisting process probably does not pose a global security threat:

> If someone is willing to hire a lawyer for a thousand dollars an hour, out himself, give his address, come to the European Court in person, then he's no longer a threat to international peace and security. The *mere fact* that he writes to the Ombudsperson, or that he writes to the European court, *alone* is a clear indication that he can no longer be as intimately involved

---

[253] Kimberly Prost, 'Remarks of the Ombudsperson at the Workshop on the UN Security Council, Sanctions and the Rule of Law' (31 May 2012), 2. Available at: bit.ly/2KiV9Hy.

[254] Interview with former member of the UN1267 Sanctions Committee, New York, June 2014 (Interview F).

[255] S/RES/1904 (2009) Annex II, para. 6.

[256] Interview I.

[257] S/RES/1904 (2009), para. 7.

with Al-Qaida as he used to be before. *He has to divulge so much information, which puts him at such a high risk . . .* that you can *easily,* every time
you have these kinds of court cases, you can delist him. What's the threat
of that guy? You know how he looks like. You know about his passport.
You know what his address is. You can call him, if you want. Where is the
terrorism threat of someone who is that known?[258]

The five rationales outlined above help explain why a small expert team of
mostly ex-intelligence and counterterrorism officials have been some of
the strongest advocates pushing to make the ISIL and Al-Qaida list more
procedurally fair and accountable. In this section I have highlighted some
of the crucially important discursive and assemblage work that the
Monitoring Team has done that has allowed the experiment of the
Ombudsperson to unfold and persist in the face of criticism. In so
doing, I have tried to disturb standard accounts of the Ombudsperson's
origins that disregard the micro-political work of the Monitoring Team
as an incidental part of a much bigger and more powerful macro-political
story. In my analysis, the Monitoring Team is an important crucible of
knowledge production shaping this domain of global law and sustaining
its techniques of governance. It performs crucial suturing work on the list
that has helped make the Ombudsperson possible.

3.4 The Compliant List: Global Constitutionalism and the UN Special Rapporteurs

One cannot understand the politics of the UN without grappling with the
divide between the hard and soft – or what Koskenniemi describes as the
conflict between 'the police' (the Security Council) and 'the Temple of
Justice' (the General Assembly):

> This dichotomy between hard UN (political activities for which the
> Security Council is mainly responsible) and soft UN (activities for
> which the General Assembly . . . is mainly responsible) is functionally
> and ideologically the most significant structuring feature of the organiza-
> tion. It governs everything from the career options of UN staff members
> and the specialization of diplomats at permanent missions . . . to the
> organization's image in the . . . mass media. It has been both a source of
> constant tension in the orientation of the UN's activities as well as an
> invaluable asset in overcoming difficult periods.[259]

---

[258] Interview F (original emphasis).
[259] Martti Koskenniemi, 'Police in the temple – order, justice and the UN: a dialectical view'
(1995) 6 *European Journal of International Law* 325, 336.

The story of the ISIL and Al-Qaida listing regime presented in this book is one of 'the police ... ransacking the temple'.[260] In Chapter 2, for example, we observed how the existential problem of defining terrorism was left with the General Assembly to argue over whilst the Security Council got on with setting up an exceptional security governance regime that did not need to define global terrorism because it could *list* it instead. And whilst the Assembly has been building a Global Counterterrorism Strategy reaffirming that 'the promotion and protection of human rights for all and the rule of law is essential',[261] the Council has expanded its listing practices in ways that allow state executives to continue to act 'unconstrained by domestic judicial review, or the international human rights treaties by which they are bound'.[262] On the whole, the General Assembly has had remarkably little influence on the evolution of the ISIL and Al-Qaida list. However, the following section highlights some of the effects that assembly-appointed officials *have had* in changing the discourse on list accountability, critiquing Council practices and conditioning this domain of global security law in important ways.

In 2005 the UN Commission on Human Rights (now the Human Rights Council) created a new Special Procedure position: the *Special Rapporteur on the promotion and protection of human rights and fundamental freedoms while countering terrorism* (hereafter, the Special Rapporteur). The Special Rapporteur is mandated to gather information on alleged violations, promote best practices, engage in dialogue and make recommendations to the Human Rights Council and General Assembly on 'the promotion and protection of human rights and fundamental freedoms while countering terrorism'.[263] There have been three post-holders since the role's inception: Martin Scheinin (2005–11), a Finnish professor of International Law and Human Rights at the European University Institute (EUI); Ben Emmerson QC (2011–17), a British barrister who co-founded Matrix Chambers in London and has litigated some of the most high-profile counterterrorism cases before

---

[260] Ibid. 348.
[261] UN Doc. A/RES/60/288, Annex Part IV, preamble (20 September 2006).
[262] UN Doc. A/67/396, Report of the Special Rapporteur on the Promotion and Protection of Human Rights and Fundamental Freedoms while Countering Terrorism (26 September 2012), para. 14.
[263] UN Commission on Human Rights Resolution 2005/80. E/CN.4/2005/L.10/Add.17 (21 April 2005), para. 14; and UN Doc. A/RES/60/251 (3 April 2006). There are currently forty-one thematic and fourteen country-specific Special Procedures appointed by the Human Rights Council on issue areas as diverse as such as food, child prostitution, self-determination, disabilities, extrajudicial killings and albinism. See: bit.ly/1S9vmxy.

the UK and EU courts;[264] and Fionnuala Ní Aoláin (2017–present), a Professor of Law from the University of Minnesota and Queen's University, Belfast, with particular specialisms in international law, counterterrorism and transitional justice.

The Special Rapporteurs play an unusual and important role within the listing assemblage. Whilst they are jurists, like the courts analysed earlier in this chapter, they are not restrained by the facts of the cases before them. They do not have to adjudicate or administer justice in specific instances, but are empowered to critique political institutions for their human rights failings. For this reason, their arguments tend to be dismissed by diplomats and listing experts as unduly 'academic' because they do not take the idiosyncrasies of Security Council politics into account. Yet their reports are a world away from the pluralism[265] and fragmentation[266] of international law and the 'global disorder of normative orders',[267] driving much of the contemporary academic legal debate on this issue. The Special Rapporteur's world is a globally constitutionalist world with clear ground rules that everyone ought to agree on. They are guardians of the Temple of Justice. Here, human rights are not just one normative order amongst many others, colliding in transnational

---

[264] For details of the professional backgrounds of Scheinin and Emmerson, see bit.ly /1N1eoBv and bit.ly/2MBHb6e. For the professional background of the current Special Rapporteur, see: bit.ly/2GIXTN4. At the time of writing, the current Rapporteur had not specifically engaged with the UN1267 listing regime, except from comments in UN Doc. A/73/361 (3 September 2018), paras. 19–21, that largely reiterated the views of her predecessors on the issue. As such, this part of the chapter focuses on the work of Martin Scheinin and Ben Emmerson as Special Rapporteurs, rather than Fionnuala Ní Aoláin.

[265] See: Krisch, *Beyond Constitutionalism*; Paul Schiff Berman, *Global Legal Pluralism: A Jurisprudence of Law beyond Borders* (Cambridge: Cambridge University Press, 2012); Peer Zumbansen, 'Defining the space of transnational law: legal theory, global governance, and legal pluralism' (2012) 21 *Transnational Law and Contemporary Problems* 305; Mireille Delmas-Marty, *Ordering Pluralism: A Conceptual Framework for Understanding the Transnational Legal World* (Oxford: Hart Publishing, 2009). A more detailed account of the global constitutionalist and pluralist literatures and debates in relation to the list is provided in Chapters 1 and 4.

[266] Martti Koskenniemi, and Päivi Leino, 'Fragmentation of international law? Postmodern anxieties' (2002) 15(3) *Leiden Journal of International Law* 553; Young, *Regime Interaction*; Andreas Fischer-Lescano and Gunther Teubner, 'Regime-collisions: the Vain search for legal unity in the fragmentation of global law' (2004) 25(4) *Michigan Journal of International Law* 999.

[267] Walker, 'Beyond boundary disputes' (emphasis added); Neil Walker, *Intimations of Global Law* (Cambridge: Cambridge University Press, 2015).

space.[268] They are master narrative, *grundnorm*,[269] foundational.[270] And as shown below in this section, their engagement with list accountability issues is animated by the idea of a legally Compliant List in accord with international human rights norms.

Whilst a lot of General Assembly work remains bogged down in lengthy intergovernmental processes, the Special Rapporteurs bypass much of that and 'tell it like it is', or rather how they see it through the powerful lens of international human rights compliance. Their findings often overlap with the courts but are even more systemically human-rights focused, which means that they have provided a constant source of critique of the Council's listing practices, saying things other actors are unprepared to say and pushing accountability debates further than they would otherwise go. And, unlike much of the General Assembly's output, their reports *do* carry considerable weight and stimulate broader public debate – especially amongst the worldwide legal community and others grappling with conflicts of security and fundamental rights. In contemporary academic-speak, their research and particular form of knowledge-production has substantial impact, public profile and valorisation.

Scheinin signalled his interest in critically engaging with the list early in his mandate.[271] In what has since become a convention of Special Rapporteur discourse, he acknowledged 'the need for preventive action is an important aspect of the fight against terrorism'.[272] But then noted with concern how the ISIL and Al-Qaida 'listing procedure infringes a number of human rights' and outlined 'basic principles and safeguards' that needed to be respected to make Security Council listing human-rights compliant.[273] Six specific lines of critique are advanced, each overlapping and building on each other.

---

[268] Fischer-Lescano and Teubner, 'Regime-collisions'. 'Rather than secure the unity of international law', according to Fischer-Lescano and Teubner, 'future endeavors need to be restricted to achieve weak compatibility between the fragments' (1045).

[269] Hans Kelsen, *Pure Theory of Law* (Berkeley CA: University of California Press, 1967).

[270] The Special Rapporteurs are, after all, appointed officials of the Human Rights Council.

[271] Special Rapporteurs are usually tasked to ensure compliance by states, not necessarily UN bodies themselves.

[272] UN Doc. A/61/267, Report of the Special Rapporteur on the Promotion and Protection of Human Rights and Fundamental Freedoms while Countering Terrorism (16 August 2006), para. 31.

[273] Ibid.

First, the 'principle of legality and legal certainty' – that is, the political problem of defining terrorism, reposed as something legally axiomatic: 'All international and national executive bodies in charge of including groups or entities on lists should be bound by a clear and precise definition of what constitutes terrorist acts and terrorist groups.'[274] Absent a definition, elastic standards like 'associated with' could be used to target 'improperly' and arbitrarily. Second, the principle of proportionality – the idea, as Lord Diplock once put it, 'that you must not use a steam hammer to crack a nut, if a nutcracker would do'.[275] The former Special Rapporteur traced the list's origins back to the humanitarian targeting of sanctions and the desire to impact 'as little as possible … the population'.[276] But implicitly rebuking the scholar-experts examined earlier, he argued that just because sanctions are 'targeted' does not mean that they are legally proportionate and fair.

Third, he noted that listing was supposed to be a temporary measure, not something 'open-ended in duration'.[277] Being legally compliant means reviewing the list annually or bi-annually to ensure all listing decisions remain 'necessary and supported by evidence'.[278] Fourth, the thorny question about appropriate standard of proof was posed. Is the list 'civil', 'criminal' or something more preemptive? What is its proper legal 'nature' and how does that shape what procedural guarantees ought to apply? But Scheinin turns the issue around and instead starts with the question of *impact*. If listing decisions apply indefinitely then their impacts must be severe. That makes them *punitive* – 'no matter how they are qualified' by the Monitoring Team and others who claim the list to be something uniquely administrative and preventative in 'nature'.[279] 'Another requirement', according to the former Special Rapporteur, is the need to transform UN listing decisions into domestic criminal prosecutions: 'if such evidence [of association with terrorism] exists … then States should have an obligation to prosecute' in accordance with 'normal rules and standards of proof'.[280] Finally, and perhaps most ambitiously, changing this preemptive security list into a criminal charge-sheet means 'transform[ing] intelligence into evidence to be used … in a court of

[274] Ibid. para. 32
[275] *R v. Goldstein* [1983] 1 WLR 151, 155.
[276] UN Doc. A/61/267, para. 33.
[277] Ibid. para. 34.
[278] Ibid.
[279] Ibid. para. 35.
[280] Ibid. para. 36.

law'.[281] Security listing is thus reframed as a way to channel speculative allegations back to the courts, where their uncertainty can be properly tested through adversarial challenge.

What is striking, on reviewing these demands, is just how far apart the former Special Rapporteur and the Security Council are in their understandings of what the ISIL and Al-Qaida list is, or ought to be. The Special Rapporteur projects the possibility of a legally Compliant List endowed with certainty and definitional clarity. But the Security Council has a list that is precisely valued for its semantic plasticity and capacity to render global terrorism into a governable object.[282] Whilst the Special Rapporteur claims listing as a means to an end, the Security Council claims listing as an end in itself: something that allows states to globally rescale preemptive security claims and effectively bypass their domestic courts. In this approach, criminal procedure is the list's antithesis, not its raison d'être. These divergences are not about one actor being right and the other being wrong. Nor are they merely different perspectives on the same basic problem. They reveal the heterogeneity of the listing assemblage and how its conflicts are as much ontological as they are normative. They show, in other words, the enactment of the list as a 'multiple object'.[283]

In his final report to the General Assembly as Special Rapporteur, Scheinin amplified his critique. Gone were the acknowledgements of work well done and gentle reminders that the Council needed to act in good faith to ensure human rights compliance. Instead, the former Special Rapporteur said the list was unlawful vis-à-vis the UN Charter and argued that it should be abolished.[284] Citing Koskenniemi's 'Police in the Temple' article,[285] the crucial issues identified now involved questions of legal competence, the proper relation between the Security Council and the General Assembly and the legal limits of Chapter VII targeting.[286] The Council's use of emergency powers 'should always be

---

[281] Ibid. para. 37.

[282] As detailed at length in Chapter 2.

[283] Mol, *The Body Multiple*.

[284] UN Doc. A/65/258, para. 57: 'the Special Rapporteur considers that sanctions regime to amount to action ultra vires, and the imposition by the Council of sanctions in individuals and entities under the current system to exceed the powers conferred on the Council under Chapter VII of the Charter'. Instead, the Council's counterterrorism resolutions – including S/RES/1373 (2001) – should be replaced by 'a single resolution, not adopted under Chapter VII', and thus not mandatory to implement (para. 2).

[285] Ibid. para. 38.

[286] On the competence issue, see: Kim Lane Scheppele, 'International standardization of national security law' (2010) 4 *Journal of National Security Law and Policy* 437; and

limited to a particular situation and should be interpreted as being of
a preliminary rather than a final character'.[287] But modifying the list after
9/11 to target all those 'associated with' terrorism around the world made
it 'no longer limited in time or space' and imbued it with a 'judicial or
quasi-judicial character'.[288] 'Such powers', according to the former
Special Rapporteur, were quite simply, 'difficult to reconcile with the
legal order of the Charter' – posited here as the 'constituent
instrument . . . [that] provides the foundation for and limit to action by
the Security Council'.[289]

The Ombudsperson had only just started operating two months before
this report was submitted. But in a stinging rebuke to the Security
Council, delivered at a time when the mechanism was attracting wide
praise for the move towards greater fairness that it signalled, the Special
Rapporteur concluded that 'the revised procedures for de-listing do not
meet the standards required to ensure a fair and public hearing by
a competent, independent and impartial tribunal established by law'.[290]
The key problem, discussed in more detail later in this chapter at Section
3.6.1, was that the Ombudsperson has no power to take decisions.
Whether someone stays on or is removed from the list is still decided
via secret political machinations of the Security Council, as it always has
been since the list's inception. For the former Special Rapporteur, solutions to the list accountability problem could come about in one of four
ways. Either (1) reform UN listing and delisting practices properly to
bring them into line with human rights norms; (2) encourage acts of 'civil
disobedience' by domestic judiciaries and support their 'indirect review'
of UN listing decisions to make the list human-rights compliant;[291]
(3) dismantle the listing regime altogether for being *ultra vires* the UN
Charter; or (4) set up a World Court of Human Rights with jurisdiction
over decisions of the UN Security Council.[292]

Cohen, *Globalization*. For present purposes, Cohen's text is best read alongside
Koskenniemi's excellent, though scathing, review of her book: Martti Koskenniemi,
'Globalization and sovereignty: rethinking legality, legitimacy and constitutionalism'
(2013) 11(3) *International Journal of Constitutional Law* 818.

[287] UN Doc. A/65/258, para. 52.

[288] Ibid.

[289] Ibid. paras. 52, 35.

[290] Ibid. para. 56.

[291] Ibid. para. 58. On judicial 'civil disobedience' in this context, see: Turkuler Isiksel,
'Fundamental rights in the EU after *Kadi* and *Al Barakaat*' (2010) 16(5) *European Law
Journal* 551; and Tzanakopoulos, *Disobeying the Security Council*.

[292] UN Doc. A/65/258, paras. 17, 80.

The reaction to such systemic critique by Council officials and other experts in the listing assemblage ranged from outright hostility to silence. The report was thoroughly dismissed by the P5 states when presented to the General Assembly. Both the USA and UK made it abundantly clear that they disagreed with the *ultra vires* argument and the idea that their Chapter VII powers could be limited in scope.[293] Russia 'categorically rejected the attempt by the Special Rapporteur to exceed his mandate and consider the legality of the Security Council as part of his functions', dismissing the report as 'superficial'.[294] Others, such as the Monitoring Team, did not even acknowledge the report at all.

But any hopes that such critiques of the list might quietly fade away were misplaced. Emmerson took over as Special Rapporteur in August 2011 and his second report to the Assembly specifically assessed whether the Ombudsperson was compatible with international human rights norms. In Chapter 1 I discussed some of the challenges and opportunities of doing this research as someone working professionally as a lawyer on this issue. One advantage is that it has opened up research sites and possibilities that otherwise would have been inaccessible.[295] Having represented people in delisting proceedings before the Ombudsperson, I was invited to London in 2011 to meet with the former UN Special Rapporteur and discuss the representation of listed persons with him. Thereafter, I was asked to convene a group of lawyers working on this issue to prepare a detailed submission, sharing our experiences of using the Ombudsperson delisting procedure. This document was then used to help the former Special Rapporteur draft his 2012 report to the General Assembly.

We were six lawyers from three countries (UK, the Netherlands and Canada) representing fifteen individuals between us who either had been, or still were, on the ISIL and Al Qaida list. Although most of us had clients who had been delisted following applications to the Ombudsperson, we all still had 'serious and shared misgivings' about the fairness of the process.[296] In almost all other analyses the experiences

---

[293] UN Doc. A/C.3/65/SR.30, United Nations General Assembly, Third Committee, Summary Record of the 30th Meeting (8 December 2010), pp. 6–7.

[294] Ibid. p. 7.

[295] As a result of helping prepare this report the Special Rapporteur facilitated introductions with a number of listing officials in New York. Some of the key interviews relied in this book come out of this collaboration.

[296] *Letter to Ben Emmerson QC, UN Special Rapporteur on Counterterrorism and Human Rights* (13 August 2012), Copy on file with author.

of lawyers who have gone through the Ombudsperson delisting procedure are notably absent. Our submission was the first attempt to fill that
gap and intervene as lawyers in the broader list accountability debate. We
highlighted a number of core deficiencies of the Ombudsperson mechanism – including the reliance on secret evidence and material allegedly
gained from torture; the lack of provision for legal aid; the punitive (after)
effects of listing; the Ombudsperson's lack of decision-making powers;
the failure to provide listed people with underlying material; and the
many other ways the delisting process operates outside of basic due
process principles and the rule of law. We argued that addressing these
concerns was a precondition for any meaningful reform of the list and
that failing to do so would only 'exacerbate the crisis of legitimacy that is
continuing to develop with respect to the UN Security Council's power to
target terrorism suspects in this way'.[297]

The Special Rapporteur's report was issued in September 2012, taking
on board many of the concerns that we had raised. The report welcomed
the 'significant due process improvements' that the Ombudsperson
mechanism has brought.[298] But its conclusions ran against the grain of
prevailing opinion by concluding that the listing regime 'continues to fall
short of international minimum standards of due process'.[299] The key
problem, according to the former Special Rapporteur, was the
Ombudsperson's lack of decision-making powers. This meant that delisting decisions were still taken by the Sanctions Committee – effectively
making the Security Council a judge in its own cause and the Office of the
Ombudsperson insufficiently independent.[300] The Ombudsperson (at
that time, Kimberly Prost) had successfully 'demonstrated independence
of mind' and made the mechanism as fair as possible 'within the limits of
her mandate'.[301] But 'the structural flaws' of the listing regime 'remain
the same' despite this 'appearance of independence'.[302] The report
argued that the recommendations of the Ombudsperson 'should be
accepted as final by the Committee and . . . the decision-making powers
of the Committee and the Council should be removed'.[303] The Office of
the Ombudsperson should then be renamed the Office of the

---

[297] Ibid.
[298] UN Doc. A/67/396, para. 33.
[299] Ibid. para. 59.
[300] Ibid. paras. 31, 35.
[301] Ibid. para. 33.
[302] Ibid. para. 34.
[303] Ibid. para. 35.

Independent Designations Adjudicator and explicitly afforded 'jurisdiction to review and overturn a designation by the Committee'.[304] In this way, the Ombudsperson would effectively be transformed into a human-rights compliant institution of international judicial review, akin to Scheinin's proposed World Court of Human Rights, with the express power to overturn Chapter VII decisions of the Security Council.[305]

I attended the launch of this report at the UN General Assembly in New York in November 2012.[306] After the former Special Rapporteur introduced the report and outlined its key findings, the floor was opened for states to provide comments. The USA and UK, essentially reading from the same script, stressed the unique nature of the listing regime and the significant procedural improvements they have made. Both cited the Ombudsperson's own assessment of her delisting procedure enshrining 'fundamental principles of fairness' as evidence to show that the accountability flaws of the list were now effectively resolved. As such, both states expressed considerable 'concern' that someone – in this case, the Special Rapporteur – could even still suggest that the list violates fundamental rights. 'In light of the Security Council's significant changes to the regime' said the USA, 'we are *somewhat concerned* by your statement that the Al-Qaida sanctions regime continues to fall short of international minimum standards of due process' (emphasis added). Similarly, the UK said, '*we were concerned at your assertion*, Mr Emmerson, that the Al-Qaida sanctions regime falls short of international minimum standards of due process' (emphasis added). The report, in other words, succeeded in breaking the emerging consensus that the due process problems of the list were a thing of the past. It successfully reclaimed the Office of the Ombudsperson as a site of political contestation, clash of divergent regimes (human rights versus collective security) and source of jurisdictional conflict.

The former Special Rapporteur's approach to this problem was animated by the idea of a legally Compliant List. Seen through this lens, the problem with the ISIL and Al-Qaida listing process:

---

[304] Ibid.
[305] See UN Doc. A/65/258, and Martin Scheinin, 'Towards a world court of human rights', *Agenda for Human Rights: Swiss Initiative to Commemorate the 60th Anniversary of the UDHR* (June 2009) Available at: bit.ly/1N7HvzO.
[306] See UN Doc. A/C.3/67/SR.26A, United Nations General Assembly, Third Committee, Summary Record of the 26th Meeting (10 January 2013). All quotes cited from this meeting are taken from the transcript of my recording of the event, which is more detailed than the meeting record listed above (copy on file with author).

is that it leaves us in a murky process where diplomacy is allowed to take the place of law . . . [Yet] at the end of the day there are parts of the world where constitutional law is applied in a manner that requires interferences with fundamental rights to be regulated by law . . . and by the bedrock of due process and not shifted to the sandy foundations of diplomatic negotiation.[307]

Notice that law is not infringing on diplomacy here. The problem is rather about diplomacy being 'allowed to take the place of law'. And the locus of analysis is the interference with human rights that listing produces, not the unique prerogatives of UN Security Council politics. This approach clearly resonates with the approach adopted by the EU courts – the ECtHR decision in *Al-Dulimi and Montana Management Inc. v. Switzerland*, for example, referred to the report's finding that the Ombudsperson was incompatible with human rights and stated that 'the Court unreservedly agrees with that conclusion of the UN Special Rapporteur'.[308] But when regimes clash, divergent versions of the list are enacted and put into relation. And because there is no 'meta-regime, directive or rule' for 'determining the frame' and deciding who ought to decide, a jurisdictional battle ensues with different actors and institutions each trying to claim *their* list as the authoritative one and embed *their* structural bias as the norm against which all listing problems are assessed.[309]

This process of 'regime collision' can be most clearly observed in the Watson Institute's reaction to the former Special Rapporteur's report.[310] In December 2012 it released *Due Process and Targeted Sanctions: An Update of the 'Watson Report'*, primarily to reframe debates about the list associated with the renewal of the Ombudsperson's mandate. But the report also sought to counter the former Special Rapporteur's claim that the Ombudsperson was unlawful, refocus the narrative of the list in light of this discursive disturbance, and bring the accountability problem back within the Institute's particular realm of expertise. After noting the former Special Rapporteur's conclusions, the first move of these scholar-experts was jurisdictional in nature:

---

[307] Ibid.

[308] *Al Dulimi*, para. 119.

[309] Koskenniemi, *The Politics*, p. 336.

[310] Koskenniemi uses the 'hegemonic contestation' to describe those situations in regime conflicts where 'what is at stake is not only what the general view is, but *who is entitled to determine it*'. See: Koskenniemi, 'Hegemonic regimes', 312. On regime collision, see: Fischer-Lescano and Teubner, 'Regime-collisions'.

> It is useful to recall the context within which this unique Ombudsperson
> mechanism functions. Targeted sanctions are political measures imposed
> by a political body, the United Nations Security Council ... Decisions to
> list individuals or entities are not legal determinations *per se*, but rather
> political findings of association with Al-Qaida.[311]

Having reasserted the appropriate political lens through which this problem
ought to be assessed, these scholar-experts could then disregard the former
Special Rapporteur's approach and reassess the Ombudsperson mechanism
in a more favourable light. Their second move thus sought to reclaim the
discursive middle-ground, differentiate their reasonable approach from the
unreasonable demands made by the former Special Rapporteur and embed
their particular list bias as normal. 'According formal judicial review by
making the Ombudsperson's decision final might be optimal from the
perspective of the courts' but, according to the Watson Institute scholars, it
'is not an even-handed approach that respects the Council's unique
prerogatives'.[312] Here the Compliant List is denigrated for imposing an
'excessively narrow and rigid institutional framework of judicial review'
and 'mechanically' transplanting national due process standards onto
a more complex, postnational political environment.[313] What the former
Special Rapporteur failed to realise, according to these scholar-experts, is that
this special domain requires 'a more flexible interpretation' to be adopted.[314]
One that recognises that 'the provision of due process has to be balanced with
the Council's responsibility to maintain international peace and security' and
that standards of procedural fairness must 'be tailored to the unique features
of the United Nations system and Security Council prerogatives', even if they
are supposed to be grounded in respect for fundamental rights.[315]

   Having differentiated flexible 'due process-lite' from its more inflexible
legalistic version and resituated the protection of fundamental rights
onto a sliding scale, the Watson Institute scholars then concluded that
'the Office of the Ombudsperson should generally be regarded as
a success'.[316] Relying on the Ombudsperson's self-assessment of their
own performance, as well as the views of 'some experts',[317] such as the

---

[311] 2012 Watson Report.
[312] Ibid. 37.
[313] Ibid.
[314] Ibid. 24.
[315] Ibid. 37.
[316] Ibid. 38.
[317] Ibid. 23: 'The Ombudsperson and some experts argue, however, that Ombudsperson's
[sic] current mandate adequately safeguards the rights of listed persons to a fair,
independent and effective process.'

Monitoring Team, the Institute argued that the Ombudsperson 'has addressed critical due process concerns', created 'a presumption of de facto authority' and provides what they call 'in essence, *de facto* judicial review'.[318] Finally, after reframing the list accountability problem, these scholars then sought to obscure the politics of this redefinition in a technical idiom and reaffirm their framework as something preordained. 'Rather than a problem to be solved', they argue, 'a more appropriate perspective' on this regime clash between security and rights 'may be that these are challenges to be managed'.[319] Bringing in the discourse of regime coordination alters the whole point of the list reform exercise. In this way, procedural reform of the list is recast as important, not because it can address egregious unfairness, but because it helps realise 'the ultimate objective' – 'strengthening the credibility of the Security Council and its instruments of targeted sanctions'.[320]

When the first Watson Report was published in 2006, the differences between these scholar-experts and the jurists calling for human rights reform seemed relatively slight. Both appeared to be on the same 'progressive' side, pushing for procedural reforms to provide targeted individuals with redress. But by 2012 the divergences between these groups were starkly drawn. This became evident to me in an interview with one of the more active scholar-experts in this field, when they critiqued the former Special Rapporteur's report on the Ombudsperson as an example of 'legal fundamentalism':

> I found [Emmerson's report] really offensive and intemperate . . . *Having played a role in the construction of the mechanism* we thought it wasn't adequately respected, recognised and researched – both by Emmerson and by the ECJ [in the 2013 *Kadi* decision]. That's what I call legal fundamentalism . . . It's easy for an International Law and Individual Human Rights person. It's clear. She does not have effective remedy. So, you either have it or you don't. Well that's a fundamentalist kind of view. It's not a matter of saying, for all intents and purposes, she *does* have effective remedy. There's been a lot of compromise and an underappreciation of how far member states, particularly the US, have come on this issue.[321]

The main problem with 'legal fundamentalism' and the Compliant List it enacts is that it threatens to undermine the Humanitarian List that these

---

[318] Ibid. 36, 37.
[319] Ibid. 40.
[320] Ibid.
[321] Interview G (emphasis added).

scholar-experts have painstakingly built since the end of the Cold War. And because of the incessant focus on individual rights, it purportedly risks taking us back to an era of civilian suffering brought about through comprehensive sanctions:

> [The Special Rapporteur's report] ... is too narrowly defined on just one issue and loses sight of ... the larger issues. What are the implications of insisting on individual rights over all other ... rights or larger communities? ... That's what worries me the most about Emmerson's report and the ECJ decision. That it's going to lead us ... back to the bad old days where, quite frankly, ... it is just easier, if its Iran, to close it out ... So, I say step back. If you're really interested in human rights, think about *all of humanity*, not just the individuals that happen to end up in the crosshairs of [this list].[322]

For these academics – who first became engaged with targeted sanctions in the 1990s motivated by humanitarian sentiments – the issue had come full circle. The former Special Rapporteur's report and 2013 *Kadi* decision brought their Humanitarian List back into view as just one contingent choice amongst many. It undermined the authority of the unique institutional experiment they helped to create. According to Larissa van den Herik: 'The high standards of judicial review that the ECJ has developed and imposed in Kadi can have unintentional and paradoxal [sic] consequences ... [including] a retreat to less targeted and more blunt sanctions.'[323] Other scholar-experts put the impact of the Compliant List enacted through these measures in similarly hyperbolic terms:

GS: So the humanitarian logic comes into play again in light of the position that Emmerson insists on. And now the danger is that we revert to comprehensive sanctions?

INTERVIEWEE: Or broader non-discriminating measures ... I've heard people speculating that in light of this, yes exactly. That in fact, okay, now we'll just go to sectoral. I mean we can just say, that sector is blocked. I mean if we're going to lose all those cases anyway. But we're not going to lose cases against the sector because there's no basis for litigation. So, the logic is that we could easily revert back to broader [measures]. *And that's ... why we've been advocating this* ... humanitarian concern that may actually be now ... tak[ing] us back to the original *Civilian Pain-Political Gain* question.[324]

---

[322] Ibid. (original emphasis).
[323] van den Herik, 'Peripheral hegemony', 446.
[324] Interview G (original emphasis). Statements about the spectre of civilian suffering and return to comprehensive sanctions have been made by various Watson Institute scholars in a range of different fora since the former Special Rapporteur's report and the 2013

When Koskenniemi suggested that the 'police are ransacking the temple', he held out the hope that things could be made otherwise. If the General Assembly was 'determinate enough', he argued, it might once more 'recover its role as the normative Temple . . . and provide the counter-weight to the [Security] Council'.[325] This section has traced the efforts of the UN Special Rapporteur on Counterterrorism to reaffirm the Assembly's power against the Police in this domain, by enacting a global security list that complies with international human rights norms. That is, a list dramatically at odds with the one the Security Council is building and divergent from the other lists examined thus far in this chapter. I have analysed these efforts to help show how the list works as a 'multiple object' and to reframe the Office of the Ombudsperson as a site of political contestation where different regimes, forms of expertise and versions of the list clash and seek to become embedded as authoritative. And I have examined my own involvement in processes of list redefinition and reform through the Special Rapporteur with other lawyers engaged in Ombudsperson delisting pro-cedures. In sum, the Special Rapporteurs are important conduits of critique that have helped to expand the realm of the possible in this context. They have been critical agents both in enabling the Office of the Ombudsperson to first emerge and then in redefining it as a rights-violating, illegitimate experiment.

3.5   The Credible List: the Security Council P5 Making the Global Exception Durable

The Security Council P5 are usually seen as the legal masterminds and architects of the Law of the List. With their unique veto powers, ability to determine threats to international peace and security and create binding Chapter VII resolutions with worldwide effect, the P5 are the most powerful of global actors. The radical transformation of collective secur-ity since 9/11 has turned the Security Council into a novel form of 'global quasi-government'.[326] The UN1267 Sanctions Committee – a subsidiary organ composed of P5 diplomats exercising delegated powers from the Security Council – has been described as exemplifying 'global hegemonic

---

Kadi decision – including by Sue Eckert, 'Smarter EU sanctions?', Workshop (University College London, 8 November 2013) and Larissa van den Herik, 'Targeted Sanctions Workshop' (University of Amsterdam, 24 February 2014).

[325] Koskenniemi, 'Globalization and sovereignty', 347.

[326] Krisch, 'The rise and fall of collective security', 879.

international law' in action, with listing procedures specifically designed to incapacitate individual suspects and 'inure to the benefit of the powerful'.[327]

Such criticisms give rise to important questions: why would such a powerful global body need to respond to critique by the courts and try to counter claims that it has overstepped its powers? Why would the Security Council build preemptive mechanisms that violate rights at the national and regional levels and disregard a global population of potentially risky subjects from legal protections on the one hand, yet set a dangerous international precedent by creating a new global governance review mechanism to offer listed individuals a modicum of redress on the other?[328] What is at stake in this apparent turn towards rights compliance and 'global administrative law' by this most powerful of international organisations?[329]

This section explores these problems by analysing how and why the Security Council P5 came to create the Office of the Ombudsperson. It does so by empirically analysing the Council's motivations and identifying what the list – and its accountability problems – means for them. What emerges is a rather different story than the one usually presented on this issue. Conventional accounts use the Ombudsperson to suggest that the Security Council is evolving into a more human-rights friendly international organisation, relying on a variety of norm diffusion models.[330] In these narratives, the Ombudsperson is put forward as

---

[327] José E. Alvarez, 'Hegemonic international law revisited' (2003) 97(4) *American Journal of International Law* 873. For Alvarez, 'the hegemon [i.e. the USA] can only do so much to alter the fundamental sources of international obligation on its own. But when acting with the Council, the hegemon can do almost anything, while still appearing to be acting consistently with the Charter's vague Principles and Purposes' (887). For a similar critique, see Kim Lane Scheppele, 'Empire of security and the security of empire' (2013) 27 *Temple International and Comparative Law Journal* 241.

[328] On the notion of disregard, see: Richard B. Stewart, 'Remedying disregard in global regulatory governance: accountability, participation and responsiveness' (2014) 108(2) *American Journal of International Law* 211. On the related idea of banishment, see: Giorgio Agamben, *Homo Sacer: Sovereign Power and Bare Life* (Stanford CA: Stanford University Press, 1998); Marieke de Goede, 'Blacklisting and the ban: contesting targeted sanctions in Europe' (2011) 42(6) *Security Dialogue* 499.

[329] On global administrative law, see note 10.

[330] See, for example: Rosemary Foot, 'The United Nations, counter terrorism and human rights: institutional adaptation and embedded ideas' (2007) 29(2) *Human Rights Quarterly* 489; Monika Heupel, 'With power comes responsibility: human rights protection in United Nations sanctions policy' (2013) 19(4) *European Journal of International Relations* 773; Adele J. Kirschner, 'Security Council Resolution 1904 (2009): A Significant Step in the Evolution of the Al-Qaida and Taliban Sanctions Regime?'

proof that the Council is institutionally learning – albeit slowly and in response to legal and political pressure – to take its human-rights obligations more seriously.

In this section I show how individuals and their fundamental rights have very little to do with how and why the Security Council has responded the way it has to this problem. I argue that accountability concerns are wholly peripheral to the P5's primary aim of ensuring state compliance with Chapter VII counterterrorism resolutions.[331] In my analysis, three issues have driven P5 engagement with this list accountability problem: credibility and state implementation, depoliticisation and ensuring longevity both of the ISIL and Al-Qaida list and the Council's counterterrorism powers more broadly. The Council, in other words, is playing the long game of strengthening its global authority over time. The Ombudsperson thus plays a crucially productive role in assembling the Law of the List. It helps to stave off critique, boost the Council's fledgling credibility vis-à-vis potentially disobedient Member States, and legitimise its novel assertions of authority in the counterterrorism domain. In other words, with the Credible List enacted by the P5, the primary beneficiaries of due process reforms are not targeted individuals who have been denied legal redress, but the Security Council itself.[332]

3.5.1   Containing Critique through Incremental Change

In the beginning, listed individuals were not informed that they were listed and there was no procedure available to petition for removal. It wasn't until 2005 that those targeted were notified in writing of the fact and the broad standard of 'associated with' was spelt out in any detail.[333] A requirement to submit a 'statement of case' – essentially, a cover sheet with the target's personal details, outlining, in generic, box-ticking terms, how they met the 'associated with' criteria – was also introduced to 'standardize listing requests' by designating states.[334] At that time, the

---

(2010) 70(3) *Zeitschrift für ausländisches öffentliches Recht und Völkerrecht* 585; Tünde Huber and Rodiles, 'An Ombudsperson in the United Nations Security Council and Biersteker, 'Targeted sanctions and individual human rights'.

[331] There are parallels here with some arguments made by the Monitoring Team, as discussed at 3.3.1 and 3.3.3 above.

[332] Cora True-Frost, 'The development of individual standing in international security' (2011) 32(4) *Cardoza Law Review* 1183.

[333] S/RES/1617 (2005), paras. 5, 2–3. Notification requirements were introduced in S/RES/1526 (2004), para. 18.

[334] Ibid. para. 4; US Embassy Cable 06USUNNEWYORK1078 (dated 26 May 2006), para. 6.

only way for individuals to be delisted was to petition their states of residence or nationality and have them take the matter up on their behalf in New York – that is, by relying on a confidential diplomatic process that was both opaque for the individuals concerned and ineffective in delivering any redress.[335]

Despite unduly optimistic claims by some academics that these initial procedural reforms strengthened the rights of targeted individuals,[336] they unsurprisingly failed to satisfy the courts. So, in 2006 the Council created a 'Focal Point' or administrative mailbox within the UN Secretariat to receive delisting requests directly from targeted individuals and groups, forward these requests to designating states and states of

---

[335] See, for example, the case of Abdirisiak Aden – one of the Somali Swedes discussed at note 131 above. The Swedish government sought delisting (on Aden's request) from the UN1267 Sanctions Committee but was initially unsuccessful – see: Per Cramer, 'Recent Swedish experiences of targeted UN sanctions: the erosion of trust in the Security Council' in Erika de Wet and Andre Nollkaemper (eds.), *Review of the Security Council by Member States* (Cambridge: Intersentia, 2003). See also the *Sayadi and Vinck* case (discussed in the Legal List section at 3.1 above) and *Youssef* v. *Secretary of State for Foreign and Commonwealth Affairs* [2016] UKSC 3 – which notes that 'from June 2009 until late 2012 the Secretary of State actively supported his removal from the Sanction Committee's Consolidated List, and attempted to persuade other members to agree, but without success' (para. 4).

[336] For Feinäugle, for example, 'the application of the "associated with" standard gives the Committee's decision-making process an impetus away from a political decision and towards a decision according to written legal standards'. It is an element providing 'legal clarity and certainty' that is 'reminiscent of domestic administrative law'. The Statement of Case is said to compel the designating state to submit 'a detailed collection of evidence that allows the Committee to assess the case objectively and to apply its "associated with" standard' – Clemens A. Feinäugle and Matthias Goldmann, 'The UN Security Council Al-Qaida and Taliban Sanctions Committee: emerging principles of international institutional law for the protection of individuals?' in Armin von Bogdandy, Rüdiger Wolfrum, Jochen von Bernstorff, Philipp Dann and Matthias Goldmann (eds.), *The Exercise of Public Authority by International Institutions* (New York: Springer, 2010), pp. 118, 129, 117. Such claims are disconnected from how the listing process works, and how the Council exercises its authority, in practice. The Sanctions Committee takes listing decisions using a no-objection procedure. There is no legal decision-making process per se that is defined by written standards. Furthermore, the targeting standard has been designed so expansively that it can readily encompass almost any link or potential form of association. Being 'associated with' someone 'associated with' Al-Qaida is now sufficient to justify being targeted – see S/RES/2083 (2012), para. 3. The 'associated with' criterion also contains an open-ended expansive clause of 'otherwise supporting'. In the 2014 Resolution against FTFs the Council made clear that 'otherwise supporting' included activities undertaken 'through information and communications technologies, such as the internet, social media, or any other means' – that is, incitement, support and potentially violent extremism on Facebook or Twitter. See: S/RES/2178 (2014), para. 7.

residence for their consideration and inform listed persons whether their requests were ultimately successful or not.[337] Leaked US Embassy cables reveal considerable debate amongst the P5 about how to best design and delimit this mechanism. The USA originally sought to have Member States create their own delisting procedures, thus outsourcing the administration of delisting to the national level. France opposed this move 'because many of the European States most concerned with "due process" wanted to shift the onus of decision-making from the national level to the sanctions committee in order to protect themselves'.[338] And it was out of these circumstances that the UN Focal Point was born as a compromise, ad hoc procedural solution.

For France, 'the Security Council [needed] to maintain control of decision-making, but not be at the "forefront" of the process', and here the Focal Point offered certain advantages.[339] It provided a '"visible" change to procedures' without actually changing existing decision-making processes, threatening substantive review of Council decisions or altering the status quo in any way.[340] 'The focal point proposal', as French diplomats explained in meetings with USUN officials, sent 'more of a "political message" than anything else'.[341] This procedure was widely discredited shortly after it was created and is not a particularly important reform in itself.[342] What *is* interesting for this chapter are the themes of *visibility* and *messaging* that emerge from the P5 debates whilst the mechanism was being constructed. Such concerns allow us to better understand the Security Council's motivations for creating procedural reforms in this area in the first place. They also help explain why the Office of the Ombudsperson was ultimately built the way it was – with all of its legal flaws and limitations.

The next round of incremental reforms came in 2008 when the Committee was required to create and post online a Narrative Summary

---

[337] S/RES/1730 (2006). The Focal Point was staffed by one person on a part-time basis only.

[338] US Embassy Cable 06USUNNEWYORK917 (dated 4 May 2006) para. 3. The key issue here was deniability. The key benefit of the Focal Point, according to the French, was that 'it removed states from a potentially "difficult position" of having to deny their own citizens de-listing requests'.

[339] US Embassy Cable 06USUNNEWYORK1078, para. 8.

[340] Ibid.

[341] Ibid.

[342] In the 2008 *Kadi* decision, for example, the ECJ dismissed the Focal Point mechanism as 'in essence diplomatic and intergovernmental' in nature – see: *Kadi and Al Barakaat*, para. 323. For a fascinating account of the intergovernmental politics of the Focal Point (in this case, between the USA and Italy), see: US Embassy Cable 07ROME2515.

of Reasons[343] for all new and existing list entries, and undertake a comprehensive review of the list over the following two years to ensure that it was as 'updated and accurate as possible'.[344] These reforms were introduced in response 'to public criticism that the Council's decisions to impose targeted sanctions are opaque'.[345] They were also aimed at convincing the EU courts to defer to the authority of the Security Council in this area because it was taking the need for 'fair and clear procedures' seriously.[346] The US government went to great lengths to curb criticism and manage the public perception of these reforms, in line with its overarching concerns about credibility and legitimacy. It pressured states that had previously voiced criticisms of the list and implored all fifteen Security Council Member States 'at the highest appropriate level' to:

> acknowledge positively and publicly the fact that we have followed through on our commitment to include new measures . . . to strengthen procedures to ensure fairness and transparency . . . We do not believe that statements emphasizing that the Council can and must do more will serve any other purpose than to cast further doubt on the Council's decisions . . . We ask that you refrain from statements focusing on the 1267 Committee's weaknesses and instead recognize the positive changes that will be implemented and encourage others to do the same.[347]

---

[343] I have already discussed the importance of Narrative Summaries at length in Chapter 2. Whilst these summaries purport to offer factual accounts of why listed persons are targeted and so address the right to be informed, they are also translation devices that transform speculative security inferences into more factually solid forms of evidence and can be highly misleading. Narrative Summaries also empower the Monitoring Team, relative to other actors in this space, because the team members are the listing experts who administer these quasi-authoritative statements of terrorist association.

[344] S/RES/1822 (2008), paras. 13, 25.

[345] US Embassy Cable 08USUNNEWYORK640 (dated 18 July 2008).

[346] On the latter point, see US Embassy Cable 08USUNNEWYORK640 and the debate between the USA and Costa Rica on the precise wording of S/RES/1822 (2008), para. 28, which 'Encourages the Committee *to continue* to ensure that fair and clear procedures exist for placing individuals and entities on the Consolidated List and for removing them' (emphasis added). Costa Rica objected because the wording suggested that fair procedures already existed with the Focal Point, when in its view they did not. For the USA amending this wording 'would have been tantamount to the Council agreeing that its own procedures for imposing targeted sanctions are not valid, and by extension the decisions to sanction those on the list were not valid. This would have provided further fodder for the criticism about the lack of "due process" in the Council's sanctions regimes, while taking the focus away from the significant improvements to the Committee's procedures.'

[347] US Embassy Cable 08STATE69684 (dated 27 June 2008). The critical states singled out for special attention in this cable were Liechtenstein, Sweden, Switzerland, Denmark, the Netherlands and Germany.

The comprehensive review was promoted by the Security Council as a way of showing that the list was preventative, not punitive, in nature and reflective of the current threat. Yet analysis of how this review was conducted shows just how inexacting it was, with very little substantive consideration by some states as to why individuals were listed or not. In one series of cables, the US government undertook a 'careful and detailed review and analysis of all available information' of a number of listings it had co-sponsored with Italy and 'determined that it currently lacks information sufficient to conclude' that those people should remain listed.[348] But Italy objected to delisting a number of these individuals simply stating, 'the GOI believes that these individuals have been and still are connected with terrorist activities'.[349] Although they arrived at differing conclusions, no further consideration appears to have been undertaken between these two designating states. No further questions were asked by the USA about the basis for this 'belief', even though in its own analysis there were no grounds for continuing listing. These cables also show Italy pushing for others to be delisted on the grounds that it was now 'actively cooperating with Italian intelligence authorities' – lending further support to the argument, discussed in Chapter 2, that UN listing is being used generatively to turn Muslim suspects into informants for security and intelligence services.[350]

After 9/11 Italy nominated around one hundred individuals for listing – 'more than any other country except the United States, UK and Russia'.[351] Yet in many cases, it did so 'at the behest' and 'on behalf of the United States' for 'purely political considerations', rather than out of concern that these individuals posed threats to international peace and security.[352] Evidently, Italy knew little about many of those it claimed were associated with Al-Qaida. So, when the comprehensive review asked nominating states to supply the Council with derogatory information to support listing decisions, the Italians understandably found themselves in trouble. Not only did the Italian government lack original supporting material capable of justifying its listing decisions, but it also lacked any 'recent information whatsoever' about many of the individuals

---

[348] US Embassy Cable 09STATE109494 (dated 22 October 2009).
[349] US Embassy Cable 09ROME1405 (dated 23 December 2009), para. 2. 'GOI' is the government of Italy.
[350] US Embassy Cable 09ROME1344 (dated 4 December 2009), para. 3.
[351] US Embassy Cable 09USUNNEWYORK474 (dated 8 May 2009), para. 6.
[352] US Embassy Cable 09ROME652, paras. 8, 2; US Embassy Cable 09ROME1404 (dated 23 December 2009), para. 3.

concerned.[353] In these circumstances, as its own lawyers plainly put it, 'it will indeed be very difficult for Italy to confirm that a listing remains appropriate'.[354] And so Italy reached out to the USA to ask for its help in providing details concerning those that the Italians had targeted. That is, Italy responded to the Security Council's request by effectively having the Council's most powerful state meet the reporting obligations on its behalf.

This review initiative was supposed to provide accountability to those listed and show that the Council was serious about fair and clear procedures. According to the Watson Institute, this was 'a serious, thorough and laborious process' of review.[355] Others, such as Rodiles, claimed the review 'was conducted thoroughly, evaluating all available information and *generating a lot of a pressure on those who had proposed the entry* or wished to maintain it to give reasons and discuss them at the Committee'.[356] Yet the picture emerging from my analysis of the US Embassy cables here is of a wholly political process fractured along strategic lines. One where states list people first without necessarily knowing why, to show political allegiance to their allies and curry favour, and only later seeking out the information they ought to have had in the first place for *post hoc* justification.

3.5.2   Forging Alignment and Stretching the International Peace and Security Envelope

The Security Council had hoped these incremental changes might be enough to satisfy the EU courts.[357] But the ECJ's 2008 decision in the

---

[353] US Embassy Cable 09USUNNEWYORK474, para. 4.

[354] Ibid. These comments were attributed to Stefano Mogini, then legal adviser of the Italian UN Mission, to USUN officials in confidence. In 2014 Mogini was appointed as a judge to the highest Italian court – the Suprema Corte di Cassazione. See bit.ly/1TzEBGh.

[355] 2009 Watson Report, p. 16.

[356] Alejandro Rodiles, 'Non-permanent members of the United Nations Security Council and the promotion of the international rule of law' (2013) 5(2) *Goettingen Journal of International Law* 333, 357 (emphasis added).

[357] See for example, US Embassy Cable 09LONDON452 (dated 20 February 2009) which notes (para. 2) that the UK's priorities as far as list reform is concerned:
     ... are to identify end-goals, pragmatically evaluate which goals are achievable and determine what approaches would avoid censure by the European Court of First Instance ... ie, will the changes from ... [Resolution] 1822 be sufficient to put off the courts once fully implemented ... Key to all their deliberations is how the European Court of Justice's decision in the Yassin Qadi case will continue to ripple through UK and EU asset-freezing regimes.

Kadi case, delivered less than three months after the adoption of Resolution 1822, definitively put such hopes to rest. In May 2008 Germany, Switzerland, the Netherlands, Denmark, Liechtenstein and Sweden came together to form the 'Group of Like-Minded States' and advocated for more far-reaching reforms to be adopted – including an external review panel of legal experts to provide recommendations to the Council on delisting requests.[358] But all P5 states were formally opposed to setting up a mechanism of this kind, primarily out of concern that it would undermine the Security Council's Chapter VII authority.[359]

Privately, the US government was lobbying extensively in European capitals and institutions to undermine the reform proposals of the Like-Minded States and convince officials that the changes introduced by Resolution 1822 would make the list sufficiently robust and legally compliant once fully implemented.[360] Although the UK had made it plain that it 'would not support the appointment of an advisory panel to opine on Council decisions',[361] it was privately studying the full range of reform options (including an independent panel) and remained confident that 'a solution [could] likely be worked out'.[362] The most important factor for the UK was 'the need to protect the credibility of the Security Council and not create a mechanism that would undermine its authority'.[363] As a former director from the UK Foreign and Commonwealth Office (FCO) who had been responsible for UN sanctions explained in interview, the prime impetus for Security Council reform from the UK perspective was neither accountability or due process but rather Member State implementation:

> We were getting cases where there were a growing number of . . . legal issues raised by individuals. And so, we thought again, as part of our wish to try to ensure the respectability of sanctions, that we really ought to allow *some* sort of appeal mechanism. So, it was introduced . . . and that

---

[358] The Like-Minded Group has since expanded to include Austria, Belgium, Costa Rica, Finland and Norway. For recent statement showing the group's approach to reform, see UN Doc. S/2014/286 (dated 21 April 2014). For a good analysis of the role played by the group in procedural improvements in this area, see: Rodiles, 'Non-permanent members'.

[359] See US Embassy Cable 08USUNNEWYORK421 (dated 12 May 2008), which recounts a meeting between the Group of Like-Minded States and the UN1267 Sanctions Committee to discuss their advisory panel proposal. Russia, France, the UK, USA and Italy all 'made clear that they did not support the idea of a panel' (para. 1).

[360] See, for example, US Embassy Cable 09BRUSSELS616 (dated 29 April 2009).

[361] US Embassy Cable 09LONDON452, para. 3.

[362] US Embassy Cable 08LONDON1690 (dated 24 June 2008) para. 3.

[363] Ibid. para. 2.

was the reason. *Let's allow some sort of appeal mechanism. And that would mean that countries would be more willing to implement the sanctions* – if they knew that there wasn't this collateral damage effect that might otherwise give them an excuse not to implement them.[364]

For the UK, enhancing list implementation was not merely about making sure there were no weak links in the chain. It was a means of embedding the Security Council's novel assertions of global authority and jurisdiction to govern terrorist threats after the end of the Cold War and events of 9/11:

> The Security Council, strictly speaking, can only deal with threats to international peace and security. Traditionally, those threats have been seen as state aggression. Come 2000, the mood was very much that the threats are different . . . On the one hand, we face new threats from state implosion, through internal rebellion. On the other, we face new threats from non-state entities that could be operating internationally. These were perceived as new issues which hitherto, the Security Council had not dealt with . . . That was when we got into the 'What is the definition of international peace and security' [issue]?[365]

For the P5 states this meant governing new transboundary threats and challenges productively in ways that could expand the scope of Security Council powers. Or, as the former FCO Director put it, when responding to new and emerging threats 'we were trying to *stretch the international peace and security envelope*'.[366] The best-known example of this 'stretching' was the R2P doctrine, which authorised preemptive action in response to international humanitarian crises and recognised the Council's right to intervene in internal conflicts.[367] But the transformation of the UN1267 list and rise of global security law were other key areas where the scope for Council intervention was dramatically expanded. After 9/11:

> Al-Qaida obviously was now seen as a transnational, international threat. It was something where we thought, well if the Security Council can deal with this, then let's try. I don't think anybody was sufficiently starry-eyed

---

[364] Interview with former UK Foreign and Commonwealth Office Director, London, April 2013 (Interview J) (emphasis added).

[365] Ibid.

[366] Ibid. (emphasis added).

[367] On R2P, see: Anne Orford, *International Authority and the Responsibility to Protect* (Cambridge: Cambridge University Press, 2011). For analysis of how R2P facilitated the Council's post-9/11 global counterterrorism campaign, see: Cohen, *Globalization*, p. 269.

to think that Security Council action on its own would solve the problem –
it was never going to do that. It was more . . . 'Can we get everyone to agree
that this is a problem'?[368]

Forging alignment between the Security Council and Member States that
global terrorism is a problem capable of being properly targeted in this
way is an important governance effect.[369] Recognising that the Council
could legitimately interfere with the lives of terrorist suspects directly and
indefinitely, wherever they were located in the world, was far-reaching in
itself.[370] Yet being able to demand that Middle-East and North-African
states take action against individuals in their territory – who may pose no
threat to them, but potentially pose a threat to the USA or UK – was
a groundbreaking legal development and novel exercise in global
governmentality.[371] What consensus on Al-Qaida (and later ISIL) *did*
'was essentially give . . . the Security Council the right to hold countries to
account' for what previously would have been considered internal issues
beyond the Council's control.[372] Or, as Cohen argues, it 'entail[ed]
a quasi-dictatorial expansion and use of Council powers without
accountability or apparent legal or institutional checks and balances' –
a global state of emergency.[373]

When the problems and reforms of the ISIL and Al-Qaida list are
reframed in this light, we can see why credibility concerns were considered so important and individual rights claims so peripheral for the P5
states. Reforming the list would enable this unique preemptive weapon to
be preserved and undermine the more far-reaching calls for change that
were being proposed. It would also bolster the authority of the Security

---

[368] Interview J (emphasis added).

[369] Here problematisation works as a translation device 'linking together the objectives of
the various parties to an assemblage, both those who aspire to govern conduct and those
whose conduct is to be conducted' – Murray Li, 'Practices of assemblage', 265. See also:
Nikolas Rose, *Powers of Freedom: Reframing Political Thought* (Cambridge: Cambridge
University Press, 1999) 48.

[370] S/RES/ 1390 (2002).

[371] Interview J. On global governmentality see: Wendy Larner and William Walters (eds.),
Global Governmentality: Governing International Spaces (London: Routledge, 2004);
Miguel de Larrinaga and Marc G. Doucet (eds.), *Security and Global Governmentality:
Globalization, Governance and the State* (London: Routledge, 2010); Yee-Kuang Heng
and Ken McDonagh, 'The other war on terror revealed: global governmentality and the
Financial Action Task Force's campaign against terrorist financing' (2008) 34(3) *Review
of International Studies* 553; Hans-Martin Jaeger, 'UN reform, biopolitics, and global
governmentality' (2010) 2(1) *International Theory* 50.

[372] Interview J.

[373] Cohen, *Globalization*, p. 19.

Council to govern individual terrorist suspects and recalcitrant Member States in unprecedented ways. Securing state compliance with Council resolutions required a Credible List. If that meant giving targeted individuals a degree of administrative standing to contest the Council's authority and providing 'the *appearance* of accountability', then so be it – that was undoubtedly a political price worth paying.[374] As the former FCO Director explained:

> The main motive for pushing [reforms] forward was . . . our sense that the legitimacy of the sanctions regime depended on us trying to address these problems . . . *We didn't want states to turn a blind eye to implementing these sanctions on the argument that actually, the courts were tearing into them, to put it bluntly.* Legitimacy was for us always absolutely key. We well understood . . . that sanctions have to be supported. It's pointless just waving a piece of paper around that the Security Council have endorsed, if some key countries are no longer supporting them. So, a key part of our argument was: if we have to adjust the procedures in order to be able to address some genuine concerns, then we must do that.[375]

The USA had originally been trenchantly opposed to reforming the list in any meaningful way. But after 2008, list reform was seized as an opportunity by the Obama Administration to show renewed commitment to multilateralism in global affairs, and the USA and UK took markedly similar approaches towards 'the hard and ongoing work of legitimation' necessary for strengthening Council authority in this area.[376] In my analysis, three key issues have driven US engagement with list accountability problems since this time: credibility and implementation, depoliticisation, and the need to ensure longevity both of the ISIL and Al-Qaida list and the Council's post-9/11 counterterrorism powers. In a confidential cable entitled '*1267: Saving the Al-Qaeda/Taliban Sanctions Regime*', the then US Ambassador to the UN (Susan Rice) outlined a package of 'bold' and 'attention-grabbing' reforms aimed at countering criticisms by various European states, human-rights NGOs and the EU courts that listing and delisting was an 'opaque, Kafkaesque process'.[377] Such critique had 'gravely undermined the regime's credibility and perceived fairness' and was facilitating the 'erosion of this tool's perceived legitimacy'.[378] Reform

---

[374] True-Frost, 'The development of individual standing', 1242 (emphasis added).
[375] Interview J (emphasis added).
[376] Murray Li, 'What is land?', 592.
[377] US Embassy Cable, 09USUNNEWYORK818, paras. 1, 9, 4. These reforms included making sanctions time-limited and giving the Monitoring Team input into listing and delisting decisions.
[378] Ibid. paras. 3, 13.

was thus primarily valued as a way for the USA to bolster the fledgling credibility of the list. And credibility was key because it allowed better implementation of the list by Member States and strengthened the Council's legitimacy to govern global terrorism in this novel way.

Second, these 'new fairness enhancements' were explicitly advanced as anti-politics measures capable of 'closing down debate about how and what to govern and the distributive effects' of current listing arrangements.[379] As Ambassador Rice plainly put it, adopting these reforms 'would go far toward restoring confidence in the regime and heading off more radical and dangerous proposals'.[380] For the US government, enhancing list credibility and depoliticising list accountability went hand-in-hand. Debates about fairness needed to be defused because they were 'undermining US interests in effective enforcement and expansion of the 1267 sanctions regime and other UN sanctions'.[381] The call by European states and NGOs to create an independent review panel was singled out as especially problematic and something that must be derailed at all costs. This panel promised a 'more thorough' review than anything the Security Council was prepared to provide, raised 'thorny issues regarding the Security Council's primacy under the UN Charter' and, according to the USA, would 'truly handicap the current sanctions regime' if it ever came to be implemented.[382]

The third aim of list accountability reform was longevity – that is, making whatever changes were necessary to placate the critics and ensure that this unique global governance tool could 'endure for yet another decade'.[383] The USA well appreciated the contradiction between a list formally justified as a targeted mechanism of temporary, preventative action against individual threats to international peace and security and a list stacked with 'low-hanging fruit' hastily targeted after 9/11 with little consideration as to why and little prospect of ever being removed.[384]

---

[379] Ibid. para. 5. The anti-politics quote comes from Murray Li, 'Practices of assemblage', 265. See also Ferguson, *The Anti-Politics Machine*.

[380] Ibid. para. 13.

[381] US Embassy Cable 06USUNNEWYORK1430 (dated 31 July 2006). Although this cable predates Rice's intervention it is revealing about the US rationale for reform and so is relevant in relation to the Ombudsperson.

[382] US Embassy Cable, 09USUNNEWYORK818; US Embassy Cable 06USUNNEWYORK1430, paras. 6, 2. The implication was that a review panel would be denied access to the classified material said to be underpinning listing decisions.

[383] US Embassy Cable 09USUNNEWYORK818, para. 15.

[384] On the problem of 'low-hanging fruit' and listing as a means of showing demonstrable progress in the war against terror, see discussion in the Living List section of this chapter at 3.3 and Suskind, *The Price of Loyalty*, p. 193.

With EU courts pushing towards substantively reviewing UN listing decisions in the *Kadi* litigation, the need to prune the list and show the preventative, rather than punitive, nature of the sanctions was becoming more acute. Yet there remained little incentive for designating states to delist, even if they knew little about why individuals were targeted in the first place.[385] Listing decisions were shielded under the secrecy of 'diplomatic discretion'[386] and the reputational risks associated with delisting encourage a practice of political inertia. As one sanctions official plainly put it: 'no government wants to be in the forefront of saying that we're about to lift sanctions on Al-Qaida. That goes without saying.'[387]

What calls for accountability and fairness provided, according to Ambassador Rice, was the opportunity to transform this reified list into 'a living process'.[388] One that 'is refreshed and renewed with additional listings, when appropriate, and delistings when individuals no longer merit being on' it.[389] But the living list idea was about more than dynamic governance and reflecting the current threat. It was about repositioning the Council to adapt, through this unique weapon and its novel targeting powers, towards whatever threat might come next. That is, renewing agreement on the problem of global terrorism in the present to allow the international peace and security envelope to be stretched through the list into the future. By 2009 it was already widely acknowledged that Al-Qaida no longer posed the threat it once did. But the Syrian civil war had not yet started and it would be five more years before the list would be repurposed as a key weapon in the global war against ISIL and 'foreign terrorist fighters'.[390] When the US government expresses concern about the longevity of this 'irreplaceable UN counter-terrorism tool', it is precisely such envelope-stretching transformations of collective security that are at stake.[391] So when countering claims that list improvement meant 'a failure to designate terrorists', Rice was adamant that such

---

[385] On this reluctance see: US Embassy Cable 09ROME652, para. 3. Italy acknowledged that it used the list to target many people 'about which they knew little' but still stated that 'Italy is not enthusiastic about delisting people from the 1267 list'.

[386] US Embassy Cable 08ROME711 (dated 4 June 2008). This cable provides an illuminating account of how states use diplomatic cover and affairs of state to foster secrecy in their security governance arrangements.

[387] Interview J.

[388] USUN, 'Remarks by Ambassador Susan E. Rice'.

[389] Ibid.

[390] S/RES/2178 (2014). This repurposing of the list is discussed in more detail at the conclusion of this book (Chapter 5).

[391] US Embassy Cable 09USUNNEWYORK818, para. 3.

criticism missed the key point of reform: '*The preservation of the tool, and the global consensus that it represents*', she argued, was '*far more important* than the designation of a handful of marginal figures'.[392]

These reform proposals discussed by Rice formed the basis for a draft Security Council Resolution presented to the other P5 states for consideration in early December 2009. Significantly, the revised draft incorporated an idea originally proposed by Denmark for an Ombudsperson post to be created within the Secretariat to receive and review delisting requests by those targeted. To assuage the concerns of Russia and China that these reforms would undermine the authority of the Council, the USA made it abundantly clear that no substantive review would take place. Instead, this mechanism would 'only have a coordinating role in the gathering of information'.[393] The prerogative to list and delist would remain vested in the Council and require P5 consensus, as had been the case since the inception of the listing regime. Nothing, in this sense, would change. Resolution 1904 (2009) was unanimously adopted by the Security Council shortly thereafter on 17 December 2009, amid much fanfare about 'fair and clear procedures'. And the Office of the Ombudsperson was finally born.

3.5.3   Credibility and the Sedimentation of Global Emergency Governance

Initially the Security Council sought to list terrorist suspects indefinitely without review and jealously guarded its Chapter VII powers from potential encroachment. The initial P5 attitude towards list accountability reform could best be described as one of disdain. Yet incremental changes were eventually introduced in an effort to placate criticisms by the liberal Like-Minded states, EU courts and human-rights NGOs. When the Office of the Ombudsperson was instituted in 2009, it was widely celebrated as a victory for fairness and respect for human rights by powerful international organisations. These changes were not perfect, but most agreed they were an improvement and an important step in the progressive movement towards 'a global rule of (administrative) law'.[394]

My analysis of P5 motivations complicates this human-rights friendly narrative. Drawing from secret embassy cables and interviews with

---

[392]   Ibid. para. 15 (emphasis added).

[393]   US Embassy Cable 09LONDON2678 (dated 2 December 2009), para. 13.

[394]   David Dyzenhaus, 'The rule of (administrative) law in international law' (2005) 68(3/4) *Law and Contemporary Problems* 127, 165.

former sanctions officials, I have shown that rights and accountability concerns have little to do with these changes, so far as the Council is concerned. The practice of the P5 states is animated by a very different kind of list. A list credible enough to be adhered to by states and able to ground their global authority through time. One that draws from the discourse of fairness in providing an 'appearance of accountability', but without offering substantive protections or altering the existing distributions of institutional power in any meaningful way.[395] In my account, list accountability reform has been embraced by the P5 for enhancing credibility and undermining critique, both of which boost state implementation. This helps forge the alignments the Law of the List needs to survive in the face of legal and political tension. Longevity of the list ultimately serves to embed the Council's jurisdictional claim to govern global terrorism in this way and allows the international peace and security envelope to be stretched again in novel ways later down the line.

As Kanishka Jayasuriya observes, the international state of emergency enacted through global security law is not so much concerned with securing 'the untrammelled exercise of sovereign power'.[396] It is the 'creation and entrenchment of new forms of administrative power and jurisdiction ... alongside, and within, existing constitutional practices' that is important.[397] My analysis of P5 procedural reform supports this account of global exceptional politics. One where reform is seized productively as an opportunity to foreclose debate and deflect critique from where it might otherwise matter most. The Office of the Ombudsperson might instinctively appeal to GAL enthusiasts because of the ways targeted individuals are given an opportunity to engage in an administrative 'dialogue' and be heard by a new global review body. But the GAL focus on transparency, participation and reasoned decision-making 'occludes awareness of the political significance of the processes under review' in this exceptional area and how procedural improvements can also work to 'obfuscate, rather than deliver rights protections for individuals at the international level'.[398]

---

[395] True-Frost, 'The development of individual standing', 1242.
[396] Kanishka Jayasuriya, 'Struggle over Legality in the midnight hour: governing the international state of emergency' in Victor Ramraj (ed.), *Emergencies and the Limits of Legality* (Cambridge: Cambridge University Press, 2008), p. 367.
[397] Ibid. pp. 367, 371.
[398] Susan Marks, 'Naming global administrative law' (2005) 37 *NYU Journal of International Law and Politics* 995, 997; True-Frost, 'The development of individual standing', 1193–4.

3.6   The Ombudsperson, Expertise and Assemblage

So far, this chapter has examined how different actors have responded to the accountability problems caused by the Security Council's post-9/11 programme of preemptive security listing. By providing a detailed praxiographic account, I have shown how divergent listing practices enact different versions of the list that prefigure conflicting aims and concerns.[399] The reform efforts of humanitarian scholars, P5 states, the courts, the Monitoring Team and UN Special Rapporteurs are animated by very different conceptions of what the list is, what list accountability problems are and how they should be addressed. In other words, the list is a 'multiple object' produced through overlapping and potentially contradictory epistemic practices that operate in conjunction but do not necessarily align.[400] However, multiplicity in global governance does not equal fragmentation. Heterogeneity is inevitably 'smoothed away',[401] reduced to organisational 'influence' or subsumed into grand narratives of international legal progress. Things 'hang together', as Mol observes, but the key 'question to be asked ... is how is this achieved?'[402] How are the different versions of the list assembled and held together, and the tensions and conflicts between the different actors in the assemblage managed, in practice?

To address this problem this final section of the chapter hones in on the Ombudsperson as a unique figure of global legal expertise. Most accounts posit the Office of the Ombudsperson as the institutional end-result of a prolonged list-accountability debate and focus on whether this review mechanism brings the Law of the List within the remit of international human rights law or not. I take a different approach to this problem and, instead, empirically examine the novel delisting practices the Ombudsperson has crafted to meet the 'fair process challenge', focusing on its decision-making processes, 'dialogue' meetings and unique evidential standards.[403] I do so by drawing primarily on

---

[399] Mol, *The Body Multiple*. Praxiography is the term that Mol uses to describe the ethnographic study of practices.

[400] Bueger, 'Making things known', 2: – defining 'epistemic practice' as 'a particular kind of practice that aims at constructing a distinct epistemic object and manipulating it'.

[401] John Law, *After Method: Mess in Social Science Research* (London: Routledge, 2004), p. 58.

[402] Mol, *The Body Multiple*, p. 55.

[403] Kimberly Prost, 'Fair process and the Security Council: a case for the office of the Ombudsperson' in Ana Maria Salinas de Frias, Katja Samuel and Nigel White (eds.), *Counter-Terrorism: International Law and Practice* (Oxford: Oxford University Press, 2012), p. 413.

interviews conducted with the first Ombudsperson (Kimberly Prost, see Figure 3.3) between 2012 and 2019 and critically reflecting on my experiences as a legal practitioner representing individuals in delisting proceedings in Tunisia before both Ms Prost (from 2011 to 2015) and Mr Kipfer Fasciati (in 2019).

My main argument is that the Office of the Ombudsperson is a crucially important mechanism that helps to contain multiplicity, absorb conflict between different actors and hold the disparate strands of the listing assemblage together. It is an institutional 'boundary object' that helps align different versions of the list that might otherwise generate legal fragmentation and political conflict.[404] Boundary objects, according to Star and Greisemer, are 'objects which inhabit several intersecting social worlds ... and satisfy the informational requirements of each of them'. They are 'plastic enough to adapt to local needs and the constraints of the several parties employing them, yet robust enough to maintain a common identity across sites'.[405] Boundary objects, in other words, are critically important translation devices in complex institutional ecologies. Analysing the Ombudsperson as a boundary object helps draws attention to the ways it cultivates and maintains coherence of the listing assemblage. The particular expertise of the Ombudsperson lies in its recombination of legal categories and practices into novel quasi-juridical forms tailored towards embedding preemptive security logics and sustaining the list in the face of political and legal critique. In my account, the Ombudsperson is a unique figure of expertise. The governance techniques and knowledge practices it has crafted to undertake review in this special environment perform crucially important list assemblage work and help make the exceptional governance of the ISIL and Al-Qaida list durable.

3.6.1   De Novo Decision-Making and Fair Adjudication

One of the key criticisms of the Ombudsperson mechanism by lawyers and the courts is that it remains procedurally weak and undertakes

---

[404] According to Star and Griesemer, 'the creation and management of boundary objects is a key process in developing and maintaining coherence across intersecting social worlds', or what they term 'institutional ecologies': Star and Griesemer, 'Institutional ecology', 393.

[405] Star and Griesemer, 'Institutional ecology', 393. See also: Susan Leigh Star, 'This is not a boundary object: reflections on the origin of a concept' (2010) 35(5) *Science, Technology and Human Values* 601.

Figure 3.3   Ms. Kimberly Prost, the UN1267 Ombudsperson from 2010 to 2015, in front of the UN headquarters in New York, September 2014. © Thomas Fricke. Reprinted with permission.

a review that is insufficiently independent to satisfy international human rights norms. The Ombudsperson can recommend whether to retain or remove a listing, but the ultimate decision still rests with the Security Council – the same body that took the listing decision in the first place. Whilst the Ombudsperson concedes that it is not the ultimate decision-maker, it does not believe this makes the Security Council a judge in its own cause. Instead, the Ombudsperson says that the decision taken by the Committee to put someone on the list and the decision taken to remove someone from the list are 'completely separate', and that the Ombudsperson only assists the Council in this latter decision by making a recommendation to the Sanctions Committee.[406] The Ombudsperson does not 'look back' or 'presume to know what was before the Committee

---

[406] Interview with the former UN 1267 Ombudsperson, Kimberly Prost. New York, November 2012 (Interview K). Although Ms Prost has been out of post since 2015 (see note 5), I still refer to her as the Ombudsperson throughout this chapter.

at the time of listing' – that is, it does not review the original listing decision as doing so, 'would be impossible and ... would not work in this context unless you have all the information the agency had that made that decision'.[407] So, whilst most literature frames the Ombudsperson as a novel review mechanism, it is important to note that the Ombudsperson does not actually review the original decision to list. Instead, its analysis and decision are solely focused on the present situation and whether 'the continued listing of the individual or entity today is justified based on all of the information now available'.[408] The Council takes 'a fresh decision on today, should this listing be maintained? And I'm feeding into that with ... considerable power'.[409]

According to the Ombudsperson, this exclusive focus on the present situation is a procedural strength rather than a weakness. It makes its unique brand of decision-making better for listed persons than conventional judicial review because it allows the Ombudsperson to 'present new information and explanations' and supposedly gives targeted persons reassurance that 'there is no issue of deference to the original decision maker' taking place.[410] For the Ombudsperson, it would be a mistake to think that conventional judicial review could possibly work in the 'very unique context' of the Security Council:

> I know [the UN Special Rapporteur's] calls for this independent judicial review process. [But] the first question I have is, *what judicial review?* What is a fair process in this particular context? Because what judicial review is in the United States ... is very, very different from what judicial review is in the European Union and it's very different from what it might be in the United Kingdom. So, my question is, in this international context, what judicial review? ... I think there is a more fundamental question. It's not so much this whole idea of there must be judicial review for it to be fair. My question is, what makes it fair in this very context? And I'm not so sure judicial review is the answer.[411]

This practice of not looking back and only focusing on the present has aided the process of individuals being removed from the list and so it underpins the mechanism's broader claims to success. As noted at the

---

[407] Ibid.
[408] Ibid.
[409] Ibid.
[410] Kimberly Prost and Elizabeth Wilmshurst, *UN Sanctions, Human Rights and the Ombudsperson*, Chatham House International Law Summary (London: Chatham House, 2013). Available at: bit.ly/25dDmrX.
[411] Interview K (original emphasis).

beginning of this chapter, by mid-2019, seventy-seven delisting requests had been made to the Office of the Ombudsperson and only nineteen had been subsequently refused by the Security Council.[412] With such impressive results, humanitarian scholar-experts, the Monitoring Team, Security Council P5 and the Ombudsperson have all effusively praised this novel '*de facto* judicial review' procedure.[413] Legal scholars have argued that in light of the 'high level of de facto judicial protection offered by the Ombudsperson ... [it] no longer seems appropriate to summarily dismiss the protection that is offered'.[414] Even EU judges have said that due to these procedural improvements it may now be finally time for the courts to adopt a more deferential stance, perform less intensive review and acknowledge that UN listing and delisting procedures 'can no longer be regarded as purely diplomatic and intergovernmental' in nature.[415]

It is important to underscore that this *de novo* approach was not written into the role, but invented by the Ombudsperson itself. The impetus for doing so was for the purpose of resolving the very practical issues, and 'avoiding the minefields', arising from its first delisting case:

> When I arrived, there was already a case. And I was thinking to myself about that case, as I approach that case, 'where are *the minefields* going to be?' And it became apparent from that case (and many others after) that going backwards and trying the classic – 'Was it [i.e. the listing decision] reasonable to begin with?' – had so many problems attached to it.[416]

When the first Ombudsperson began the role, the delisting procedure had not yet been spelled out – 'they [i.e. the Security Council] didn't give me any of that procedural stuff to fill in'.[417] This procedural lacuna was important because it meant the individual Ombudsperson 'had the

---

[412] Office of the Ombudsperson of the Security Council's 1267 Committee, *Ombudsperson to the ISIL (Da'esh) and Al-Qaida Sanctions Committee: Status of Cases*. Available at: bit.ly/2ZgDBSu.

[413] For impassioned support of the Ombudsperson as procedural improvement, see: 2012 Watson Report; van den Herik, 'Peripheral hegemony'; Devika Hovell, *The Power of Process: The Value of Due Process in Security Council Sanctions Decision-Making* (Oxford: Oxford University Press, 2016).

[414] Cuyvers, 'Give me one good reason', 1786.

[415] Joined Cases C-584/10P, C-593/10P and C-595/10P, *Commission, Council and United Kingdom* v. *Kadi* [2013], Opinion of AG Bot, para. 82.

[416] Interview with the former UN1267 Ombudsperson, Kimberly Prost (via Skype), July 2019 (Interview S) (emphasis added).

[417] Ibid.

choice', creative latitude and requisite expertise to design the Ombudsperson role in the ways they thought to be most productive. The first Ombudsperson had extensive experience in international politics, having previously worked on numerous multilateral treaty negotiations in Canada, including the Rome Statute: 'So, I knew a lot about big-P Politics, and little-p politics. That kind of context.'[418] Having such a political background was 'very instrumental' and 'extremely important' – both for success in the role more broadly and for the specific creative task of designing the delisting procedures.[419] First, because it was politics that allowed the Ombudsperson to be able to identify and avoid (or engage with) the potential 'minefields' associated with the role – for example, state sensitivities associated with the use of intelligence as evidence and P5 sensitivities around protecting the unique prerogatives of the Council and ensuring its Chapter VII decisions were not reviewed. 'Avoiding minefields', in this sense, is best thought of as an assemblage practice concerned with managing conflicts, authorising assumptions of the UNSC and containing critiques of the list. Second, politics here means being pragmatic, rather than principled, in approach and being willing to accommodate 'sensitivities' associated with the 'minefields' of the list:

GS: Were there times when your background as a judge was an obstacle to the work?
OMBUDSPERSON: I don't think so . . . because I had the balance. I had worked in other contexts internationally, not just as a judge. If I had come in and just applied a purely judicial approach, it wouldn't have gone anywhere, because you did need to have some [politics]. You know how I conducted certain things. You had to have a bit of a pragmatic approach and practicality. I would always reach independent conclusions. But how I might frame things would take into account sensitivities.[420]

Attending to such 'sensitivities' and 'minefields' helps to align divergent versions of the list enacted by different actors in the assemblage. But *de novo* decision-making also introduces an important temporal gap into the delisting procedure that generates three key effects. First, it frees designating states and the Security Council from ever having to explain the underlying basis for their listing decisions and claims of terrorist association to those that they target, whilst assuaging concerns the threat

[418] Ibid.
[419] Ibid.
[420] Ibid.

of independent review. Whilst promising fairness and greater account-ability, this practice also consolidates the list as an exceptional govern-ance technology. As the former Ombudsperson notes:

> The fact that I focus my analysis on present day circumstances solely has been very important. I would not have been in the job long if I had attempted to start reviewing ... I keep completely out of the question and I avoid ... the whole issue of what was the basis for the listing. Because ... there is all sorts of information in these cases, [or] in many of these cases that I'm not receiving ... It's very important that I can say [to states]: 'I accept that when you listed this person you may have known all sorts of things [and that] you may still know all sorts of things, but this is all I'm looking at today'.[421]

As a result of this temporal cut, individuals can be listed by the Council for many years and then delisted without ever really knowing why they were targeted in the first place or removed in the end. Indeed, this has been the experience of some of my clients in Ombudsperson delisting proceedings – which operated entirely by written procedure with little to no input from either the Ombudsperson, designating states or the 1267 Sanctions Committee. In one case, I was directed to a story that my client had 'liked' on his Facebook page as evidence that he was 'associated with' an Al-Qaida affiliate group and so constituted a threat to international peace and security. In another, I was presented with generic allegations drawn from a Narrative Summary that appeared to be loosely based upon someone else's trial proceedings. When my clients were finally removed from the list, following a wholly opaque process, no reasons were given despite the Council being required to do so.[422] The sole reason for delisting given to one client, who had been listed for more than eight years, was the following: 'There is nothing in the Petitioner's personal circumstances to indicate that his lack of current involvement with Al-Qaida is attributable to anything other than a personal choice.'[423] Whilst my clients clearly welcomed the final decision to lift the sanctions against them, they all nonetheless experienced the Ombudsperson delisting procedure as opaque and unfair. They left the process with little more understanding of why they had been targeted than when they had started.

---

[421] Interview K.

[422] S/RES/2161 (2014), Annex II, para. 16 required the Committee to convey whether the measures are retained or terminated, *setting out reasons*.

[423] *Letter from UN 1267 Ombudsperson* (21 December 2012), copy on file with author. This explanation still remains entirely baffling to me. My client also said that he had no idea what it meant.

In this way, there are no possibilities for wrongful listings to be acknowledged or for financial compensation to ever be paid to delisted individuals as a result. Both of these important issues are 'left open' by this carefully assembled delisting process and its exclusive focus on present-day circumstances.[424]

This inability for listed persons to find out the reasons why they have been listed has been a problem that successive Ombudspersons have also encountered and critiqued. After the Sanctions Committee had taken its ultimate decision to delist or retain the listing, it was previously required to write to the Ombudsperson 'setting out reasons and including any further relevant information'.[425] In practice, however, it rarely did so. After the delisting of one of my clients in 2014, for example, the former Ombudsperson wrote to inform me about the non-disclosure of reasons in my client's case:

> Regrettably, the communication from the Committee, while it references the reasons for the recommendation of the Ombudsperson, does not set out those reasons or any other. In my opinion, this is contrary to the plain wording of paragraph 16 of Annex II to resolution 2161 (2014), through which the Security Council has mandated the Committee to convey whether the measures are retained or terminated, *setting out reasons*.[426]

The lack of disclosure of substantive reasons for decisions taken by the Sanctions Committee has been a persistent objection in the Ombudsperson's regular reports to the Security Council. It has been criticised for perpetuating the view that the delisting process is arbitrary, 'unnecessarily shrouded in mystery' and for presenting an ongoing 'lacuna in terms of fair process'.[427] The prevalent view in the Committee had been that, if individuals were ultimately delisted, then they 'got what they wanted' and so should not complain about not being provided with reasons. Yet, as the former Ombudsperson noted in her final report to the Council: 'a fair process – by its nature and nomenclature – relates not to the result achieved, but to the fairness of the process

---

[424] Remarks by Catherine Marchi-Uhel, Ombudsperson, Security Council ISIL (Da'esh) and Al-Qaida Sanctions Committee at the meeting of the EU Council Working Group on Public International Law (COJUR), Brussels (2 June 2016), 8. Available at: bit.ly/2OEVMAE.

[425] S/RES/2161 (2014), para. 16. This reporting process has since changed. See: S/RES/2368 (2017), paras. 16–18.

[426] Letter from UN1267 Ombudsperson (25 August 2014) (original emphasis), copy on file with author.

[427] UN Doc. S/2015/80 (2 February 2015), paras. 41, 56; UN Doc. S/2016/96 (2 February 2016), para. 38.

by which the outcome was attained. To this end, a reasoned explanation for the decision taken is relevant and necessary to fairness in both delisting and retention cases.'[428] In interview, she was more frank: 'Trying to explain to them that a reasoned decision has to be demonstrated in a reasonable process and you needed reasons for that ... was just impossible. It was like banging your head against a wall.'[429] Yet this issue of non-disclosure of reasons is arguably a problem of the Ombudsperson's making. The *de novo* approach to review, which the Ombudsperson crafted, looks only to present risk and not back to reasons for listing. It was specifically designed to accommodate such sensitivities and is supported by states for this reason.[430]

Second, the *de novo* review procedure also provides a pragmatic, face-saving solution for delisting individuals for whom the original reasons for listing were either manifestly unfounded or unknown. As discussed earlier, the Sanctions Committee does not hold the classified material underpinning its own listing decisions. Instead, it approves proposed designations using a confidential 'no-objection' procedure that precludes substantive consideration of the grounds.[431] The Ombudsperson's *de novo* approach to delisting complements this process by providing a mechanism for annulling unfounded listing decisions without the risk of creating damaging precedent through adverse court findings:

> A state can choose whatever information they want to give me. I know states are choosing not to give me certain pieces of information and that's fine. It might not even be classified information ... Some states have just decided: 'Well we had this information way back then, but we don't want to bother [because] we are not opposed to delisting'. So, they just don't give me information and that's also perfectly fine ... Can I do a proper

---

[428] UN Doc. S/2015/533 (14 July 2015), para. 42.

[429] Interview S.

[430] Ibid: 'Ultimately, the United States became a huge supporter of the de novo standard. For obvious reasons, they liked that very much. As did other states.' Whilst the process for disclosing reasons has since changed (see S/RES/2368 (2017), paras. 16–18), problems still persist. For a recent call for reform, see: UN Doc. S/2018/1094, Letter from the Group of Like-Minded States on Targeted Sanctions to the President of the Security Council (11 December 2018), paras. 11–21.

[431] Simon Chesterman, 'The spy who came in from the Cold War: intelligence and international law' (2006) 27 *Michigan Journal of International Law* 1071, 1115; Vanessa Baehr-Jones, 'Mission possible: how intelligence evidence rules can save UN terrorist sanctions' (2011) 2 *Harvard National Security Journal* 447. Statements of Case must now be provided with each proposed listing, but the information to be disclosed is still generic.

review? I *can* do a proper review of the decision I have to make . . . because it will be based solely on what they give me.[432]

According to the former Ombudsperson, more than half of all delisting applications she handled were accepted by the Sanctions Committee without any objections being raised or counter-material provided. And in a significant proportion of delisting cases, states provided no response at all.[433] This means that the majority of delisting cases are effectively dealt with *ex parte*, with little to no input from the other side. So, not only does this unique review refrain from reviewing the listing decision, but it also often takes place using material provided by those who are listed and little else. How can we account for the limited engagement by states in this de facto 'review' process? In May 2019 one of my clients was delisted following an application to the Ombudsperson, after more than fifteen years on the list. He was then provided with a brief summary of the Ombudsperson's analysis, which the Committee emphasised was 'not attributable to the Committee or any individual Committee member'.[434] The summary noted that: 'There was no information before the Ombudsperson in this proceeding which would justify the petitioner's listing, other than that which concerned criminal charges in Italy fifteen years ago.'[435] This historical criminal conviction appeared to be the only basis for my client's ongoing 'preventative' listing and argument by states (either the USA, Tunisia and/or Italy) that they stay on the list. Yet in this case, the *de novo* standard worked to my client's advantage:

> Member State support for the petitioner's continued listing was based on the rationale that because of the petitioner's criminal record, the possibility of future association with Al-Qaida or its affiliates could not be excluded. Analysed against the Ombudsperson's standard of review, this is not a sufficient basis to justify continued listing. Sufficiency requires more than a hypothetical possibility extrapolated from historic events. The circumstances must be considered presently, and to be sufficient, the information must demonstrate a link to the petitioner's current situation.[436]

---

[432] Interview K (original emphasis).
[433] Interview with the former UN 1267 Ombudsperson, Kimberly Prost. New York, June 2014 (Interview L).
[434] Letter to the Ombudsperson from the Chair of the 1267 Sanctions Committee (23 May 2019), copy on file with author.
[435] Summary of the analysis, observations, arguments and recommendations set out in the Ombudsperson's report, in accordance with para. 16 of Annex 11 to Resolution 2368 (2017) (23 May 2019), copy on file with author.
[436] Ibid.

The Office of the Ombudsperson is valued for the important list-pruning function it provides. As discussed earlier, getting off the ISIL and Al-Qaida list is far more difficult than getting on. The collective inertia of states to delist, the indefinite application of the sanctions, the lack of *pro bono* lawyers doing this kind of defence work and the reduced 'scrutiny from the press and NGO community because "even human rights groups don't want to stand up for terrorists"',[437] all mean that once someone is listed they will likely *remain* listed forever, irrespective of why they were listed in the first place.[438] As the above quote reveals, there is real reluctance to delist individuals because the 'possibility of future association' with ISIL, Al-Qaida or affiliated groups cannot be excluded. The Ombudsperson's *de novo* techniques bypass these political obstacles and help to trim the list of 'low-hanging fruit'. This mitigates the threat of judicial review – by dissipating potential norm conflicts before they reach court – and so strengthens the Council's global listing authority. After the 2013 *Kadi* decision, when the ECJ did not give recognition to the Office of Ombudsperson, states became less supportive of the post. In response, the Ombudsperson argued with states that the mechanism was valuable because it helped avoid cases getting to court.[439] *De novo* review is central to that process.

Third, and most importantly, this temporal cut allows the Ombudsperson to argue that its decision-making processes are fair because they allow listed persons to know the case against them. This claim comes, however, with an important caveat: 'when I say that I believe that listed individuals have been told about the case, it's the case against them *such as has been given to me*'.[440] The Ombudsperson's understanding of the cases, however, is partial and fragmentary at best. As noted above, it is often based on the 'general, unsubstantiated, vague and unparticularised'[441] Narrative Summary of Reasons and/or Statement of Case released by the Committee 'and nothing more. That does not mean that there *is* nothing more, but that I *have* nothing more.'[442] For the Ombudsperson, this disparity does not create an

---

[437] US Embassy Cable 09LONDON452, para. 5 (recounting dialogue between UK FCO and US diplomatic officials on list accountability reform).

[438] With the exception of those individuals who have the money to engage legal counsel (such as Mr Kadi).

[439] Interview S.

[440] Interview K (emphasis added).

[441] *Kadi* v. *Commission*, para. 157.

[442] Interview K (original emphasis).

inequality of arms between the Council and those it targets because the Ombudsperson's recommendation and the Sanctions Committee's decision are based on exactly the same information – 'If that wasn't the case, [then] I would say that it is an unfair process.'[443]

This idea of symmetry between the Ombudsperson and Council resonates with conventional ideas of review, where decision-makers decide upon findings of fact and accepted evidence. But how can one assume that in this exceptional domain these two very different bodies base their delisting decisions on the same material? The relation between Council and Ombudsperson is unlike the relation between executive decision-maker and court. I suggest that in the 'emergency context within which the Security Council necessarily operates',[444] this idea of symmetry is little more than wish-fulfilment. The Ombudsperson claims that 'the mechanisms in place give significant weight to [her] . . . recommendations'.[445] But there are no rules restricting the types of information the Council can consider or that limit its discretion in any way. The Council remains effectively 'unbound by law'.[446] Its deliberations on delisting are undertaken in secret, ordinarily through discrete bilateral exchanges or in state capitals, outside of the 1267 Sanctions Committee meeting framework altogether.[447]

This myth of symmetry anchors claims of procedural fairness and so helps assuage legal critics. But the Ombudsperson and Security Council are very different institutions with no 'constitutional connective tissue' binding them together – they are fundamentally asymmetrical.[448] There are any number of pragmatic or political reasons why the Security Council might choose to remove people from the list (or not). As

---

[443] Ibid.
[444] Hovell, *The Power of Process*, p. 50.
[445] S/2013/452 (31 July 2013), para. 57.
[446] Gabriël H. Oosthuizen, 'Playing the devil's advocate: the United Nations Security Council is unbound by law' (1999) 12(3) *Leiden Journal of International Law* 549. See, however: UN1267 Sanctions Committee, *Guidelines of the Committee for the Conduct of Its Work* (5 September 2018). These guidelines do not restrict Council decision-making and are non-enforceable.
[447] This is an effect of the 'no-objection' procedure. As one Committee member explained: 'We usually have Committee meetings once every two or three weeks. We'll discuss Monitoring Team trip reports, Monitoring Team recommendations and the substance of [Monitoring] Team reports. *Listing and delisting requests typically are not handled within the Committee.*' – Interview F. See also: UN1267 Sanctions Committee, *Guidelines* (5 September 2018), paras. 6(n), 7(f).
[448] Daniel Halberstam, 'LJIL Symposium Vol 25–2: Beyond Constitutionalism? A Comment by Daniel Halberstam', *Opinio Juris* (6 July 2012). Available at: bit.ly/1saeEHm.

a lawyer of listed individuals, I have worked at length to prepare detailed arguments setting out why my clients were not 'associated with' ISIL or Al-Qaida, as any defence lawyer would. Yet, throughout the delisting process, I was continually reminded – through the procedural irregularities and novelties of this mechanism – that this was a political and at best quasi-juridical procedure where my legal submissions may ultimately have little bearing on the end-result. Decisions to retain or remove listings may have nothing to do with the arguments put forward by listed parties or the Ombudsperson. As the former Chair of the 1267 Committee plainly acknowledged: 'At the end of the day, it's a political decision based on a political process.'[449] Avoiding precedent-setting litigation and consolidating the Security Council's authority to govern global terrorism in this way are more likely catalysts for many of the delisting decisions undertaken to date.

3.6.2   Speculative Standards

The Ombudsperson delisting process is strengthened by the novel evidential standards that are used. These standards are unique and were crafted by the Ombudsperson in its role as a judicial expert.

When considering delisting requests the Ombudsperson applies an evidential standard of whether there is 'sufficient information to provide a reasonable and credible basis for the continued listing'.[450] Whilst this standard is loosely based 'on concepts generally accepted as fundamental across legal systems',[451] it is novel insofar as it has no direct equivalent in either domestic or international law. As the Ombudsperson has candidly said: 'I made it up.'[452] The nominal reason for doing so was to create 'an international standard appropriate in this context'.[453] One that could

---

[449] On the political nature of UN listing, see also AG Bot's 2013 opinion in *Commission, Council and United Kingdom* v. *Kadi*, para. 80:
   It is true that listing is based on evidence indicating how the conduct of a person or an entity has a link with a terrorist organisation and therefore constitutes a threat to international peace and security, but it also has regard more generally to strategic and geopolitical interests ... Listings are thus part of a political process which goes beyond any individual case.

[450] Office of the Ombudsperson of the Security Council's 1267 Committee, *Approach and Standard*. Available at: bit.ly/2YkOUwC.

[451] Ibid.

[452] Hovell, *The Power of Process*, p. 150.

[453] Interview L.

blend and synthesise elements from different jurisdictions without being necessarily tied to any one of them:

> This a standard being used at the international level. So, what it cannot be is simply lifted from a legal system. Whether they acknowledge it or not, the FATF [for example] has always used language that is common law language, because of who they were driven by and that causes problems when you're dealing with other countries that don't come from that tradition. Like 'reasonable grounds to believe' means something to me, but it doesn't mean a heck of a lot to the French. And so, what I wanted to do is get away from . . . things that were familiar in one system and move to something that has those concepts, but that is in language that everyone can understand . . . So that everyone can say, 'Okay, that for me means this and that for me means that'.[454]

Part of the motivation for creating such a unique legal standard was pragmatic: 'I wanted to make sure that it was a standard that was realistic and practical for the states that were responsible for a number of listings.'[455] To that end, the former Ombudsperson first consulted with 'states that that had a lot of listings and states of the European Union who obviously had a great interest in how this would work' to ensure this evidential standard would be acceptable to them, before rolling it out.[456]

Part of the motivation was about avoiding the 'minefield' of legal debate associated with whether one should adopt an evidential standard of 'reasonable grounds to believe' as against a standard of 'reasonable grounds to suspect'. After studying the jurisprudence on this issue, principally from the UK, the former Ombudsperson 'knew I didn't want to go anywhere near that, because I don't want to get caught up in that. So, using other language [was important].'[457] This evidential standard, in other words, was carefully assembled by the first Ombudsperson to address the specific challenges and sensitivities of handling and assessing intelligence as evidence in this 'special environment'. This cosmopolitan approach, of crafting a novel standard that resonates with existing national approaches but is confined to none of them, not only purports to foster greater inclusivity, but also expands the Ombudsperson's discretion as expert by deflecting the reach of domestic and regional laws of proof:

---

[454] Ibid.
[455] Interview S.
[456] Ibid.
[457] Ibid. On the UK debate on this issue, see: *HM Treasury* v. *Ahmed and Others* [2010] UKSC 2.

GS: What kind of work can you do with this that you couldn't do with reasonable suspicion or balance of probabilities standard?

OMBUDSPERSON: What it does for me is that it doesn't restrict me to what might be developed case law in any particular jurisdiction ... I don't have to go into whole reams of, you know, 'what does the case law in five common law jurisdictions say about X'? It gives me, quite frankly, freedom and the flexibility to say, 'I'm just using the common definition of what's reasonable, what's credible'. And *that*, in *this* area, is much more *practical* ... There are people who make the point to me ... that I'm not a judge [and] this isn't a legal process. So, I say, 'OK. This isn't a standard that you use in any particular court ... or judicial context. It's an international standard appropriate in this context. It also helps me *that* way.[458]

So, just as the Ombudsperson's unique decision-making processes are forged from the dissensus surrounding international judicial review and hold together different versions of the ISIL and Al-Qaida list, its novel evidential standards are designed to suture together localised legal elements into something distinct, quasi-juridical yet familiar and recognisably global. However, as with any pragmatic compromise solution, something important is lost in the translation from formality to practicality. In this case, the resulting standard is so elastic that it can readily allow just about any material into the delisting procedure, whilst at the same time failing to provide targeted individuals with any clarity about how they might go about getting off the list.[459] The Ombudsperson's recurring emphasis on practicality also reflects a functionalist approach to this deeply political issue. Existing standards of proof are reassembled as 'technique[s] of pragmatic governance', based on an apparent common-sense understanding of what is reasonable in the circumstances.[460] Yet, as Koskenniemi points out, 'if people were able to agree on what is

---

[458] Ibid (original emphasis).

[459] In 2016, the second Ombudsperson, Ms Catherine Marchi-Uhel, drafted further guidance on the Ombudsperson's approach to the analysis and assessment of information to 'lift some of the unnecessary mystery in which the process before the Ombudsperson remains shrouded'. See: Ombudsperson to the ISIL (Da'esh) and Al-Qaida Sanctions Committee, *Approach to Analysis, Assessment and Use of Information*. Available at: bit.ly /2Yrags0; Ms Catherine Marchi-Uhel, Ombudsperson of the ISIL (Da'esh) and Al-Qaida Sanctions Committee, Statement to the 51st meeting of the Committee of Legal Advisers on Public International Law (CAHDI) of the Council of Europe (4 March 2016) 4. Available at: bit.ly/2YliWAe.

[460] Martti Koskenniemi, 'Occupied zone – "a zone of reasonableness"?' (2008) 41(1–2) *Israel Law Review* 13, 17.

reasonable . . . no courts or law would ever be needed'.[461] Listing is grounded in inferential, speculative and contested preemptive security practices. In such a setting, 'reasonableness' and the discourse of practicality does work to absorb these uncertainties and help recast the list in apolitical terms.

The internationalism of the evidential standard is also used by the Ombudsperson to justify her distinct approach to assessing material tainted by torture. Because listing is often based on local information drawn from security and intelligence actors in regions where torture is endemic, reliance on tainted material is an ever-present risk in this area. 'Intelligence from torture has', according to the former UN Special Rapporteur on Counterterrorism, 'been used to justify the designation of individuals' on the ISIL and Al-Qaida list.[462] The use of torture evidence is ordinarily firmly prohibited by judicial bodies. It is both *jus cogens* and contrary to the UN Convention against Torture (UNCAT), which requires states to 'ensure that any statement which is established to have been made as a result of torture shall not be invoked as evidence in any proceedings'.[463]

But because these prohibitions are designed for national states, there is uncertainty about whether they apply to the global context where UN listing and delisting takes place. Defence lawyers for listed persons and the former UN Special Rapporteur on Counterterrorism have both argued for clear rules to be adopted to make plain that torture evidence must be excluded from listing and delisting procedures. But the Ombudsperson argues that 'the measures applied by the Security Council are preventative in nature and thus "exclusionary rules" are not appropriate',[464] and that 'even more significantly [because] this is an international mechanism ... it should not be premised upon, or reflective of, specialized rules arising from one legal system'[465] – that is, the common law tradition:

---

[461] Ibid. 22.

[462] UN Doc. A/67/396, para. 49.

[463] UN Convention against Torture and Other Cruel, Inhuman or Degrading Treatment or Punishment (UNCAT), Article 15. For decisions concerning the exclusion of torture evidence at the domestic level, see: *A and Others* v. *Secretary of State for the Home Department (No 2)* [2005] UKHL 71; Oberlandesgericht (OLG), OLG Hamburg, Decision of 14 June 2005, reprinted in (2005) 58 *Neue Juristische Wochenzeitschrift* 2326; *Hamdan* v. *Rumsfeld*, 548 US 577.

[464] Letter from the UN1267 Ombudsperson (dated 12 November 2012), copy on file with author.

[465] Ibid.

> I am not prepared to apply any exclusionary rules of evidence because that takes me down a path that I do not want to go down ... My job is more like an investigating judge in the civil-law context than the traditional Ombudsperson ... I gather all the information and I look at the individual pieces of it for questions like reliability and credibility. A key issue would be if the petitioner says, 'Listen ... I was tortured', those kinds of cases come up. So, I look at all those factors, but not in this common-law tradition of exclusion – even though I know that's coming from the Torture Convention. I look at it more of, you know, looking at all the factors.[466]

Following external pressure and criticism, the first Ombudsperson made a public statement on the issue in 2013 stating that if her Office is 'satisfied to the relevant standard that the information has been obtained through torture' then it will not rely on it in its analysis.[467] But because the sources of underlying information are never disclosed to the Ombudsperson, it remains unclear how such an assessment could realistically be undertaken and findings of 'inherent unreliability' drawn. States are under no obligation to proactively disclose potentially tainted and exculpatory material.[468] How can the Ombudsperson realistically assess claims of torture – even in accordance with its own very elastic standards – if it lacks 'information' to do so?[469] As Lord Bingham of the House of Lords has observed in the comparable context of UK Special Immigration Appeals Commission (SIAC) proceedings: 'despite the universal abhorrence expressed for torture and its fruits, evidence procured by torture *will* be laid before SIAC because its source will not have been "established"'.[470] Moreover, in an interview in 2012, the Ombudsperson expressed a much more cavalier attitude towards the use of torture material, seemingly at odds with her later public statements on this issue – an attitude driven by the preemptive logics of the list rather than considerations about the unreliability of the evidence:

---

[466] Interview K.

[467] Ombudsperson to the ISIL (Da'esh) and Al-Qaida Sanctions Committee, *Approach to Analysis*.

[468] On the issue of exculpatory material in the context of security listing, see: UN Doc. A/67/396, para. 45; Forcese and Roach, 'Limping into the future', 266; Jared Genser and Kate Barth, 'Targeted sanctions and due process of law' in Jared Genser and Bruno Stagno Ugarte (eds.), *The United Nations Security Council in the Age of Human Rights* (Cambridge: Cambridge University Press, 2014), pp. 231–2.

[469] Genser and Barth, 'Targeted sanctions'.

[470] *A and Others* v. *Secretary of State for the Home Department*, para. 59 (emphasis added).

> Jack Bauer, you know, on 24. He tortured a lot of people [and] he got information [that] there is a bomb about to go off. Nobody would suggest that you shouldn't use or rely on that information and go look for the bomb. So, taking that in a preventative context here, if . . . you've got information and it indicates from a preventative point of view that you should be using the sanctions, I don't think anyone would argue that you shouldn't, from a prevention point of view, rely on that information.[471]

This novel standard has been rightly criticised by jurists for being too vague and setting the evidential threshold too low given the 'quasi-penal consequences' that flow from being on the list.[472] But, for the Ombudsperson, the applicable standard in this domain has to be kept 'a bit fuzzy and a bit lower'[473] than conventional criminal or civil standards because the list is 'preventative in nature' and its assessment seeks to hybridise two very different kinds of information – intelligence and evidence:

> [With intelligence] you have to be looking at what the inferences are much more than you do with evidence. With evidence, you know you're looking at concrete facts . . . But here, it's more about can you draw inferences from . . . certain activities? . . . It's not just [in] the information but in the inference [that petitioners] have a chance to respond . . . and explain.[474]

The anomalies of assessing intelligence-as-evidence are discussed at length in Chapter 4. For now, I merely highlight how the Ombudsperson's novel standard is a speculative standard that facilitates the drawing and assessment of inferences, potential associations and dangers. A mosaic standard capable of imbuing disparate fragments of information from the past with cumulative purpose and future effect. This quasi-juridical measure is designed 'a bit fuzzy', not just because of the 'international context' of the list, but because the list is a preemptive security technology animated by logics of possibility, rather than probability.[475] It is important to recall that people are not listed here for what they have done, but rather for what they might do in the future – this is what the list being 'preventative in nature' effectively means. Listed persons are not 'known terrorists' as such but rather *emergent* and 'dividuated' subjects made up of fragments of risk

---

[471] Interview K.
[472] UN Doc. A/67/396, para. 55.
[473] Interview K.
[474] Ibid.
[475] Louise Amoore, *The Politics of Possibility: Risk and Security Beyond Probability* (Durham Duke NC: University Press, 2013), p. 102.

and inferences of potential threat.[476] The speculative standard used by the Ombudsperson helps actualise this potential terrorist and correlate their associations to make them amenable to quasi-legal assessment. This is not so much a standard of proof directed towards establishing the truth, in the conventional sense. It is better thought of as what David Dyzenhaus has termed 'an imaginative experiment in institutional design' arising from conditions of global emergency.[477] An experiment that reassembles existing legal standards in accordance with the pre-emptive logics of global security, loosely tethering the list to claims of legality and further entrenching it as an exceptional governance technology.

3.6.3   Inquisitorial Dialogue and Speculative Lawyering

After gathering information from the Committee and other relevant bodies,[478] the Ombudsperson delisting procedure enters what is known as the 'dialogue phase': a two-month period of engagement where listed persons are said to be 'made fully aware of the case against him or her and be afforded the opportunity to respond fully to it'.[479] This dialogue is held out as a 'critical part of the process in terms of fairness'[480] that enables the Ombudsperson to meet both 'the right to be informed and the right to be heard'.[481] It is the phase where the listed person 'can tell his side of the story'.[482] As scholars like Hoerauf have enthusiastically observed, this dialogue is not 'just an exchange between the listee and some organ somewhat participating in the delisting process, but a hearing before

---

[476] Ibid. On 'dividuation', see: Gilles Deleuze, 'Postscript on the societies of control' (1992) (59) *October* 3.

[477] Dyzenhaus, *The Constitution of Law*, p. 215.

[478] S/RES/1904 (2009), Annex II, paras. 1–4. During this initial four-month period, 'members of the Committee, designating State(s), State(s) of residence and nationality or incorporation, relevant UN bodies, and any other States deemed relevant by the Ombudsperson' are asked to provide information relevant to the delisting request and their views on whether the request should be granted (para. 2). The Monitoring Team is also engaged by the Ombudsperson to scrutinise the delisting request, provide relevant information from the Monitoring Team's own extensive records and provide 'questions or requests for clarification' that the Ombudsperson should ask (para. 3). The information-gathering period can be extended by an additional two-months if needed (para. 4).

[479] Prost, 'Fair process and the Security Council', 422.

[480] Prost and Wilmshurst, *UN Sanctions, Human Rights and the Ombudsperson*, p. 6.

[481] Prost, 'Fair process and the Security Council', 422.

[482] Natacha Wexels-Riser, 'The Security Council's ISIL (Da'esh) and Al-Qaida Sanctions regime: the human dimension', paper presented to the Max Planck Institute for Foreign and International Criminal Law (2 December 2017), 7. Available at: bit.ly/2yCOO48.

a neutral de facto decision-maker'.[483] Such effusively positive accounts present the 'dialogue phase' of the Ombudsperson's delisting procedure as a model example of international due process in action. In my experience, however, it is more inquisitorial and exceptional than dialogical and cathartic in nature. The dialogue phase is where the speculative standards of the Ombudsperson are really put into effect. The following section illustrates how, by sharing my own experiences as a lawyer representing listed people in Ombudsperson delisting proceedings.

In 2014 one of my clients was asked to participate in a 'dialogue meeting' with the former Ombudsperson in Tunisia. Letters were exchanged prior to the meeting in an attempt to narrow down and clarify the key issues to be determined, as is the norm with pre-action correspondence between lawyers in litigation. My client had been subjected to domestic criminal proceedings in Italy more than ten years prior to the meeting for alleged association with terrorism. The criminal proceedings had been based on conduct occurring five years before the trial – that is, almost fifteen years before the Ombudsperson dialogue meeting in Tunisia. In the end, my client was cleared of these terrorism charges by the Court for want of evidence. We had therefore assumed that his listing by the UN must have been based on some other allegations and were pushing the Ombudsperson to disclose the underlying basis of his UN terrorist listing to us so that we could adequately respond. Yet, over the course of our correspondence, it slowly became clear that the allegations of terrorist association underneath my client's UN listing decision were primarily (if not exclusively) based on the domestic judicial findings that had already found those same allegations to be unfounded. Moreover, many of the allegations advanced by the Ombudsperson as to why my client was 'associated with' Al-Qaida were drawn from the very preliminary stage of the criminal investigation in which he had not formally participated or been able to put forward a defence. In other words, the allegation that my client constituted a threat to international peace and security under Chapter VII of the UN Charter was apparently based on submissions prepared by a local prosecutor for an investigating Italian

---

[483] Dominic Hoerauf, 'United Nations Al-Qaida Sanctions regime after UN Resolution 1989: due process still overdue' (2012) 26(2) *Temple International and Comparative Law Journal*, 213, 227–8. See also Prost and Wilmshurst, *UN Sanctions, Human Rights and the Ombudsperson*, p. 6: 'The Ombudsperson noted that it was very striking how much this meeting means for the petitioners. On several occasions she has been told by petitioners that it is the first time after many years of being on the list that anyone has listened to their side of the story.'

magistrate to decide (in secret) whether there was sufficient circumstantial evidence and prima facie grounds to order pre-trial detention in my client's criminal case. Most of the findings made by this investigating magistrate were either later dismissed by the appellate courts or were not ultimately pursued in trial. Yet they were nonetheless recycled by the Ombudsperson during the 'dialogue phase' more than ten years later to try and demonstrate why my client was an international terrorist.

When we made our concerns plain and explained to the Ombudsperson that many of these initial findings had been drawn from closed *in absentia* proceedings and had either been later overturned following detailed examination or otherwise abandoned, we were told that 'for all judicial or administrative decisions it is *the underlying information revealed by it*, as opposed to the conclusions or reasoning, which is of significance' to the Ombudsperson in the dialogue phase. And that the Ombudsperson's analysis 'will ultimately consider the *cumulated* material and *the inferences to be drawn* from the same', and that this approach was appropriate because the list was preventative in nature.[484] This is one part of the 'dialogue' where the speculative evidential standards of the Ombudsperson can be put to coercive effect as a jurisdictional device.[485] Material used as evidence in domestic proceedings to try and show terrorist association in accordance with conventional legal standards and burdens of proof can effectively be rerun at the global level in accordance with the extremely broad and unique standards crafted by the Ombudsperson. In this special context, there is no double jeopardy rule and judicial findings or considerations of evidence are 'not in any way determinative', even if they end up in acquittal.[486] Rather, what

---

[484] Letter from the UN 1267 Ombudsperson (dated 15 August 2013) (emphasis added), copy on file with author.

[485] According to Mariana Valverde, jurisdiction is best understood as a kind of sorting process that divides events into different classes to make things amenable to legal governance and ensure the 'smooth functioning of law'. It is not only about grounding authority claims. It also 'conceals from view the qualitative differences in governance that the discussion of scale has canvassed' and transforms disputes about 'the qualitative features of governance … into seemingly mundane and technical questions'. Jurisdiction does not only decide *who* governs a particular situation, but 'also determines *how* something is to be governed' and so retains a 'magical power to depoliticize governance' – Mariana Valverde, *Chronotopes of Law: Jurisdiction, Scale and Governance* (London: Routledge, 2015), pp. 83–4. It is in this sense that the Ombudsperson's delisting standards operate as a jurisdictional device. They rescale localised trial material to a global site whilst altering its temporal orientation in critical ways – from alleged past criminal activities to uncertain future threats – through technical means.

[486] Letter from the UN 1267 Ombudsperson (dated 15 August 2013).

matters are the correlations that can potentially be drawn anew in the Ombudsperson's fresh assessment of the 'underlying information'.

One week before our meeting the Ombudsperson put forward a new allegation against my client: 'There is evidence that Mr X recently met with a Tunisian extremist.'[487] Our requests for more information about this allegation – for example, whom did he meet with, when and in what circumstances, what was the alleged purpose of the meeting – were all rebuffed: 'I am unable to disclose the source.'[488] And yet an inference was being clearly drawn from this unsourced allegation that my client was 'associated with' terrorism. Given the vagueness of the claim, we were unable to take instructions and present a counter-argument capable of interfering with the inference. What should one do as a defence lawyer in such extraordinary circumstances, duty bound to advance the best interests of your client? In the end we refused to respond to this 'spectral evidence', whilst pushing for an assurance from the Ombudsperson that no adverse inferences would be drawn as a result (which was duly provided).[489] But if our client *had* answered by guessing, then anyone mentioned might, by inference and association, be flagged as a potential terrorist or terrorist associate, end up on a no-fly list or become a person of security interest. Here 'dialogue' is a means of generating new intelligence and it is this generative capacity that may explain why the Council has been so encouraging of the Ombudsperson to reach out and engage with listed persons in this way.

The material purportedly underlying the listing is never seen by listed individuals. Since 2008, there have been Narrative Summaries, but they are expressly designed to exclude all confidential information and are too vague to enable listed persons to effectively defend themselves.[490] The Ombudsperson seeks to improve this process by putting questions to the listed during the 'dialogue' that aim to work out what they know of the classified material into their background. According to the Ombudsperson, this process – which is closely vetted by the states involved – allows listed individuals to know 'the contours of the case',

---

[487] Letter from the UN 1267 Ombudsperson (4 September 2013), copy on file with author.

[488] Ibid.

[489] Spectral evidence is evidence based on dreams and apparitions. It was first rendered admissible in English courts during the Bury St Edmunds Witch Trials in Suffolk during the seventeenth century and was then famously deployed during the Salem Witch trials in Massachusetts, USA, during the same period. I am indebted to Amir Attaran for drawing the analogy between the use of spectral evidence in witch trials and speculative material in the Ombudsperson delisting procedures.

[490] *Kadi* v. *Commission*, paras. 157, 177.

whilst being sensitive to the concerns of targeting states by excluding the relevant 'details' and 'particulars'.[491]

In practice this means that 'dialogue meetings' can be spent trying to rebut adverse inferences drawn from unseen material in accordance with the broadest and most elastic of associational standards. In my client's case, this involved responding to claims by the Ombudsperson built on allegations previously made by prosecutors using fragments of telephone intercept material more than fifteen years old and that had, in many instances, already been deemed to be of little probative value by the courts. Neither the original intercept material or transcripts were provided, and so the basis and context for the inferences being put to my client were often left entirely unclear, thus reducing his capacity to defend himself and exacerbating the unfairness of the whole process. Our dialogue meeting lasted over eight hours. The more unseen intercept material the Ombudsperson relied upon throughout the course of the day, the stronger the inferences being drawn seemed to become. Although much of the information used was openly acknowledged by the Ombudsperson to be 'broad and vague [in] nature'[492] and could be explained individually, when the fragments and scraps were associated together a cumulative inference of a potential terrorist threat could be drawn.

My client consistently denied all knowledge of and links with terrorism, as he had done before the Italian courts many years before, but this dialogue was an altogether different and more exceptional process. When one infers from inferences and associates from associations using possibilistic forms of reasoning and without disclosing the basis for the inferences and associations being drawn to the other side, it is extremely difficult to mount what most lawyers consider to be a proper defence. In my experience, these 'dialogue meetings' required a particular form of speculative security lawyering that bore little resemblance to the judicial review litigation to which I was accustomed in the English courts. This was not 'de facto judicial review' or an opportunity for my client to share his side of the story, as supporters of the Ombudsperson mechanism suggest, but an inquisitorial and exceptional quasi-legal procedure more akin to a postmodern Star Chamber.[493] Comparable mechanisms of

---

[491] Interview K. According to the Ombudsperson: 'sometimes they will say, "This is the only way we would allow that information to be put" or I might say "I'm going to ask this question, is that okay?"'.

[492] Letter from the UN 1267 Ombudsperson (dated 15 August 2013).

[493] The Star Chamber was an English Royal Prerogative court active from the fifteenth–seventeenth centuries. It was infamous for its secrecy, inquisitorial methods, use of

secret justice (such as Closed Material Procedures in the UK) at least have special advocates who can try to mitigate this inequality of arms by accessing the underlying material and making submissions on the defendant's behalf. No such mechanism exists here. There is only Ombudsperson dialogue. As Lord Bingham has observed: 'It is inconsistent with the most rudimentary notions of fairness to blindfold a man and then impose a standard which only the sighted could hope to meet.'[494] Yet requiring the listed to explain themselves to an inferential standard applied by the Ombudsperson in secret to material that they will never see is, in my experience, precisely what this dialogue phase is all about.

3.7 Multiplicity and Experimentation in Global Exceptional Governance

Since the end of the Cold War the Security Council's powers have dramatically expanded to encompass a diverse array of novel and diffuse global threats. UN sanctions – previously criticised as a 'blunt instrument' that engendered widespread humanitarian suffering – were recalibrated as targeted or 'smart'. The 9/11 attacks accelerated these processes of 'stretching the international peace and security envelope', with individuals suspected of being nodes in global terrorist networks transformed into objects of legal intervention by the Security Council for the first time. But when IOs 'pierce the state veil' and begin exercising coercive powers over individuals, the dynamics of the international system radically change.[495] Individual rights are interfered with without the possibility of redress. Executive decision-making is detached from domestic and regional review mechanisms and 'drifts upward' into 'global administrative space' where conventional legal constraints no longer apply.[496]

---

torture and reliance on involuntary confessions. As such, the Star Chamber has become synonymous with the worst excesses of exceptional medieval justice and is often used by common law jurists to account for the constitutional origins of due process principles and procedural justice.

[494] *A and Others* v. *Secretary of State for the Home Department*, para. 59.

[495] Emma Dunlop, 'Globalization and sovereignty: global threats and international security', in Sabino Cassese (ed.), *Research Handbook on Global Administrative Law* (Cheltenham: Edward Elgar Publishing, 2016), p. 468.

[496] On 'upward drift' see: Gráinne de Búrca, 'The European Court of Justice and the international legal order after Kadi' (2010) 51 *Harvard International Law Journal* 1, 3. On 'global administrative space' see: Kingsbury et al., 'The emergence of global administrative law', 25–7.

The ISIL and Al-Qaida list, in other words, has come to entrench
a global state of exception. Giving individuals the means to challenge
their listing and bring the Security Council to account has thus become
the key fault-line and litmus test of the Council's global security law-
building project.[497]

The creation of the Office of the Ombudsperson in 2009 was designed to
resolve this accountability dilemma, and for many it did. Scores of individuals were delisted following recommendations by the Ombudsperson
and the Security Council has now moved away from due process concerns
towards list implementation issues, fighting ISIL and FTFs and extending
the travel ban around the globe. The Ombudsperson has been held up as an
accountability success, despite the continued reservations of the courts and
constitutionalist scholars. The history of the Security Council due process
debate has now been written, and reiterated innumerable times, as one of
conflict leading to incremental improvements by the Council, institutional
learning and responsive global governance.

Key actors may disagree on the most appropriate response to take
and whether the procedural protections offered by the Ombudsperson
go far enough. But we can all seemingly agree that this experiment has
been a step in the right direction and provided something better than
the legal black hole that existed before.[498] As GAL lawyers, legal pluralists and functionalists continually remind us, there is no '"one size fits
all" or "universally applicable" model of procedural fairness' for resolving postnational accountability problems.[499] Rights protections needs
to be recast onto 'a more flexible gliding scale' when we are dealing with
global security law norm conflicts.[500] De facto judicial review by the
Ombudsperson might not be ideal, in other words, but it is good
enough.

This chapter has challenged this teleological narrative and claim that
the Ombudsperson is 'as good as it gets' by providing a genealogical
account of this institutional experiment's emergence.[501] This allowed me
to 're-orientate the received narrative of this institution' as something
more complex and contingent, placing the reproduction of power

---

[497] On individual rights as a 'fault line' in this domain, see: Elspeth Guild, EU Counter-
Terrorism Action: A Fault line between law and politics?' (Brussels: CEPS Liberty and
Security in Europe Series, April 2010).

[498] On the idea of the legal black hole, see: Dyzenhaus, *The Constitution of Law*.

[499] Hovell, *The Power of Process*, p. 35.

[500] Cuyvers, 'Give me one good reason', 1786.

[501] Rodiles, 'The design of UN sanctions'.

through practice at the centre of my analysis.[502] It helped me highlight divergences between different actors to underscore my key argument: that the list is a multiple object enacted through the diverse practices of those in the listing assemblage with a stake in this accountability problem. Academic scholar-experts concerned with the humanitarian effects of targeted sanctions and judges in the EU courts vested to protect fundamental rights, for example, produce entirely divergent notions of what this list is, what its key accountability problems are and how they can best be resolved. This is not just a question of plurality, or of different perspectives on the same set of problems, but also a problem of multiplicity.

Existing accounts acknowledge the differences in this domain, but contain them in various ways. For Devika Hovell, for example, the 'debate about due process in Security Council decision-making has played out for well over a decade' and 'increasingly resembles a conversation of the deaf' – with courts and lawyers on one side and the Council on the other talking at cross-purposes.[503] For Hovell, this 'intransigence' is essentially 'a question of (flawed) methodology' and thus something that might be resolved.[504] But only if we cease asserting claims to fundamental rights in the international realm and embrace a 'contextual approach' to due process that primarily aims to 'support institutional practice' and enhance the legitimacy of Security Council action.[505] For others, the protracted nature of the list accountability debate reflects the diversity of disciplinary and epistemic frames involved. As one interviewee closely involved in the Office of the Ombudsperson reform process put it:

> There's a real divide here and this is somewhat disciplinary ... There is a law side – and I say that it's easy for the lawyers because there's a right and wrong here. But on the other side – the political side, the policy side, the sanctions side – there's a *different* kind of logic where, 'Well, isn't this close enough to effective remedy?'. There is this fundamental disciplinary [divide] in some of these debates ... Sometimes the argument gets reduced to: 'The Americans want this'. No. The lawyers all share an epistemic community and way of thinking about the issues. The political scientists have a different way. The policy practitioners concerned with

---

[502] Ben Golder, 'The responsibility to protect: practice, genealogy, biopolitics' (2013) 1(1) *London Review of International Law* 158, 163.
[503] Hovell, *The Power of Process*, p. 1.
[504] Ibid. p. 2.
[505] Ibid. p. 4.

> abuse of power [have another] . . . So many of the divisions actually fall
> into almost disciplinary understandings of the problem.[506]

This is the familiar problem of 'regime interaction' or 'international policy coordination'.[507] Such accounts adopt a managerial approach to global jurisdictional conflicts, suggesting that differences 'can be overcome by coordinating and adjusting the operation of single regimes so as to ensure the smooth functioning of the whole' – as Hovell's argument outlined above suggests.[508] The key problem with these functional accounts of world politics is that they leave their reality fundamentally intact. They permit 'mutually exclusive perspectives, discrete, existing side by side, in a transparent space', as Hovell's 'conversation of the deaf' analogy suggests. 'While in the centre, the object of many gazes' – in this case, the list and its accountability problems – 'remains singular, intangible, untouched'.[509]

When we foreground the assemblage practices, expertise and governance techniques of different actors and follow how and what they enact, a more textured and complex topology of the global emerges. Performing reality through technologies and practices, as STS scholars have observed, fractures and multiplies it. Drawing from such insights, this chapter has provided a praxiographic account of the listing assemblage in action, in efforts to resolve persistent accountability problems. I have argued that differences between actors in the assemblage are not just epistemological, but have a crucially important ontological dimension as well. We have a Legal List, a Humanitarian List, a Living List, a Compliant List and a Credibility List all vying to resolve an accountability problem framed in their own terms and bring it within it their control. The 'politics of redefinition' that Koskenniemi argues is driving jurisdictional conflicts in the postnational present is not only a question of expert idiom, perspectives and authority.[510] Because 'objects come into being . . . with the practices in which they are manipulated . . . [and] are not the same from one site to another', there is also an ontological politics

---

506 Interview G (original emphasis).
507 This literature is vast. For an overview, see: Young, *Regime Interaction*; John G. Ruggie, 'Territoriality and beyond: problematizing modernity in international relations' (1993) 47(1) *International Organization*, 139; Andreas Antoniades, 'Epistemic communities, epistemes and the construction of (world) politics' (2003) 17(1) *Global Society* 2.
508 Koskenniemi, 'Hegemonic regimes', 305.
509 Mol, *The Body Multiple*, p. 76.
510 Koskenniemi, *The Politics*, p. 67.

to conflicts of the list and hard assemblage work involved in seeking to overcome them.[511]

Having developed a critical genealogy of the list accountability problem, this chapter then advanced a second key argument: that the Ombudsperson is a unique figure of global legal expertise that contains multiplicity, absorbs conflict and holds the listing assemblage together in the face of tension. Drawing from interviews with the former post-holder (Ms Kimberly Prost) and my own experiences as a practitioner representing listed individuals, I sought to take the reader beyond the vapid claim that this mechanism offers 'fair and clear' accountability procedures. Three elements specifically crafted by the Ombudsperson to work in this 'special' environment were subjected to empirical scrutiny: their decision-making processes, 'dialogue' meetings and speculative evidential standards. Each element involves the recombination of existing legal categories usually associated with judicial review (reasoned decision-making, transparency, standards of proof, etc.) into novel quasi-juridical forms aimed at entrenching preemptive security, avoiding political 'minefields' and attending to state and UNSC sensitivities. These legal knowledge practices, in other words, are deeply political and do important work smoothing out the conflicts of the list. In my analysis, the Ombudsperson is an institutional 'boundary object', fostering coherence across the 'intersecting social worlds' of the list and gluing disparate strands of the assemblage together.[512]

These findings problematise the pervasive claim that the Ombudsperson is a normatively positive improvement and step in the right direction. In 2016 the Watson Institute finally conceded that the listing regime, which it has invested so much effort in reforming and defending, had 'evolved into the realm of the permanent exception'.[513] This followed the former Special Rapporteur's conclusion that the list is a 'permanent tool . . . more closely resembling a system of international law enforcement than [the] temporary political measure' it was originally designed to be.[514] In my account, this list is a far-reaching experiment in global emergency law and the Ombudsperson attenuates and fortifies this global exception in important ways, through their assemblage practices and delisting processes.

---

[511] Mol, *The Body Multiple*.

[512] Star and Griesemer, 'Institutional ecology'.

[513] Thomas Biersteker, Sue Eckert and Marcos Tourinho, 'Conclusion' in Biersteker, Eckert and Tourinho (eds.), *Targeted Sanctions: The Impacts and Effectiveness of United Nations Action* (Cambridge University Press, 2016), p. 273.

[514] Un. Doc. A/67/396, para. 12.

4

Complexity in the Courts: the Spatiotemporal Dynamics of the List*

> Given the difficulties of sharing intelligence . . . the UN is inherently a highly limited mechanism for conducting counter-terrorism operations . . . On the other hand, the UN's global reach and the Security Council's Chapter VII authority are valuable assets . . . [G]oing forward, the US has a two-fold task – to improve the current UN system and use it more effectively as a weapon in the war against terrorism.
>
> US Embassy Cable, War on Terrorism – The Security Council's Role – Making it Work for the US[1]

Previous chapters have analysed listing expertise across various sites to show the complex, contingent and contradictory ways it produces global security law. Chapter 2 showed how the mundane technical work of the ISIL and Al-Qaida Monitoring Team and the technology of the list condition this regime in crucially important ways. Chapter 3 provided a detailed genealogical account of the Ombudsperson's emergence and showed how this unique experiment seeks to resolve list accountability conflicts but ends up embedding preemptive logics and security practices. Each chapter has followed the list and its protagonists to particular sites to show how the problems negotiated there *produce* this domain of global security law in distinctive ways. The Law of the List, as I have shown, is more than the Security Council edicts that bestow it with formal authority. It is an assemblage of norms, knowledges and techniques produced and held together by an array of localised practices at different sites and scales.

But what might it mean to think of this listing assemblage as a novel kind of global legal weapon, as the cable above suggests? Something

---

* Parts of this chapter were previously published in: Gavin Sullivan and Ben Hayes, *Blacklisted: Targeted Sanctions, Preemptive Security and Fundamental Rights* (Berlin: ECCHR, 2011); Gavin Sullivan, 'Transnational legal assemblages and global security law: topologies and temporalities of the list' (2014) 5(1) *Transnational Legal Theory* 81; and Gavin Sullivan, 'Secret justice inside the EU courts' *Al-Jazeera* (online, 19 April 2014).
[1] US Embassy Cable 06USUNNEWYORK1609 (dated 22 August 2006).

formally tethered to rules of international law but deployed in radical new ways to incapacitate individuals who might pose a threat in the future. What qualities might make the list work 'more effectively' in these terms? And how might existing legal principles and judicial practices be rearranged to better realise its potential coercive effects? What happens when the preemptive security logics and governance of radical uncertainty embedded in the list meet the principles of judicial proof and procedural justice long used and protected by the courts? How do the courts perform judicial review when there is no executive 'decision' to review? What legal and political changes can be made to resolve or accommodate fundamental conflicts of this kind? And what might these transformations tell us about how global security law works in action?

   This chapter probes these problems by bringing the latent spatiotemporal dynamics of the list to the analytical surface. It follows the list to the site of the EU courts trying to undertake judicial review of this unique legal weapon.[2] Drawing from interviews with judges, sanctions officials and classified US Embassy cables, I analyse the EU courts as a localised site deeply entangled in the production of global security law.[3] My key argument is that the technology of the list is driven by dynamics of nonsynchrony and dis-location and a mosaic epistemology. Understanding how these elements work is crucially important because they are operating underneath the radar of formal law to generate legal conflict and stretch the scope of this exceptional governance regime in practice. Building on previous chapters, I argue that detailed micro-level empirical

---

[2] Technically the EU courts do not review the ISIL and Al-Qaida list, because they cannot review Chapter VII measures of the Security Council. Rather, they review the EU decision to implement the UN list into the EU legal order.

[3] The literature on local sites producing the global is vast and has been discussed in the introductory chapter (Chapter 1). See, for example: Bruno Latour, *Reassembling the Social: An Introduction to Actor-Network-Theory* (Oxford: Oxford University Press, 2005), pp. 173–90; Anna Tsing, 'The global situation' (2000) 15(3) *Cultural Anthropology* 327; Richard Warren Perry and Bill Maurer (eds.), *Globalization under Construction: Governmentality, Law and Identity* (Minneapolis MN: University of Minnesota Press, 2003); Aihwa Ong and Stephen J. Collier (eds.), *Global Assemblages: Technology, Politics and Ethics as Anthropological Problems* (Oxford: Blackwell Publishing, 2008); George E. Marcus, 'Ethnography in/of the world system: the emergence of multi-sited ethnography' (1995) *Annual Review of Anthropology* 95; Saskia Sassen, *The Global City: New York, London, Tokyo* (Princeton NJ: Princeton University Press, 2001); Annelise Riles, *The Network Inside Out* (Anne Arbor MI: University of Michigan Press, 2001); Sally Engle Merry, 'New legal realism and the ethnography of transnational law' (2006) 31(4) *Law and Social Inquiry* 975.

analysis of how listing conflicts are negotiated reveals important insights into how this global security regime is being assembled.

Time and space have long been recognised as central vectors of globalisation. Yet they remain almost entirely neglected in global legal scholarship, which continues to posit law in positivist terms abstracted from time and space.[4] This reductionism impoverishes conceptions of what global law is and funnels legal scholarship into a zero-sum debate between the One (global constitutionalism) and the Many (global legal pluralism).[5] This chapter instead draws on the sociological research of Saskia Sassen, who argues that globalisation proceeds through the emergence of novel spatiotemporal assemblages that stimulate legal fragmentation and conflict.[6] But, whereas Sassen's work is pitched at a macro-level of historical change, this chapter maps dynamics and effects operating at a more granular scale – contributing to debates on the transformations of law under conditions of globalisation by showing how global security regimes are being built.

To develop these claims the chapter is divided into two interrelated sections. The first section ('4.1 Non-Synchronous Law') highlights the temporal dynamics of the list by exploring problems associated with using intelligence-as-evidence as the basis for listing decisions. The idea of non-synchronicity draws on the groundbreaking work of Boaventura de Sousa Santos, who argues that law is never singular but always an effect of the 'interaction and intersection among legal spaces' or 'interlegality'.[7] For Santos, law is 'a highly dynamic process' because the sites and networks that clash and constitute it 'are *non-synchronic* and

---

[4] There is little literature that takes spatiotemporal dynamics seriously in relation to global law. See, however: Neil Walker, 'Out of place and out of time: law's fading co-ordinates', Working Paper No 2009/01 (Edinburgh: University of Edinburgh School of Law, 2009); Hans Lindahl, *Fault Lines of Globalization: Legal Order and the Politics of A-Legality* (Oxford: Oxford University Press, 2013); Mireille Delmas-Marty, *Ordering Pluralism: A Conceptual Framework for Understanding the Transnational Legal World* (Oxford: Hart Publishing, 2009).

[5] The global constitutionalism versus global legal pluralism debates were discussed in Chapter 1. Framing these debates as the One and the Many is drawn from: Desmond Manderson, 'Beyond the provincial: space, aesthetics and modernist legal theory' (1995) 20 *Melbourne University Law Review* 1049, 1060.

[6] Saskia Sassen, 'Neither global nor national: novel assemblages of territory, authority and rights' (2008) 1(1–2) *Ethics and Global Politics* 61; Saskia Sassen, *Territory, Authority, Rights: From Medieval to Global Assemblages* (Princeton NJ: Princeton University Press, 2006).

[7] Boaventura de Sousa Santos, 'Law: a map of misreading. Toward a postmodern conception of law' (1987) 14(3) *Journal of Law and Society* 279, 288.

thus result in uneven and unstable mixings of legal codes'.[8] This chapter extends this insight to the empirical study of conflicting legal temporalities. In my account, non-synchronous law is best thought of as a form of legality composed of divergent temporal logics that are literally 'out of sync'. I argue that the ISIL and Al-Qaida list is a paradigmatic example of non-synchronous law because of the ways it interlaces different temporal logics and epistemic practices associated with intelligence and evidence together into productive relation.

To show how this relation plays out in practice I focus my analysis on the EU courts. But, instead of adding to the already voluminous literature on the *Kadi* case, I examine the reform of the EGC's procedural rules to allow the European judiciary to handle closed, security-sensitive material for the first time. This mundane reform process has hardly been discussed in the legal literature to date. But I argue that these minor technical changes on evidential rules are extremely important. The key question I ask is: how was a court vested to protect fundamental rights so readily enlisted to build, what is in effect, a legally authorised state of exception? The answers I provide do not look towards some sovereign decision or inexorable preemptive turn, but to the bona fide efforts of the judiciary to ameliorate practical problems of legal governance. I argue that the spatiotemporal dynamics and mosaic epistemology of the list are in friction with conventional legal practices (like judicial review) and forms of inductive reasoning that underpin principles of legal proof. Managing these problems stimulates new recombinant legal practices and forms of reasoning that were not possible before. In other words, the list is altering, at a very granular level, the ways judges produce 'legal truth'. It is also taking judicial reasoning into the uncertain terrain of the contemporary security mosaic, with its logics of correspondences and associations.

The common view – in security studies and criminology concerned with risk governance – is that with the increasing shift towards preemption and governing of future threats, conventional legal principles and practices stand to be abandoned. So, we need either radical new forms of jurisprudence and politics or a renewed commitment to liberal legality to protect ourselves from the perils of 'Future Law' and restrain the inexorable rise of the preventative state.[9] This chapter contributes to these

---

[8] Ibid. 298 (emphasis added).

[9] See, for example: Lucia Zedner, 'Preventive justice or pre-punishment? The case of control orders' (2007) 60(1) *Current Legal Problems* 174; Claudia Aradau and Rens van Munster, 'Governing terrorism through risk: Taking precautions, (un)knowing the future' (2007) 13(1)

debates by showing that when pre-emption and rule of law come into contact one does not necessarily supplant the other. Risk and pre-emption, in other words, are not monolithic or emanating from the logic of late modernity in ways that herald an epochal shift. Instead, legal knowledges and modes of governance are reorganised in different ways through this encounter. My analysis suggests that global sociolegal scholarship should be empirically attentive to the forms this reorganisation takes if we want to understand the complexities of law in the present.

The second section of this chapter ('4.2 Dis-Located Law') examines how this non-synchronicity confounds and reorders the spatial dynamics of judicial review. The prevailing literature suggests that the EU courts have robustly defended the rule of law against this UN listing regime. Yet, in my analysis, the list is both reordering how the EU judiciary produces legal knowledge and altering the judicial review process itself in potentially far-reaching ways. Judicial review is usually retrospectively orientated towards the 'decision' of the authority under challenge. But I show how using intelligence-as-evidence for terrorism-listing effectively defers this space of decision and challenges the judicial process because the decision supposedly under review is, strictly speaking, not there. I use the term 'dis-located law' to capture this dynamic process because it draws attention to both the location of legal process and the sense of legal fracture occasioned through this deferral. My analysis here highlights this process of evacuation and shows how key sites of formal decision-making across the listing assemblage are rendered baseless as a result. When the list is analysed through the lens of the Security Council resolutions that constitute it, the global is projected as something 'broadly encompassing, seamless and mobile' and representative of the 'international community'.[10] But my micro-analysis of how preemptive security problems are being mediated by the courts shows that this global security regime is something far more 'patchy' or 'partial and situated' than most accounts suggest.[11]

I analyse two recent listing case decisions by the EU courts to show these dynamics at work and highlight the confusion that they are generating in the courts. The first case (*Kadi II*) tries to locate a listing decision for the purposes of review by bringing it *forward in time* and

European Journal of International Relations 89, 106; Louise Amoore, *The Politics of Possibility: Risk and Security beyond Probability* (Durham NC: Duke University Press, 2013), p. 85.

[10] Stephen J. Collier and Aihwa Ong, 'Global assemblages, anthropological problems' in Ong and Collier, *Global Assemblages*, p. 12.

[11] Ibid.

into the litigation process itself. I argue that this stands to transform the EU judicial review process into something much more plastic and fluid than has usually been the case. The second decision (*Abdulrahim*) moves in an altogether opposite direction, by looking backwards towards a listing decision presumed to have taken place in the past. Whilst the prevailing literature suggests that the EU courts are robustly defending the rule of law from attack via this UN listing regime, my analysis suggests that the relation between the two is more complicated and co-productive in practice. I show that, through this encounter, the list is modulating and reordering, in potentially far-reaching ways, the EU judicial review process itself. This is not merely a matter of 'force yield[ing] place to law' or vice versa, but of pre-emptive security governance techniques reassembling the ways that justice is done.[12]

The spatiotemporal dynamics of the list are deeply entangled in assembling a novel form of global exceptional governance: one that carries the weight of the UN collective security system yet remains without foundation – a legal weapon that enables listing authorities to wield legal violence over individuals without any real consideration as to why. It is an exception that mutates and expands through legal efforts (however well-intentioned) to ameliorate its worst effects, defying attempts to fill its 'legal black holes'[13] with law. Building on the tradition of critical legal and security scholarship that emphasises the co-production of law and emergency politics,[14] this chapter shows how mapping the fragmented spatiotemporal dimensions of legal governance can provide important insights into how global emergencies come to be normalised, stretched and rendered durable through legal techniques.

---

[12] Cian Murphy, 'Secret evidence in EU security law: special advocates before the Court of Justice?' in David Cole, Federico Fabbrini and Arianna Vedaschi (eds.), *Secrecy, National Security and the Vindication of Constitutional Law* (Cheltenham: Edward Elgar Publishing, 2013), pp. 268, 282.

[13] David Dyzenhaus, *The Constitution of Law: Legality in a Time of Emergency* (Cambridge: Cambridge University Press, 2006).

[14] See, for example: Fleur Johns, *Non-legality in International Law: Unruly Law* (Cambridge: Cambridge University Press, 2013); Derek Gregory, 'The black flag: Guantanamo Bay and the space of exception' (2006) 88(4) *Geografiska Annaler* 404; Susanne Krasmann, 'Law's knowledge: on the susceptibility and resistance of legal practices to security matters' (2012) 16(4) *Theoretical Criminology* 379; Louise Amoore, 'Risk before justice: when the law contests its own suspension' (2008) 21(4) *Leiden Journal of International Law* 847; and Nasser Hussain, *The Jurisprudence of Emergency: Colonialism and the Rule of Law* (Ann Arbor MI: University of Michigan Press, 2009).

4.1   Non-Synchronous Law and the Use of Intelligence-As-Evidence

Evidence is integral to the production of legal knowledge. It is collected in relation to specific acts alleged to have taken place in the past and ordinarily used to 'aid the court in establishing the probability of past events into which it must inquire'.[15] Legal evidence is therefore retrospectively orientated, as it comes to be used to 'establish that a version of what occurred has an acceptable probability of being correct'.[16] In judicial review emphasis is placed upon 'evidence which was before, or available to, the public body at the time of its impugned action' – that is, relevant evidential questions are intimately tied to the nature of the executive decision-making under challenge.[17] Legal evidence is evaluated publicly by judges in accordance with established forensic standards of proof – usually to either determine guilt beyond reasonable doubt (the criminal standard) or liability on the balance of probabilities (the civil standard).[18] To rely on evidence in court, certain rules must be satisfied – hearsay, for example, cannot be relied upon – yet these rules differ significantly depending on the legal systems where they are used.[19] Whilst common law systems use exclusionary rules to prohibit reliance

---

[15] Richard Glover, *Murphy on Evidence* (14th edn, Oxford: Oxford University Press, 2015), p. 3. See also William Twining, 'Evidence as a multi-disciplinary subject' (2003) 2 *Law, Probability and Risk* 91: 'disputed trials are typically concerned with inquiries into past events in which the hypotheses are defined in advance by law' (at 103).

[16] Glover, ibid. at 3. My discussion here is introductory, focused on evidence in law rather than evidence more generally and aimed at differentiating evidence and intelligence as typologies of knowledge to assist in my analysis of the Al-Qaida listing regime. It is beyond the scope of this chapter to analyse the logic of proof and the complex relations between evidence, inference and proof in the detail it deserves. For an excellent study on these issues, see: Terence Anderson, David Schum and William Twining, *Analysis of Evidence* (2nd edn, Cambridge: Cambridge University Press, 2005).

[17] Michael Fordham, *Judicial Review Handbook* (4th edn, Oxford: Hart Publishing, 2004), p. 331.

[18] Whilst I use the English legal system as the typology here, degrees of proof are acknowledged within both standards in that context.

[19] Hearsay is generally excluded, but the evidential rules on this issue are more complicated than presented here. In the USA hearsay is generally excluded in both civil and criminal matters. In the UK hearsay is expressly admissible in civil proceedings (see Civil Procedure Rules, Part 33, and Civil Evidence Act 1995, s. 2) and admissible on exceptional grounds in certain criminal matters (see Criminal Procedure Rules, Part 34, and Criminal Justice Act 2003, s. 114). Article 6(3)(d) of the European Convention on Human Rights generally prohibits the use of hearsay in criminal matters, as those charged have the right 'to examine or have examined witnesses against him and to obtain the attendance and examination of witnesses on his behalf under the same conditions as witnesses against him'. However, this right has been limited in recent case law – see, for example:

upon certain types of evidence, civil law systems tend to admit evidence more freely and accord weaker material less probative value or weight. Evidence, the sources used to obtain it and any exculpatory material must all usually be disclosed so litigants can undertake cross-examination or mount an effective defence, and judges can evaluate the probative value of the material to make evidence-based findings of fact.

Intelligence is a rather different form of knowledge.[20] Although evidence and intelligence are both species of inferential reasoning, intelligence is primarily concerned with future threats and risk possibilities, rather than specific acts undertaken in the past. It is orientated speculatively rather than retrospectively.[21] Intelligence is kept secret to protect the sources and methods used to obtain it and is internally evaluated in relation to the importance of the risk, rather than externally and publicly verified in accordance with a forensic standard of proof. Intelligence is therefore a much more conjectural form of knowledge than is the case with evidence.[22] It openly admits opinion and hearsay and allows loose correlations from a disparate array of unverified data sources to be freely relied upon.

During the Cold War intelligence usually involved inductive processes of 'puzzle-solving' and 'looking for additional pieces to fill out a mosaic of understanding whose broad shape was a[lready] given'.[23] It tended to deal with probabilistic risks and problems that could be solved with a degree of certainty given access to the right information.[24] Yet in the post-9/11 period of the global war on terror, the nature of risks and threats, and therefore that of intelligence, have dramatically changed. The shift from targeting states to targeting transnational non-state actor networks that traverse domestic and international boundaries, for example, presents 'mysteries' that lack both 'a shared story that would facilitate

Al-Khawaja and Tahery v. *United Kingdom* App. Nos. 26766/05 and 22228/06 (ECtHR, 15 December 2011).

[20] I draw upon the valuable work of Kent Roach on this issue. See Kent Roach, 'The eroding distinction between intelligence and evidence in terrorism investigations' in Andrew Lynch, Nicola McGarrity and George Williams (eds.), *Counter-Terrorism and Beyond* (London: Routledge, 2010), p. 48.

[21] Twining, 'Evidence as a multi-disciplinary subject', 104. On the speculative, see: Marieke de Goede, *Speculative Security: The Politics of Pursuing Terrorist Monies* (Minneapolis MN: University of Minnesota Press, 2012).

[22] On conjectural reasoning in the war on terror, see Claudia Aradau and Rens van Munster, *Politics of Catastrophe: Genealogies of the Unknown* (London: Routledge, 2011).

[23] Gregory F. Treverton, *Intelligence for an Age of Terror* (Cambridge University Press, 2009) 3.

[24] Ibid.

analysis and communication' and a definable location because transnational terrorist networks are dynamic and both 'here' at home as well as 'over there' or abroad.[25] So the risks of global terrorism are experienced as more amorphous and unbounded than those of the Cold War. Donald Rumsfeld's invocation of 'unknown unknowns' speaks to this heightened epistemic complexity, as does the 9/11 Commission's finding that the US intelligence community's failure to properly 'connect the dots' contributed to the 11 September 2001 terrorist attacks.[26] In response to the mass surveillance and algorithmic data-governance techniques exposed by Edward Snowden, this idea of dot-connecting has been reposed in the era of big data as the problem of 'finding the needle in a haystack' of electronic communications. But, unlike the traditional detective work of finding particular clues and using them to unveil the whole story, here intelligence agencies 'argue that the hay field – all the data – is needed to derive both expectations about normality and the anomalous elements. Big data is the new whole.'[27] The contemporary security mosaic, in other words, presupposes a very different epistemology than the inductive reasoning that marked earlier forms of intelligence analysis. It relies on logics of association and correspondence and practices of pattern-discovery through 'drawing things together' in order to identify unknown potential future terrorists and risky persons.[28]

The ISIL and Al-Qaida list is a form of global security law that collapses the distinction between intelligence and evidence. Its format (the list) is one of the most archaic ordering devices. But it is a governance device produced with the epistemology of the contemporary security mosaic. On the one hand, the list is a preemptive security instrument designed to counter potential terrorist threats before they emerge and act in advance

---

[25] Ibid. pp. 4, 28.

[26] Rumsfeld's statement was made in the lead-up to the 2003 invasion of Iraq in relation to the lack of evidence linking Saddam Hussein's regime to the supply of weapons of mass destruction to terrorist groups:

As we know, there are known knowns; there are things we know we know. We also know there are known unknowns; that is to say we know there are some things we do not know. But there are also unknown unknowns – the ones we don't know we don't know. And if one looks throughout the history of our country and other free countries, it is the latter category that tend to be the difficult ones.

For the transcript of Rumsfeld's briefing, see: bit.ly/2TgzymU. The *Final Report of the National Commission on Terrorist Attacks Upon the United States* (2004) is available at: bit.ly/1jGQbS2.

[27] Claudia Aradau, 'The signature of security: big data, anticipation, surveillance' (2015) 191 *Radical Philosophy* 21.

[28] Ibid.

of any legal determination of culpability through risk-based techniques of 'disruption, restriction and incapacitation'.[29] Criminal due process standards are inapplicable in this domain because these sanctions have been deemed to be preventative, rather than punitive, measures.[30] According to the guidelines of the UN1267 Sanctions Committee, for example: '*A criminal charge or conviction is not a prerequisite for listing as the sanctions are intended to be preventative in nature.*'[31] In practice, this means that listing decisions are based on intelligence suggesting that the listed individual is in some way 'associated with' ISIL, Al-Qaida or their associates.[32]

This underlying material, as discussed in Chapter 2, is diffusely produced through an array of different security agencies, counterterrorism experts and national institutional actors.

On the other hand, the UN list is not self-enforcing and must be implemented. And it is a core principle of the rule of law that when individuals are targeted by executive action they are entitled to certain due process protections, such as the right to an effective remedy. But, to exercise these rights in any meaningful way, one must be informed of the material underneath the accusation. So, listing decisions are formally

---

[29] Jude McCulloch and Sharon Pickering, 'Pre-crime and counter-terrorism: imagining future crime in the "war on terror"' (2009) 49(5) *British Journal Of Criminology* 628, 629; Marieke de Goede, 'The politics of preemption and the war on terror in Europe' (2008) 14(1) *European Journal of International Relations* 161; Amoore, 'Risk before justice', 847; International Commission of Jurists (ICJ), *Assessing the Damage, Urging Action: Report of the Eminent Jurists Panel on Terrorism, Counter-Terrorism and Human Rights* (Geneva: ICJ, 2009), pp. 91–122.

[30] On the preventative/punitive distinction, see Case T-85/09, *Kadi v. Commission* [2010] ECR II 5177, at para. 150:

It might even be asked whether – given that now nearly 10 years have passed since the applicant's funds were originally frozen – it is not now time to call into question the finding of this Court … [that] the freezing of funds is a temporary precautionary measure … The same is true of the statement of the Security Council … that the measures in question 'are preventative in nature and are not reliant upon criminal standards set out under national law'. In the scale of a human life, 10 years in fact represent a substantial period of time and the question of the classification of the measures in question as preventative or punitive, protective or confiscatory, civil or criminal seems now to be an open one.

[31] UN1267 Sanctions Committee, 'Guidelines for the Committee for the Conduct of its Work' (5 September 2018), para. 6(d) (emphasis added). See also UNSC S/RES/1822 (2008), Preamble.

[32] David Cole, 'Terror financing, guilt by association and the paradigm of prevention in the war on terror' in Andrea Bianchi and Alex Keller (eds.), *Counterterrorism: Democracy's Challenge* (Oxford: Hart Publishing, 2008); Cian Murphy, *EU Counterterrorism Law: Pre-Emption and the Rule of Law* (Oxford: Hart Publishing, 2012), pp. 142–4.

taken by the UN1267 Sanctions Committee, putatively on the basis of closed *intelligence*, but are implemented by Member States and regional bodies (such as the EU) in circumstances where individuals are entitled to disclosable *evidence*. The ISIL and Al-Qaida list therefore works as a hybrid legal technology by using *intelligence-as-evidence*, collapsing these traditionally distinct forms of knowledge and generating conflict between international security and human rights law in the process.

The use of intelligence-as-evidence is of course not unique to the ISIL and Al-Qaida listing regime, but one of the defining features of post-9/11 counterterrorism law.[33] There are two broad approaches to resolving the problems associated with using intelligence-as-evidence: either change the nature of the intelligence underneath the list so it can be used in court proceedings or change the nature of court proceedings so that this material can be relied upon without disclosure.[34]

As discussed in Chapter 3, the various decisions taken by the EU courts in the *Kadi* case – and much of the European sanctions case law annulling listing decisions for violating defence rights – have tended to endorse the first approach to resolving this problem. In the 2010 *Kadi* decision, for example, the EGC held that the Narrative Summary of Reasons put forward as the grounds for justifying the listing decision was composed of 'vague and imprecise allegations' that prevented Mr Kadi from knowing and effectively contesting the case against him. Listed individuals were entitled to an 'in principle, full review' that extended to 'the substantive assessments of the Sanctions Committee itself and the *evidence* underlying' its decision.[35] On appeal, in its 2013 *Kadi II* decision the ECJ confirmed that judicial review could only be based on evidence that has been disclosed. According to the Court, 'in principle, full review' required judicial 'verification of the allegations' to enable an assessment of 'the probative value of the information or evidence' and a determination as to whether the underlying reasons, 'or at the very least, one of those

---

[33] For an overview see: ICJ, *Assessing the Damage*, pp. 67–90; Justice, *Secret Evidence* (London: Justice, 2009).Available at: bit.ly/2ZMfL1b. For a cross-jurisdictional analysis, see: Cole et al., *Secrecy*.

[34] On analysing legal governance through problematisation, see: Nikolas Rose and Mariana Valverde, 'Governed by law?' (1998) 7(4) *Social and Legal Studies* 541: 'While it might seem obvious to begin by asking "what does law govern?", from the perspective of government we would not start from law at all. Instead we would start from problems or problematizations – [that is] . . . way[s] in which experience is offered to thought in the form of a problem requiring attention' (at 545).

[35] *Kadi v. Commission*, paras. 173–4 and 129–33 (emphasis added).

reasons', could be 'substantiated'.[36] That is, only disclosure of the closed material underneath the listing decisions (to the Court, if not the listed parties) could ultimately remedy the intelligence-as-evidence problem.

These decisions sent shockwaves through world capitals and the international legal community for challenging the supreme authority of the UN Security Council in this area. Leaked US Embassy cables warned that, 'we cannot risk losing the use of one of our few non-military coercive tools because the EU courts believe that they are somehow illegitimate' and called for a 'coordinated US interagency strategy' targeting EU leaders to 'protect these policies from legal challenge'.[37] Targeted sanctions experts and advocates despaired that these decisions eroded the legitimacy of the Council's Chapter VII UN Charter powers,[38] undermining 'the legal authority of the Security Council in all matters, not just in the imposition of sanctions'.[39] If the ISIL and Al-Qaida list was to survive scrutiny by the EU courts then something clearly had to give. And, eventually, something did.

Whilst robustly protecting fundamental rights in these high-profile *Kadi* cases, the EU courts discretely developed other technical initiatives that threatened to undermine them. Between 2012 and 2015 the EGC worked with the European Commission and Council in dialogue with the ECJ to review its procedural rules so that judges could handle intelligence material without disclosure to targeted individuals – that is, they quietly pursued the second strategy for resolving the *intelligence-as-evidence* problem. These changes passed unnoticed by most scholars working on this issue because they frame legal conflicts through the prism of legal doctrine. But an assemblage lens shifts the analytical focus towards the prosaic sites of legal practice operating underneath the radar of formal law and brings them more clearly into view. In section 4.1.1 I examine

---

[36] Joined Cases C-584/10P, C-593/10P and C-595/10P *Commission, Council and United Kingdom v. Kadi* [2013] ECLI:EU:C:2013:518, para. 124 (hereafter, '*Kadi II*').

[37] US Embassy Cable 09BRUSSELS616 (dated 29 April 2009).

[38] For Biersteker and Eckert: 'There is a real, and growing, political problem associated with the legitimacy, not only of the instrument of targeted sanctions, *but increasingly of actions taken under Chapter VII by the UN Security Council itself*. This is a fundamental challenge to an essential instrument of the international community to counter threats to international peace and security' (emphasis added) – Thomas Biersteker and Sue Eckert, *Addressing Challenges to Targeted Sanctions: An Update of the 'Watson Report'* (Geneva: Graduate Institute Watson Institute for International Studies, 2009), p. 4.

[39] UN Doc S/2011/245 (13 April 2011), Eleventh Report of the Analytical Support and Sanctions Implementation Monitoring Team established pursuant to Security Council Resolution 1526 (2004), para. 30.

this reform process through interviews undertaken with key actors as the proposals were being negotiated. I argue that these procedural reforms are jurisgenerative and reveal key spatiotemporal features of this form of global security law.

4.1.1   Procedural Exceptions and the Forging of Alignments

Until relatively recently, using evidence in the EU courts required full disclosure. Article 67(3) of the Procedural Rules of the EGC stated that only documents provided to all parties could be relied on as evidence, enshrining what is known as the 'adversarial principle'.[40] The reforms examined in this chapter specifically amend this provision 'by laying down a special procedural regime for situations in which the security of the Union or of its Member States or the conduct of their international relations is at issue'.[41] Now, in exceptional circumstances, the executive and judiciary can see underlying closed material that is deemed essential for determining the case but those targeted by intelligence that bring legal challenges cannot.

The reforms refrain from setting up a mechanism (like a Special Advocates procedure)[42] to compensate for the adverse effects of secrecy.[43] Instead, the EGC has simply said it will 'take account of the fact that a main party has not been able to make his views on [the secret material] known' and therefore 'has not been fully able to exercise his rights of defence'[44] when they 'weigh up' the different elements to 'make a reasoned order specifying the procedures to be adopted'.[45] This exception, according to the Court, constitutes a 'significant

---

[40] A similar rule applies in the ECJ (Article 54a, Rules of Procedure of the Court of Justice (OJ C 177, 2.7.2010)).

[41] ST 7795 2014 INIT, *Draft Rules of Procedure of the General Court,* 14 March 2014 (Article 101). Although the changes are designed to meet the problems generated by sanctions litigation, they extend beyond this domain to all matters where the security of the EU, its Member States and/or their international relations are in issue.

[42] Special advocates are security-vetted lawyers who can see the classified material and make submissions to the Court about it, but are prevented from disclosing it to listed parties. For discussion of the viability of special advocates in this context, see Murphy, 'Secret evidence'; and Christina Eckes, 'Decision-making in the dark? – Autonomous EU sanctions and national classification' Legal Studies Research Paper 64 (Amsterdam: Amsterdam Law School 2012).

[43] Armin Cuyvers, '"Give me one good reason": the unified standard of review for sanctions after Kadi II' (2014) 51(6) *Common Market Law Review* 1759, 1779.

[44] *Draft Rules,* Articles 104 and 102.

[45] Ibid. Article 105(6).

innovation'.[46] In February 2015, with the UK government abstaining,[47] the EU Council of Ministers finally approved these reforms. The EGC signed off on the changes shortly thereafter and the new court rules finally entered into force on 1 July 2015.[48]

There is little available information that explains the rationale for this exception to the longstanding principle of open justice or that sheds light on the political and legal complexities underneath these reforms.[49] Until the Council of the EU posted the final draft amendments online in March 2014, the reform process remained almost entirely opaque and shrouded in confidentiality.[50] The proposals approved by the EGC suggest a fairly innocuous process of micro-procedural adjustment. But my empirical analysis of this process reveals a much more complicated negotiation involving a wide range of actors navigating deep-seated conflicts and complexities associated with the list. This procedural reform process, in other words, is best understood as a listing assemblage practice aimed at managing contradictions.

This complexity has been rendered partly visible through listing litigation. EU court cases overturning listing decisions for violating fundamental rights have been a key catalyst for these reforms. The core problems of using intelligence-as-evidence in this domain were identified by the EGC as early as 2006 in *Organisation des Modjahedines du peuple*

---

[46] Ibid. Article 104.

[47] The UK government abstained for two reasons. First, concern that once intelligence material was admitted as evidence it might not be able to be withdrawn at any later stage. Second, there were not procedures in place for EU court judgments and orders made using intelligence-as-evidence to be vetted by the security services. See Comments by Rt Hon D. Lidington MP, Minister for Europe, *House of Lords Select Committee on the European Union Sub-Committee E, Plans for New Court Rules and Conduct of EU Sanctions* (2 March 2015). Available at: bit.ly/1L90118.

[48] See General Court of the European Union, *Press Release No 73/15* (19 June 2015). Available at: bit.ly/1TADREh.

[49] For material discussing these reforms, see Nik de Boer, 'Case C-300/11, ZZ v. Secretary of State for the Home Department. Judgment of the Court (Grand Chamber) of 4 June 2013' (2014) 51(4) *Common Market Law Review* 1235, 1252–6; Stephan Hollenberg, 'The Security Council's 1267/1989 targeted sanctions regime and the use of confidential information: a proposal for decentralization of review' (2015) 28(1) *Leiden Journal of International Law* 49; Alice Riccardi, 'Revisiting the role of the EU judiciary as the stronghold for the protection of human rights while countering terrorism' (2018) 18(2) *Global Jurist* 1; Cuyvers, 'Give me one good reason'.

[50] See, however, posts on the weblog *European Sanctions: Law and Practice* maintained by one of Kadi's lawyers, Maya Lester (available at bit.ly/1CYk37j and bit.ly/2ZMzUEf) and Laurence Norman, 'EU governments approve secret evidence in sanctions cases', *Wall Street Journal* (10 February 2015). Available at: on.wsj.com/2M9bfqx.

d'Iran v. *Council* (the *OMPI* case) – a case involving an Iranian group's challenge to its inclusion on the EU autonomous terrorism list on the basis of material the French government refused to disclose to either the group or the Court.[51] In its decision, the EGC (then Court of First Instance) acknowledged that 'the use of confidential information may be necessary when national security is at stake' but said that this did not free executive bodies from judicial review in terrorism-related matters.[52] 'The Community Courts', the EGC held, '*must* be able to review the lawfulness and merits of the measures to freeze funds without it being possible to raise objections that the evidence and information used by the Council is secret or confidential'.[53] Yet how this imperative of review could be realised in relation to the list was left unclear in this case. Closed material might be provided to the Court 'in accordance with a procedure that remains to be defined', but the issue was ultimately deferred until later.[54]

The possibility of attenuating this problem through procedural design was revisited by the ECJ in its famous 2008 *Kadi* decision. Echoing the sentiments of the EGC in the *OMPI* case, the ECJ acknowledged that in terrorism-listing 'overriding considerations to do with safety or the conduct of the international relations of the Community and of its Member States may militate against the communication of certain matters to the persons concerned'.[55] But it went on to state that 'that does not mean, with regard to the principle of effective judicial protection, that restrictive measures such as those imposed by the contested regulation escape all review by the Community judicature'.[56] Instead, in such exceptional circumstances, the Court should be able to apply special 'techniques which accommodate, on the one hand, legitimate security concerns about the nature and sources of information taken into account ... and, on the other, the need to accord the individual a sufficient measure of procedural justice'.[57] So, although the problem was identified here in *Kadi*, it was again left unresolved. What such

---

[51] Case T-228/02, *Organisation des Modjahedines du peuple d'Iran* v. *Council of European Union* [2006] ECR II-04665.

[52] Ibid. para. 156.

[53] Ibid. para. 155 (emphasis added).

[54] Ibid. para. 158.

[55] Joined Cases C-402P and 415/05P *Kadi and Al Barakaat* v. *Council and Commission* [2008] ECR I 6351, para. 342.

[56] Ibid. para. 343.

[57] Ibid. para 344.

'techniques' for handling intelligence-as-evidence might look like was again left as an open question by the Court.

The *Kadi* case provoked a massive wave of EU listing litigation, increasing the risk that UN and autonomous sanctions might not be implemented in the EU. According to one member of the Commission Legal Service, providing intelligence to EU judges was critical to stemming this potential flood of litigation and protecting terrorist listing policies from further attack:

COMMISSION: The problem that we have ... [is that] we are seeing hundreds of cases that we lost approaching. And we think that these cases could have been won if there was the information. But Member States say it is classified and they cannot give it to the Council ... And [so] we start from the end (the end is the court), by trying to introduce rules of the court that will allow the court to receive classified information.

GS: Presumably the Commission are hoping that re-drafting the rules will allow states to feel more confident to disclose. But ... if states are reluctant to even share [closed material] with Council at the moment in a confidential working party, what would make you think that they would share it with the court if confidential rules apply?

COMMISSION: The fact ... that they will lose a hundred and fifty cases. And if they lose a hundred and fifty cases then the regime will fall apart (any regime would fall apart) .... Fortunately, we don't have any UN listing challenges at the court right now ... If the UN is challenged it is sure ... that they will lose it and then it will have the effect of a [House of Cards].[58]

This threat of regime 'collapse' was widely shared by listing experts within the UN Security Council and powerful states outside the EU, such as the USA. As one former member of the UN ISIL and Al-Qaida Monitoring Team described the impact of the ECJ's 2008 *Kadi* decision:

If EU isn't going to implement, no one is going to implement. Come on, why should Africa or the Middle East implement? So, you'd be left with permanent members implementing and moaning that nobody else is. What's the point of having a ... regime like that? So, these court decisions are *incredibly* important, they're fundamental to survival of the sanctions regime.[59]

---

[58] Interview with member of European Commission Legal Service, Brussels, November 2012 (Interview M). These comments were given before the 2013 *Kadi II* decision, which arguably provides a more optimistic outlook for EU institutions.

[59] Interview with former member of the UN 267 Monitoring Team, New York, November 2012 (Interview A) (emphasis added).

Leaked Embassy Cables reveal the extent of US government concerns about EU judicial review of terrorism listing and suggest that the USA was deeply involved behind the scenes pushing for EU procedural reform on this issue. In one cable entitled '1267: Saving the Al-Qaeda/Taliban Sanctions Regime', former US National Security Adviser Susan Rice warned: 'Bold action is needed to salvage the UN's 1267 al-Qaeda ... targeted sanctions regime ... [which] has been seriously undermined by criticisms – and adverse European court rulings – asserting that procedures for listing and delisting ... are not adequately fair and clear.'[60] According to another cable:

> We cannot risk losing the use of one of our few non-military coercive tools because EU courts believe that they are somehow illegitimate ... The US has an interest in actively engaging the EU to overcome the gap that is developing between us on this issue. We must support and supplement existing EU sanctions ... by sharing substantive information on our ... targets ... and *comparing strategies to protect these policies from legal challenge* ... Without the political will and commitment of EU leaders in the coming year, and *a coordinated US interagency strategy to effect this*, we will fall short of our intended mark on vital national security and foreign policy goals.[61]

Another cable dispatched after the ECJ's 2008 *Kadi* decision stressed how EU judicial review is adversely affecting 'USG proposals to the EU for listings and terrorist sanctions' and suggested new methods of US–EU intelligence-sharing might resolve the issue:

> EU ... courts are rendering judgments that may hinder our ability to secure EU-wide designations of terrorist entities. The new problem for us is the higher standards of evidence and the judicial review of the sufficiency of that evidence, that will make the EU and its member States less responsive to our request for terrorist designations and accompanying asset freezes. As we pursue the valuable foreign and security policy tool of terrorist designations, we may need to ramp up our intelligence sharing on terrorist entities against which we seek EU action. ... We must confront the possibility that working with the Council on designations may entail enabling the EU court to access unclassified or even classified information to review the legality of the EU listing by a standard yet to be fully determined.[62]

---

[60] US Embassy Cable 09USUNNEWYORK818 (dated 4 September 2009), para. 4.
[61] US Embassy Cable 09BRUSSELS616 (dated 29 April 2009) (emphasis added).
[62] US Embassy Cable 09BRUSSELS41 (dated 13 January 2009).

Such intelligence-sharing has long been a key talking point in collaborative US–EU work on listing policy. One cable – entitled 'EU Intelligence and Classified Information Sharing' – documents a meeting in Brussels in February 2010 between US inter-agency sanctions officials and the European Commission Legal Service which aimed to identify how the EU and USA could best work together to strategically offset the adverse effects of the (then) upcoming decision of the EGC in the *Kadi* case.[63] In its action points the cable states:

> Intelligence and classified information sharing between EU institutions and Member States is among the most sensitive and least developed areas of EU policy and procedure, a last bastion of national sovereignty. *EU level implementation of UN and autonomous counterterrorism sanctions is testing the limits of how long the EU can hold out against confronting the practical implications of handling these issues* ... Given US security and foreign policy equities in EU sanctions and other counter-terrorism policies, we should expand US–EU legal expert discussions ... addressing the institutional underpinnings necessary to preserve EU measures before their courts.[64]

It was against this political backdrop of US–EU conflict and secrecy concerns that ECJ AG Sharpston issued her opinion in the case of *French Republic* v. *PMOI* suggesting that 'serious consideration' be given to amending the Court's procedural rules to allow for 'the production of evidence that is truly confidential'.[65] In her opinion, AG Sharpston – who previously represented the British government in national security cases before the Special Immigration Appeal Commission (SIAC)[66] – outlined a broad range of reform scenarios, intimating that special advocates and closed material procedures similar to those used in the UK might provide the key to resolving the intelligence-as-evidence problem.[67] Her opinion – which aimed 'to assist those who will have to engage with the question of how precisely to deal with this conundrum'[68] – proved highly influential. According to one leading EGC judge, it really 'pushed us to talk about these things' and helped

---

[63] US Embassy Cable 10USEUBRUSSELS212 (dated 24 February 2010).

[64] Ibid. (emphasis added).

[65] Case C-27–09 P *French Republic* v. *PMOI* [2011] ECLI:EU:C:2011:482, Opinion of AG Sharpston, para. 186.

[66] See, for example: *Secretary of State for the Home Department* v. *Rehman* [2001] UKHL 47, paras. 22–6.

[67] AG Sharpston, *French Republic* v. *PMOI*, paras. 171–86, 244. For discussion on this opinion see: Murphy, 'Secret evidence'.

[68] Ibid. para. 190.

influence the court's initial decision to review its rules of procedure on this issue.[69]

In July 2013 the ECJ delivered its long-awaited appeal decision in the *Kadi* case on the appropriate standard of review to be adopted by the EU courts in sanctions cases.[70] The EGC had previously held that the EU courts must undertake an 'in principle, full review' of listing decisions that included judicial access to the underlying evidential material relied upon. The ECJ's 2013 decision, however, overturned this approach and set out a novel formula for handling the intelligence-as-evidence problem in listing cases. Instead of 'full review', the EU courts only needed one substantiated ground for listing disclosed to them for judicial review.[71] In language that closely mirrors the draft procedural reforms the courts had been negotiating in private with the Commission and Council, the ECJ noted that in listing cases 'overriding considerations to do with the security of the European Union or of its Member States or with the conduct of their international relations may preclude the disclosure of some information or some evidence to the person concerned'.[72] When confronted with such security-sensitive dilemmas, the court must:

> apply, in the course of the judicial review to be carried out, techniques which accommodate, on the one hand, legitimate security considerations about the nature and sources of information taken into account in the adoption of the act concerned and, on the other, the need sufficiently to guarantee to an individual respect for his procedural rights.[73]

Just what such 'techniques' might mean, however, was again left unclear. Beyond echoing its earlier pronouncements in the 2008 *Kadi* decision, the only possibility entertained by the ECJ was 'disclosure of a summary outlining the information's content or that of the evidence in question'.[74] It would be up to the courts to 'assess whether and to what the extent the failure to disclose confidential information or evidence to the person concerned' would affect 'the probative value of the confidential evidence'.[75]

The procedural reforms enabling the judicial handling of intelligence provide the missing piece to this puzzle, effectively 'codif[ying] the

---

[69] Interview with member of the EGC, Luxembourg, March 2013 (Interview N).
[70] *Kadi II.*
[71] Ibid. para. 130.
[72] Ibid. para. 125.
[73] Ibid.
[74] Ibid. para. 129.
[75] Ibid.

approach' taken by the ECJ in *Kadi II*.[76] Interestingly, the initiative for EU judges to review intelligence-as-evidence originated as a proposal made by the EGC itself.[77] The Commission then wrote to the Court in the context of its procedural review requesting that serious consideration be given to making the necessary amendments for handling classified material.[78] On the Commission's view, the reform process was envisaged as something fairly straightforward. First, it wrote to the EGC leaving it open to the Court to lead on this issue by suggesting how it would best like to handle the matter, but asking it to consider the viability of an EU Special Advocate regime and mechanisms for using closed material like those used in the UK.[79] Following internal discussion and debate it was then thought the Court would formulate its specific options for reform. Finally, once the Court had made its views known, 'it will become a Council Regulation'.[80] For Commission lawyers, the reforms were clearly aimed at resolving the problem of using intelligence-as-evidence in sanctions cases – which was seen as 'the most difficult decision of all' for the EU Courts to grapple with following the *Kadi* decision.[81]

But members of the EU judiciary interviewed on this issue expressed quite different understandings of the complexities involved and had very real concerns about how the reform process should best be handled. As one member of the EGC explained in early 2013:

> We are currently in the throes of a review of our rules of procedure covering a whole range of measures. And one of the issues that has come up is the existence of the present rule which says that as between the principal parties everything has to be made available to everyone ... Although no final decision has been taken ... I think the current attitude is that we *could* envisage an exception to that rule being made.[82]

For the courts, unlike the Commission, this reform process was far from straightforward. Proactively designing techniques for handling intelligence potentially compromised the Court's role as guardian of fundamental rights and raised problems of judicial independence:

---

[76] Cuyvers, 'Give me one good reason'.

[77] 'The Court made a suggestion, "Is this worth looking into?" And so, the Commission began looking into it': Interview with member of the EEAS, Brussels, March 2013 (Interview O).

[78] Interview M.

[79] Ibid.

[80] Ibid.

[81] Ibid.

[82] Interview N (original emphasis).

> Where one is going to be formulating a set of procedural rules which are
> probably at the upstream stage going to involve limiting . . . the procedural
> rights of the applicant . . . it's absolutely clear that we are going to be faced
> with arguments that this involves infringements of fundamental rights
> guaranteed by the Charter . . . [So] we are going to have to be slightly
> careful here because we don't want to find ourselves in a position whereby
> we have implicitly approved a model which is then challenged . . . and we
> find that our hands are notionally tied – having said that this is an
> excellent idea and then we do something else.[83]

As one member of the ECJ explained, *who* crafts the exception is critically
important: 'I don't want to have to design their architecture for them
because I might have to . . . [determine] whether it is sufficient . . . [But]
I am a bit nervous about people designing architecture who . . . don't
realise what the implications *are* of judicial scrutiny.'[84] If the reform
process was left for the executive to resolve, the end result would likely
violate fundamental rights. But being too involved in designing this
exception might unwittingly place the courts in a conflicting and con-
stitutionally compromising position.[85]

These reforms were also difficult for the courts because they fore-
grounded the problem of intelligence-sharing. As one EGC judge put
it: 'When the Commission takes a decision, does that mean that all
members of the Commission are going to have the right of access to
that material, or their *Chef de Cabinet*? How is the security clearance
going to be done and so on? You can see all these problems.'[86] Providing
underlying material to the Council was seen as even more problematic
because it would require confidential material to be shared amongst the
executives of twenty-eight EU Member States. This threat of disclosure
was a critical issue for sanctions officials interviewed in the European

---

[83] Ibid.

[84] Interview with a member of European Court of Justice, Luxembourg, March 2013
      (Interview P) (emphasis in original).

[85] This judicial uncertainty was the focal point of resistance by a number of influential legal
      and human rights advocacy organisations – including the Law Society and Bar Council of
      England and Wales, JUSTICE and Liberty – who were in private correspondence with the
      EU courts in an effort to persuade them to engage in public consultation on the proposals.
      See, variously, Letter to the President of the Court of Justice of the EU (21 May 2013);
      Letter to the Chairman of the Bar Council of England and Wales (18 June 2013); Letter to
      the President of the Court of Justice of the EU (22 July 2013), copies on file with author.
      This group argued that the proposals could have 'a serious substantive impact on the rule
      of law and rights of defence, which may affect the validity and legality of the amendments'
      (letter dated 22 July 2013).

[86] Interview N.

External Action Service (EEAS), who predicted that any reforms requiring closed material to be shared amongst the Council would be vociferously opposed by the UK and France – who, as P5 members, have long guarded Security Council prerogatives in the EU.[87]

4.1.2 Reassembling the Courts and the Epistemology of the Security Mosaic

Given these complexities, how *did* the EU courts actually end up forging these amendments? What techniques allowed these changes to unfold and what are their likely governance effects? How was a court vested to protect fundamental rights so readily enlisted to build, what is in effect, a legally authorised state of exception? And why – when the *Kadi* case has been 'one of the most discussed judgments in ECJ history'[88] – have scholars paid so little attention to the potentially far-reaching consequences of these procedural reforms?

As detailed in Chapter 1, most literature on the ISIL and Al-Qaida sanctions focuses on the normative conflict between UN counterterrorism law and EU human rights law epitomised in cases like *Kadi* and how it supports competing claims about global security law. But the tension these reforms aim to resolve is more than just a clash of competing norms. I argue that it is also a problem of the conflicting temporal dynamics embedded in the list: one being reactive, evidence-led, disclosure-driven and based on a 'past–present axis', and the other proactive, intelligence-led, secret and based on a 'present–future axis'.[89] Using intelligence-as-evidence entangles preemptive and retrospective logics together and produces this list as a form of non-synchronous or 'asynchronous' law,[90] and it is these divergent legal temporalities and their disordering capabilities that the EU procedural reforms seek to manage. Consider how one member of the ECJ explained the distinction they thought *ought* to be drawn between intelligence and evidence to resolve problems generated by the Law of the List:

> I want to make a distinction between intelligence/surveillance material and material underpinning a decision that is going to be susceptible to judicial review. In terms of surveillance, anything you can get your paws

---

[87] Interview O.
[88] Murphy, 'Secret evidence', 115.
[89] Brian Massumi, 'The future birth of the affective fact' *Conference Proceedings: Genealogies of Biopolitics* (2005), copy on file with author.
[90] Delmas-Marty, *Ordering Pluralism*, pp. 119–32.

on is good. You evaluate its credibility, its weight etc. But you have not got problems about admissibility or challenge. Because . . . surveillance material is kind of like a sponge . . . – you get [it] in and the problem is then working out what is right, what is wrong, what is false lead, what is deliberately misleading.

I think . . . that is sharply to be distinguished from: 'I am going to take an executive decision, which is going to have certain adverse consequences for that person. I know before I take that decision . . . that the system under the rule of law of which I'm part is going to afford that person the right to challenge my decision'.

If I know all of that, then I need to be asking myself, *upstream* of taking the decision, 'What is the material on which I'm going to base that decision'? And I need to ask . . . whether I think that material will stand up scrutiny. And at that moment *I mustn't confuse which hat I'm wearing.* It is *not the same* as looking at surveillance material and deciding that X is probably a bad egg and needs watching. It's not the same, . . . it's *a completely different function* . . .

The problem is: [this] distinction . . . is one that *needs to be* accepted. And, therefore, needs to inform what goes in upstream into the process of making the decision. You can't unmake the omelette starting from this end![91]

Demanding the demarcation of intelligence and evidence as something that 'needs be accepted' to resolve the problem tells us that the opposite is, in fact, likely to be the case. For the judiciary, the conflation and use of intelligence-as-evidence is driving legal conflict in this domain.[92] We are told that this problem should properly be dealt with by the executive further 'upstream' – and the Ombudsperson experiment discussed at length in Chapter 3 is one effort in that direction. But the fact these procedural reforms have been initiated, co-designed and adopted by the judiciary suggests that core principles of the EU justice system are also being altered to 'unmake' these conflicts through the courts.

When such problems arise in academic accounts they are usually framed in terms of secrecy and posed as something that can be remedied by the transparency of constitutional and human rights law.[93] The locus

---

[91] Interview P (emphasis in original).

[92] For analyses recognising the centrality of the intelligence-as-evidence problem in this domain see: Craig Forcese and Kent Roach, 'Limping into the future: the UN 1267 terrorism listing process at the crossroads' (2010) 42 *George Washington International Law Review* 217; Vanessa Baehr-Jones, 'Mission possible: how intelligence evidence rules can save UN terrorist sanctions' (2011) 2 *Harvard National Security Journal* 447; Hollenberg, 'The Security Council's 1267/1989 targeted sanctions regime'.

[93] See, for example: Cole et al., *Secrecy*.

of the problem, we are told, is one of visibility. If only the 'gist'[94] of material hidden behind the classified curtain could be revealed, then a proper defence could be mounted by targeted individuals and their lawyers and the underlying normative conflicts resolved.[95]

But intelligence and evidence do not just differ in degrees of visibility. They are also distinct knowledge forms with quite different epistemic and temporal qualities. Though hinged together here in the singular format of the list, these are dynamics that cannot easily be made commensurable. They move in different directions and at different speeds, carrying radically divergent assumptions about the proper relation between suspicion and proof.[96] As the EGC held in the 2010 *Kadi* decision: 'the assessments in question here are complex and require an evaluation of the measures necessary to safeguard international and internal security. They require the know-how of the intelligence services and the political acumen which, in the Council's submission, only governments possess.'[97] Thus, as one ECJ member explained when discussing the review of listing cases, using intelligence-as-evidence demands legal standards and forms of reasoning that are altogether more preemptive in orientation:

> If you say to me this person was involved in violent anti-government demonstrations that is an assertion of fact and ... I'm going to want something that I can recognise judicially as evidence ... because you're building this part of your case on an allegation of a specific fact. If you say to me, 'The material suggests that they've been involved in a number of groups and therefore the inference is that they represent [or are] probably thinking of violent Jihadi tactics' ... Well at that stage it's not that they were a member of that demonstration. *It's much more a chain of little*

---

[94] *A and Others* v. *United Kingdom* App. No. 3455/05 (ECtHR, 19 February 2009). In this case the Strasbourg court held that individuals 'must be given sufficient information about the allegations against him to enable him to give effective instructions to the special advocate – that is, the "gist" of the underlying allegations' (para. 220).

[95] For some (like Fabbrini and Hollenberg) the answer lies in decentralised review by domestic courts with mechanisms in place for reviewing secret intelligence without disclosure. For others (like Baehr-Jones) only new mechanisms and universal standards for reviewing intelligence at the UN level can assuage US concerns about handing the secret evidence underneath the ISIL and Al-Qaida list for review. See, respectively: Hollenberg, 'The Security Council's 1267/1989 targeted sanctions regime'; Federico Fabbrini, 'Global sanctions, state secrets and supranational review: seeking due process in an interconnected world' in Cole et al., *Secrecy,* p. 284; Baehr-Jones, 'Mission possible'.

[96] Justice, *Secret Evidence,* p. 236: 'It is often assumed that, secrecy aside, the evidence in ... [SIAC] cases is no different from that put forward in an ordinary criminal trial or civil hearing. Nothing could be further from the truth.'

[97] *Kadi* v. *Commission*, para. 106.

scraps, little mosaic scraps which have led you to the inference. [And] there ... I'm going to have a problem, aren't I? Because I'm not a security agent and I don't have the training to put it together?[98]

The mosaic form is an increasingly pervasive feature of contemporary security governance. It is grounded in a 'theory of informational synergy' that assumes that 'disparate items of information, though individually of limited or no utility to their possessor, can take on added significance when combined with other items of information'.[99] From e-borders[100] and targeted killing[101] to global surveillance and algorithmic data-mining initiatives,[102] uncertain future threats are identified and rendered actionable through informational fragments and otherwise innocuous details associated together in novel ways to bring emergent dangerous subjects into view. This mosaic presupposes very different kinds of knowledge and spatiotemporal dynamics from conventional forms of inductive reasoning and logics of proof. As Louise Amoore observes in her analysis of biometric bordering, 'the lines of association that are drawn here are not linear and causal but temporally and spatially fractured'.[103] For Claudia Aradau the mosaic form is best thought of as a kind of 'divination rather than detection' and its epistemology 'has more in common with the "pseudo-rationality" of astrology than the method of clues' usually associated with the detective work of intelligence analysis.[104]

For most security scholars the mosaic's temporal and epistemic logics remain exogenous to the law. According to Aradau and Rens van Munster, as 'computation of the future ... become[s] decisional' under contemporary conditions of precautionary risk, it becomes untenable for courts to determine liability in terrorism cases through 'careful

---

[98] Interview P (emphasis added).

[99] David E. Pozen, 'The mosaic theory, national security, and the Freedom of Information Act' (2005) 115 (3) *Yale Law Journal* 628, 633 and 630.

[100] Amoore, *The Politics of Possibility*.

[101] Jeremy Scahill and Glenn Greenwald, 'The NSA's secret role in the US assassination program', *The Intercept* (10 February 2014). Available at: bit.ly/1zeKzrV; Ian Cobain, 'Obama's secret kill list – the disposition matrix', *The Guardian* (London: 14 July 2013). Available at: bit.ly/QBfJ7A; Cori Crider, 'Killing in the name of algorithms: how big data enables the Obama Administration's drone war', *Al Jazeera America* (4 March 2014). Available at: bit.ly/1BgYFum.

[102] National Security Agency, 'Summary of DNR and DNI Co-Travel Analytics' (1 October 2012), available at: bit.ly/1GHNuxh; Barton Gellman and Laura Poitras, 'US, British intelligence mining data from nine US Internet companies in broad secret program', *The Washington Post* (7 June 2013), available at: wapo.st/1gIS8gu.

[103] Amoore, *The Politics of Possibility*, p. 94.

[104] Aradau, 'The signature of security'.

consideration of evidence' and the use of 'burdens of proof'. Fighting terrorism with techniques like administrative detention thus reveal 'the inadequacy of law to deal with situations of precautionary risk'. 'What counts', they suggest, 'is a coherent scenario of catastrophic risk and imaginary description of the future'.[105] In her analysis of SIAC proceedings in the UK, Amoore makes a similar argument. Whilst astutely observing how decisions at the border are increasingly 'drawn through [the] . . . joining of dots and lines of associated elements', she argues that 'decisions on the assembly of the mosaic' remain 'untraceable and unrecognizable in the conventions of legal evidence and burdens of proof'.[106]

And yet here we find the mosaic form embedded right at the heart of the EU justice system guiding the production of legal truth and being used to explain how intelligence-as-evidence is transforming judicial functions. Law is not contained in some privileged rampart here – standing above the turbulent sea of preemption, receding in the face of exception[107] and incalculable risk[108] or set apart from the security practices it seeks to temper. Rather, legal practices and techniques are being put into motion and recalibrated at the most granular of levels so that courts can assess uncertain future risks, possible associations and inferences *as* judicial evidence.[109] Judicially reviewing this form of non-synchronous law (the list) brings retrospective evidential standards and preemptive security practice into co-productive relation,[110] enlisting the judiciary into the radically uncertain process of identifying unknown future terrorists without the training to put the pieces of the security mosaic together.[111]

---

[105] Aradau and van Munster, 'Governing terrorism', 106.

[106] Amoore, *The Politics of Possibility*, p. 85. See, however: Amoore, 'Risk before justice' – where the confluence of risk and juridical is underscored.

[107] Carl Schmitt, *Political Theology: Four Chapters on the Concept of Sovereignty* (Chicago IL: University of Chicago Press, 2005), p. 12.

[108] Ulrich Beck, *Risk Society: Towards a New Modernity* (London: Sage, 1992); Ulrich Beck, 'The terrorist threat: world risk society revisited' (2002) 19(4) *Theory, Culture and Society* 39.

[109] The opinion of AG Bot in the *Kadi II* appeal is instructive in this regard: 'the fight against terrorism cannot lead democracies to abandon or dent their founding principles, which include the rule of law. However, it does cause them to make the changes to them that the preservation of the rule of law requires'. *Kadi II*, Opinion of AG Bot, para. 6.

[110] Sheila Jasanoff (ed.), *States of Knowledge: The Co-production of Science and Social Order* (London: Routledge, 2004).

[111] On the relation between the mosaic form and the 'emergent subject', see: Amoore, *The Politics of Possibility*, pp. 79–104. For examples of critical security scholarship

These procedural changes may well end up allowing a degree of secret material to be made available for judicial assessment in listing cases and rendering visible some of what has hitherto been kept hidden.[112] But the core problems associated with non-synchronicity that the list brings out will undoubtedly persist. How can judges decide whether listing decisions are justified by assessing both past acts (using evidence sufficiently detailed to close the gap between suspicion and proof) and radically uncertain future possibilities (assembled from 'little mosaic scraps' organised according to preemptive logics of potential risk and threat)? How can the proportionality of action taken 'not in response to but in anticipation of wrongdoing' be judicially assessed with any kind of legal certainty?[113] When can suspicions from past actions become (or cease to become) future threats sufficient to warrant listing, and what possible standard of proof (if any) could apply to such non-quantifiable claims?[114] Conventional forms of legal knowledge grounded in inductive reasoning and linear time are destabilised and reordered when confronted by a list that governs the contingencies of the future by acting on the present under epistemic conditions of 'objective uncertainty'.[115]

Unsurprisingly, the revised rules are vague about how judges should actually perform their judicial review functions under heightened conditions of epistemic and temporal complexity. They merely provide the court with broad ad hoc discretion to assess listing decisions by weighing up the different interests involved. 'These are', as Armin Cuyvers observes, 'highly factual and complex questions of a rather executive nature . . . [that] make it difficult for the EU courts to set a clear standard for review'.[116] Yet this idea of intelligence-as-evidence rendering the application of legal standards problematic, as Cuyvers suggests, might be unduly optimistic. According to Lord Hoffmann, former UK Supreme Court judge, it is questionable whether standards can play any meaningful

---

highlighting this co-productive relation, see: Marieke de Goede and Beatrice de Graaf, 'Sentencing risk: temporality and precaution in terrorism trials' (2013) 7(3) *International Political Sociology* 313; and Krasmann, 'Law's knowledge'.

[112] Under the principles laid out by the ECJ in the 2013 *Kadi* appeal decision, for example, only one substantiated ground must be provided to justify a listing decision: *Kadi II*, para. 130.

[113] Zedner, 'Preventive justice', 198.

[114] Cuyvers, 'Give me one good reason', 1770. 'Possibilistic' refers to the important work of Louise Amoore on this issue: Amoore, *The Politics of Possibility*.

[115] Brian Massumi, 'Potential politics and the primacy of preemption' (2007) 10(2) *Theory and Event* 13, 24.

[116] Cuyvers, 'Give me one good reason', 1772–3 and 1774.

role when judges are required to assemble fragments and 'little mosaic scraps' as evidence of uncertain future threat in security cases:

> the whole concept of a standard of proof is not particularly helpful in a case such as the present. In a criminal or civil trial in which the issue is whether a given event happened, it is sensible to say that one is sure that it did, or that one thinks it more likely than not that it did. But the question in the present case is *not whether a given event happened but the extent of future risk* ... [This] cannot be answered by taking each allegation seriatim and deciding whether it has been established to some standard of proof. It is a question of evaluation and judgment.[117]

The more profound effects of these procedural reforms are therefore not in what they may or may not make visible, but rather how the effort of doing so serves to reorder or modulate legal institutions in alignment with broader security rationalities and epistemologies. By more deeply embedding preemptive logics and decision-making techniques into the EU legal system I argue that these reforms stand to change the temporal ordering of the legal system itself by requiring judges to use more associational, inferential practices oriented towards countering future risk. The application of conventional standards of proof, retrospective modes of legal-reasoning and the delivering of public judgments are all made more difficult to sustain when the courts are concerned with assembling chains of 'little mosaic scraps' and risk fragments to evaluate whether individuals are 'associated with' global terrorism.[118]

My point here is not to claim that law is being replaced by security or evidence supplanted by intelligence. It is that in bringing intelligence and evidence (and their divergent legal temporalities) together, the list functions *jurisgeneratively* – stimulating new problems and recombinant legal practices that were not possible before. The list is changing, at a very granular level, the ways judges come to produce 'legal truth' in concrete cases and is taking legal-reasoning into the very uncertain terrain of the contemporary security mosaic. These effects are not the inevitable end result of law's decline in the face of preemptive security or the rise of risk

---

[117] *Rehman*, para. 56 (emphasis added). The case concerned the use of intelligence-as-evidence in SIAC proceedings, which is comparable and relevant for the current context.

[118] As detailed earlier, one of the key objections of the British government to these proposals concerned the inability of security services to vet EU judgments for unwarranted disclosure of security-sensitive material – see: Lidington, *House of Lords Select Committee*. In 2013 the UK Supreme Court held that it was appropriate to hear evidence in closed session for the first time on appeal, with serious misgivings expressed by the judiciary. See *Bank Mellat v. HM Treasury* [2013] UKSC 38.

in late modernity – they are more site-specific and provisional than that. My analysis shows judges in the EU courts doing their best to try and pragmatically resolve a particular legal problem. But doing so requires them to grapple with the radically different episteme of the mosaic that is stimulating changes in the ways they reason and judge.

As Pat O'Malley points out, analysing risk governance techniques means 'attending to their natures as the products of contingency and invention' – not black-boxing them as 'the effects of an inescapable "logic" of moder-nity', as theorists like Ulrich Beck suggest.[119] Similarly, for Michel Foucault, understanding security governance requires analysis of 'the point[s] where power surmounts the rules of rights that organize and delimit it and extends itself beyond them' and 'invests itself in institutions' and procedures that are then 'displaced, extended and modified'.[120] Only by mapping how governmental practices emerge, transform and cohere around particular problems at the microphysical level can we properly understand how new forms of power and authority are formed. Similarly, my analysis of this procedural reform process shows how the list works to stretch the terrain of exceptional security politics by reordering established rule of law principles and methods of legal knowledge production.

As discussed earlier in our analysis of the Ombudsperson experiment, most scholarship posits law and exception in antithetical terms. States of exception are represented as 'lawless' and forged by transferring the power of security intervention and determinations of guilt or innocence from the established conventions of the juridical order to the realm of arbitrary sovereign decision.[121] These reforms highlight how problematic sweeping claims that explain exceptional politics as 'suspension[s] of the juridical order itself' are.[122] As detailed in Chapter 3, laws and norms are not locked in a zero-sum game but are hybridised through the proble-matics of government.[123] Or as Foucault put it, law and legal institutions

---

[119] Pat O'Malley, *Risk, Uncertainty and Government* (London: Glasshouse Press, 2004), p. 7.
[120] Michel Foucault, *The Birth of Biopolitics: Lectures at the Collège de France, 1978–1979* (London: Springer, 2008), p. 3.
[121] Liam Stockdale, 'Imagined futures and exceptional presents: a conceptual critique of "pre-emptive security"' (2013) 25(2) *Global Change, Peace and Security* 141.
[122] Giorgio Agamben, *The State of Exception* (Chicago IL: University of Chicago Press, 2005), p. 4.
[123] Rose and Valverde, 'Governed by law?', 546. On the co-constitutive relation between the legal and extra-legal, see: Johns, *Non-legality in International Law*. See also the vast literature on autopoietic systems theory: Nikolas Luhmann, *Law as a Social System* (Oxford: Oxford University Press, 2004); Gunther Teubner, 'The two faces of legal pluralism' (1992) 13 *Cardozo Law Review* 1443.

do not fade into the background under conditions of security but instead come to operate 'more and more as a norm' and are 'increasingly incorporated into a continuum of apparatuses'.[124] These reforms help to show how exceptional governance is made durable through the 'novel recombination[s] of already existing ... mechanisms and modalities of power' and inscribed through the concrete re-articulation of legal practices in accordance with preemptive security logics and concerns about the effective administration of justice, rather than an abstract movement away from 'the Law'.[125]

Members of the EU judiciary interviewed about these procedural reforms, for example, downplayed the secret review of intelligence-as-evidence by likening it to existing procedures for reviewing legally privileged communications in competition law disputes:

> In reality we have, in many contexts, to have discussion with the parties about how to treat various items of evidence in *all sorts* of situations, [including] commercially confidential material. And in that connection, I don't see why one shouldn't have discussions as to whether, for the purpose of this particular case, looking at that material how it should be handled in order to preserve confidentiality.[126]

Reference was made to procedures that were developed out of earlier EU case law on the confidentiality of documents subject to legal professional privilege.[127] If companies claimed that written communications were privileged and European Commission antitrust inspectors disagreed, the disputed documents could be sealed and sent to the EGC for determination:

> The procedure was improvised. Ok, ... we have problem. Here is a stack of documents. They [i.e. the company] are saying *this is* legal advice and is covered. The Commission is saying, 'Our inspector wants to see it. We will take those documents and we will ... both watch [while] we put it into an

---

[124] Michel Foucault, *The Will to Knowledge: The History of Sexuality, Vol. 1* (London: Penguin, 1979), p. 144.

[125] Much of the Agamben scholarship on preemptive security reproduces a reified conception of law that excludes administrative measures as extra-legal – hence, my use of the term, 'the Law'. See Gavin Sullivan and Marieke de Goede, 'Between law and the exception: the UN 1267 Ombudsperson as a hybrid model of legal expertise' (2013) 26 (4) *Leiden Journal of International Law* 833, 838.

[126] Interview N (original emphasis).

[127] C-155/79, *Australian Mining and Smelting Europe Ltd* v. *Commission*, [1982] ECR 1575; Joined Cases T-125–03 and T-253–03, *Akzo Nobel Chemicals Ltd and Akcros Chemicals Ltd* v. *Commission* [2007] ECR II 3523.

envelope [and] seal it.' The envelope goes to the court. The court opens
the envelope and it assesses the content and nature of each document.[128]

For the judiciary, this example highlighted how the EU courts had
previously developed pragmatic techniques for resolving confidentiality
problems that parallel those of the present. In this way, changing the rules
of the court to handle intelligence-as-evidence could be framed as con-
stitutionally insignificant, and simply 'a more extreme case of what we
have to do in many cases [already] where one has stock market sensitive
material'.[129]

Judges are professionally predisposed to reasoning by analogy. But the
differences between assessing commercially confidential material and
intelligence-as-evidence are quietly subsumed when these procedural
innovations are discursively sutured together this way. Reviewing privileged communications and intelligence-as-evidence both require confidentiality. But because of the mosaic epistemology of the list, reviewing
intelligence-as-evidence demands temporally complex processes of contingent legal knowledge production. Whilst the assessment of privileged
communications can readily fit within the existing judicial review framework, the assessment of intelligence-as-evidence requires the review
process itself to be altered in significant ways. Both issues engage questions of fundamental rights, but they do so with profoundly distinct
consequences. Commercially confidential material might prove important, for example, in securing a company's competitive advantage. But
listing information is sometimes procured through torture, so when
judges assess it without knowledge of its source, they risk embedding
torture material within the EU justice system.[130]

---

[128] Interview P (original emphasis).

[129] Interview N. By way of contrast, the introduction of closed material procedures in the
UK (through the Justice and Security Act 2013) was subjected to considerable public and
parliamentary debate due to the risks these changes posed to the rule of law, principles of
natural justice and the protection of fundamental rights.

[130] On the use of torture material in terrorism listing see: Case T-306/10, *Yusef
v. Commission* [2014] ECLI:EU:T:2014:141; UN Doc. A/67/396, Report of the Special
Rapporteur on the Promotion and Protection of Human Rights and Fundamental
Freedoms while Countering Terrorism (26 September 2012). As the former Special
Rapporteur notes, 'intelligence derived from torture has been used to justify the designation of individuals' (para. 47). As Lord Bingham of the UK House of Lords observed in
the case of *A and Others*: 'despite the universal abhorrence expressed for torture and its
fruits, evidence procured by torture *will be* laid before SIAC because its source will not
have been "established"': *A and Others* v. *Secretary of State for the Home Department*
(No 2) [2005] UKHL 71, para. 59, in dissent (emphasis added). On the risk of relying on

When procedures for reviewing legally privileged communications and intelligence-as-evidence are conflated this way, the judiciary helps bring preemptive security logics and EU justice principles into practical alignment. Such discursive moves perform important legitimation and legal assemblage work by linking divergent objectives and 'smoothing out contradictions so that they seem superficial rather than fundamental'.[131] The proliferation of exceptional governance is often explained as a 'migration of anti-constitutionalist ideas' from the exceptional core (such as the USA, UK or UNSC) to the rule-of-law periphery (such as the EU).[132] But these procedural reforms suggest that in the global war on terror legal agency is more distributed and multidirectional than that. Just as the Monitoring Team and Ombudsperson examined in earlier chapters embedded and stretched this form of law in novel ways by trying to resolve problems of the List, these reforms similarly show the EU courts assembling and extending the Law of the List in important ways by seeking to ameliorate its worst effects and improve the administration of justice.

4.2   Dis-Located Law: Taking Listing Decisions beyond the Vanishing Point of Review

The preceding section examined how the list's non-synchronous dynamics generate conflicts and introduce complexities into the EU judicial review process. Yet temporal shifts always enact corresponding spatial changes because 'time' and 'space' are integrated and inseparable dimensions in legal governance. As Valverde observes, 'different legal times create or shape legal spaces and vice versa ... [and] the spatial location and spatial dynamics of legal processes in turn shape law's time'.[133] The challenge for global sociolegal scholarship is thinking through the 'temporal and spatial dimensions of governance *at the*

---

torture material as a result of these procedural changes, see also: Cuyvers, 'Give me one good reason', 1776.

[131] Tania Murray Li, 'Practices of assemblage and community forest management' (2007) 36(2) *Economy and Society* 263, 265.

[132] As suggested in Cian Murphy, 'Counter-terrorism and the culture of legality: the case of special advocates' (2013) *King's Law Journal* 19–37, 21; following Kim Lane Scheppele, 'The migration of anti-constitutional ideas: the post-9/11 globalisation of public law and the international state of emergency' in Sujit Choudry (ed.), *The Migration of Constitutional Ideas* (Cambridge: Cambridge University Press, 2007).

[133] Mariana Valverde, *Chronotopes of Law: Jurisdiction, Scale and Governance* (London: Routledge, 2015), pp. 17–18.

same time', rather than reifying time-space binaries, privileging one dimension over the other or representing different governance scales as mutually exclusive.[134]

This section builds on this insight by analysing how the spatial dynamics of judicial review are challenged and reordered through the divergent temporalities of intelligence-as-evidence. Administrative 'decisions' are almost always the focal point of judicial review, such that it is often claimed that 'absent a "decision", judicial review will not lie'.[135] EU annulment proceedings in sanctions cases are similarly decision-orientated and directed at the legality of EU institutional acts.[136] Grounds of administrative legal challenge are therefore usually inextricably tied to the nature and quality of executive decision-making. So, what happens when this constitutive relation between decision and review is emptied out or severed? This problem of (dis-)location of the listing decision is explored in the remainder of this chapter.

Earlier in this chapter I discussed some of the key divergences in resolving the intelligence-as-evidence problem. To reiterate: one approach (endorsed by the ECJ's 2008 *Kadi* decision) suggests that closed material underneath the list should either be declassified or transformed so it can be used as evidence in judicial proceedings. The other approach (implicit in the reform of the EGC's rules) suggests that EU judicial procedures should themselves be changed to allow reliance on closed material without risk of disclosure. Crucially, both approaches assume that the material underpinning UN listing decisions is actually *held* by the UN1267 Sanctions Committee and so could potentially be disclosed to the European Council, Commission and courts. But on closer analysis, this assumption – of there being some kind of 'upstream' space of substantive assessment or decision-making that reviews the merits of individual listing decisions – appears to be unfounded.

4.2.1   Emptiness of the UN Sanctions Committee Decision-Making process

In his 2013 opinion in the *Kadi II* appeal Advocate General Bot of the ECJ claimed that 'the listing and delisting procedures in the Sanctions Committee allow for a careful examination of whether listings are

---

[134] Ibid. p. 36 (emphasis added).
[135] Fordham, *Judicial Review Handbook*, p. 138.
[136] Summaries of EU Legislation, 'The Action for Annulment'. Available at: bit.ly/1MIslBE.

justified and whether or not it is necessary to maintain them'.[137] I argue that this claim is little more than a blind and unfounded assertion. It shows the extent of mainstream thinking about the Law of the List and how far removed it is from listing practice.

The UN1267 Sanctions Committee does not access the classified material that purportedly underpins its own listing decisions.[138] Instead, it is standard practice of the Committee to simply approve proposed designations provided to it by states using a confidential 'no-objection' procedure – where 'if no State has opposed a listing proposal (or has put it "on hold") within 10 working days, the individual or entity will be added to the list'[139] – that precludes any substantive consideration of the grounds.[140] Whilst the Committee appears to require states to structure their designation requests in a particular format, including basic identifying information and generic allegations of terrorist association (the 'Statement of Case'), the underlying material supposedly supporting the allegations is neither collectively presented nor substantively assessed. As one former member of the Monitoring Team stated:

> Intelligence sharing always has a limitation as to the level of trust between states. You are never going to get a degree of intelligence sharing within fifteen members, random members more or less, of the international community, which anyone is going to regard as able to protect a secret … Any idea that the UN could *keep* a secret let alone share one, I mean, is ridiculous. It just will never happen here … We've had very bad experiences of people giving intelligence, so-called, to the Security Council, like in the run up to the Iraq war. It's not a mechanism that works, [and] quite frankly … should be avoided.[141]

4.2.2 Speculating from inside the Lacuna: The UN Office of Ombudsperson

In light of the Committee's 'rubber-stamping' process, some commentators argue that the Ombudsperson mechanism examined in Chapter 3 helps fill

---

[137] AG Bot in *Kadi II*, para. 86.

[138] UN Doc. A/67/396, para 26; Lisa Ginsborg and Martin Scheinin, 'Judicial powers, due process and evidence in the Security Council 1267 terrorist sanctions regime: the *Kadi II* conundrum', *EUI Working Papers: RSC* (San Domenico di Fiesole: European University Institute, 2011), pp. 9–10.

[139] UN Doc. A/67/396.

[140] Simon Chesterman, 'The spy who came in from the Cold War: intelligence and international law' (2006) 27 *Michigan Journal of International Law* 1071, 1115.

[141] Interview A (emphasis in original).

this decisional void. Whilst Sue Eckert and Thomas Biersteker observe that 'a thorough analysis of all available information is critical for due process' and securing access to information has been a 'significant challenge', they nonetheless argue that 'with the creation and enhancement of the Office of the Ombudsperson ... the rights of individuals to be informed, have access to, and be heard, appear to have been addressed'.[142] There is a presumption that the Ombudsperson is proximate to the source material underneath the list. As one member of the Commission Legal Service explained in interview: 'the Ombudsperson is the closest to the decision-taking and therefore ... best placed to make the review ... The review that she does is ... the best one a listed person can have ... *We don't pretend that the Commission makes a more substantive review than the Ombudsperson. It's the other way around.*'[143]

As detailed in Chapter 3, the former Ombudsperson also claimed that its decision-making process is fair because it enables listed individuals to know the case against them.[144] These claims to fairness, however, come with two important caveats. First, '[W]hen I say that I believe [listed individuals] have been told about the case, it's the case against them *such as has been given to me*.'[145] The former Ombudsperson acknowledged that the organisation is often given the summary of reasons compiled by the Committee and Monitoring Team 'and nothing more'.[146] Second, and more importantly for the purposes of this chapter, the Ombudsperson does not actually review the original listing decision, as discussed at length in Chapter 3. For the Ombudsperson, reviewing listing decisions would 'be impossible ... in this context unless you have all the information the agency had that made the decision'.[147]

Bilateral agreements have been forged by the Ombudsperson with particular states for accessing closed material, but these states are selective about what material they provide.[148] 'Even then', as one former

---

[142] Sue Eckert and Thomas Biersteker, *Due Process and Targeted Sanctions: An Update of the 'Watson Report'* (Geneva: Watson Institute for International Studies, Brown University and the Graduate Institute, 2012), pp. 22–3.

[143] Interview M (emphasis added).

[144] For a detailed analysis of the problems associated with the Ombudsperson's delisting processes, see Sullivan and de Goede, 'Between law and the exception' and discussion in Chapter 3.

[145] Interview with Kimberly Prost, former UN 1267 Ombudsperson, New York, November 2012 (Interview K, emphasis added).

[146] Ibid.

[147] Ibid.

[148] Interview A.

Monitoring Team member notes, 'she's not going to go and interrogate the sources, she's not going to go and look through the files'.[149] There is no assessment of the veracity and reliability of the material supposedly underlying individual entries. In short, claims that the Ombudsperson fills this gap by undertaking a substantive assessment of the underlying material are problematic. As Stephan Hollenberg observes in his analysis of this issue: 'it is difficult to see how the problem of not sharing confidential information underlying an individual's designation could ever be solved at the UN level'.[150]

4.2.3 EU Listing Decisions and the Politics of Executive Box-Ticking

If the material supposedly justifying the listing decision is not held or assessed at the UN level by the Sanctions Committee or Ombudsperson then it cannot be passed from there to EU institutions implementing the list.[151] Contrary to popular assumption, there is no movement of underlying material from supranational 'core' to regional 'periphery'. The same kind of empty decision-making taking place in the UN is replicated, in exacerbated form, in the EU.

Leaked US Embassy cables highlight the extent of this emptiness. One cable documents a February 2010 meeting between US Justice, Treasury and State department officials and senior civil servants from the EU Council and Commission on the dangers that EU judicial review poses to UN listing. A key 'area of high risk', according to Council lawyers, is the 'multiple cases involving UN designations' before the EU courts where 'EU institutions have little or no [supporting] information'.[152] Other cables between Italian security officials and the US Consulate in Rome explain that 'on behalf of the US, Italy had proposed numerous candidates for designation' on the UN1267 list 'about which they knew little'. In the event of an EU legal challenge, Italy will have difficulty justifying these listing decisions 'unless they get ... [background] information'[153] from the USA – even though designating states are 'generally expected to have

---

[149] Ibid.
[150] Hollenberg, 'The Security Council's 1267/1989 targeted sanctions regime', 63. See also: Forcese and Roach, 'Limping into the future'.
[151] Ginsborg and Scheinin, 'Judicial powers', p. 18.
[152] US Embassy Cable 10BRUSSELS219 (dated 25 February 2010).
[153] US Embassy Cable 09ROME652 (dated 9 June 2009).

reviewed the underlying evidence' before nominating people to be listed.[154]

EU case law on terrorist listing and interviews with key European actors provide further support to the argument that EU listing procedures are bereft in substance. In the 2010 *Kadi* decision the EGC frankly acknowledged that 'at the hearing, the Commission confirmed ... that it did not have any of the evidence in question' and that 'a request for the production of evidence must, in its view, be made to the United Nations States which hold it'.[155] On appeal, the ECJ noted that 'the Commission was not ... put in possession of evidence other than [the] ... summary of reasons',[156] before setting out the new review standard it thought ought to be applied in listing cases.

Trying to get underlying information out of the UN ISIL and Al-Qaida Sanctions Committee, according to one member of the Commission Legal Service, was 'very difficult': 'it takes a lot of time to get a reply and the reply is telegraphic. Most of the time, there is nothing.'[157] On the rare occasions when information *is* forthcoming, the Commission only sees redacted versions of documents at best. Sources and methods used to obtain information remain unknown, posing problems for EU institutions bound to refrain from relying on torture material.[158] In sum, the Commission 'doesn't have any institutional role when it comes to classified information. We have access, now and then, ... [but only] because there is an interest from one of the states to win a case. Otherwise we wouldn't have *any* access at all.'[159] Another European Council official confirmed in interview that 'there is no dossier of justifying information' supporting ISIL and Al-Qaida listing decisions or any kind of substantive decision-making taking place within the EU. Instead, listing decisions are wholly taken within the capitals of key Member States who only share information bilaterally with their trusted partners.[160] According to this official, if the EU courts keep pushing to see something resembling a proper decision, 'they will not find it'. Such pressure will more likely lead to

---

[154] Special Rapporteur (n 130) para. 26.
[155] *Kadi* v. *Commission*, para. 95.
[156] *Kadi II*, 110.
[157] Interview M.
[158] Ibid.
[159] Ibid. (emphasis in original).
[160] Interview with member of Council of the European Union, Brussels, March 2013 (Interview Q).

'abandon[ing] the use of targeted sanctions as a [counterterrorism] tool' altogether.[161]

It is precisely this kind of empty decision-making that has confounded the EU judiciary when reviewing terrorist listing cases and driven them to overturn implementation of UN listing decisions and try to improve EU listing procedures. As a result of the ECJ's 2008 *Kadi* decision, for example, EU institutions could no longer simply automatically implement the ISIL and Al-Qaida list into the EU legal order. Instead, they were to undertake an independent assessment of their own to determine whether their implementation was consistent with fundamental rights. In April 2009 a new Council Regulation was introduced to change European listing practice from one of 'automatic compliance' to 'controlled compliance'.[162] Individuals or groups added to the list were to be sent 'without delay' a copy of the Statement of Reasons and invited to express their views on the listing decision. The Commission was then obliged to take these views into account, as well as the opinion of an advisory committee of experts from the Member States, before taking the final decision to designate them on the list.[163]

This procedure appears to facilitate some kind of independent EU decision-making, but in practice it has continued to remain elusive. One Embassy cable documenting a 2009 meeting between the US Mission to the EU, Francesco Fini (of the former EU Council Secretariat Directorate General for External and Politico-Military Affairs) and Richard Szostak (of the Council Legal Service) recounts how this EU listing procedure was explained to US officials:

> Fini and Szostak insisted that the Council would never reject a UN decision, since any Member State obstructing UN sanctions would have to defend itself directly in New York and would not have recourse to the EU de-listing process. In their view, the EU would limit its objections to requests for additional information from UN institutions and Member States. Such exchanges would address EU concerns (e.g., factual inaccuracies), 'without putting the UN in a difficult situation.'[164]

---

[161] Ibid.

[162] Regulation (EU) No 1286/2009, amending Regulation (EC) No 881/2002.

[163] Those who were already on the EU list implementing Resolution 1267 prior to the *Kadi* judgment were also empowered to ask for a statement of reasons and invited to submit representations that the Commission must take into account before taking their final decision on continued designation.

[164] US Embassy Cable 09BRUSSELS1524 (13 November 2009). Fini later became Head of Sanctions at the EEAS.

Limiting decision-making to requests for basic factual information and fettering discretion because of the political 'difficulties' this might pose for the Security Council is quite removed from what is usually thought of as lawful administrative decision-making. The flaws in this procedure were made plain in 2010 when the EGC annulled the Commission's renewed decision to freeze Mr Kadi's assets. The Court held that this EU 'decision' was patently inadequate and rights-compliant 'only in the most formal and superficial sense' because the Commission 'in actual fact considered itself strictly bound by the Sanctions Committee's findings and therefore at no time envisaged calling those findings into question in the light of the applicant's observations'.[165] For the Court, the new listing procedure underscored, rather than remedied, the fundamental emptiness of the situation. Following this decision:

> the Regulations broadly remained in place, but now sort of slightly more had been done by way of explaining what had happened. Though the peculiarity is: *in what way is it relevant for the Council to be explaining what someone else has done?* I mean what does that add to the validity of the legal exercise that the Council, or the Commission, goes through before putting someone on the list?[166]

An EGC judge involved in this decision explained the Court's approach in the following terms – reproduced at length, because it's a rare instance of a judge candidly explaining (outside the confines of formal judgment) the impetus for their reasoning in UN terrorist listing cases:

> One of the peculiarities about the situation that was created as a result of the post-9/11 legislation adopted by the EU was that ... it provided ... that the listing of someone by the 1267 Committee was a sufficient basis for the UN to require states under Chapter VII ... to take certain action vis-à-vis those individuals. And the Member States, through the Regulations in question, ... did precisely that. So, when in *Kadi* the issue arose: 'Well, what *was* the material that on the basis of which the *Council* had made its decision to put someone on the list?' – the situation *wasn't one* in which it had applied its mind to the underlying material that had led the 1267 Committee to impose the sanctions ... *There was no sort of looking at the evidence.* It was merely, in its express terms, there was an external obligation to take *these* measures against *these* people once *this* factual condition is fulfilled: [namely] that X's name appears on the list established by the United Nations.

---

[165] *Kadi* v. *Commission*, para. 171.
[166] Interview N (emphasis in original).

... I think many of the commentators slightly misunderstood what we were saying in our [2010] judgment. Effectively what we were saying was: 'We are here as the Administrative Court of the European Union whose task is review the legality of acts of the EU institutions'. To do that job properly what we have to do is actually have a look to see what the institutions *have*, in fact, *done* and to see whether that accords with whatever legal constraints they may be under. And from that point of view, what the Council did is effectively no more than simply say, 'Well where is Mr Kadi's name? Yes, we see it. It's on the list. Tick box one ... no other boxes to tick. Well that's it' ... The issue wasn't ... whether we *can* or *can't* review decisions of the Security Council – we clearly can't, not in any normal sense of review ... This actually went to the *legality* of the base regulation itself: namely ... [does] a measure of this type ... nonetheless require *something further beyond the mere box-ticking exercise?* ... [It was] the legal regime set up by [the EU Regulation] – which did no more than require that box-ticking process – [that] was arguably the *real vice* in that case.[167]

This encounter succinctly highlights some of the problems faced by courts when trying to judicially review global security laws with complex spatiotemporal dynamics. We can see the EU judiciary looking back here to the executive act implementing the ISIL and Al-Qaida list and rightly asking for the evidence relied on to arrive at that decision, as per its mandate as EU Administrative Court. But what it found was that 'the decision' was not really there at all and so 'there was no ... looking at the evidence' in the conventional sense. The mosaic method for putting someone's name on the list had effectively shifted the 'source' of decision elsewhere. The non-synchronous and dis-locating dynamics of the list are, in other words, mutually constitutive processes. What's left for the courts to review is nothing other than a pro forma 'box-ticking exercise' which enables EU institutions to exercise coercive control over listed individuals without any real consideration as to why. It is empty decision-making.

Unsurprisingly, this situation was viewed by the Court as an intolerable exception in a polity based on the protection of fundamental rights. The quote from the EGC judge above also suggests that the judiciary objected to the loss of power and control to properly determine these issues as a result of the Security Council's counterterrorism policies. Yet, as even this judge acknowledged, the solution proposed in the case (full substantive review) was optimistic and provisional. Dis-location was seen as an enduring feature of the list and a core problem that

---

[167] Ibid. (emphasis in original).

'we are going to have to come back to … in the context of *Kadi II*, and possibly post-*Kadi II*, when we are saying: "Well, *what precisely is it that the Council is doing*? On what material is it going to have to be acting and how then is this material going to be handled?"'[168]

4.2.4 'What Precisely Is it that the [Courts] Are Doing?'

When the *Kadi II* appeal judgment was delivered in July 2013 the ECJ's proposed solution to this problem was made clear. Listing decisions were to be re-localised by the Court enacting a uniform standard of review applicable to both UN and EU sanctions cases. The case was received as a victory for EU transparency over UN Security Council secrecy. It highlighted the unlawfulness of empty decision-making by affirming that EU institutions are 'under an obligation to examine, carefully and impartially, whether the alleged reasons are well-founded', taking into account exculpatory material or evidence provided by listed parties and even by seeking information from the ISIL and Al-Qaida Sanctions Committee or relevant Member States if required.[169] Following *Kadi II*, the EU courts are now obliged to review 'the factual basis of listings, so the relevant authorities will have to provide sufficient evidence to support the reasons given for listing. No evidence means no sanction.'[170] Following the decision, Commission officials planned high-level meetings in the USA with the ISIL and Al-Qaida Sanctions Committee, Ombudsperson and US counter-terrorism officials to try and forge classified information-sharing agreements.[171] Security and sanctions officials were predictably shocked by scope of the ECJ's decision. According to the former coordinator of the ISIL and Al-Qaida Monitoring Team, Richard Barrett:

> This ruling presents a direct challenge to the ability and authority of the Security Council to impose targeted sanctions … [It] means that any individual or institution under Security Council sanction can avoid the consequences within the EU by taking the case to court. The Security Council will not readily submit its decisions in such matters to the second-guessing of the EU courts and may ask what article 103 of the UN Charter actually means.[172]

---

[168] Ibid. (emphasis in original).
[169] *Kadi II*, para. 114.
[170] Cuyvers, 'Give me one good reason', 1771.
[171] Interview with a member of the Commission Legal Service, Brussels, October 2013 (Interview R).
[172] Richard Barrett, Comments in relation to *Kadi II* judgment (29 July 2013), *Economic Sanctions Listserve* (copy on file with author).

Yet, whilst pushing towards greater disclosure with one hand, the Court narrowed the potential effects of this move with the other, altering the EU judicial review process in crucially important ways. The EGC had previously held that listed persons were entitled to 'an in principle, full review' extending to 'the substantive assessments of the Sanctions Committee itself and the evidence underlying' its decisions.[173] In *Kadi II* the ECJ found this review to be too expansive and held that the EGC had erred by failing to consider 'the many material obstacles that exist to the communication' of underlying material from the UN to the EU – including that 'the source of that information and evidence is . . . subject to a requirement of confidentiality due to its sensitivity'.[174]

So, in what is arguably the most far-reaching aspect of its decision, the ECJ held that the only information needed for EU institutions to put or maintain someone on the list was the 'statement of reasons' provided by the UN ISIL and Al-Qaida Sanctions Committee.[175] That is, the short summary excluding all underlying material, previously dismissed by the EGC as nothing more than 'general, unsubstantiated [and] vague' allegations,[176] was now accepted as a valid basis for listing. Crucially, it is only when listed individuals commence judicial review proceedings that EU institutions are actually expected to turn their minds to whether the reasons for listing are well founded. And it is only then that one substantiated ground must be given to the Court so it can subject the listing decision to judicial review.[177]

This judicial innovation aimed at resolving core problems of the list produces four important effects. First, it affirms that empty box-ticking decision-making is lawful for the overwhelming majority of listed individuals who do not, or cannot, challenge their listing before the EU courts. Second, it frees executives from the burden of having to disclose all relevant material, allowing them to strategically cherry-pick what they would like to reveal and hide from the court. If there is torture material justifying the listing decision or material indicating the listed person is

---

[173] *Kadi* v. *Commission*, paras. 173–4 and 129–33.

[174] *Kadi II*, para. 79. Whilst in this citation the Court is referring to the submissions of the Commission, Council and UK, it is clear that this position is implicitly accepted by the Court in its reasoning at paras. 117–29 and by its regard for 'the preventative nature of the restrictive measures at issue' (para. 130).

[175] Ibid. para. 111.

[176] *Kadi* v. *Commission*. The ECJ qualified this requirement in *Kadi II* (at paras. 116–18) by insisting that the statement of reasons must be specific and concrete enough to comply with Article 296 Treaty on the Functioning of the European Union.

[177] *Kadi II*, para. 130.

not associated with ISIL or Al-Qaida, for example, this need not be disclosed.[178]

Third, by alleviating EU institutions from having to take reasoned decisions when placing someone on the list and lowering the standard of review, the Court dramatically diminished its own power to indirectly challenge the legitimacy of the UN listing regime, as it had done in the 2008 *Kadi* case. By dissolving the threat of 'regime collapse' through diluting what can be expected of the Commission and Council, the ECJ fortified the ISIL and Al-Qaida list in the EU legal order. According to one member of the Commission Legal Service interviewed, this depoliticisation was the most profound effect of the decision. After the EGC's 2010 *Kadi* decision, I was told that further EU legal challenges by UN listed individuals might cause the listing regime to fall apart.[179] But when we spoke after *Kadi II* this official was remarkably upbeat. Whilst 'there was widespread pessimism after the judgment' from states like France and the UK, 'the Commission was, surprisingly, the only one not so pessimistic because we highlighted ... that there are certain positive aspects in the decision' – including that 'everything doesn't collapse' now in the event of further legal challenge.[180] According to this official, listing litigation will now only pose specific problems to be determined 'on a case by case basis' – 'either we will win or we will lose. But the whole regime does not collapse.'[181] *Kadi II* was therefore crucial for diminishing the conflict of the list to a more manageable 'battle of one by one'.[182] Put differently: whatever generative political space the 2008 decision succeeded in prising open on this issue, the 2013 decision effectively closed down.

Finally, *Kadi II* disrupted the conventional nexus between judicial review and its object (an executive act of administrative decision) and altered the temporal orientation of review by bringing the listing decision *forward in time* and making it more processual. Through this judgment, the site of decision is relocated as something that can unfold during the litigation itself rather than something prior to legal proceedings and

---

[178] As Cuyvers points out, allowing the executive to 'select which evidence is presented and which is withheld ... may undermine the court's ability to establish the material truth' by enabling, for example, exculpatory material or material obtained through torture to be excluded from the review process – Cuyvers, 'Give me one good reason', 1775.

[179] Interview A.

[180] Interview R.

[181] Ibid.

[182] Ibid.

'when the box was ticked', as had been the case. It's a discrete temporal move, but one that stands to alter the rationale of EU judicial review in significant ways. Before these reforms and decision, for example, an EGC judge whom I interviewed described their role in listing litigation in the following terms:

> Remember *we are reviewing what the Commission has done*. If the Commission is saying, 'We are not looking at it' [i.e. intelligence-as-evidence], we are going to say: 'Excuse me. We are an Administrative Court reviewing the legality of your acts. We are not making our separate assessment of whether if you had looked at that material you could have come to that conclusion. *We are just looking at what you say you did and . . . the materials that supported you in doing what you were saying you were doing'*. . . . We are not a first instance court making our own assessment . . . We can only review what they have actually done.[183]

In this quote, judicial review is represented in its traditional form as a retrospective process hinged upon a prior act of executive decision with evidence informing it. But the *Kadi II* case disaggregates decision and evidence and brings them both into a more fluid judicial process. The idea of the EU courts 'just looking at what you say you did' no longer holds with respect to the Law of the List. As with cases concerning uncertain future environmental risks where 'the Court is forced by the grounds invoked to judge the scientific validity and the conclusiveness of the scientific arguments' raised,[184] the EU judiciary must likely now make its own assessments as to whether potential fragments, inferences and 'little mosaic scraps' can be assembled in ways that allow the future threats of global terrorism to emerge. Judicial fact-finding, in other words, now comes to be concerned with assembling a security mosaic. This spatiotemporal move – performed for the first time in the *Kadi II* case and consolidated via reform of the rules of the Court – translates and embeds preemptive security knowledge practices into the EU judicial review legal fact-finding procedure.

The 2015 EGC decision in the case of *Abdulrahim*, however, suggests that we can expect *more* uncertainty in the EU courts about what the proper judicial role in listing litigation is.[185] The case, brought by an individual listed as a suspected member of the Libyan Islamic Fighting Group (LIFG), provided a testing ground for the new post-*Kadi II* review

---

[183] Interview N (emphasis in original).

[184] Marjolein van Asselt and Ellen Vos, 'The precautionary principle and the uncertainty paradox' (2006) 9(4) *Journal of risk Research* 313, 326.

[185] Case T-127/09 RENV *Abdulrahim* v. *Council and Commission* [2015] ECLI:EU:T:2015:4

procedures to be applied.[186] But the EGC's review was limited because the Summary of Reasons provided failed to show that Abdulrahim was 'associated with' Al-Qaida 'on the date he was listed',[187] and the Commission failed to provide any further relevant material in support of the allegations. Crucially, what additional information the Commission *did* provide – consisting of press and academic articles, witness statements from earlier UK legal proceedings and public statements about the merger of the LIFG and Al-Qaida – was dismissed by the Court as:

> ... *a priori of no relevance since, for the most part, they post-date both the listing* of Mr Abdulrahim's name in the Sanctions Committee list and the adoption of Regulation No 1330/2008 and since they *consequently could not have been taken into consideration*, by either the Sanctions Committee or the Commission, in order to assess whether the freezing of Mr Abdulrahim's funds was appropriate.[188]

So, whilst in *Kadi II* the ECJ brought the listing decision *forward in time* as something assembled during the judicial review process itself, in Abdulrahim the EGC *looked back* towards material 'taken into consideration' by executive actors (the Sanctions Committee and the European Commission) when putting someone on the list and excluded subsequent material as irrelevant. But the substance of the listing decision could not actually be evaluated because the Court did not know what material was used when it was taken. And as the decision was not appealed, this divergence is now effectively settled into EU law. For the ISIL and Al Qaida Monitoring Team, the *Abdulrahim* case is significant because it 'demonstrates that European Union courts have no interest in reversing course following the momentous decision of the Court of Justice of the European Union in *Kadi II*'.[189] But it is also worrisome because it signals that the EU courts might 'require more substantial and timely evidence than may have been envisaged following the *Kadi II* decision', although 'it remains to be seen just how much and what type of evidence will be regarded as adequate'.[190]

---

[186] Ibid. paras. 62–71.
[187] Ibid. para. 89.
[188] Ibid. para. 90 (emphasis added).
[189] UN Doc. S/2015/441 (16 June 2015) 'Seventeenth Report of the Analytical Support and Sanctions Monitoring Team concerning Al-Qaida and Associated Individuals and Entities', para. 45.
[190] Ibid.

But the issue arising from this case is not merely one of evidential quantity and quality. It is a more complex problem concerning the proper relation between UN listing decisions, the use of intelligence-as-evidence and the EU judicial review process. Is UN terrorist listing something amenable to traditional judicial review or something co-produced by the courts through legal challenge due to its particular spatiotemporal and epistemological features? If the former, how can this retrospective movement (as seen in *Abdulrahim*) be adequately reconciled with the preemptive security logic of the list and its mosaic epistemology? And if the latter (as suggested in *Kadi II*), how does this exceptional procedure discretely rearrange the judicial fact-finding function? EU court procedures for handling intelligence were reformed to specifically resolve contradictions and conflicts of the Law of the List. But these procedural innovations have not resolved these issues. Instead, the EU judiciary has altered the list by extending its scope and embedding its preemptive security logics more deeply into the EU justice system. As with the reform efforts examined in previous chapters, we again see bona fide efforts towards improvement of the list acting in parallel to broaden, modify and entrench the list's reach and rule. Reforming the Law of the List reassembles it.

At the time of writing, the new procedural rules of the EGC had not yet been used. But both the EGC and ECJ have formally set out procedures clarifying how they will handle secret information that comes to them from cases where the new procedural rules have been invoked.[191] These procedures effectively reframe the EU courts as security and intelligence agencies tasked with the handling of classified material to be shared only on a 'need to know' basis with those appropriately briefed on their security responsibilities.[192] Classified information is to be held in a secure location guarded by an intrusion detection system and protected from electronic eavesdropping.[193] It cannot be transmitted digitally or viewed on equipment connected to computerised networks or the Internet. National Security authorities from Member States relying on

---

[191] See: Decision (EU) 2016/2387 of the General Court of 14 September 2016 concerning the security rules applicable to information or material produced in accordance with Article 105(1) or (2) of the Rules of Procedure. O.J. 2016, L 355/18; Decision (EU) 2016/2386 of the Court of Justice of 20 September 2016 concerning the security rules applicable to information or material produced before the General Court in accordance with Article 105 of its Rules of Procedure. O.J. 2016, L 355/5.

[192] Ibid. Decision (EU) 2016/2386, preambular para. 6 and Article 7(1).

[193] Ibid. Annex II.

the security exceptions in the new procedural rules are expressly authorised to vet those identified by the Court as being able to access the secret material to ensure 'nothing adverse is known that would call into question the[ir] loyalty, trustworthiness or reliability' and can revoke their security clearance at any time.[194] These are rules clearly aimed at reassuring states that the use of intelligence-as-evidence by the EU judiciary can be controlled by intelligence services to ensure secret material is not inadvertently disclosed.[195]

4.2.5   Knowledge Circulation and Scalar Complexity in Legal Governance

'Knowledges', as Mariana Valverde, Ron Levi and Dawn Moore point out, 'are always circulating, changing, being taken apart and reassembled in new shapes by new actors' and legal sites provide fertile terrain for new risk knowledges to take root and spread.[196] In such conditions, the aim of sociolegal research is 'to try and capture this creative movement in our analysis' through dynamically mapping 'the different effects of particular circuits of risk information' that emerge through these hybrid encounters.[197] One effect of the entanglement of preemption and rule of law that my analysis of the EU judiciary highlights is the process of 'dis-location'. As discussed above, judicial review is usually orientated retrospectively towards the 'decision' of the authority under challenge. But using intelligence-as-evidence for terrorism listing shifts this site of decision-making elsewhere and challenges the judicial process because the decision supposedly under review is, strictly speaking, not there – as the 'box-ticking' example above succinctly shows. Wherever one looks for some kind of independent list decision-making process, as the EU courts have persistently done, one instead finds emptiness and deferral to some other actor further along the transnational chain of command and presumably closer to the 'source' of the decision. Yet the 'source' of the decision is never made plain – either because it is generated through the

---

[194] Ibid. Annex 1, Article 5.

[195] The rules directly respond, for example, to the security concerns previously raised by the UK. See note 47.

[196] Mariana Valverde, Ron Levi and Dawn Moore, 'Legal knowledges of risk' in Law Commission of Canada (ed.), *Law and Risk* (Vancouver: University of British Columbia Press, 2005), p. 89.

[197] Ibid.

diffuse knowledge practices of listing experts examined earlier or the apparent use of secret intelligence material as evidence.

I use the term 'dis-located law' to refer to this spatiotemporal move. This term is intended to both draw attention to the site of decision-making that is taken elsewhere and denote a fracture with the way things ordinarily work. Judicial review proceedings commonly challenge the legality of executive decisions, for example, on the grounds that irrelevant considerations were taken into account or relevant considerations were not. In so doing the first question the court asks is: 'What material did the decision-maker have before them at the time that they took their decision'? Did they fail to take something relevant into account? Did they give each element its proper weight etc?' But when the source of the listing decision is not made apparent this evaluative process starts breaking down. How can judicial review work when answering this most basic of evidential questions is obscured through preemptive logics and security concerns? The ISIL and Al-Qaida list is, in my account, a *dis-located* form of law that eludes consideration by the courts. Judicial review persists but is increasingly emptied of substance by a discrete spatiotemporal move and the use of intelligence-as-evidence.

In light of this dis-location, one might well ask: 'where precisely *is* the site of decision-making located here?' Comments provided by the former UK Minister for Europe, David Lidington MP, when explaining why the EU court rules were being changed to allow the use of closed material, provide an illuminating response to this question. Whilst his interlocutors kept stressing that protecting the secrecy of national intelligence was *the* critical factor justifying these procedural reforms, Lidington pointed towards other crucially important reasons:

> It would be wrong to think that when we are talking about confidential material we are talking only about material that might have an intelligence origin. *Sanctions that have been imposed originally at UN level are quite likely to have been based on information contained in a confidential report from a UN-mandated group of experts.* It is very possible that disclosure of that material in detail could lead to witness intimidation or damage international relations. Individuals, Governments or organisations might have given information in confidence to that UN group of experts, and the CMP [Closed Material Procedure] provisions in Article 105 should help to ensure the secrecy and confidentiality of that UN information.[198]

---

[198] Lidington, *House of Lords Select Committee*, p. 10 (emphasis added). On CMPs, see: Civil Procedure Rules, Part 82, Closed Material Procedure. Available at: bit.ly/2KG5D3F.

Here, it is the deformalised processes of expert-led global listing examined in Chapter 2 that provide *the* critical source of listing information,[199] not the formal deliberations of the Sanctions Committee and their P5 foreign ministries in conjunction with national intelligence agencies, as is commonly suggested. As I have shown, these global listing processes are marked by 'distributed knowledge production' practices and a 'diffusion of evaluative labour'.[200] If this is what provides the key 'source' of list decision-making it is little wonder the EU courts have had such problems locating 'a decision' to review. 'Liquid authority', as Nico Krisch has observed, 'is dynamic, difficult to locate and thus hard to grasp for actors who seek to challenge it'. When 'there is no one point of decision-making, but instead ... process[es] in which standards are made and remade by different actors', review inevitably 'suffer[s] from the lack of a suitable target'.[201] Judicial review becomes, in other words, dis-located.

If this is correct, then it is executive agencies and security officials within select national states and listing experts relatively autonomous from the formal political apparatus of the UN Security Council that are populating the list with its targets. Preemptive security decisions taken by subnational actors enrolled into new transnational networks are given the force of global law, with the Security Council providing little more than a shell of institutional cover for this rescaling and governing process. This enables national accountability constraints to be weakened, loosens the 'shackles' of international lawmaking based on sovereign equality and state consent and may help explain why global security law seen such a remarkable uptake by states around the world since 9/11.[202] But the strategic advantages enabled here go both ways. Aligning disparate actors into a common security project and building a new optic for governing

---

[199] For Koskenniemi, deformalisation, refers to 'the increasing management of the world's affairs by flexible and informal, non-territorial networks within which decisions can be made rapidly and effectively': Martti Koskenniemi, 'Global governance and public international law' (2004) 37(3) *Kritische Justiz* 241, 243.

[200] Anya Bernstein, 'The hidden cost of terrorist watch lists' (2013) 61 *Buffalo Law Review* 461, 464 and 485.

[201] Nico Krisch, 'Authority, solid and liquid, in postnational governance' in Roger Cotterrell and Maksymilian Del Mar (eds.), *Authority in Transnational Legal Theory: Theorising across Disciplines* (Cheltenham: Edward Elgar Publishing, 2016), p. 46.

[202] For an overview, of literature charting the decline of classical international lawmaking and rise of informal global governance, see: Koskenniemi, 'Global governance'; Joost Pauwelyn, Ramses A. Wessel and Jan Wouters, 'When structures become shackles: stagnation and dynamics in international lawmaking' (2014) 25(3) *European Journal of International Law* 733.

global terrorism also extends the authority of the Council and the technical experts administering the list. The net effect of global security law, as Kim Lane Scheppele points out, 'has been an increase in the power of transnational bodies and an increase in the power of domestic governments at the same time'.[203] Security governance capabilities are being stretched at both scales through new legal weapons like the ISIL and Al-Qaida listing regime.

4.3 Spatiotemporal Dynamics and Global Legal Assemblage

So, what can empirically studying legal spatiotemporal dynamics tell us about the kind of global law the ISIL and Al-Qaida list is? The first part of this chapter analysed the list as a non-synchronous form of law that uses intelligence-as-evidence and brings divergent temporal dynamics and epistemic practices together into productive relation. Most research on the list foregrounds the normative conflicts between international security and human rights law in cases like *Kadi* and suggests that the legal problems with the list can be adequately resolved through existing constitutional frameworks.[204] Whilst this conflict is important, I have argued that it is driven and shaped in large part by the temporal complexities of the list and its mosaic epistemology. Intelligence material is orientated towards a radically uncertain future, reframed in the present as dots to be connected and potential associations to be drawn through imaginative, abductive reasoning. Evidence is orientated retrospectively to demonstrate, through inductive reasoning, that an act did or did not take place in accordance with a given standard of proof. Because the list brings intelligence and evidence together, it generates both temporal and epistemological conflict. This problem is not merely a clash of norms.

I have argued that changing the rules of the EGC to allow judges to handle closed material without disclosure is an attempt to attenuate the conflicting temporal dynamics at play that are driving these legal conflicts between the UN and EU. My interviews with members of the EU

---

[203] Kim Lane Scheppele, 'The international state of emergency: challenges to constitutionalism after September 11', Yale Legal Theory Workshop (21 September 2006) (unpublished manuscript), 9.

[204] For Cian Murphy, citing Euripides, 'the EU rule of law remains robust in the field of targeted sanctions. In the EU, in this field, "force yields place to law"' – Murphy, 'Secret evidence', 282. For Justice Garlicki the 'constitutional law of today is better-than-ever prepared to address the challenge of national security, including issues relating to how to handle secret information and intelligence' – Justice L. Garlicki, 'Concluding remarks' in Cole et al., *Secrecy*, p. 337.

judiciary and analysis of recent EU case law, however, show that this experiment in problem management is not as straightforward as it may seem. In trying to ameliorate the worst effects of the ISIL and Al-Qaida list, the judiciary is forging recombinant techniques that embed and stretch it in novel ways. It is often said that the rise of preemption brings with it a corresponding decline in the rule of law and that legal and political institutions recede in the face of incalculable risks. But when preemption is studied empirically as a governmental technology and way of taming uncertain threats, a more textured account of legal change emerges. In my analysis, law does not stand apart from the security practices it seeks to temper, but is rather reorganised at a very granular level as a result of this encounter. Being attentive to these shifts in legal knowledge production and 'practices of reference'[205] can provide important insights into how jurisdictional conflicts are diffused, global security law is enacted and preemptive security governance is made more durable and expansive.

The second part of the chapter explored how this non-synchronicity reorientates the spatial dynamics of EU judicial review. Following critical examination of baseless decision-making at key nodes in the assemblage, I argue that the mosaic epistemology of the list generates particular spatial effects – namely, it works to perpetually defer or shift the source of formal decision-making elsewhere. The list's reliance on intelligence-as-evidence, in other words, enacts a corresponding dynamic of dis-location. Two recent EU listing decisions by the EU courts were scrutinised to show these dynamics at work. The first case (*Kadi II*) tried to locate a listing decision for the purposes of review by bringing it *forward in time* and into the litigation process itself. This move stands to transform the conventional rationale for EU judicial review – i.e. a retrospective process hinged upon a prior act of executive decision and the evidence informing it – into something more plastic and fluid. The second case (*Abdulrahim*) took a different approach and *looked backwards* towards a listing decision presumed to have taken place in the past. Whilst the prevailing literature suggests that the EU courts are defending the rule of law from attack via this UN listing regime, my analysis suggests this relation is more complicated in practice. The list is not only changing how the judiciary produces legal knowledge but also modulating and altering, in potentially far-reaching ways, the EU judicial review process itself.

---

[205] Johns, *Non-legality in International Law*, p. 23.

My empirical findings in this chapter show a global regime that is 'patchy', composed through diverse knowledge practices and temporal dynamics and enacted through preemptive security networks. Because it uses intelligence-as-evidence, the political relations that constitute it are more fragmented and bilateral than all-encompassing and global. Analysing the list through the lens of the EU courts trying to attenuate the intelligence-as-evidence problem and perform judicial review reveals a complexity of scale often observed in other transnational governance arrangements. I argue that the Law of the List is 'neither national nor international ... at the same time as being both'.[206] Or, as Sassen suggests in her study of global assemblages, it 'continue[s] to inhabit ... the nation-state and the inter-state system' but is 'no longer part' of both 'as historically constructed'.[207]

Realist state-centred approaches to international law and governance therefore fail to adequately capture how this listing regime works. In my account, the national is not so much engaged here as a sovereign state determinative of relations in a Westphalian international sphere, but as networks of executive actors and experts aligned through a particular governance technology and taking preemptive security action 'that is more across, beyond or through states than it is between' them.[208] IR scholars have highlighted how national executives 'collusively delegate'[209] and pool their authority at the supranational level to 'loosen domestic political constraints'[210] and increase their autonomy vis-à-vis other actors in the domestic sphere.[211] With the Law of the List, I argue that this delegation and loosening is closely linked with the task – as this chapter's epigraph points out – of using global law and international

---

[206] Craig Scott, '"Transnational law" as proto-concept: three conceptions' (2009) 10(7) *German Law Journal* 868.

[207] Sassen, 'Neither global nor national', 63 and 61.

[208] Scott, 'Transnational law'. As Krisch observes, 'the UN sanctions regime today bears little resemblance to the classical ways in which international law is created and implemented': Nico Krisch, *Beyond Constitutionalism: The Pluralist Structure of Postnational Law* (Oxford: Oxford University Press, 2012), p. 156.

[209] Mathias Koenig-Archibugi, 'International governance as the new raison d'état? The case of the EU common foreign and security policy' (2004) 10(2) *European Journal of International Relations* 147.

[210] Ibid.

[211] Klaus Dieter Wolf, 'The new raison d'état as a problem for democracy in world society' (1999) 5(3) *European Journal of International Relations* 333.

organisations 'more effectively as a weapon in the war against terrorism'.[212]

The spatiotemporal dynamics of the ISIL and Al-Qaida list have particular epistemic and legal governance effects. They transform existing legal knowledge production processes, dis-locate decision-making sites and enable an array of listing authorities to exercise legal violence over individuals without any consideration as to why.[213] That is, whether by design or unintended consequence, the spatiotemporal dynamics of this list are deeply entangled in assembling a form of global exceptional security governance. Exceptional not in terms of some lawless black hole or sovereign decision, but rather as something prosaic and incredibly coercive, yet legally assembled.[214]

For constitutionalist scholars such effects comprise the dark logical flipside of the 'responsibility to protect' (R2P) doctrine and the post-Cold War transformation of the Security Council's Chapter VII powers into an 'enforcement model' grounded in 'global law and community values, rather than international peace per se'.[215] According to Jean Cohen, 'we really only face two choices today: strengthened international law or imperial projects by existing and future superpowers'.[216] Whilst Martti Koskenniemi disagrees with the

---

[212] US Embassy Cable 06USUNNEWYORK1609 (dated 22 August 2006). This is not to suggest that international law was not already 'weaponised'. As Kennedy argues: 'Law and force flow into one another. We make war in the shadow of law, and law in the shadow of force': David Kennedy, *Of War and Law* (Princeton NJ: Princeton University Press, 2006), p. 165. The alternative to 'weaponising' international law is to work outside it. The 2010 US National Security Strategy (May 2010) speaks of 'the shortcomings of international institutions that were developed to deal with the challenges of an earlier time' and urges the government to instead 'harness a new diversity of instruments, alliances, and institutions' (at pp. 3 and 46). Available at: bit.ly/2MUum76.

[213] 'Public' is used broadly here with reference to 'any kind of governance activity ... [which] determines individuals, private associations, enterprises, states, or other public institution'. Armin Von Bogdandy, Philipp Dann, and Matthias Goldmann, 'Developing the publicness of public international law: towards a legal framework for global governance activities' (2008) 9 *German Law Journal* 1375, 1376.

[214] David Dyzenhaus, 'The rule of (administrative) law in international law' (2005) 68(3/4) *Law and Contemporary Problems* 127, 164. On the legally assembled exception, see note 14.

[215] Jean Cohen, *Globalization and Sovereignty: Rethinking Legality, Legitimacy, and Constitutionalism* (Cambridge: Cambridge University Press, 2012), p. 270.

[216] Jean Cohen 'Whose sovereignty? Empire versus international law' (2004) 18(3) *Ethics and International Affairs* 1, 24.

'conceptual architectonics'[217] of UN Charter reform, he argues that these effects are a clear consequence of the 'fall'[218] of international law and its replacement by functional regimes and their expertise. The key critical legal task ahead involves contesting the instrumentalism of global governance by redeeming international law's promise as a project of critical universalism and 'placeholder for the vocabularies of justice and goodness'.[219] For Neil Walker, global security law is problematic because it 'sets aside the symmetrical logic of both particularism and universalism' – it struggles both 'to speak in the name of . . . a new putative global community' and 'justify itself . . . in the name of timeless universal values'.[220] Whilst this 'unsettles much of what we imagine the moral and cognitive high ground of law to be', it also opens an important 'threshold debate' about whether the global security law issued by the UN Security Council 'deserves the title of "legislation"' or whether it is merely 'a centralised form of coercion by influential powers' executed through legal means.[221]

These cosmopolitan turns and lament for the loss of the magisterial in international law may well be valid concerns, but I argue that global security law and governance regimes might just as well be critiqued by better understanding the complexities of how they work. That is, by ethnographically remapping the particular techniques, spatiotemporal moves, legal knowledges and practices through which these legal ensembles achieve their effects – in short, by delving more deeply into the dynamics of nascent global legal governance arrangements, rather than flying away from them, as some have suggested. Examining how global security law is materially assembled is both a descriptive and critical endeavour. It can highlight the 'frailty'[222] of new arrangements of power, reappraise what 'existing technical knowledge does . . . and what latent possibilities it might hold'[223] and empirically chart 'the transformations that had to

---

[217] Martti Koskenniemi, 'Globalization and sovereignty. Rethinking legality, legitimacy and constitutionalism' (2013) 11(3) *International Journal of Constitutional Law* 818, 821.

[218] Martti Koskenniemi, *The Gentle Civilizer of Nations: The Rise and Fall of International Law 1870–1960* (Cambridge: Cambridge University Press, 2001).

[219] Martti Koskenniemi, *The Politics of International Law* (Oxford: Hart Publishing, 2011), p. 361.

[220] Walker, 'Out of place and out of time', p. 43.

[221] Ibid. pp. 44, 45.

[222] Latour, *Reassembling the Social*, p. 176.

[223] Annelise Riles, *Collateral Knowledge: Legal Reasoning in the Global Financial Markets* (Chicago IL: University of Chicago Press, 2011), p. 224.

take place in order for new structures of knowledge to have emerged'.[224] Studying global legal assemblages, in other words, enables us to 'experience the international legal field afresh and, potentially, to acquire a new "feel" for the political possibilities available within it'.[225]

---

[224] Arnold I. Davidson, 'Structures and strategies of discourse: remarks towards a history of Foucault's philosophy of language' in Arnold Ira Davidson (ed.), *Foucault and His Interlocutors* (Chicago IL: University of Chicago Press, 1997), p. 11. Cited in Anne Orford, 'In praise of description' (2012) 25(3) *Leiden Journal of International Law* 609, 618.

[225] Johns, *Non-legality in International Law*, p. 27.

5

Conclusions

The primary aims of this book have been to understand how the UN ISIL and Al-Qaida listing regime works as a form of global security law and governance and to explore what happens when legality becomes entangled with preemptive security and orientated towards the countering of uncertain future threats. To that end, each chapter has followed the list to different sites to examine the problems being negotiated there by ensembles of diverse actors and empirically analysed the techniques and assemblage practices they are forging to manage problems of the list. My aim has been to show how these discrete practices produce, shape and sustain this domain of law in distinctive ways. I have argued that the Law of the List is a unique legal weapon in the global war against terrorism and a far-reaching form of global security law. It is transforming the relation between national and international legal orders, building powerful preemptive security networks and authorising new forms of expertise, enabling new global-bordering capabilities and forms of data collection and analysis to spread and stretching what the collective security system is capable of doing in practice. It is generating new governance techniques, knowledge practices and security mechanisms that are reconfiguring how legality works at a granular level. The ISIL and Al-Qaida list is a radical form of global exceptional governance – a temporary preventive measure that lasts indefinitely and that is plastic enough to be reshaped to govern new threats as they emerge.

This final chapter is structured in three parts. First, I revisit the key arguments developed by providing a brief summary of each chapter. Second, I highlight six original contributions that this book makes to the study of global security law and governance. Finally, I close by pointing the way ahead for the Law of the List and highlighting potential areas of further research.

5.1 The Law of the List: Key Arguments

Chapter 1 introduced the scope of this study and set out my key research questions. It explained how I first came to this research project as a human rights lawyer representing people on the ISIL and Al-Qaida list and why I wanted to understand this novel domain of global law as a form of *productive* power, rather than merely some new global governance technique that violates fundamental rights. After highlighting the limitations of existing legal scholarship on this issue, the three key analytical moves of this book were introduced: studying global law as an assemblage; examining risk and preemption as practices of governmentality; and rethinking the problem of exceptional governance. I argue that these analytical moves set this sociolegal study of UN terrorism listing apart from the other existing research on this issue. They also help generate broader insights about the nature of global law and global governance of relevance to those working in different fields – including international law, sociology, anthropology and critical security studies.

The introduction also positioned this book as a methodological experiment in situated knowledge production. Drawing on STS scholarship, I have argued that methods are not just epistemological tools. They are also performative and enact different ontologies. They interfere with and help constitute the worlds they describe, and so are intensely political. This led to a discussion about how my own subject positioning within this assemblage as a practising lawyer has conditioned and shaped my findings. But rather than trying to discount this as something that detracts from the veracity of the study, as is the case in traditional social science research which values dispassionate detachment, my positioning as a practitioner and advocate within the listing regime has helped bring new insights to the fore and fostered a research ethic of situated and sustained engagement.

Three distinct methodological moves of this book were highlighted and then developed in the chapters that followed. First, studying the list as a multisited research object and the global as 'an emergent dimension of arguing about the connection between sites'.[1] Second, empirically examining the crucial and constitutive role of *practices* in global security law and governance. And, finally, using leaked documents to assemble

---

[1] George E. Marcus, 'Ethnography in/of the world system: the emergence of multi-sited ethnography' (1995) 24 *Annual Review of Anthropology* 95, 99.

my research fields and open the black box of an area of law that would have otherwise remained obscured in secrecy.

Chapter 2 examined the crucial role of background listing expertise in global security governance. We followed the list to two specific sites where the UN1267 Monitoring Team was undertaking list implementation work – in 'consultation meetings' with security and intelligence officials, aimed at populating the list with potential targets, and in collaboration with other IOs to make the list interoperable with global policing data (Interpol) and the passenger data of the global aviation industry (ICAO and IATA). I argue that these seemingly innocuous practices of list implementation are doing far-reaching global security governance work. They are not just implementing the list but stretching the scope of what this listing regime can do in profound ways. The mundane technical practices of UN listing expertise, in other words, are important and jurisgenerative. The ISIL and Al-Qaida list emerges from this analysis as a crucial actant of global security law. It exerts agency in its own right, performs important legal assemblage work, builds new ensembles of relations and helps to make the potential future threats of global terrorism governable in the present.

Chapter 2 also analysed how the technology of the list works as an inscription device and 'global optic' for quantifying and ordering global terrorism into something amenable to intervention. We followed the process of how the list enrols a diverse array of actors into new global preemptive security networks to see the threat in the same way. The list performs crucial governance work in bypassing the vexing problem of having to define what terrorism is. The listing format also allows individuals and groups that may ordinarily have no relation to each other to be associated together, made commensurable and governable. Drawing from STS and governmentality scholarship, I argued that list and listing expertise work together to produce a 'centre of calculation' for enabling new forms of 'government at a distance' to take place.[2] The Security Council emerges from this account as an IO that governs transboundary problems like terrorism through epistemic techniques and practices, not just binding Chapter VII counterterrorism resolutions.[3]

---

[2] Bruno Latour, *Science in Action: How to Follow Scientists and Engineers through Society* (Cambridge MA: Harvard University Press, 1987) 215–57; Peter Miller and Nikolas Rose, 'Governing economic life' (1990) 19(1) *Economy and Society* 1.

[3] On this point, see also: Christian Bueger, 'Making things known: epistemic practices, the United Nations and the translation of piracy' (2015) 9 *International Political Sociology* 1.

We also saw how UN listing experts aimed to counter unknown future terrorist threats by establishing an 'equilibrium of possibilities'.[4] This entailed targeting a very broad potential threat population deemed 'at risk' of radicalisation, which is dramatically at odds with the discourse of 'targeted' governance usually justifying UN sanctions policy and the notion of 'concrete threat' thought to limit Chapter VII intervention to particular situations. I argue that this shows how the list works as a novel programme of global biopolitical management, not just a disciplinary tool of immiseration aimed at individual suspects. My analysis of these 'consultation meetings' changes the locus of where we should look to find global security law unfolding – not just in the formal doctrine of IOs and their norm conflicts in the courts, but in the complex assemblages of instruments, calculation and expertise enabled through particular IO interventions.[5] It underscores the urgent need for more empirical research on global governance technologies and the constitutive role of technical practices in global lawmaking.

My analysis of list interoperability – developed towards the end of Chapter 2 – highlighted the crucial importance of the politics of formatting. Analysing the problem of trying to 'build the third hurdle' to better implement the list travel ban shows technical reformatting to be a creative, jurisgenerative and profoundly political governance move that performs what STS scholars call a 'translation'.[6] Reformatting does not simply move the list from context A to context B – it *changes* the list in accordance with the new ordering practices, listing criteria and spatiotemporal dynamics that condition the different formats. Translation, in other words, is a legally and politically generative process. My argument is that empirically unpacking and examining the politics of translation is critically important because it shows us how global security law can be embedded and stretched through listing practices, without attributing agency to powerful actors or deferring to some kind of master-plan.[7] This helps to explain how global security law continues

---

[4] Interview with former member of the UN 1267 Monitoring Team, New York, June 2014 (Interview B).

[5] Guy Fiti Sinclair, *To Reform the World: International Organizations and the Making of Modern States* (Oxford: Oxford University Press, 2017), p. 11.

[6] On translation, see, for example: Michel Callon and Bruno Latour, 'Unscrewing the big Leviathan: how actors macro-structure reality and how sociologists help them to do so' in Aaron Victor Cicourel and Karin Knorr-Cetina (eds.), *Advances in Social Theory and Methodology: Toward an Integration of Micro and Macro-Sociologies* (London: Routledge, 1981), pp. 277, 279.

[7] Tania Murray Li, 'Practices of assemblage and community forest management' (2007) 36 (2) *Economy and Society* 263.

to expand into new regulatory domains and informally absorb a plethora of diverse discourses, institutions and practices into its remit, despite sustained criticism by reform-orientated states, human rights advocates and the courts. In other words, studying the micro-politics of translation and 'taking on the technicalities of law', as Riles puts it, are critically important global sociolegal research strategies.[8]

Chapter 3 shifted focus to the problem of accountability in global governance and provided a detailed genealogical account of the emergence of the UN1267 Office of the Ombudsperson – the procedural mechanism created in 2009 to allow targeted individuals and groups to make delisting requests to the Security Council. Most literature posits the Ombudsperson as an improvement and a much-needed step in the right direction towards realising 'fair and clear procedures' in UN sanctions. My account complicates this teleological narrative of legal progress and reframes the Office of the Ombudsperson as a governance effect arising from multiple conflicts across the listing assemblage: a composite figure born out of institutional struggles between diverse actors under conditions of international legal fragmentation.

My analysis in Chapter 3 shows that the divergences between actors in this domain run deeper than usually suggested. The list accountability conflict isn't just about different perspectives on the same problem, in a process ultimately mediated by the Security Council. Drawing from the STS insight that objects are differentially enacted through practice, I argue that the different actors across the listing assemblage engaged in this conflict enact fundamentally different, or ontologically distinct, versions of the list. What we see in this accountability conflict is not just a clash of regimes or epistemic communities, but a multiplicity of divergent realities colliding. To get at this heterogeneity, I analysed five different versions of the list enacted through this conflict – including the Legal List of the courts, the Humanitarian List of targeted sanctions scholar-experts, the Living List of listing experts, the Compliant List of the UN Special Rapporteurs on Counterterrorism, and the Credible List of the P5 states. As my 'praxiographic' study shows, each version of the list frames the accountability conflicts of the ISIL and Al-Qaida sanctions regime in radically different ways and seeks procedural redress for

---

[8] Annelise Riles, 'A new agenda for the cultural study of law: taking on the technicalities' (2005) 53 *Buffalo Law Review* 973. See also: Gavin Sullivan, '"Taking on the technicalities" of international law – practice, description, critique: a response to Fleur Johns' (2017) 111 *AJIL Unbound* 181.

divergent purposes.[9] My analysis reframes the list as a multiple object and reveals the heterogeneity of the listing assemblage. When the Law of the List is fractured this way, a key question becomes: how are the different versions of the list assembled and held together, and the tensions and conflicts between the different actors in the listing assemblage managed in practice?

To address this problem, the latter part of Chapter 3 analysed the Ombudsperson as a unique figure of global legal expertise and closely examined their important assemblage work. Drawing from interviews with the former position-holder and my own professional experience representing targeted individuals in delisting proceedings, I examined the novel decision-making processes, 'dialogue' meetings and evidential standards that the Ombudsperson has crafted to work in this special environment. I argue that these inventive practices help mute underlying political and legal tensions, avoid 'minefields', accommodate political sensitivities and hold the disparate strands of the listing assemblage together. In my account, the Ombudsperson performs crucially important legal assemblage work by facilitating convergence between the different versions of the list and smoothing over list conflicts and contradictions that might otherwise engender fragmentation and political conflict. The particular expertise of the Ombudsperson lies in their recombination of existing legal categories and practices into novel quasi-juridical forms tailored towards embedding preemptive security logics. Existing scholarship suggests that the Ombudsperson provides a mechanism of 'de facto judicial review' and 'fair and clear procedures' to listed persons. Drawing from my own experience representing listed individuals, I argue that such accounts show little understanding of the inequities and asymmetries that this experimental review mechanism creates in practice.[10] So, whilst most scholarship frames the Ombudsperson as a procedural improvement and postnational accountability solution, my analysis recasts it as a unique conduit of global exceptional governance and an ongoing political and legal problem.

---

[9] Annemarie Mol, *The Body Multiple: Ontology in Medical Practice* (Durham NC: Duke University Press, 2002).

[10] See for example: Sue Eckert and Thomas Biersteker, *Due Process and Targeted Sanctions: An Update of the 'Watson Report'* (Geneva: Watson Institute for International Studies, Brown University and the Graduate Institute, 2012), p. 37; Devika Hovell, *The Power of Process: The Value of Due Process in Security Council Sanctions Decision-Making* (Oxford: Oxford University Press, 2016); Larissa van Den Herik, 'Peripheral hegemony in the quest to ensure security council accountability for its individualized UN sanctions regimes' (2014) 19(3) *Journal of Conflict and Security Law* 427.

Finally, in Chapter 4 we followed the list to the EU courts and closely examined the practices of judicial review. This chapter explored what happens when the preemptive security logics and mosaic epistemology of the list meet the principles of judicial proof and fact-finding that the courts have long used to establish legal truth. Most legal scholarship on the Law of the List focuses on the high-profile clash between the EU courts and the UN Security Council in the *Kadi* case, with global constitutionalists and global legal pluralists battling it out to determine whether the courts got the answers to that norm conflict 'right' or 'wrong'. My analysis goes beneath the legal reasoning of the courts to empirically study their procedural practices, by charting the reform of the courts' rules to allow judges to handle intelligence material as evidence without disclosure to listed persons for the first time.

The key puzzle that this chapter sought to understand was how a court vested to protect fundamental rights was so readily enlisted to construct this legally authorised state of exception? This problem was analysed by bringing the latent spatiotemporal dynamics and epistemic qualities of the list to the analytical surface. Drawing on the work of Boaventura de Sousa Santos, I argued that the listing assemblage is a paradigmatic form of non-synchronous law – that is, a legal form composed of divergent temporalities that are literally 'out of sync'. Using intelligence-as-evidence pulls the Law of the List in radically different temporal directions. Evidence is grounded on a 'past–present axis' and tethered to acts undertaken in the past, whilst intelligence is hinged on a 'present–future axis' and orientated towards making radically uncertain futures knowable.[11] I argue that bringing these two knowledge forms and temporal logics together in the format of the list puts non-synchronous dynamics in play and generates legal conflict.

These procedural reforms aim to allow EU judges to manage this conflict, but my analysis of recent case law showed that they stand to engender further complexity in practice. Judicial review is retrospectively orientated towards a 'decision' that has taken place in the past. But Chapter 4 showed how reliance on intelligence-as-evidence defers this space of decision and confounds this process because the decision supposed to be under review is literally not there. The phrase 'dis-located law' was used to try and capture this dynamic process of fracture and deferral. My empirical analysis highlighted how this process of dis-

---

[11] Brian Massumi, *The Future Birth of the Affective Fact*, Conference Proceedings: Genealogies of Biopolitics (2005), copy on file with author.

location works in practice to render key sites of formal decision-making across the assemblage substantively empty. Building on insights from sociolegal and globalisation studies, I argued that empirically mapping the spatiotemporal dimensions of legal governance can provide important insights into how global security law is extended in scope and how global emergencies are normalised, stretched and made durable through legal means.[12]

When we analyse the ISIL and Al-Qaida list through the lens of IO doctrine and the UN Security Council Resolutions that formally constitute it, global security law seems broadly encompassing and representative of the international community it purports to protect. But empirically analysing how preemptive security problems are being mediated by the courts, and closely following the assemblage practices of the judiciary trying in good faith to ameliorate the normative defects of the list, shows this global security regime to be something far more 'patchy', dynamic and fragmented. I argue that such complexities can provide fertile terrain for global sociolegal research and that if we want to understand how global law works we need to take the spatiotemporal dynamics of legal governance more seriously.

In what follows I highlight six original contributions that this book brings to the study of global security law and governance. Rather than specifically focusing on the ISIL and Al-Qaida listing regime and the scholarly debates associated with it, I have underscored parts of this book that readers from related fields (such as postnational law, IO studies, global governance, critical security and sociolegal studies) may find valuable for their own research projects.

5.2 The Law of the List: Original Contributions

5.2.1   Global Legal Assemblage

Most scholarship in this area examines IO doctrines and the relevant UN Security Council Resolutions and tracks how they have been indirectly challenged by domestic and regional courts. Legal conflicts are highlighted (such as in the *Kadi* case) and normative theories for resolving those conflicts – global constitutionalism, global legal pluralism, regime theory and global administrative law – are debated. These discussions are

---

[12] Mariana Valverde, *Chronotopes of Law: Jurisdiction, Scale and Governance* (London: Routledge, 2015); Saskia Sassen, *Territory, Authority, Rights: From Medieval to Global Assemblages* (Princeton NJ: Princeton University Press, 2006).

important, but this book also shows that they are limited and reduction-ist. They reveal only a small part of what are more complex legal and political problems and tell us little about why human rights have such limited purchase over this form of preemptive security governance.

So, the first contribution of this study lies in opening up a very different way of understanding global security law. This book has studied the Law of the List as an assemblage of knowledge practices, governance techniques, spatiotemporal dynamics, artefacts and novel legal relations, or what Nikolas Rose and Mariana Valverde call a 'legal complex'.[13] This approach removes us from the reified terrain of static models and normative debates about whether the courts were 'right' or 'wrong' and allows us to examine global security law as something very much emer-gent, expansive and in motion. As I have shown, moving outside the positivist world of legal doctrine, judicial reasoning and the Chapter VII decrees of the Security Council allows more variegated and textured conceptions of global security law to come into view. Globalisation is driven by dynamics situated within the interstate and nation-state system that transform old capabilities into new organising logics and governance capabilities.[14] It is not a zero-sum game between the 'national' and 'global', but something marked by processes and practices of recomposi-tion and rearrangement. Reframing the ISIL and Al-Qaida list as a legal assemblage helps us to get at these novel processes of reordering. What emerges is a global regime that inhabits, yet exceeds, existing frames of international and national law. One that is tethered to the UN Charter powers of the Security Council yet stretching the collective security system in practice.

By honing in on EU judicial review and the problem of assessing intelligence-as-evidence in Chapter 4, for example, we were able to see that there are no decisions (in the public law sense) animating this regime, despite its public international law origins. Instead, we have intelligence agencies and executive actors sharing information bilaterally or not at all, on a need-to-know basis and circulating 'Narrative Summaries' to placate targeted individuals, regime critics and courts. Dis-locating listing decisions in this way has confounded the EU judi-ciary and prompted far-reaching changes to its evidential rules. Judges accustomed to conventional retrospective processes of judicial proof

---

[13] Nikolas Rose and Mariana Valverde, 'Governed by law?' (1998) 7(4) *Social and Legal Studies* 541, 542–3.

[14] Sassen, *Territory, Authority, Rights.*

must now assemble future-orientated security mosaics from informational scraps and inferences. Global security law is thereby embedded and stretched through micro-processes of reorganisation. And the list is changing the ways that justice is done inside the EU courts. Analysing the Law of the List from this site allowed us to see how fragmented, novel and jurisgenerative it is. The ISIL and Al-Qaida list is unlike any other UN sanctions regime or international law instrument. It is a unique preemptive legal weapon in the global war against terrorism and is generating profound legal and political effects.

Analysing global assemblage practices sheds a very different light on how governmental programmes are constructed. The key insight drawn from STS scholarship here is that objects are produced through practice.[15] This means that, when faced with conflicts in postnational governance about particular institutions or governmental programmes, we are not only dealing with different perspectives on the same legal or political problem. Instead, we have multiplicities and different versions of reality clashing and coming into conflict. That is, differences between actors are not just epistemological but ontological as well. This is what makes assemblages *heterogeneous* and why the hard work of pulling divergent strands together into contingent wholes is so important. Enlisting and aligning different actors into networks, managing conflicting claims, authorising the expertise of some and marginalising the knowledge of others or otherwise translating their will to your own: this is how global security law and governance is materially assembled and reproduced.

Most legal accounts reduce these differences to questions of normative interpretation or compliance. Analyses of the UN1267 Ombudsperson, for example, argue about whether this institution brings UN sanctions within the remit of human rights law and whether courts should show more deference to the Security Council as a result. GAL scholars see the Ombudsperson mechanism in prefigurative and evolutionary terms as an important step in the right direction, sanitising its contested history and problems. Analysing global law as an assemblage, however, allows us to grasp differences as something more radical and generative. When actors clash in postnational legal space it is not only a conflict of norms, but also competing versions of reality that are in friction and vying for dominance. The techniques and practices through which divergences are

---

[15] Mol, *The Body Multiple.*

glued together and conflicts contained becomes part of the empirical puzzle to be explained, rather than extraneous background work.

Numerous scholars have called for more innovative approaches to understand how globalisation and the governance of transboundary problems are transforming law.[16] Others are reorientating the study of IOs and emergence of new forms of international executive rule as assemblages of practice.[17] This book has engaged with such calls by performing an important analytical reorientation – shifting focus from normative and positivist questions like 'what is global law?' or 'what ought global law be?' to the more mundane, empirical question of 'how is global law assembled and sustained?' in the face of ongoing tension. I argue that this shift is important not only for those interested in global security law, but also for those studying postnational legal problems more generally. When global law is reframed as 'a practical and contingent achievement', our attention is drawn to the diverse practices, alignments, translations and techniques involved in making that achievement possible.[18] Decentring the Law, in other words, prompts a much-needed 'expansion of the dimensions of legality'.[19] And I argue that this kind of expansion is critically important in making sense of the complexities of global legal-ordering unfolding in the present. We need to broaden our understandings of what law is and experiment with constructing theories from the material conditions and conflicts that global law creates and inhabits. It is this kind of empiricism that allows us to 'find the conditions under which something new is produced' and

---

[16] See, for example: Peer Zumbansen, 'How, where and for whom? Interrogating law's forms, locations and purposes', *Inaugural Lecture, King's College London* (28 April 2016); Eve Darian-Smith, *Laws and Societies in Global Contexts: Contemporary Approaches* (Cambridge: Cambridge University Press, 2013); Mireille Delmas-Marty, *Ordering Pluralism: A Conceptual Framework for Understanding the Transnational Legal World* (Oxford: Hart Publishing, 2009); Boaventura de Sousa Santos, *Toward a New Legal Common Sense: Law, Globalization and Emancipation* (Cambridge: Cambridge University Press, 2002).

[17] See, for example: Fiti Sinclair, *To Reform the World*; Dimitri Van Den Meerssche, 'Performing the rule of law in international organizations: Ibrahim Shihata and the World Bank's turn to governance reform' (2019) 32(1) *Leiden Journal of International Law* 47; Anne Orford, *International Authority and the Responsibility to Protect* (Cambridge: Cambridge University Press, 2011).

[18] Andrew Barry, *Material Politics: Disputes Along the Pipeline* (Oxford: Blackwell Publishing, 2013), p. 183.

[19] Sally E. Merry, 'New legal realism and the ethnography of transnational law' (2006) 31(4) *Law and Social Inquiry* 976.

to think about how new global security regimes might be made otherwise.[20]

5.2.2   Studying the Global from Global Structure-Making Sites

A second contribution that this book makes concerns scale and the politics of scale production. Law is often implicitly spatialised through logics of verticality and encompassment – with the global up on top, the regional and national further below, and the local down the bottom.[21] Because each scale is thought to encompass the other as one ascends the international hierarchy of norms, more of one is usually taken to mean less of the other. And so, the local, national and global scales through which legal-ordering and governance are arranged end up being reified and locked into a zero-sum game. If international lawyers and political geographers are asked to explain a particular global problem, for example, they would likely give dramatically different responses tied to differing notions of scale. The geographers might talk about logistics chains, algorithmic architectures, geopolitical stacks or flows of infrastructural space.[22] Complex topologies would be outlined showing how 'heterogeneous techniques, technologies, material elements, and institutional forms are taken up and assembled'.[23] But the lawyers will still likely frame the problem jurisdictionally and in abstract normative terms, talking about the global as if it is something 'up there' and local 'down here'. Describing law in this way can offer helpful shortcuts when discussing legal issues and be a useful figure of speech. But global law and the politics of legal scale are just not as straightforward as that in practice. I argue that postnational norm conflicts and the rapid spread of informal legal-ordering are underscoring just how analytically ill-equipped conventional forms of legal analysis are in grappling with fluid global

---

[20] Gilles Deleuze and Claire Parnett, *Dialogues* (London: The Athlone Press, 1987), p. vii.

[21] James Ferguson and Akhil Gupta 'Spatializing states: toward an ethnography of neoliberal governmentality' (2002) *American Ethnologist* 981.

[22] See, respectively: Deborah Cowen, *The Deadly Life of Logistics: Mapping Violence in Global Trade* (Minneapolis MN: University of Minnesota Press, 2014); Luciana Parisi, *Contagious Architecture: Computation, Aesthetics and Space* (Cambridge MA: MIT Press, 2013); Benjamin Bratton, *The Stack: On Software and Sovereignty* (Cambridge MA: MIT Press, 2015); Keller Easterling, *Extrastatecraft: The Power of Infrastructure Space* (New York: Verso, 2014).

[23] Stephen Collier, 'Topologies of power: Foucault's analysis of political government beyond "governmentality"' (2009) 26(6) *Theory, Culture and Society* 78, 89–90.

governance problems that are multi-scalar, technologically complex and transboundary in nature.

This book addresses this problem of scale by taking 'the global' in global security law seriously. It has followed the list to local sites where global structure-making practices are constructed and put into circulation. And it has shown how governance scales are empirical problems that require detailed examination, not a priori background conditions that can be taken for granted in our analyses.

As we saw in Chapter 2, powerful new forms of global counterterrorism governance are being made from localised sites through fragile alignments of knowledge practices, techniques, infrastructures and relations. By aligning diverse actors into preemptive security networks through the technology of the list, for example, UN listing experts are constructing new ways of seeing and governing global terrorism that were not possible before. In my analysis, list and listing expertise are working together to build what Bruno Latour has called a 'centre of calculation' for enabling 'action at a distance' to take place.[24] We also saw how making the ISIL and Al-Qaida list interoperable with the biometric data used by states and Interpol and the aviation data used by ICAO and the global airline industry dramatically expands its scope and governance possibilities. Reformatting the list does more than move it from context A to context B. It performs an act of translation that is crucially important, as discussed in more detail below at Section 5.2.4. In the imaginary of the 'third hurdle', the list need not be applied at national borders, because it is enacted electronically at points of sale when someone buys an airline ticket. Ensembles of different experts, private trade bodies (IATA, the Biometrics Institute), IOs (UNSC, ICAO, Interpol) and global regulatory regimes (UNSC Resolutions, ICAO SARPs, UN CTED best-practice guidelines) are brought into novel relation through the mundane technical work of list reformatting.

These examples draw attention to the hard work of making global law operative and powerful. Bringing ANT into this domain helps us to 'flatten the landscape' of global security governance.[25] The key insight drawn from STS scholarship throughout this book is that 'global' actors are not necessarily 'bigger' than any other, but are made more powerful by virtue of their relative connectedness and the inscription technologies

---

[24] Latour, *Science in Action*; Miller and Rose, 'Governing economic life'.

[25] Bruno Latour, *Reassembling the Social: An Introduction to Actor-Network Theory* (Oxford: Oxford University Press, 2005), p. 182.

they use.[26] In other words, the Law of the List is made global and powerful through scale-producing practices and techniques that can be empirically scrutinised. I argue that, when we cease taking governance scales for granted, we can get a much better sense of how they are being rearranged and repurposed through new forms of legal-ordering. And this can provide us with a much richer sense of how laws and legal institutions are being transformed through globalisation.

The other effect of this approach to scale is more forensic and political in nature. If powerful actors are made powerful through their scale-producing activities and practice of making others small in comparison, then empirically charting how such processes work opens a space for disturbance or what Michel Callon and Latour call 'unscrewing the big Leviathan'.[27] Showing how global structures are produced reveals the material conditions through which actors can 'dominate on a large scale'.[28] Such an approach reminds us that global law is not merely something that powerful global actors hold and wield to their strategic advantage, but a series of relational effects and material constructions that are more contingent and potentially reversible than usually suggested.[29] 'To take the fabrication of various scales as our main center of interest', as Latour notes, 'is to place the practical means of achieving power on a firm foundation'.[30] By taking scale production seriously, as this book does, powerful international institutions and agency in global governance are recast as effects of practice.

5.2.3   Following the Politics of Expertise in Global Law-Making

Much contemporary legal scholarship is concerned with managing anxieties surrounding international legal fragmentation. This book has instead tried to show what the fragmentation and functional differentiation of international law looks like in practice. Analysing how transboundary threats of global terrorism are being countered through novel governance techniques and practices takes us squarely into the politics of expertise. The kind of technical legal assemblage work examined in this

---

[26] Callon and Latour, 'Unscrewing the big Leviathan'.

[27] Ibid.

[28] Bruno Latour, 'Visualization and cognition: drawing things together' (1986) 6 *Knowledge and Society* 12.

[29] Michel Foucault, *Power/Knowledge: Selected Interviews and Other Writings 1972–1977* (New York: Pantheon, 1980), p. 98.

[30] Latour, 'Visualization and cognition', 27.

book is usually dismissed by legal scholars as something peripheral and extra-legal. But my analysis suggests that the background workings of functional expertise need to be closely examined and taken much more seriously in global legal research, because this is where some of the most experimental and expansive global security lawmaking and preemptive security governance is being assembled. So, a third key related insight to be drawn from this book is that global security law is not only powerful because it is issued by the Security Council under Chapter VII of the UN Charter. It is *made* powerful through the mundane assemblage work of functional experts and the knowledge practices and artefacts they are crafting. So, 'background' expertise requires close empirical analysis.

In Chapter 2, for example, we saw how UN listing experts performing seemingly prosaic tasks (like enhancing list implementation) are stretching the list in far-reaching ways and transforming it into a powerful global legal weapon. Improving implementation of the travel ban requires altering global aviation standards, building new bordering capabilities and putting new preemptive security arrangements in place that affect all travellers worldwide. This is not just a functional problem about enhancing the implementation of a list. It is global lawmaking and security governance in motion. But because it is seen as technical work, the politics of listing expertise goes largely unnoticed and unchallenged. In Chapter 3 we analysed how academic experts motivated by the possibility of global humanitarian reform became enrolled into targeted sanctions policy. And how, after 9/11, these scholars were revalorised as counterterrorism finance experts. I argued that the assemblage work these scholar-experts have performed has been crucial for the Law of the List. They have enlisted a diverse range of actors into their networks, framed debates about the accountability problems of the list in managerial terms and shaped this domain of global security law in profound yet largely unacknowledged ways.

For Martti Koskenniemi the main problem with international law's deferral to expertise is that it instrumentalises law and recasts it in a technical idiom. As such, the key critical task we now face involves redeeming international law as 'a placeholder for the vocabularies of justice and goodness' and reclaiming law as a transcendent project that embodies 'the regulative idea of universal community'.[31] David Kennedy identifies three ways to challenge the hegemony of expertise in global

---

[31] Martti Koskenniemi, *The Politics of International Law* (Oxford: Hart Publishing, 2011), pp. 360–1.

governance. We must identify the interests animating experts, render their latent assumptions visible and reframe expertise as something individuals have discretion and political responsibility over to encourage 'a form of expertise which could experience politics as its vocation'.[32]

These accounts offer important ways of challenging expertise, but the critical stance adopted in this book operates in a different register and direction. Rather than transcending the technicalities of expertise by turning towards law's promise of universality, I argue that we might develop new forms of *immanent critique* that revalorise the technicalities of expertise as powerful and jurisgenerative. Studying global law through the artefacts, knowledge practices and performative effects of expertise reorientates us towards a different set of questions than those usually asked by legal scholars: 'what productive work do they do as they circulate? What forms of social action are they able to mobilise, and how? What subjects, objects and situations are produced in the manner of their circulation and deployment and how?'.[33] Addressing such questions, and charting the politics of expertise empirically as it unfolds in specific sites, is politically important because it shows how small shifts in knowledge practices at a micro-level can provide important sources of legal change in macro-organisations like the UN Security Council. And it reveals how institutions become powerful by translating the will of others, building centres of calculation and forging new forms of domination through technical means. As Kennedy notes, 'we need better maps of expertise', but 'mapping the knowledge of experts is complex and technical work'.[34] This book contributes to this task by studying the politics of the list and listing expertise to better understand how this domain of global security law is being assembled, often through mundane technical and infrastructural work.

5.2.4   Governance Technologies As Legal Actants and the Politics of Translation

A fourth related contribution to current debates that this book makes is to show that the governance technologies used to deal with transboundary

---

[32] David Kennedy, 'Challenging expert rule: the politics of global governance' (2005) 27 *Sydney Law Review* 5, 24.

[33] Andrew Lang, 'International lawyers and the study of expertise: representationalism and performativity' in Mosche Hirsch and Andrew Lang (eds.), *Research Handbook on the Sociology of International Law* (Cheltenham: Edward Elgar Publishing, 2018), p. 149.

[34] Kennedy, 'Challenging expert rule', 14.

problems are not just means to an end but are in themselves crucial agents of global lawmaking. Drawing on governmentality and STS scholarship, and building on the growing literature on global indicators, standards and informal law, I have shown that the ISIL and Al-Qaida list is a powerful protagonist in this domain, deeply entangled in the knowledge objects that come into being through its use. The problem of defining terrorism – and determining whether it should extend to include armed national liberation movements or state terrorism – was one of the key political divides of the decolonising world in the late twentieth century. More than sixty proposed definitions were put forward for international agreement between 1936 and 1981 without success.[35] Yet my analysis has shown how this definitional problem has now been effectively bypassed. Global terrorism is now something rendered visible, actionable and governable through the technology of the list.

The list is one of the most archaic ordering devices. It is innocuous and simple, yet malleable and – as I have shown throughout this book – capable of performing crucially important governance work. After 9/11 it was the list that helped to 'quantify a threat that no-one could easily quantify' and generate actionable results in the global war on terror.[36] My analysis has shown how the list works as a performative technology that enables uncertain future threats to be made visible and governed in the present. The list produces global terrorism as an object of legal intervention by making diverse threats commensurable, optically consistent and targetable. When global constitutionalists and pluralists argue about how the effects of legal fragmentation in this area can best be normatively contained, the list is either nowhere to be found or relegated to the status of inert instrument. Drawing on the work of Annelise Riles, Fleur Johns, Sally Engle Merry, Mariana Valverde and others working in the sociology of knowledge tradition and charting the importance of things in configuring world politics, I argue that legal technicalities and tools should be reappraised as important agents of legal change in their own right. Technologies of governance like the list are not just appendages of powerful actors that organise preexisting phenomenon, but actants that help constitute and condition the very problems they purport to represent or target. As I have shown, studying the politics of performativity, or

---

[35] Mark Muller, 'Terrorism, proscription and the right to resist in the age of conflict' (2008) 20 *Denning Law Journal* 113.

[36] Interview with former member of the UN1267 Monitoring Team, New York, November 2012 (Interview A).

the ways that 'things' enable and shape global law and governance, can be a fruitful endeavour.[37]

Whilst debates about the lack of a definition of terrorism are still important, this book suggests they are somewhat missing the point. In the current era, global terrorism is something that is listed, not defined. Failure to define terrorism is not a source of lack but a condition of possibility. Those interested in global counterterrorism law might benefit from closely analysing how listing works as a knowledge production and ordering technique. So, the fourth insight to be gleaned from this book is that understanding global law requires paying close empirical attention to the governance technologies through which it is enacted. This means using analytical tools that can break down conventional distinctions between subjects and objects and structure and agency. Each chapter of this book has shown how non-human things – artefacts, technologies, instruments – actively participate in the making of legal and political relations and allow new forms of government to emerge and intervene. Understanding the power asymmetries and violence of global security governance requires more than attributing influence to hegemonic world powers (like the USA and other P5 states). It requires empirical analysis of the inscriptions and technologies being used to make new forms of action at a distance possible – that is, detailed study of the seemingly mundane technicalities of global legal work.[38]

Highlighting the agency of things also helps make the politics of translation visible. That is, the ways that objects, techniques, practices and relations are aligned in particular ways to make new security knowledges and forms of governance possible. Lawyers and political scientists are accustomed to looking for causative mechanisms to explain the phenomena that they study. Their focus is usually on norms, institutions and the authority of powerful actors. But, as shown in this book, this misses much of how global law and governance unfolds in practice and

---

[37] Dimitri Van Den Meerssche, 'International organizations and the performativity of measuring states: discipline through diagnosis' (2018) 15(1) *International Organizations Law Review* 168; Lang, 'International lawyers and the study of expertise'; Annelise Riles, *Collateral Knowledge: Legal Reasoning in the Global Financial Markets* (Chicago IL: University of Chicago Press, 2011).

[38] Riles, *Collateral Knowledge*; Mariana Valverde, 'Jurisdiction and scale: legal "technicalities" as resources for theory' (2009) 18(2) *Social and Legal Studies* 139; Fleur Johns, *Non-Legality in International Law: Unruly Law* (Cambridge: Cambridge University Press, 2013).

the ways in which extending practices and moving objects across different empirical sites can generate new knowledge and governance possibilities. Studying how potential threats from around the world are collected, transported and sedimented through the technology of the list, to enable global terrorism to be calculated and governed, shows how new regimes of global power are constructed and made durable through diffuse translation practices that operate underneath the radar of formal law and authority. When the list is reformatted and made interoperable with aviation data, for example, it does not stay the same. Changing the material conditions and practices through which the list performs its security work changes the list as well and opens up new avenues of intervention.

If power and agency are effects of such practices, and not only features deriving from institutional authority, then the politics of translation and the agency of governance technologies need to be rigorously examined. This book has contributed to this task by studying the ways things (like lists and technical formats and inscription practices) make global security law and governance possible and by arguing that we need to not only study the law but also conditions of emergent causality. Michel Foucault showed us that the state was constituted 'on the basis of multiple and very diverse processes which gradually coagulate[d] and form[ed] an effect' – that is, through governmental practices.[39] Timothy Mitchell has shown how 'the economy did not come about as a new name for the processes of exchange that economists had always studied' but rather through 'the reorganization and transformation of those and other processes into an object that had not previously existed'.[40] This book has sought to bring something similar to the study of global security law by deepening our understanding of what difference the technology of the list can make.

5.2.5 Preemptive Security Logics and Novel Rearrangements of Legal Practice

This book has also analysed the ISIL and Al-Qaida listing regime to understand how preemptive security affects conventional legal practices and principles when they inevitably come into conflict. There has been

---

[39] Michel Foucault, *Security, Territory, Population: Lectures at the College de France 1977–1978* (Basingstoke: Palgrave Macmillan 2007), p. 248.

[40] Timothy Mitchell, *Rule of Experts: Egypt, Techno-Politics, Modernity* (Berkeley CA: University of California Press, 2002), p. 5.

little empirical study on how law is transformed through countering unknown risks and future terrorist threats. Most accounts suggest that preemption is supplanting liberal principles of legality and that we need a new jurisprudence of Future Law to grapple with the specific problems it generates.[41] The assumption – in most sociology, criminology and critical security studies literature – is that law is receding in the face of radically uncertain risks. This has understandably led to calls to defend liberal legality and the rule of law from undue encroachment by preemptive security politics.

As a human rights lawyer who represents targeted individuals in this domain, I am very supportive of the idea that legal protections of listed persons ought to be strengthened. As discussed in Chapter 3, for example, in my experience the Ombudsperson mechanism is not a form of 'de facto judicial review' that allows for 'fair and clear procedures' but an experiment in global exceptional governance more akin to a postmodern Star Chamber of our times. Yet, as I have shown throughout this book, preemption is not supplanting existing legal practices and principles so much as rearranging them into novel hybrids and amalgams. In Chapter 4, for example, we saw how EU judges changed their procedural rules to handle intelligence-as-evidence for the first time. We observed how the future-orientated mosaic epistemology of the list and retrospective processes of judicial proof were becoming commingled into new knowledge production practices to judicially review the list and resolve its problems. The outcome of this entanglement is not preordained but something more contingent and uncertain. Global security law is indeed putting principles of liberal legality into motion. But it is also stimulating processes of legal reordering – new ways of assessing intelligence-as-evidence (Chapter 4), novel mechanisms for reviewing listing decisions and holding IOs to account (Chapter 3) and new techniques for governing global travel (Chapter 2). It is not eroding the foundational principles of liberal legality, but modulating and rearranging them in new ways.

Analysing risk and preemption as practices of governmentality, as I have done throughout this book, helps us chart these novel recombinations and grasp how global security law works as a form of productive power. It provides a useful antidote to the epochal claims made about law's inexorable disappearance in the face of risk, and instead prompts us

---

[41] Lucia Zedner, 'Preventative justice or pre-punishment? The case of control orders' (2007) 60(1) *Current Legal Problems* 174.

to theorise global security law and governance from the empirical problems and problem-management techniques it is generating. As Claudia
Aradau argues:

> Critical work needs to become more analytically attentive to the prefix
> 're' – to what gets reconfigured, recomposed or rearticulated. While
> technologies of (in)security often appear different, novel, unprecedented,
> critical work needs to reformulate analytical tools that can grasp the
> reconfiguration and recomposition of discourses, technologies and
> practices.[42]

Showing global governance effects to be contingent to the problems they
attend also underscores the fact that things could be otherwise. The novel
practices being forged, and that I have highlighted in this study, may end
up being critical in enabling new forms of global intervention to become
embedded or inconsequential. My broader point here is that, if we want
to understand global security law and the ways it is transforming other
bodies of law (international human rights norms, domestic constitutional law, IOs law and collective security) we need to empirically examine how it is being materially conditioned. Being attentive to the
'heterogeneous recompositions and reconfigurations' through which
global security governance is enacted through its entanglement with
law opens up new avenues of analysis and critique.[43] We cannot rely
on static models or normative theories to define what global security law
is or ought to be. Instead, I argue that it is more productive to theorise
global security law immanently from inside the empirical problems,
novel reconfigurations and fragmented international legal landscape
that we are currently situated within.

5.2.6   Rethinking the Global Exception

The sixth contribution this book seeks to make is to rethink the problem
of the exception. The ISIL and Al-Qaida listing regime is formally built
upon resolutions of the UN Security Council adopted pursuant to emergency provisions in Chapter VII of the UN Charter. As Chapter VII
measures, listing decisions cannot be reviewed and they must be strictly
implemented by Member States even if they come into conflict with
domestic or constitutional requirements. The listing regime 'provides

---

[42] Claudia Aradau, 'Politics of technoscience and (in)security' in Mark Salter (ed.), 'Horizon
Scan: Critical Security Studies for the next 50 years' (2019) 50(4) *Security Dialogue* 23, 24.
[43] Ibid.

a ready means by which individual states can make executive decisions with far reaching consequences, apparently unconstrained by domestic judicial review or the international human rights treaties by which they are bound'.[44] Listed individuals are targeted for things that designating states believe they might do in the future and are not afforded any real opportunity to contest the allegations supposedly made against them. The listing regime, in other words, functions as a novel form of global exceptional governance – albeit one that does not easily fit in the existing ways that exceptions are understood.[45]

This book has argued that understanding the violence of global security governance and the ways that exceptions become the norm in postnational space requires us to think more innovatively about how emergency law and politics unfolds. Instead of looking for 'states' of emergency declared by sovereign decisions and defined by the absence of law, I have suggested that security exceptions should be studied empirically as processes and networks of relations that are legally assembled, often through relatively banal techniques and security practices. Humanitarian scholars working on 'smart sanctions' and deflecting political critique of the regime (Chapter 3); EU court officials developing procedures for judges to handle secret intelligence-as-evidence, ostensibly to improve the administration of justice (Chapter 4); security experts translating 'global terrorism' into novel fields of intervention and global aviation bodies implementing the list through new techniques for preemptively targeting travellers (Chapter 2): each of these examples may not amount to much on their own. But, when sutured together as an assemblage of co-functioning elements, I argue that we can see a variegated topology of global exceptional governance emerging. One that is provisional and diffuse yet dense, jurisgenerative and powerful.

The adverse effects of global governance are often framed as deficits of (democratic) accountability. But, in the global security domain – where security actors work secretly through opaque transnational networks and IOs to target terrorism suspects in ways that may be unlawful if pursued

---

[44] UN Doc. A/67/396, Report of the Special Rapporteur on the Promotion of Human Rights and Fundamental Freedoms while Countering Terrorism (26 September 2012), p. 5.

[45] On Chapter VII measures as exceptional, see: Jared Schott, 'Chapter VII as exception: Security Council action and the regulative ideal of emergency' (2007) 6(1) *Northwestern University Journal of International Human Rights* 24; Simon Chesterman, 'Unaccountable – the United Nations, emergency powers, and the rule of law' (2009) 42 *Vanderbilt Journal of Transnational Law* 1509.

domestically – democratic deficit discourse cannot adequately capture the politics of what is at stake. As the Edward Snowden revelations plainly revealed, we need new ways of conceptualising global emergency rule – not only in relation to global mass surveillance, but also with other global security arrangements like targeted killing, countering violent extremism and global terrorism listing regimes.

I argue that reframing exceptional governance as assemblages of relations can help us to rethink global emergency rule and open up potential new avenues of contestation. This book makes three contributions to that project. First, it shows how uncoupling the exception from sovereignty allows us to better analyse how *global* emergencies unfold. With their shared emphasis on national sovereign decision, neither Carl Schmitt nor Giorgio Agamben (nor the bodies of emergency scholarship they have spawned) offer much help in thinking through postnational exceptional politics. If we are always looking for 'decisions', then we easily miss how exceptions are forged through *practices*. But when we analyse the practices that 'make a difference' in any given domain – that is, if we take an assemblage approach to agency in global security governance – a more dynamic and textured field of exceptional law and politics emerges.[46] I have argued in this book that analysing how such fields are stabilised and stretched is critical for understanding how exceptions are materially reproduced and made durable.

Second, foregrounding assemblage practices in this way allows us to see how the well-intentioned activities of different actors situated at different sites and scales can work together to produce dangerous results. As shown throughout this book, exceptions are not just effects of sovereign rule. Different actors working in good faith to resolve problems of list administration have forged new techniques that enable the listing regime to grow in novel and inventive ways. Judges, technical experts and academics have all engaged with the list with good intentions, but the problem-management techniques and practices they have constructed have allowed the list to evolve into new amalgams and made these actors important conduits of exceptional governance. Thinking about the exception as something globally assembled has the advantage of prompting us to look for emergency politics in unexpected places and asking different sorts of

---

[46] According to Latour, an actor or actant is any thing that 'makes a difference': 'The questions to ask about any agent are simply the following: does it make a difference in the course of some other agent's action or not?' – Latour, *Reassembling the Social*, p. 71.

research questions: how are the techniques and practices being constructed to resolve particular security problems embedding new
forms of preemptive security? How are sites of contestation and
challenge to global security regimes neutralised or muted to make
them more durable or achieve more effective results? How are
different domains brought together into productive relation or rendered commensurable in ways that enable emergency powers to
become more entrenched, transform and grow? Asking these kinds
of questions opens the exception up as an empirical problem that
needs investigation.

Finally, this approach helps us think about the exception in material,
rather than normative, terms. Most legal scholarship on the state of
exception aims to identify the legal limits or constraints that ought to be
used to properly contain emergency rule. The key question pursued in
that work is how to reconcile and balance illiberal security governance
with liberal principles of legality. This work is important from the
perspective of normative theory, but it sheds little light on how global
exceptional governance unfolds and might be challenged in practice.
What we need, in other words, is to rethink problems of exceptional
governance more concretely. This book contributes to this task and
adds to the growing body of scholarship analysing emergencies empirically through the material effects and practices they produce. As I have
shown in Chapter 4, by analysing how the use of intelligence-as-
evidence and dis-location of decision-making worked together to
make the list globally powerful yet substantively baseless and beyond
the scope of judicial review, global exceptions are not lawless black
holes, but saturated and conditioned by legality. To paraphrase Walter
Benjamin, we must attain to a conception of global security law that is in
keeping with this insight.[47]

5.3   From Al-Qaida to ISIL and Beyond: the Global
Law of Endless War

This study began in 2011, shortly after Osama bin Laden was killed by
US Special Forces in Pakistan. At that time, there was speculation that
Bin Laden's death and the weakening of 'Al-Qaida central' might
prompt post-9/11 legal measures aimed at countering Al-Qaida to be

---

[47] Walter Benjamin, *Illuminations* (New York: Random House, 1968) 266.

wound down. The global war on terror, so the argument went, had now realised its key objectives. So, the state of emergency used to fight that war could finally be brought to an end and a state of normality restored.

Two weeks after Bin Laden's death, however, the Security Council issued a press release making it plain that the Al-Qaida sanctions regime would be continuing on regardless. According to the then Chair of the UN1267 Sanctions Committee, whilst Bin Laden's death was a turning point 'it is neither the end of Al-Qaida nor the end of terrorism'.[48] Through a series of subsequent list modifications adopted incrementally over a two-year period (2013–15) the global war against Osama bin Laden and Al-Qaida was repurposed and extended to combat a new threat and enemy of humanity: the movement of FTFs from around the world joining ISIL and the Al-Nusrah Front (ANF) in Syria.[49]

Many of the measures introduced by the Council to combat FTFs stretch and reorder features of the list. And the list has enabled a diverse array of new actors, institutions and practices to be brought within the remit of the Council's global war against FTFs. As we saw in Chapter 2, for example, the travel ban on listed individuals (long criticised for being wholly ineffective) is being recalibrated to build a 'third hurdle' to stem the flow of FTF travel, with all states now being required to collect, analyse and share API, PNR and biometric data for the purposes of preventing the movement of listed persons and FTFs from their territories.[50] The FTF threat and global circulation of 'risky 'persons, in other words, is

---

[48] UN Doc. SC/10252 (16 May 2011), *Anti-Terrorism Committees Must Continue to Strengthen Efforts, Despite Death of Osama Bin Laden, Security Council Told.* Available at: bit.ly/2H1pzx1.

[49] In May 2013 the UN Security Council quietly amended its listing of Al-Qaida in Iraq (AQI), first designated in October 2004, to include two new akas: ANF for the People of Levant and ISIL. The following year this listing was modified again to separate AQI and ANF into two distinct entries. By the time Resolution 2170 was adopted in September 2014, the two groups controlling much of Syria and Iraq had already been listed by the UN1267 Sanctions Committee as being 'associated with' Al-Qaida. In December 2015 the UN1267 listing regime was formally renamed the 'ISIL (Da'esh) & Al-Qaida Sanctions List'. See, respectively: UN Doc. SC/11019 (dated 30 May 2013); UN Doc. SC/11397 (dated 14 May 2014); S/RES/2253 (2015).

[50] S/RES/2178 (2014), para. 9; S/RES/2396 (2017), paras. 11, 12, 15. The collection of biometric data is 'to responsibly and properly identify terrorists, including foreign terrorist fighters': ibid. para 15.

continuing to open up new avenues for the Law of the List to grow and creating new domains to secure and govern.

In 2006–7, for example, the USA sought to extend the list to target Islamists providing ideological support to terrorism through a project described as the 'radical ideologue initiative'.[51] But countries that were trying to co-opt radical Imams and turn them into informants or monitoring radical forums to map domestic terrorist networks were worried that listing ideological extremists as global terrorists, de facto members of Al-Qaida and threats to international peace and security would prove to be counterproductive.[52] The global listing regime against FTFs, however, conflates these targeting categories. Being 'associated with' ISIL or Al-Qaida for UN terrorism listing now includes those who express support for ISIL and the movement of FTFs on the Internet and social media.[53] In addition, social media platforms (such as Facebook) now use the ISIL and Al-Qaida list as a key tool for defining and removing terrorist and extremist content online.[54] In these ways, the distinctions between extremism and terrorism, or ideological and material support, are being actively blurred. And the ISIL and Al-Qaida list continues to be extended and modified through its reappropriation.

As suggested throughout this book, the Law of the List will never be wound down. It is a unique global counterterrorism tool with the enduring capacity to align the Security Council P5 states, and an increasingly diverse ensemble of private actors, against a globally diffuse yet common enemy. Because the list defines and produces the object of global terrorism that it targets, it has a plasticity that allows it to be transformed and modified to fight emerging security threats in the years ahead. It is not driven by meeting specific policy objectives or instrumental criteria like other sanctions.

This book has analysed the Law of the List at a particular historical conjuncture. Yet it is hoped that the insights generated here are forensically valuable in navigating the terrain of global security law and

---

[51] See, for example: US Embassy Cable 06PARIS5732 (dated 25 August 2006).

[52] See, for example: US Embassy Cable 07RIYADH305 (dated 13 February 2007), 06ROME1708 (dated 7 June 2006) and 06RIYADH8416 (dated 24 October 2006).

[53] S/RES/2178 (2014), para. 18.

[54] Comments by Erin Saltman, Facebook Counter Terrorism policy lead, 'Technology against terrorism: how to respond to the exploitation of the internet', Chatham House (12 July 2017). Available at: bit.ly/2WhPitM. See also: Brian Fishman, 'Crossroads: counterterrorism and the internet' (2019) 2(2) *Texas National Security Review* 82, 88–90. Facebook also use the US list of Foreign Terrorist Organisations and its own internal list of 'dangerous organisations and individuals'.

governance to come. The war against FTFs and violent extremism is authorising new forms of expertise, generating new mechanisms of informal governance and building new global infrastructures for data collection and analysis. It is stimulating new networks of public and private actors and domestic and international institutions, as well as novel recombinations of preemption and legality across different areas of practice. The need to depart from formal law and authority, by empirically studying the governance techniques and knowledge practices of global legal assemblages, will undoubtedly persist into the future, as we try to make greater sense of this fractured legal terrain.

I came into this study as a disenchanted human rights lawyer keen to know how this form of global security law might be challenged, and this book does not offer a silver-bullet answer to that question. But, it has deepened our understanding of the list and provoked us to 'experience the international legal field afresh' by studying how this form of global security law is being assembled.[55] By providing a granular account of legal conflict and change in the Law of the List, my hope is that this book allows us 'to acquire a new "feel" for the political possibilities' within it.[56] As Foucault reminds us, 'the role for theory today ... [is] not to formulate the global systematic theory which holds everything in place, but to analyse the specificity of mechanisms of power, to locate the connections and extensions [and] to build little by little a strategic knowledge'.[57] This book is an experiment in strategic knowledge production and an invitation for more situated studies of global security law and power to emerge.

[55] Johns, *Non-Legality in International Law*, p. 27.
[56] Ibid.
[57] Foucault, *Power/Knowledge*, p. 145.

BIBLIOGRAPHY

Abbott, K. and Snidal, D., 'International regulation without international government: improving IO performance through orchestration' (2010) 5 *Review of International Organizations* 315

Abeyratne, R., *Aviation Security Law* (New York: Springer, 2010)

Abrahamsen, R. and Williams, M., *Security beyond the State: Private Security in International Politics* (Cambridge: Cambridge University Press, 2011)

Ackerman, B., 'The emergency constitution' (2004) 113(5) *Yale Law Journal* 1029
  Before the Next Attack: Preserving Civil Liberties in an Age of Terrorism (New Haven CT: Yale University Press, 2006)

Ackerman, S., 'Obama maintains Al-Qaida and Isis are "one and the same" despite evidence of schism' *The Guardian* (London, 2 October 2014). Available at: bit.ly/2aYW39l

Acuto, M. and Curtis, S. (eds.), *Reassembling International Theory: Assemblage Thinking and International Relations* (Basingstoke: Palgrave Pivot, 2013)

Adler, E. and Pouliot, V. (eds.), *International Practices* (Cambridge: Cambridge University Press, 2011)

Agamben, G., *Homo Sacer: Sovereign Power and Bare Life* (Stanford CA: Stanford University Press, 1998)
  State of Exception (Chicago IL: University of Chicago Press, 2005)

Ali, N. T., *Regulatory Counter-Terrorism: A Critical Appraisal of Proactive Global Governance* (London: Routledge, 2018)

Allen, J., 'Powerful assemblages' (2011) 43(2) *Area* 154

Alvarez, J. E., 'Hegemonic international law revisited' (2003) 97 *American Journal of International Law* 873
  International Organizations as Law-Makers (Oxford: Oxford University Press, 2005)

Aly, G., Roth, K., Black E. and Oksiloff, A., *The Nazi Census: Identification and Control in the Third Reich* (Philadelphia PA: Temple University Press, 2004)

Ambrus, M., Arts, K., Hey, E. and Raulus, H. (eds.), *The Role of 'Experts' in International and European Decision-Making Processes: Advisors, Decision Makers or Irrelevant Actors?* (Cambridge: Cambridge University Press, 2014)

Amicelle, A., Aradau, C. and Jeandesboz, J., 'Questioning security devices: performativity, resistance, politics' (2015) 46(4) *Security Dialogue* 293

Amoore, L., 'Risk before justice: when law contests its own suspension' (2008) 21(4) *Leiden Journal of International Law* 847

'Data derivatives: On the emergence of a security risk calculus for our times' (2011) 28(6) *Theory, Culture and Society* 24

The Politics of Possibility: Risk and Security beyond Probability (Durham NC: Duke University Press, 2013)

Amoore, L. and de Goede, M. (eds.), *Risk and the War on Terror* (London: Routledge, 2008)

'Transactions after 9/11: the banal face of the preemptive strike' (2008) 33(2) *Transactions of the Institute of British Geographers* 173

Anderson, T., Schum, D. and Twining, W., *Analysis of Evidence* (2nd edn, Cambridge: Cambridge University Press, 2005)

Angiolelli, L., *IATA Campaign Results: Passenger Data* (2012) (copy on file with author)

Antoniades, A., 'Epistemic communities, epistemes and the construction of (world) politics' (2003) 17 *Global Society* 2

Appadurai, A., 'Grassroots globalization and the research imagination' in Arjun Appadurai (ed.), *Globalization* (Durham NC: Duke University Press, 2001)

Aradau, C., 'Law transformed: Guantanamo and the "other" exception' (2007) 28(3) *Third World Quarterly* 489

'The signature of security: big data, anticipation, surveillance' (2015) *Radical Philosophy* 191

Aradau, C. and Huysmans, J., 'Critical methods in international relations: the politics of techniques, devices and acts' (2014) 20(3) *European Journal of International Relations* 596

Aradau, C. and Van Munster, R., 'Governing terrorism through risk: taking precautions, (un)knowing the future' (2007) 13(1) *European Journal of International Relations* 89

Politics of Catastrophe: Genealogies of the Unknown (London: Routledge, 2011)

Asselt, M. van and Vos, E., 'The precautionary principle and the uncertainty paradox' (2006) 9 *Journal of Risk Research* 313

Atia, M., 'In whose interest? Financial surveillance and the circuits of exception in the war on terror' (2007) 25 *Environment and Planning D: Society and Space* 447

Baehr-Jones, V., 'Mission possible: how intelligence evidence rules can save UN terrorist sanctions' (2011) 2 *Harvard National Security Journal* 447

Barnett, M. and Finnemore, M., *Rules for the World: International Organizations in Global Politics* (Ithaca NY: Cornell University Press, 2004)

Barr, M. S. and Miller, G. P., 'Global administrative law: the view from Basel' (2006) 17(1) *European Journal of International Law* 15

Barrett, R., 'Time to reexamine regulation designed to counter the financing of terrorism' (2009) 41 *Case Western Reserve Journal of International Law* 7

Comments in relation to Kadi II judgment' (29 July 2013), *Economic Sanctions Listserve*

Barry, A., *Political Machines: Governing a Technological Society* (London: The Athlone Press, 2001)

Material Politics: Disputes Along the Pipeline (Oxford: Blackwell Publishing, 2013)

'The translation zone' (2013) 41 *Millennium: Journal of International Studies* 413

BBC, 'Text of Colin Powell's speech to the UN Security Council' *BBC News* (5 February 2003). Available at: bbc.in/1GXm9pF

Beck, U., *Risk Society. Towards a New Modernity* (London: Sage Publications, 1992)

World Risk Society (Bristol: Polity Press, 1999)

'The terrorist threat: world risk society revisited' (2002) 19(4) *Theory, Culture and Society* 39

Belcher, O. and Martin, L. L., 'Ethnographies of closed doors: conceptualising openness and closure in US immigration and military institutions' (2013) 45 (4) *Area* 403

Bellanova, R. and Duez, D., 'A different view on the "making" of European security: the EU Passenger Name Record system as a socio-technical assemblage' (2012) 17 *European Foreign Affairs Review* 109

Benjamin, W., *Illuminations* (New York: Random House, 1968)

Bennett, J., *Vibrant Matter: A Political Ecology of Things* (Durham NC: Duke University Press, 2010)

Berman, P., 'Global Legal Pluralism' (2007) 80 *Southern California Law Review* 1155

Global Legal Pluralism: A Jurisprudence of Law beyond Borders (Cambridge: Cambridge University Press, 2012)

Bernstein, A., 'The hidden cost of terrorist watch lists' (2013) 61 *Buffalo Law Review* 461

Biersteker, T. J., 'Targeted sanctions and individual human rights' (2010) 65(1) *International Journal: Canada's Journal of Global Policy Analysis* 99

'Scholarly participation in transnational policy networks: the case of targeted sanctions' in Mariano E. Bertucci and Abraham Lowenthal (eds.), *Narrowing the Gap: Scholars, Policy-Makers and International Affairs* (Baltimore MD: John Hopkins University Press, 2012)

Biersteker, T. J. and Eckert, S., *Addressing Challenges to Targeted Sanctions: An Update to the 'Watson Report'* (Geneva: Graduate Institute Watson Institute for International Studies, 2009)

Biersteker, T. J., Eckert, S. and Tourinho, M. (eds.), *Targeted Sanctions: The Impact and Effectiveness of United Nations Action* (Cambridge: Cambridge University Press, 2016)

Bigo, D. Carrera, S., Guild, E. and Walker, R., 'The changing landscape of European liberty and security: the mid-term report of the CHALLENGE Project' (2007) 59(192) *International Social Science Journal* 283

Black, E. and Wallace, B., *IBM and the Holocaust: The Strategic Alliance between Nazi Germany and America's Most Powerful Corporation* (New York: Crown Publishers, 2001)

Boon-Kuo, L., Hayes, B., Sentas, V. and Sullivan, G., *Building Peace in Permanent War: Terrorist Listing and Conflict Transformation* (Amsterdam: Transnational Institute, 2015)

Bowker, G. and Leigh Star, S., *Sorting Things Out: Classification and Its Consequences* (Cambridge MA: MIT Press, 1999)

Bratton, B., *The Stack: On Software and Sovereignty* (Cambridge MA: MIT Press, 2015)

Braun, B. and Whatmore, S. J., 'The stuff of politics: an introduction' in Bruce Braun and Sarah J. Whatmore (eds.), *Political Matter: Technoscience, Democracy and Public Life* (Minneapolis MN: University of Minnesota Press, 2010)

Braverman, I., 'The regulatory life of threatened species' in Irus Braverman (ed.), *Animals, Biopolitics, Law: Lively Legalities* (London: Routledge, 2016)

Bueger, C., 'Pathways to practice: praxiography and international politics' (2014) 6 *European Political Science Review* 383

'Making things known: epistemic infrastructures, the United Nations and the translation of piracy' (2015) 9 *International Political Sociology* 1

'Territory, authority, expertise: global governance and the counter-piracy assemblage' (2018) 24(3) *European Journal of International Relations* 614

Bueger, C. and Gadinger, F., *International Practice Theory: New Perspectives* (Basingstoke: Palgrave Macmillan 2014)

Bush, G. W., 'Address to Joint Session of Congress and the American People' (21 September 2001). Available at: cnn.it/2JigZeY

'Graduation speech at West Point Military Academy' (1 June 2002). Available at: nyti.ms/2akwrsh

'State of the Union Address' (20 January 2004). Available at: wapo.st/2XqCumm

Callon, M., 'Some elements of a sociology of translation: domestication of the scallops and the fisherman of St-Brieuc Bay' in John Law (ed.), *Power, Action and Belief: A New Sociology of Knowledge?* (London: Routledge & Kegan Paul, 1986)

The Laws of the Markets (Oxford: Blackwell Publishing, 1998)

Callon, M. and Latour, B., 'Unscrewing the big Leviathan: how actors macro-structure reality and how sociologists help them to do so' in Aaron Victor

Cicourel and Karin Knorr-Cetina (eds.), *Advances in Social Theory and Methodology: Toward an Integration of Micro and Macro-Sociologies* (London: Routledge & Kegan Paul, 1981)

Cameron, I., *Targeted Sanctions and Legal Safeguards*, Report to the Swedish Foreign Office (October 2002)

'Targeted sanctions and legal safeguards' (2003) 72 *Nordic Journal of International Law* 159

Cassese, S., *Research Handbook on Global Administrative Law* (Cheltenham: Edward Elgar Publishing, 2016)

Chesterman, S., 'Does the UN have intelligence?' (2006) 48 *Survival* 149

'Shared Secrets: intelligence and collective security', Lowy Institute Paper 10 (Double Bay NSW: Lowry Institute, 2006)

'The spy who came in from the Cold War: intelligence and international law' (2006) 27 *Michigan Journal of International Law* 1071

'Globalization rules: accountability, power, and the prospects for global administrative law' (2008) 14(1) *Global Governance* 39

'Unaccountable – the United Nations, emergency powers, and the rule of law' (2009) 42 *Vanderbilt Journal of Transnational Law* 1509

Christiansen, D. and Powers, G. P., 'Unintended consequences' (1993) 49 *Bulletin of the Atomic Sciences* 41

Clawson, P., 'Sanctions as punishment, enforcement and prelude to further action' (1993) 7 *Ethics and International Affairs* 20

Cloatre, E., *Pills for the Poorest: An Exploration of TRIPS and Access to Medication in Sub-Saharan Africa* (Basingstoke: Palgrave Macmillan, 2013)

Cobain, I., 'Obama's secret kill list – the disposition matrix' *The Guardian* (London, 14 July 2013). Available at: bit.ly/QBfJ7A

Cohen, J., 'Whose sovereignty? Empire versus international law' (2004) 18(3) *Ethics and International Affairs* 1

Globalization and Sovereignty: Rethinking Legality, Legitimacy and Constitutionalism (Cambridge: Cambridge University Press, 2012)

Cole, D., 'Terror financing, guilt by association and the paradigm of prevention in the war on terror' in Andrea Bianchi and Alex Keller (eds.), *Counterterrorism: Democracy's Challenge* (Oxford: Hart Publishing, 2008)

Cole, D. and Lobel, J., *Less Safe, Less Free: Why America Is Losing the War on Terror* (New York: New Press, 2007)

Coleman, R. and Ringrose, J., 'Introduction: Deleuze and research methodologies' in Rebecca Coleman and Jessica Ringrose (eds.), *Deleuze and Research Methodologies* (Edinburgh: Edinburgh University Press, 2013)

Collier, S. J., 'Topologies of power: Foucault's analysis of political government beyond "governmentality"' (2009) 26 *Theory, Culture and Society* 78

Collier, S. J. and Ong, A., 'Global assemblages, anthropological problems' in Aihwa Ong and Stephen J. Collier (eds.), *Global Assemblages: Technology, Politics, and Ethics as Anthropological Problems* (Oxford: Wiley-Blackwell, 2004)

Comras, V. D., *Flawed Diplomacy: The United Nations and the War on Terrorism* (Lincoln NE: Potomac, 2010)

Cortright, D. and Lopez, G. A. (eds.), *Smart Sanctions: Targeting Economic Statecraft* (Lanham MD: Rowman & Littlefield, 2002)

   The Sanctions Decade: Assessing UN Strategies in the 1990s (Boulder CO: Lynne Rienner, 2000)

   Uniting against Terror: Cooperative Nonmilitary Responses to the Global Terrorist Threat (Cambridge MA: MIT Press, 2007)

Cortright, D., Lopez, G. A., Stellingwerf, G., Fackler, E. and J. W, Persinger, *Human Rights and Targeted Sanctions: An Action Agenda for Strengthening Due Process Procedures* (Sanctions and Security Research Program, November 2009). Available at: bit.ly/2MuNtVf

Cowen, D., *The Deadly Life of Logistics: Mapping Violence in Global Trade* (Minneapolis MN: University of Minnesota Press, 2014)

Cramer, P., 'Recent Swedish experiences of targeted UN sanctions: the erosion of trust in the Security Council' in Erika De Wet and André Nollkaemper (eds.), *Review of the Security Council by Member States* (Cambridge: Intersentia, 2003)

Craven, M., 'Humanitarianism and the quest for smarter sanctions' (2002) 13 *European Journal of International Law* 43

Crider, C., 'Killing in the name of algorithms: how big data enables the Obama Administration's drone war' *Al Jazeera America* (4 March 2014). Available at: bit.ly/1BgYFum

Cuyvers, A., '"Give me one good reason": the unified standard of review for sanctions after Kadi II' (2014) 51(6) *Common Market Law Review* 1759

Darian-Smith, E., *Laws and Societies in Global Contexts: Contemporary Approaches* (Cambridge: Cambridge University Press, 2013)

Davidson, A. I., 'Structures and strategies of discourse: remarks towards a history of Foucault's philosophy of language' in Arnold Ira Davidson (ed.), *Foucault and his Interlocutors* (Cambridge: Cambridge University Press, 1997)

Davis, K. E., Fisher, A., Kingsbury, B. and Merry, S. E. (eds.), *Governance by Indicators: Global Power through Classification and Rankings* (Cambridge: Cambridge University Press, 2012)

Davis, K. E., Kingsbury, B. and Merry, S. E., 'Indicators as a technology of global governance' (2012) 46 *Law and Society Review* 71

De Boer, N., 'Case C-300/11, ZZ v. Secretary of State for the Home Department. Judgment of the Court (Grand Chamber) of 4 June 2013' (2014) 51(4) *Common Market Law Review* 1235

De Búrca, G., 'The European Court of Justice and the international legal order after Kadi' (2010) 51 *Harvard International Law Journal* 1

De Goede, M., 'Hawala discourses and the war on terrorist finance' (2003) 21 *Environment and Planning D: Society and Space* 513

'The politics of preemption and the war on terror in Europe' (2008) 14(1) *European Journal of International Relations* 161

'Blacklisting and the ban: contesting targeted sanctions in Europe' (2011) 42(6) *Security Dialogue* 499

Speculative Security: The Politics of Pursuing Terrorist Monies (Minneapolis MN: University of Minnesota Press, 2012)

De Goede, M. and De Graaf, B., 'Sentencing risk: temporality and precaution in terrorism trials' (2013) 7 *International Political Sociology* 313

De Goede, M. and Sullivan, G., 'The politics of security lists' (2016) 34(1) *Environment and Planning D: Society and Space* 67

De Goede, M., Leander, A. and Sullivan, G. (eds.), 'The politics of the list: law, security, technology' (2016) [Special Issue] 34 *Environment and Planning D: Society and Space* 3

De Goede, M. and Simon, S., 'Governing future radicals in Europe' (2013) 45 *Antipode* 315

De Larrinaga, M. and Doucet, M. G. (eds.), *Security and Global Governmentality: Globalization, Governance and the State* (London: Routledge, 2010)

Dean, M., 'A genealogy of the government of poverty' (1992) 21 *Economy and Society* 215

De Sousa Santos, B., 'Law: a map of misreading: toward a postmodern conception of law' (1987) 14(3) *Journal of Law and Society* 279

Toward a New Legal Common Sense: Law, Globalization and Emancipation (Cambridge: Cambridge University Press, 2002)

De Wet, E., 'The role of European Courts in the development of a hierarchy of norms within international law: evidence of constitutionalisation?' (2009) 5(2) *European Constitutional Law Review* 284

'Human rights considerations and the enforcement of targeted sanctions in Europe: the emergence of core standards of judicial protection' in Bardo Fassbender (ed.), *Securing Human Rights: Achievements and Challenges of the UN Security Council* (Oxford: Oxford University Press, 2011)

'From Kadi to Nada: judicial techniques favouring human rights over United Nations Security Council sanctions' (2013) 12 *Chinese Journal of International Law* 787

De Wet, E. and Vidmar, J. (eds.), *Hierarchy in International Law: The Place of Human Rights* (Oxford: Oxford University Press, 2012)

Deleuze, G., 'Postscript on the Societies of Control' (1992) 59 *October* 3

Deleuze, G. and Guattari, F., *A Thousand Plateaus: Capitalism and Schizophrenia* (Minneapolis MN: University of Minnesota Press, 1987)

Deleuze, G. and Parnet, C., *Dialogues* (London: The Athlone Press, 1987)

Delmas-Marty, M., *Ordering Pluralism: A Conceptual Framework for Understanding the Transnational Legal World* (Oxford: Hart Publishing, 2009)

Dershowitz, A., *Why Terrorism Works: Understanding the Threat, Responding to the Challenge* (New Haven CT: Yale University Press, 2002)

   Preemption: A Knife That Cuts Both Ways (London: W.W. Norton & Company, 2006)

Desrosières, A., *The Politics of Large Numbers: A History of Statistical Reasoning* (Cambridge MA: Harvard University Press, 1998)

Dezalay, Y. and Garth, B. G., *Dealing in Virtue: International Commercial Arbitration and the Construction of a Transnational Legal Order* (Chicago IL: University of Chicago Press, 1998)

   The Internationalization of Palace Wars: Lawyers, Economists, and the Contest to Transform Latin American States (Chicago IL: University of Chicago Press, 2002)

Dorsett, S. and McVeigh, S., *Jurisdiction* (London: Routledge, 2012)

Drezner, D. W., 'Sanctions sometimes smart: targeted sanctions in theory and practice' (2011) 13 *International Sanctions Review* 96

Dunlop, E., 'Globalization and sovereignty: global threats and international security' in Sabino Cassese (ed.), *Research Handbook on Global Administrative Law* (Cheltenham: Edward Elgar Publishing, 2016)

Dyzenhaus, D., 'The rule of (administrative) law in international law' (2005) 68(3/4) *Law and Contemporary Problems* 127

   The Constitution of Law: Legality in a Time of Emergency (Cambridge: Cambridge University Press, 2006)

Easterling, K., *Extrastatecraft: The Power of Infrastructure Space* (New York: Verso, 2014)

Eckert, S., 'The US regulatory approach to terrorist financing' in Thomas J. Biersteker and Sue Eckert (eds.), *Countering the Financing of Terrorism* (London: Routledge, 2008)

   'Smarter EU sanctions?', Workshop (University College London, 8 November 2013)

Eckert, S. and Biersteker, T., *Due Process and Targeted Sanctions: An Update of the 'Watson Report'* (Geneva: Watson Institute for International Studies, Brown University and the Graduate Institute, 2012)

Eckes, C., 'Decision-making in the dark? – Autonomous EU sanctions and national classification' *Legal Studies Research Paper* 64 (Amsterdam: Amsterdam Law School, 2012)

Emmerson, B., 'Ben Emmerson Curriculum Vitae'. Available at: bit.ly/2MBHb6e

   'Statement by Ben Emmerson, Special Rapporteur on Countering Terrorism' (UN General Assembly, 21 November 2012)

Eriksson, M., 'Unintended consequences of targeted sanctions' in Christopher Daase and Cornelius Friesendorf (eds.), *Rethinking Security Governance: The Problem of Unintended Consequences* (London: Routledge, 2010)

Espeland, W. N. and Stevens, M. L., 'Commensuration as a social process' (1998) 24 *Annual Review of Sociology* 313

'A sociology of quantification' (2008) 49 *European Journal of Sociology* 401

European Parliament News, 'EU Passenger Name Record (PNR) Directive: an overview' (1 June 2016) bit.ly/2xXe2dg

Fabbrini, F., 'Global sanctions, state secrets and supranational review: seeking due process in an interconnected world' in David Cole, Federico Fabbrini and Arianna Vedaschi (eds.), *Secrecy, National Security and the Vindication of Constitutional Law* (Cheltenham: Edward Elgar Publishing, 2013)

Fassbender, B., 'Targeted sanctions and due process. The responsibility of the UN Security Council to ensure that fair and clear procedures are made available to individuals and entities targeted with sanctions under Chapter VII of the UN Charter', Study Commissioned by the United Nations Office for Legal Affairs (New York: Office of the Legal Counsel, 2006)

'Targeted sanctions imposed by the UN Security Council and due process rights' (2006) 3 *International Organizations Law Review* 437

Fassin, D., *Humanitarian Reason: Moral History of the Present* (Berkeley CA: University of California Press, 2012)

Feinäugle, C. A. and Goldmann, M., 'The UN Security Council Al-Qaida and Taliban Sanctions Committee: emerging principles of international institutional law for the protection of individuals?' in Armin von Bogdandy, Rüdiger Wolfrum, Jochen von Bernstorff, Philipp Dann and Matthias Goldmann (eds.), *The Exercise of Public Authority by International Institutions* (New York: Springer, 2010)

Ferguson, J., *The Anti-Politics Machine: Development, Depoliticization, and Bureaucratic Power in Lesotho* (Cambridge: Cambridge University Press, 1990)

Ferguson, J. and Gupta, A., 'Spatializing states: toward an ethnography of neoliberal governmentality' (2002) 29(4) *American Ethnologist* 981

Finnemore, M. and Sikkink, K., 'International norm dynamics and political change' (1998) 52 *International Organization* 887

Fischer-Lescano, A. and Teubner, G., 'Regime-collisions: the vain search for legal unity in the fragmentation of global law' (2004) 25(4) *Michigan Journal of International Law* 999

Fishman, B., 'Crossroads: counterterrorism and the internet' (2019) 2(2) *Texas National Security Review* 82

Fiti Sinclair, G., *To Reform the World: International Organisations and the Making of Modern States* (Oxford: Oxford University Press, 2017)

Foot, R., 'The United Nations, counter terrorism and human rights: institutional adaptation and embedded ideas' (2007) 29 *Human Rights Quarterly* 489

Forcese, C. and Roach, K., 'Limping into the future: the UN 1267 terrorism listing process at the crossroads' (2010) 42 *George Washington International Law Review* 217

Fordham, M, *Judicial Review Handbook* (4th edn, Oxford: Hart Publishing, 2004)

Forensic Architecture Project. Available at: bit.ly/2a8EOmZ

Foucault, M., *Discipline and Punish: The Birth of the Prison* (London: Allen Lane, 1977)

'Nietzsche, genealogy, history' in Donald Bouchard (ed.), *Language, Counter-Memory, Practice: Selected Essays and Interviews* (Ithaca NY: Cornell University Press, 1977)

The History of Sexuality. Vol. 1 (New York: Pantheon, 1978)

The Will to Knowledge: The History of Sexuality. Vol. 1 (London: Penguin, 1979)

Power/Knowledge: Selected Interviews and Other Writings, 1972–1977 (New York: Pantheon, 1980)

'Space, knowledge and power' in Paul Rabinow (ed.), *The Foucault Reader* (New York: Pantheon, 1984)

'What is enlightenment?' in Paul Rabinow (ed.), *The Foucault Reader* (New York: Pantheon Books, 1984)

'Governmentality' in Graham Burchell, Colin Gordon and Peter Miller (eds.), *The Foucault Effect: Studies in Governmentality* (Chicago IL: University of Chicago Press, 1991)

'Questions of method' in Graham Burchell, Colin Gordon and Peter Miller (eds.), *The Foucault Effect: Studies in Governmentality* (Chicago IL: University of Chicago Press, 1991)

'The subject and the power' in James D. Faubian (ed.), *Essential Works of Foucault 1954–1984. Vol. 3: Power* (New York: New Press, 2000)

Society Must Be Defended: Lectures at the Collège de France, 1975–1976 (London: Picador, 2003)

Security, Territory, Population: Lectures at the Collège de France 1977–1978 (Basingstoke: Palgrave Macmillan, 2007)

The Birth of Biopolitics: Lectures at the College de France 1978–1979 (London: Springer, 2008)

Foucault, M. and Deleuze, G., 'Intellectuals and power' in Donald Bouchard (ed.), *Language, Counter-Memory, Practice: Selected Essays and Interviews by Michel Foucault* (Ithaca NY: Cornell University Press, 1977)

Galanter, M., 'Justice in many rooms: courts, private ordering and indigenous law' (1981) 13(19) *Journal of Legal Pluralism and Unofficial Law* 1

Garlicki, Justice L., 'Concluding remarks' in David Cole, Federico Fabbrini and Arianna Vedaschi (eds.), *Secrecy, National Security and the Vindication of Constitutional Law* (Cheltenham: Edward Elgar Publishing, 2013)

Geertz, C., 'Thick description: toward an interpretive theory of culture' in Michael Martin and Lee C McIntyre (eds.), *Readings in the Philosophy of Social Science* (Cambridge MA: MIT Press, 1994)

Gellman, B. and Poitras, L., 'US, British Intelligence mining data from nine US internet companies in broad secret program' *The Washington Post* (Washington, 7 June 2013). Available at: wapo.st/1gIS8gu

General Court of the European Union, Press Release No 73/15 (19 June 2015). Available at: bit.ly/1TADREh

Genser, J. and Barth, K., 'When due process concerns become dangerous: the Security Council's 1267 regime and the need for reform' (2010) 33 *Boston College International and Comparative Law Review* 1

'Targeted sanctions and due process of law' in Jared Genser and Bruno Stagno Ugarte (eds.), *The United Nations Security Council in the Age of Human Rights* (Cambridge: Cambridge University Press, 2014)

Ginsborg, L. and Scheinin, M., 'Judicial powers, due process and evidence in the Security Council 1267 terrorist sanctions regime: the Kadi II conundrum' (EUI Working Papers: RSC, 2011)

'You can't always get what you want: the Kadi II conundrum and the Security Council 1267 terrorist sanctions regime' (2011) 8 *Essex Human Rights Review* 7

Giumelli, F., *Coercing, Constraining and Signalling: Explaining UN and EU Sanctions after the Cold War* (Colchester: ECPR Press, 2011)

Global Counterterrorism Forum (GCTF). Available at: bit.ly/1DgUeLZ

Glover, R., *Murphy on Evidence* (14th edn, Oxford: Oxford University Press, 2015)

Golder, B., 'The responsibility to protect: practice, genealogy, biopolitics' (2013) 1 *London Review of International Law* 158

Foucault and the Politics of Rights (Stanford CA: Stanford University Press, 2015)

Goldstein, R. J., *American Blacklist: The Attorney General's List of Subversive Organizations* (Lawrence KA: University Press of Kansas, 2008)

González, R. J., 'Anthropology and the covert: methodological notes on research-ing military and intelligence programmes' (2012) 28(2) *Anthropology Today* 21

Goody, J., *The Domestication of the Savage Mind* (Cambridge: Cambridge University Press, 1977)

Goold, B. J. and Lazarus, L. (eds.), *Security and Human Rights* (London: Bloomsbury Publishing, 2007)

Gowlland-Debbas, V., 'The Security Council as enforcer of human rights' in Bardo Fassbender (ed.), *Securing Human Rights? Achievements and Challenges of the UN Security Council* (Oxford: Oxford University Press, 2011)

Greenstock, J., 'The Security Council in the post Cold-War world' in Vaughan Lowe and Dominik Zaum (eds.), *The United Nations Security Council and War: The Evolution of Thought and Practice since 1945* (Oxford: Oxford University Press, 2010)

Gregory, D., 'The black flag: Guantanamo Bay and the space of exception' (2006) 88 *Geografiska Annaler* 404

Gross, O., 'The normless and exceptionless exception: Carl Schmitt's theory of emergency powers and the "norm-exception" dichotomy' (2000) 21 *Cardozo Law Review* 1825

Guild, E., *EU Counter-Terrorism Action: A Fault Line between Law and Politics?* (Brussels: CEPS Liberty and Security in Europe Series, 2010)

Hacking, I., *The Emergence of Probability: A Philosophical Study of Early Ideas about Probability, Induction and Statistical Inference* (Cambridge: Cambridge University Press, 1975)

Halberstam, D., 'LJIL Symposium Vol 25–2: beyond constitutionalism? A comment by Daniel Halberstam' *Opinio Juris* (6 July 2012). Available at: bit.ly/1saeEHm

Halberstam, D. and Stein, E., 'The United Nations, the European Union, and the King of Sweden: economic sanctions and individual rights in a plural world order' (2009) 46 *Common Market Law Review* 13

Haraway, D., *Simians, Cyborgs, and Women: The Reinvention of Nature* (London: Routledge, 1991)

Harlow, C., 'Global administrative law: the quest for principles and values' (2006) 17(1) *European Journal of International Law* 187

Headrick, D. R., *The Tools of Empire: Technology and European Imperialism in the Nineteenth Century* (Oxford: Oxford University Press, 1981)

Heath-Kelly, C., 'Counter-terrorism and the counterfactual: producing the "radicalisation" discourse and the UK PREVENT strategy' (2013) 15 *British Journal of Politics and International Relations* 394

Heng, Y.-K. and McDonagh, K., 'The other war on terror revealed: global governmentality and the Financial Action Task Force's campaign against terrorist financing' (2008) 34(3) *Review of International Studies* 553

Risk, Global Governance and Security: The Other War on Terror (London: Routledge, 2009)

Heupel, M., 'With power comes responsibility: human rights protection in United Nations sanctions policy' (2013) 19(4) *European Journal of International Relations* 773

High Level Review of UN Sanctions. Available at: bit.ly/2KydUb1

Hoerauf, D., 'United Nations Al-Qaida Sanctions regime after UN Resolution 1989: due process still overdue' (2012) 26(2) *Temple International and Comparative Law Journal* 213

Hollenberg, S., 'The Security Council's 1267/1989 targeted sanctions regime and the use of confidential information: a proposal for decentralization of review' (2015) 28 *Leiden Journal of International Law* 49

Hovell, D., 'A dialogue model: the role of the domestic judge in Security Council decision-making' (2013) 26 *Leiden Journal of International Law* 579

'Kadi: king-slayer or king-maker? The shifting allocation of decision-making power between the UN Security Council and courts' (2016) 79 *Modern Law Review* 147

The Power of Process: The Value of Due Process in Security Council Sanctions Decision-Making (Oxford: Oxford University Press, 2016)

Huber, K. T. and Rodiles, A., 'An Ombudsperson in the United Nations Security Council: a paradigm shift' (2012) *Anuario Mexicanode Derecho Internacional: Décimo Anniversario* 107

Hussain, N., 'Beyond norm and exception: Guantanamo' (2007) 33(4) *Critical Inquiry* 734

The Jurisprudence of Emergency: Colonialism and the Rule of Law (Ann Arbor MI: University of Michigan, 2009)

Huysmans, J., 'What's in an act? On security speech acts and little security nothings' (2011) 42(4–5) *Security Dialogue* 371

IATA, 'Passenger Data Exchange: the basics'. Available at: bit.ly/2M5kC9U

'Cautious optimism extends into 2019 – airlines heading for a decade in the black', Press Release No. 72 (12 December 2018). Available at: bit.ly/2MlFj1 j

IATA/Control Authorities Working Group, 'Guidelines for the removal of inadmissible passengers'. Available at: bit.ly/1xiMprt

ICAO, ICAO Resolution A36-20, A36-WP/336 and Plenary Action Sheet No. 3 *Making an ICAO Standard*. Available at: bit.ly/1pmY2sI

The Universal Security Audit Programme Continuous Monitoring Approach (USAP-CMA) and Its Objective. Available at: bit.ly/1xiMwDl

Annex 9 to the Convention on International Civil Aviation: Facilitation, 15th edn, International Standards and Recommended Practices (October 2017), SARP 9.5–9.16

Doc. 10118, *Global Aviation Security Plan* (2017)

International Commission of Jurists, *Assessing the Damage, Urging Action: Report of the Eminent Jurists Panel on Terrorism, Counter-Terrorism and Human Rights* (Geneva: ICJ, 2009)

Isiksel, N. T., 'Fundamental rights in the EU after *Kadi* and *Al Barakaat*' (2010) 16(5) *European Law Journal* 551

Jaeger, H.-M., 'UN reform, biopolitics, and global governmentality' (2010) 2(1) *International Theory* 50

Jamal, A. and Nasr, A. (dirs.), *The Long Way Home* (2017). Available at: imdb.to/2K7mnlo

Jasanoff, S. (ed.), *States of Knowledge: The Co-Production of Science and Social Order* (London: Routledge, 2004)

Jayasuriya, K., 'Struggle over legality in the midnight hour: governing the international state of emergency' in Victor V Ramraj (ed.), *Emergencies and the Limits of Legality* (Cambridge: Cambridge University Press, 2008)

Johns, F., *Non-Legality in International Law: Unruly Law* (Cambridge: Cambridge University Press, 2013)

    'The turn to data analytics and international law' (2014) 3 *ESIL Reflections* 6

    'The list plus algorithm as global law' (2016) 34 *Environment and Planning D: Society and Space* 126

Justice, *Secret Evidence* (London: Justice, 2009)

Kassem, R. and Azmy, B., 'Spying or no flying' *Al Jazeera* (7 May 2014). Available at: bit.ly/30DROsP

Keller, H. and Fischer, A., 'The UN anti-terror sanctions regime under pressure' (2009) 9(2) *Human Rights Law Review* 257

Kelsen, H., *Pure Theory of Law* (Berkeley CA: University of California Press, 1967)

Kennedy, D., 'The forgotten politics of international governance' (2001) *European Human Rights Law Review* 117

    'Reassessing international humanitarianism: the dark sides', The Allen Hope Southey Memorial Lecture (University of Melbourne Law School, 8 June 2004) Available at: bit.ly/1H2WOwm

    'Challenging expert rule: the politics of global governance' (2005) 27 *Sydney Law Review* 5

    Reassessing International Humanitarianism (Princeton NJ: Princeton University Press, 2005)

    Of War and Law (Princeton NJ: Princeton University Press, 2006)

    'One, two, three, many legal orders: legal pluralism and the cosmopolitan dream' (2007) 31 *New York University Review of Law and Social Change* 641

    A World of Struggle: How Power Law and Expertise Shape Global Political Economy (Princeton NJ: Princeton University Press, 2016)

Kennedy, Duncan, *A Critique of Adjudication* (Cambridge MA: Harvard University Press, 1997)

Kessler, O. and Werner, W., 'Extrajudicial killing as risk management' (2008) 39(2–3) *Security Dialogue* 289

Kingsbury, B., 'The concept of "law" in global administrative law' (2009) 20 *European Journal of International Law* 23

Kingsbury, B. and Casini, L., 'Global administrative law dimensions of international organizations law' (2009) 6(2) *International Organizations Law Review* 319

Kingsbury, B., Krisch, N. and Stewart, R. B., 'The emergence of global administrative law' (2005) 68(3/4) *Law and Contemporary Problems* 15

Kirchner, S., 'Effective law-making in times of global crisis – a role for international organizations' (2010) 2 *Goettingen Journal of International Law* 267

Kirschner, A. J., 'Security Council Resolution 1904 (2009): a significant step in the evolution of the Al-Qaida and Taliban sanctions regime?' (2010) 70(3) *Zeitschrift für ausländisches öffentliches Recht und Völkerrecht* 585

Knorr-Cetina, K., *Epistemic Cultures: How the Sciences Make Knowledge* (Cambridge MA: Harvard University Press, 1999)

'Objectual practice' in Theodore R Schatzki, Karin Knorr-Cetina and Eike Von Savigny (eds.), *The Practice Turn in Contemporary Theory* (London: Routledge, 2001)

Knorr-Cetina, K. and Cicourel, A. V. (eds.), *Advances in Social Theory and Methodology* (London: Routledge, 1981)

Koenig-Archibugi, M., 'International governance as the new raison d' état? The case of the EU common foreign and security policy' (2004) 10(2) *European Journal of International Relations* 147

Koh, H., *The Trump Administration and International Law* (Oxford: Oxford University Press, 2019)

Kokott, J. and Sobotta, C., 'The *Kadi* case: constitutional core values and international law – finding the balance?' (2012) 23(4) *European Journal of International Law* 1015

Koskenniemi, M., 'Police in the temple – order, justice and the UN: a dialectical view' (1995) 6 *European Journal of International Law* 325

'Letter to the editors of the symposium' (1999) 93 *American Journal of International Law* 351

The Gentle Civilizer of Nations: The Rise and Fall of International Law 1870–1960 (Cambridge: Cambridge University Press, 2001)

'Global governance and public international law' (2004) 37 *Kritische Justiz* 241

'Occupied zone – "a zone of reasonableness"?' (2008) 41(1–2) *Israel Law Review* 13

The Politics of International Law (Oxford: Hart Publishing, 2011)

'Hegemonic regimes' in Margaret A. Young (ed.), *Regime Interaction in International Law: Facing Fragmentation* (Cambridge: Cambridge University Press, 2012)

'Globalization and sovereignty: rethinking legality, legitimacy and constitutionalism' (2013) 11(3) *International Journal of Constitutional Law* 818

Koskenniemi, M. and Leino, P., 'Fragmentation of international law? Postmodern anxieties' (2002) 15(3) *Leiden Journal of International Law* 553

Krasmann, S., 'Law's knowledge: on the susceptibility and resistance of legal practices to security matters' (2012) 16(4) *Theoretical Criminology* 379

Krasner, S., 'Structural causes and regime consequences: regimes as intervening variables' in Stephen Krasner (ed.), *International Regimes* (Ithaca NY: Cornell University Press, 1983)

Krisch, N., 'The rise and fall of collective security: terrorism, US hegemony, and the plight of the Security Council' in Christian Walter, Silja Vöneky, Volker Röben and Frank Schorkopf (eds.), *Terrorism as a Challenge for National and International Law: Security versus Liberty?* (New York: Springer, 2004)

Beyond Constitutionalism: The Pluralist Structure of Postnational Law (Oxford: Oxford University Press, 2012)

'The decay of consent: international law in an age of global public goods' (2014) 108 *American Journal of International Law* 1

The Structure of Postnational Authority (SSRN 2564579, 2015)

'Authority, solid and liquid, in postnational governance' in Roger Cotterrell and Maksymilian Del Mar (eds.), *Authority in Transnational Legal Theory: Theorising across Disciplines* (Chletenham: Edward Elgar Publishing, 2016)

Krisch, N. and Kingsbury, B., 'Introduction: global governance and global administrative law in the international legal order' (2006) 17 *European Journal of International Law* 1

Kruse, B., 'Zivile Todesstrafe' (12 November 2007) bit.ly/30m2z39

Kuus, M., 'Foreign policy and ethnography: a sceptical intervention' (2013) 18(1) *Geopolitics* 115

Lang, A., 'Legal regimes and professional knowledges: the internal politics of regime definition' in Margaret A. Young (ed.), *Regime Interaction in International Law: Facing Fragmentation* (Cambridge: Cambridge University Press, 2012)

'International lawyers and the study of expertise: representationalism and performativity' in Mosche Hirsch and Andrew Lang (eds.), *Research Handbook on the Sociology of International Law* (Cheltenham: Edward Elgar Publishing, 2018)

Larner, W. and Walters, W. (eds.), *Global Governmentality: Governing International Spaces* (London: Routledge, 2004)

Latour, B., 'The powers of association' in John Law (ed.), *Power, Action and Belief: A New Sociology of Knowledge* (London: Routledge, 1986)

'Visualization and cognition: drawing things together' (1986) 6 *Knowledge and Society* 1

Science in Action: How to Follow Scientists and Engineers through Society (Cambridge MA: Harvard University Press, 1987)

The Politics of Nature: How to Bring the Sciences into Democracy (Cambridge MA: Harvard University Press, 1987)

The Pasteurization of France (Cambridge MA: Harvard University Press, 1993)

Reassembling the Social: An Introduction to Actor-Network Theory (Oxford: Oxford University Press, 2005)

The Making of Law: An Ethnography of the Conseil d'État (Bristol: Polity Press, 2010)

Latour, B. and Woolgar, S., *Laboratory Life: The Construction of Scientific Facts* (Princeton NJ: Princeton University Press, 1986)

Law, J., 'Notes on the theory of the actor-network: ordering, strategy, and heterogeneity' (1992) 5(4) *Systems Practice* 379

Ordering and Obduracy (Lancaster: Lancaster University Centre for Science Studies, 2001)

After Method: Mess in Social Science Research (London: Routledge, 2004)

'Collateral realities' in Fernando Dominguez Rubio and Patrick Baert (eds.), *The Politics of Knowledge* (London: Routledge, 2012)

Law, J. and Callon, M., 'Engineering and sociology in a military aircraft project: a network analysis of technological change' (1998) 35(3) *Social Problems* 284

Law, J. and Ruppert, E., 'The social life of methods: devices' (2013) 6(3) *Journal of Cultural Economy* 229

Law, J., Ruppert. E, and Savage. M., 'Reassembling social science methods: the challenge of digital devices' (2013) 30(4) *Theory, Culture and Society* 22

Law, J. and Urry, J., 'Enacting the social' (2004) 33(3) *Economy and Society* 390

Leander, A. and Aalberts, T. (eds.), 'International Legal Theory: Symposium: Expertise, Uncertainty, and International Law' (2013) 26(4) *Leiden Journal of International Law* 783

Lester, M., 'EU Member States approve new European Court rules'. Available at: bit.ly/1Ff7svs

'EU to approve new court rules to permit secret hearings' Available at: bit.ly/1CYk37j

Lidington, D. MP, Minister for Europe, *House of Lords Select Committee on the European Union Sub-Committee E, Plans for New Court Rules and Conduct of EU Sanctions* (2 March 2015). Available at: bit.ly/1L901I8

Lindahl, H., *Fault Lines of Globalization: Legal Order and the Politics of A-Legality* (Oxford: Oxford University Press, 2013)

Lopez, G. A., 'More ethical than not: sanctions as surgical tools' (1999) 13 *International Affairs* 143

Lopez, G. A., Cortright, D., Millar, A. and Gerber-Stellingwerf, L., *Overdue Process: Protecting Human Rights while Sanctioning Alleged Terrorists*, Report to Cordaid from the Fourth Freedom Forum and Kroc Institute for International Peace Studies (Notre Dame NI: University of Notre Dame, April 2009)

Löwenheim, O., 'Examining the state: a Foucauldian perspective on international "governance Indicators"' (2008) 29 *Third World Quarterly* 255

Luhmann, N., *Law as a Social System* (Oxford: Oxford University Press, 2004)

Mallard, G., 'Antagonistic recursivities and successive cover-ups: the case of private nuclear proliferation' (2018) 69(4) *British Journal of Sociology* 1007

Manderson, D., 'Beyond the provincial: space, aesthetics and modernist legal theory' (1995) 20 *Melbourne University Law Review* 1049

March, J. G. and Simon, H. A., *Organizations* (New York: John Wiley and Sons, Inc., 1958)

Marchi-Uhel, C., Ombudsperson, Security Council ISIL (Da'esh) and Al-Qaida Sanctions Committee, Remarks at the meeting of the EU Council Working Group on Public International Law (COJUR), Brussels (2 June 2016). Available at: bit.ly/2OEVMAE

   Ombudsperson, Security Council ISIL (Da'esh) and Al-Qaida Sanctions Committee, Statement to 51st Meeting of the Committee of Legal Advisers on Public International Law (CAHDI) of the Council of Europe (4 March 2016). Available at: bit.ly/2YliWAe

Marcus, G. E., 'Ethnography in/of the world system: the emergence of multi-sited ethnography' (1995) 24 *Annual Review of Anthropology* 95

   'Multi-sited ethnography: notes and queries' in Mark-Anthony Falzon (ed.), *Multi-Sited Ethnography: Theory, Praxis and Locality in Contemporary Research* (Farnham: Ashgate, 2009)

Marks, S., 'Naming global administrative law' (2005) 37 *NYU Journal of International Law and Politics* 995

Marty, D., Council of Europe Parliamentary Assembly Report, *United Nations Security Council and European Union Blacklists*, Doc. 11454 (2007)

Massumi, B., *The Future Birth of the Affective Fact*, Conference Proceedings: Genealogies of Biopolitics (copy on file with author)

   'Potential politics and the primacy of preemption' (2007) 10 *Theory and Event* 13

McCulloch, J. and Pickering, S., 'Pre-crime and counter-terrorism: imagining future crime in the "war on terror"' (2009) 49(5) *British Journal of Criminology* 628

McKeen Edwards, H. and Porter, T., *Transnational Financial Associations and the Governance of Global Finance: Assembling Wealth and Power* (London: Routledge, 2013)

Mendelsohn, B., *Combating Jihadism: American Hegemony and Interstate Cooperation in the War on Terrorism* (Chicago IL: University of Chicago Press, 2009)

   'Threat analysis and the UN's 1267 Sanctions Committee' (2015) 27 *Terrorism and Political Violence* 609

Merry, S. E., 'New legal realism and the ethnography of transnational law' (2006) 31(4) *Law and Social Inquiry* 976

   'Measuring the world' (2011) 52 *Current Anthropology* 83

Merry, S. E. and Coutin, S. B., 'Technologies of truth in the anthropology of Conflict: AES/ APLA Presidential Address, 2013' (2014) 41 *American Ethnologist* 1

Mezzadra, S. and Neilson, B., *Border as Method, or, the Multiplication of Labor* (Durham NC: Duke University Press, 2013)

Michaels, R., 'Global legal pluralism' (2009) 9 *Annual Review of Law and Social Sciences* 243

Mikuriya, K., 'API and PNR: two key words on the global security agenda', *WCO News* (No. 77, June 2015)

Milanovic, M., 'The Human Rights Committee's views in Sayadi v Belgium: a missed opportunity' (2009) 3 *Goettingen Journal of International Law* 519

'European Court decides Nada v Switzerland', *EJIL Talk weblog* (14 September 2012). Available at: bit.ly/1MLJGvL

Milde, M., *International Air Law and ICAO. Vol. 4* (The Hague: Eleven International Publishing, 2008)

Millar, A. and Gerber-Stellingwerf, L., *Overdue Process: Protecting Human Rights while Sanctioning Alleged terrorists*, Report to Cordaid from the Fourth Freedom Forum and Kroc Institute for International Peace Studies (Notre Dame NI: University of Notre Dame, April 2009). Available at: ntrda.me/1OEFhvd

Miller, G. and De Young, K., 'In Syria, Obama stretches legal and policy constraints he created for counterterrorism' *Washington Post* (Washington, 23 September 2014). Available at: wapo.st/2bbx32h

Miller, P. and Rose, N., 'Governing economic life' (1990) 19(1) *Economy and Society* 1

Minear, L. and Weiss, T. G., 'Groping and coping in the Gulf crises: discerning the shape of a new humanitarian order' (1992) 9 *World Policy Journal* 755

Minnella, C., 'Human rights in the counter-terrorist sanctions regime' in *Imperfect Socializers: International Institutions in Multilateral Counter-Terrorist Cooperation* (DPhil thesis, University of Oxford)

Mintrom, M., 'Policy entrepreneurs and the diffusion of innovation' (1997) *American Journal of Political Science* 738

Mitchell, T., *Rule of Experts: Egypt, Techno-Politics, Modernity* (Berkeley CA: University of California Press, 2002)

Mitsilegas, V., 'The value of privacy in an era of security: embedding constitutional limits on preemptive surveillance' (2014) 8(1) *International Political Sociology* 104

Moghaddam, F. M., 'The staircase to terrorism: a psychological exploration' (2005) 60 *American Psychologist* 161

Mogini, S., 'LinkedIn Profile'. Available at: bit.ly/1TzEBGh

Mol, A., 'Ontological politics: a word and some questions' in John Law and John Hassard (eds.), *Actor Network Theory and After* (Oxford: Blackwell Publishers, 1999)

'Ontological politics. a word and some questions' (1999) 47(S1) *Sociological Review* 74

The Body Multiple: Ontology in Medical Practice (Durham NC: Duke University Press, 2002)

Mueller, J. and Mueller, K., 'Sanctions of mass destruction' (1999) 78 *Foreign Affairs* 43

Muller, M., 'Terrorism, proscription and the right to resist in the age of conflict' (2008) 20 *Denning Law Journal* 111

Müller, M., 'Assemblages and actor-networks: rethinking socio-material power, politics and space' (2015) 9(1) *Geography Compass* 27

Mundy, M. and Pottage, A. (eds.), *Law, Anthropology, and the Constitution of the Social: Making Persons and Things* (Cambridge: Cambridge University Press, 2004)

Murphy, C., *EU Counterterrorism Law: Pre-Emption and the Rule of Law* (Oxford: Hart Publishing, 2012)

'Secret evidence in EU security law: special advocates before the Court of Justice?' in David Cole, Federico Fabbrini and Arianna Vedaschi (eds.), *Secrecy, National Security and the Vindication of Constitutional Law* (Cheltenham: Edward Elgar Publishing, 2013)

Murray, S. K., 'The contemporary presidency: stretching the 2001 AUMF: a history of two presidencies' (2015) 45 *Presidential Studies Quarterly* 175

Murray Li, T., 'Practices of assemblage and community forest management' (2007) 36(2) *Economy and Society* 263

The Will to Improve: Governmentality, Development and the Practice of Politics (Durham NC: Duke University Press, 2007)

'What Is land? Assembling a resource for global investment' (2014) 39(4) *Transactions of the Institute of British Geographers* 589

National Commission on Terrorism Attacks upon the United States, *9–11 Commission Report*. Available at: bit.ly/1jGQbS2

National Security Agency, 'Summary of DNR and DNI co-travel analytics'. Available at: bit.ly/1GHNuxh

Neal, A., *Exceptionalism and the Politics of Counter-Terrorism: Liberty, Security and the War on Terror* (London: Routledge, 2009)

Ní Aoláin, F., 'The UN Security Council, global watch lists, biometrics, and the threat to the rule of law', *Just Security* (17 January 2018). Available at: bit.ly/32YnD1K

Nietzsche, F., *On the Genealogy of Morals and Ecce Homo* (New York: Vintage, 2010)

Nollkaemper, A., 'Inside or out: two types of international legal pluralism' in Jan Klabbers and Touko Piiparinen (eds.), *Normative Pluralism and International Law: Exploring Global Governance* (Cambridge: Cambridge University Press, 2013)

Norman, L., 'EU governments approve secret evidence in sanctions cases' *Wall Street Journal* (New York, 10 February 2015)

Office of the Ombudsperson of the Security Council's 1267 Committee, *Approach and Standard* (2011). Available at: bit.ly/1POIqfr

Office of the Ombudsperson of the Security Council's 1267 Committee, *Approach to Analysis, Assessment and Use of information*. Available at: bit.ly/2Yrags0

Office of the Ombudsperson of the Security Council's 1267 Committee, *Ombudsperson to the ISIL (Da'esh) and Al-Qaida Sanctions Committee: Status of Cases*. Available at: bit.ly/2YkOUwC

O'Malley, P., 'Risk, power and crime prevention' (1992) 21(3) *Economy and Society* 252

    Risk, Uncertainty and Government (London: Glasshouse Press, 2004)

Ong, A. and Collier, S. J. (eds.), *Global Assemblages: Technology, Politics, and Ethics as Anthropological Problems* (Oxford: Wiley-Blackwell, 2004)

Oosthuizen, G.H., 'Playing the devil's advocate: the United Nations security council is unbound by law' (1999) 12(3) *Leiden Journal of International Law* 549

Ophir, A., 'The politics of catastrophization: emergency and exception' in Didier Fassin and Mariella Pandolfi (eds.), *Contemporary States of Emergency: The Politics of Military and Humanitarian Interventions* (New York: Zone Books, 2010)

Orford, A., *International Authority and the Responsibility to Protect* (Cambridge: Cambridge University Press, 2011)

    'In praise of description' (2012) 25(3) *Leiden Journal of International Law* 609

Paglen, T., 'Goatsucker: toward a spatial theory of state secrecy' (2010) 28(5) *Environment and Planning D: Society and Space* 759

Paglen, T. and Solnit, R., *Invisible: Covert Operations and Classified Landscapes* (New York: Aperture, 2010)

Parisi, L., *Contagious Architecture: Computation, Aesthetics and Space* (Cambridge MA: MIT Press, 2013)

Pauwelyn, J., Wessel, R. A. and Wouters, J. (eds.), *Informal International Lawmaking* (Oxford: Oxford University Press, 2012)

    'When structures become shackles: stagnation and dynamics in international lawmaking' (2014) 25(3) *European Journal of International Law* 733

Petersmann, E.-U., 'Do judges meet their constitutional obligations to settle disputes in conformity with "principles of justice and international law"' (2007) *European Journal of Legal Studies* 1

Porter, T. M., *The Rise of Statistical Thinking: 1820–1900* (Princeton NJ: Princeton University Press, 1986)

Power, M., *The Audit Society: Rituals of Verification* (Oxford: Oxford University Press, 1999)

'Evaluating the audit explosion' (2003) 25 *Law and Policy* 185

Pozen, D. E., 'The mosaic theory, national security, and the Freedom of Information Act' (2015) 115 *Yale Law Journal* 628

President, Secretary of the Treasury O'Neill and Secretary of State Powell on Executive Order, 'President Freezes Terrorists' Assets' (Washington: US Department of State, 24 September 2001). Available at: bit.ly /31DjUoC

Price, D. H., 'Anthropological research and the Freedom of Information Act' (1997) 9(1) *Field Methods* 12

Privacy International, *Eyes Wide Open: Special Report* (2013). Available at: bit.ly /2NCffBos

Prost, K., 'Fair process and the Security Council: a case for the office of the Ombudsperson' in Maria Salinas De Frias, Katja Samuel and Nigel White (eds.), *Counter-Terrorism: International Law and Practice* (Oxford: Oxford University Press, 2012)

'Remarks of the Ombudsperson at the Workshop on the UN Security Council, Sanctions and the Rule of Law'. Available at: bit.ly/2KiV9Hy

Prost, K. and Wilmshurst, E., *UN Sanctions, Human Rights and the Ombudsperson, Chatham House International Law Summary* (London: Chatham House, 2013). Available at: bit.ly/25dDmrX

Ragazzi, F., 'Suspect community or suspect category? The impact of counter-terrorism as "policed multiculturalism"' (2016) 42(5) *Journal of Ethnic and Migration Studies* 724

Ramraj, V. V. (ed.), *Emergencies and the Limits of Legality* (Cambridge: Cambridge University Press, 2008)

Rancière, J., 'Who is the subject of the rights of man?' (2004) 33(2–3) *South Atlantic Quarterly* 297

On Dissensus: Politics and Aesthetics (London: Bloomsbury Publishing, 2010)

Raphael, S., Black, C., Blakeley, R. and Kostas, S., 'Tracking rendition aircraft as a way to understand CIA secret detention and torture in Europe' (2016) 20(1) *International Journal of Human Rights* 78

Ratner, S. R. and Slaughter, A. M., 'Appraising the methods of international law: a prospectus for readers' (1999) 93 *American Journal of International Law* 291

Riccardi, A., 'Revisiting the role of the EU judiciary as the stronghold for the protection of human rights while countering terrorism' (2018) 18(2) *Global Jurist* 1

Riles, A., *The Network Inside Out* (Ann Arbor MI: University of Michigan Press, 2001)

'New agenda for the cultural study of law: taking on the technicalities' (2005) 53 *Buffalo Law Review* 973

Collateral Knowledge: Legal Reasoning in the Global Financial Markets (Chicago IL: University of Chicago Press, 2011)

Roach, K., 'The eroding distinction between intelligence and evidence in terrorism investigations' in Andrew Lynch, Nicola McGarrity and George Williams (eds.), *Counter-Terrorism and Beyond* (London: Routledge, 2010)

The 9/11 Effect: Comparative Counter-Terrorism (Cambridge: Cambridge University Press, 2011)

Rodiles, A., 'Non-permanent members of the United Nations Security Council and the promotion of the international rule of law' (2013) 5(2) *Goettingen Journal of International Law* 333

'The design of UN sanctions and the interplay with informal arrangements' in Larissa Van Den Herik (ed.), *Research Handbook on International Law and United Nations Sanctions* (Cheltenham: Edward Elgar Publishing, 2017)

Coalitions of the Willing and International Law: The Interplay between Formality and Informality (Cambridge: Cambridge University Press, 2018)

Rodiles, A. and Sullivan, G., 'Global security assemblages: international counter-terrorism law in motion' (forthcoming, draft on file with author)

Roele, I., 'Disciplinary power and the UN Security Council Counter Terrorism Committee' (2014) 19(1) *Journal of Conflict and Security Law* 49

Rosa, H. and Scheuerman, W. E. (edss), *High Speed Society: Social Acceleration, Power and Modernity* (Penn State Park PA: Pennsylvania State University Press, 2009)

Rosand, E., 'The Security Council's efforts to monitor the implementation of Al Qaeda/ Taliban sanctions' (2004) 98(4) *American Journal of International Law* 745

'The UN-led multilateral institutional response to jihadist terrorism: is a global counterterrorism body needed?' (2006) 11 *Journal of Conflict and Security Law* 399

Rose, N., *Powers of Freedom: Reframing Political Thought* (Cambridge: Cambridge University Press, 1999)

Rose, N. and Miller, P., 'Political power beyond the state: problematics of government' (1992) 43(2) *British Journal of Sociology* 173

Rose, N. and Valverde, M., 'Governed by law?' (1998) 7(4) *Social and Legal Studies* 541

Rottenburg, R. and Merry, S. E., 'A world of indicators: the making of govern-mental knowledge through quantification' in Richard Rottenburg, Sally Engle Merry, Sung-Joon Park and Johanna Mugler (eds.), *The World of*

Indicators: The Making of Governmental Knowledge through Quantification (Cambridge: Cambridge University Press, 2015)

Ruggie, J. G., 'Territoriality and beyond: problematizing modernity in international relations' (1993) 47(1) *International Organization* 139

Ryan, P. and Dundan, T., 'Case research interviews: eliciting superior quality data' (2008) *International Journal of Case Method Research and Application* 443

Salter, M. and Mutlu, C. E. (eds.), *Research Methods in Critical Security Studies: An Introduction* (London: Routledge, 2013)

Saltman, E., 'Technology against terrorism: how to respond to the exploitation of the internet', Chatham House (12 July 2017). Available at: bit.ly /2WhPitM

Sarooshi, D. and Tzanakopoulos, A., 'United Kingdom' in August Reinisch (ed.), *The Privileges and Immunities of International Organizations in Domestic Courts* (Oxford: Oxford University Press, 2013)

Sassen, S., 'Spatialities and temporalities of the global: elements for a theorization' in Arjun Appadurai (ed.), *Globalization* (Durham NC: Duke University Press, 2001)

The Global City: New York, London, Tokyo (Princeton NJ: Princeton University Press, 2001)

Territory, Authority, Rights: From Medieval to Global Assemblages (Princeton NJ: Princeton University Press, 2006)

'Neither global nor national: novel assemblages of territory, authority and rights' (2008) 1(1–2) *Ethics and Global Politics* 61

'Bordering Capabilities versus borders: implications for national borders' (2009) 30 *Michigan Journal of international Law* 567

Saul, B., 'Terrorism and international criminal law: questions of (in)coherence and (il)legitimacy' in Gideon Boas, William Schabas and Scharf (eds.), *International Criminal Justice: Legitimacy and Coherence* (Cheltenham: Edward Elgar Publishing, 2012)

Scahill, J. and Greenwald, G., 'The NSA's Secret role in the US assassination program', *The Intercept* (10 February 2014). Available at: bit.ly/1zeKzrV

Scheinin, M., 'Curriculum Vitae: Martin Scheinin'. Available at: bit.ly/1N1eoBv

Human Rights/Counter Terrorism: The New UN Listing Regimes for the Taliban and Al-Qaida – Statement by the Special Rapporteur on Human Rights and Counter Terrorism (29 June 2011). Available at: bit.ly/2Z4yyHZ

'Towards a World Court of Human Rights', *Agenda for Human Rights: Swiss Initiative to Commemorate the 60th Anniversary of the UDHR* (June 2009). Available at: bit.ly/1N7HvzO

Scheper-Hughes, N., 'The last commodity: post-human ethics and the global traffic in "fresh" organs', in Aihwa Ong and Stephen J. Collier (eds.), *Global*

Assemblages: Technology, Politics, and Ethics as Anthropological Problems (Oxford: Wiley-Blackwell, 2004)

Scheppele, K. L., 'The international standardization of national security law' (2001) 4 *Journal of National Security Law and Policy* 437

'The international state of emergency: challenges to constitutionalism after September 11', Yale Legal Theory Workshop (21 September 2006) (unpublished manuscript)

'The migration of anti-constitutional ideas: the post-9/11 globalisation of public law and the international state of emergency' in Sujit Choudry (ed.), *The Migration of Constitutional Ideas* (Cambridge: Cambridge University Press, 2007)

'The empire of security and the security of empire' (2013) 27 *Temple International and Comparative Law Journal* 241

Scheuerman, W. E., *Liberal Democracy and the Social Acceleration of Time* (Baltimore MD: John Hopkins University Press, 2004)

Schmitt, C., *Political Theology: Four Chapters on the Concept of Sovereignty* (Cambridge MA: MIT Press, 1985); (Chicago IL: University of Chicago Press, 2005)

Schott, J., 'Chapter VII as exception: Security Council action and the regulative ideal of emergency' (2007) 6(1) *Northwestern University Journal of Human Rights* 24

Scott, C., '"Transnational law" as proto-concept: three conceptions' (2009) 10(7) *German Law Journal* 868

Sending, O. J. and Neumann, I. B., 'Banking on power: how some practices in an international organization anchor others' in Emanuel Adler and Vincent Pouliot (eds.), *International Practices* (Cambridge: Cambridge University Press, 2011)

Shaffer, G., 'A transnational take on Krisch's pluralist structure of postnational law' (2012) 23(2) *European Journal of International Law* 565

Slaughter, A. M., 'The real new world order' (1997) 76 *Foreign Affairs* 184

Staeheli, U., 'Listing the global: dis/connectivity beyond representation?' (2012) 13 *Distinktion: Scandinavian Journal of Social Theory* 233

Stampnitzky, L., *Disciplining Terror: How Experts Invented Terrorism* (Cambridge: Cambridge University Press, 2013)

Star, S. L., 'This is not a boundary object: reflections on the origin of a concept' (2010) 35 *Science, Technology and Human Values* 601

Star, S. L. and Griesemer, J. R., 'Institutional ecology, translations and boundary objects: amateurs and professionals in Berkeley's Museum of Vertebrate Zoology 1907–39' (1989) 19 *Social Studies of Science* 387

Stewart, R. B., 'Remedying disregard in global regulatory governance: accountability, participation and responsiveness' (2014) 108(2) *American Journal of International Law* 211

Stockdale, L., 'Imagined futures and exceptional presents: a conceptual critique of "pre-emptive security"' (2013) 25 *Global Change, Peace and Security* 141

Stollenwerk, E., Dörfler, T. and Schibberges, J., 'Taking a new perspective: mapping the Al Qaeda network through the eyes of the UN Security Council' (2016) 28(5) *Terrorism and Political Violence* 950

Stone-Sweet, A., 'A cosmopolitan legal order: constitutional pluralism and rights adjudication in Europe' (2011) 1 *Journal of Global Constitutionalism* 53

Sullivan, G., 'Secret justice inside the EU courts' *Al-Jazeera Online* (19 April 2014)
  'Transnational legal assemblages and global security law: topologies and temporalities of the list' (2014) 5(1) *Transnational Legal Theory* 81
  'Rearranging global law: reflections on laws and societies in a global context' (2017) 13(4) *International Journal of Law in Context* 553
  '"Taking on the technicalities" of international law – practice, description, critique: a response to Fleur Johns' (2017) 111 *AJIL Unbound* 181

Sullivan, G. and de Goede, M., 'Between law and the exception: the UN 1267 Ombudsperson as a hybrid model of legal expertise' (2013) 26(4) *Leiden Journal of International Law* 833

Sullivan, G. and Hayes, B. *Blacklisted: Targeted Sanctions, Preemptive Security and Fundamental Rights* (Berlin: ECCHR, 2011)

Suskind, R., *The Price of Loyalty: George W. Bush, the White House and the Education of Paul O'Neill* (New York: Simon & Schuster, 2004)
  The One Percent Doctrine: Deep Inside America's Pursuit of Its Enemies Since 9/11 (New York: Simon & Schuster, 2006)

Szasz, P., 'The Security Council in the post Cold-War world' (2002) 96 *American Journal of International Law* 901
  'The Security Council starts legislating' (2002) 96(4) *American Journal of International Law* 901

Talmon, S., 'The Security Council as world legislature' (2005) 99(1) *American Journal of International Law* 175

Teubner, G., 'The two faces of legal pluralism' (1992) 13 *Cardoza Law Review* 1443
  'Global Bukowina: legal pluralism in the world society' in Gunther Teubner (ed.), *Global Law without a State* (Aldershot: Ashgate Publishing, 1997)

Thrift, N., 'Movement-space: the changing domain of thinking resulting from the development of new kinds of spatial awareness' (2004) 33 *Economy and Society* 582

Tomuschat, C., 'The Kadi case: what relationship is there between the universal legal order under the auspices of the United Nations and the EU legal order?' (2009) 28 *Yearbook of European Law* 654

Treverton, G. F., *Intelligence for an Age of Terror* (Cambridge: Cambridge University Press, 2009)

True-Frost, C., 'The development of individual standing in international security' (2011) 32(4) *Cardoza Law Review* 1183

Tsing, A., 'The global situation' (2000) 15(3) *Cultural Anthropology* 327

Twining, W., 'Evidence as a multi-disciplinary subject' (2003) *Law, Probability and Risk* 91

Tyner, J., *The Politics of Lists: Bureaucracy and Genocide under the Khmer Rouge* (Morgantown WV: West Virginia University Press, 2018)

Tzanakopoulos, A., 'An effective remedy for Josef K: Canadian judge "defies" Security Council sanctions through interpretation', *EJIL Talk weblog* (19 June 2009). Available at: bit.ly/1IaS2HX

   'United Nations sanctions in domestic courts from interpretation to defiance in Abdelrazik v. Canada' (2010) 8 *Journal of International Criminal Justice* 249

   Disobeying the Security Council: Countermeasures against Wrongful Sanctions (Oxford: Oxford University Press, 2011)

UN1267 Sanctions Committee (5 September 2018), 'Guidelines for the Committee of the Conduct of Its Work'. Available at: bit.ly/37L43be

UN Commission on Human Rights Resolution 2005/80. E/CN.4/2005/L.10/ Add.17 (21 April 2005)

UN Doc. A/50/60-S/1995/18221 (3 January 1995), *Supplement to an Agenda for Peace*

UN Doc. A/60/887-S/2006/331 (14 June 2006), Identical letters dated 19 May 2006 from the Permanent Representatives of Germany, Sweden and Switzerland to the United Nations addressed to the President of the General Assembly and the President of the Security Council

UN Doc. A/61/267 (16 August 2006), Report of the Special Rapporteur on the Promotion and Protection of Human Rights and Fundamental Freedoms while Countering Terrorism

UN Doc. A/62/891 – S/2008/428 (2 July 2008), Identical letters dated 23 June 2008 from the Permanent Representative of Switzerland to the United Nations addressed to the President of the General Assembly and the President of the Security Council

UN Doc. A/65/258 (6 August 2010), Report of the Special Rapporteur on the Promotion and Protection of Human Rights and Fundamental Freedoms while Countering Terrorism

UN Doc. A/67/396 (26 September 2012), Report of the Special Rapporteur on the Promotion and Protection of Human Rights and Fundamental Freedoms while Countering Terrorism

UN Doc. A/73/361 (3 September 2018), Report of the Special Rapporteur on the Promotion and Protection of Human Rights and Fundamental Freedoms while Countering Terrorism

UN Doc. A/ C.3/65/SR.30 (8 December 2010), United Nations General Assembly, Third Committee, Summary Record of the 30th Meeting

UN Doc. A/ C.3/67/SR.26A (10 January 2013), United Nations General Assembly, Third Committee, Summary Record of the 26th Meeting

UN Doc. A/Res/60/1 (24 October 2005), Resolution adopted by the General Assembly on 16 September 2005, World Summit Outcome

UN Doc. A/RES/60/251 (3 April 2006), Resolution adopted by the General Assembly, 60/251 Human Rights Council

UN Doc. A/RES/60/288 (20 September 2006), Resolution adopted by the General Assembly on 8 September 2006, The United Nations Global Counter-Terrorism Strategy

UN Doc. S/2005/83 (15 February 2005), Second Report of the Analytical Support and Sanctions Monitoring Team appointed pursuant to Resolution 1526 (2004) concerning Al-Qaida and the Taliban and associated individuals and entities

UN Doc. S/2005/572 (9 September 2005), Third Report of the Analytical Support and Sanctions Monitoring Team appointed pursuant to Resolution 1526 (2004) concerning Al-Qaida and the Taliban and associated individuals and entities

UN Doc. S/2006/154 (10 March 2006), Fourth Report of the Analytical Support and Sanctions Monitoring Team appointed pursuant to Security Council Resolutions 1526 (2004) and 1617 (2005) concerning Al-Qaida and the Taliban and associated individuals and entities

UN Doc. S/2007/132 (8 March 2007), Sixth Report of the Analytical Support and Sanctions Monitoring Team appointed pursuant to Security Council Resolutions 1526 (2004) and 1617 (2005) concerning Al-Qaida and the Taliban and associated individuals and entities

UN Doc. S/2007/677 (20 November 2007), Seventh Report of the Analytical Support and Sanctions Monitoring Team appointed pursuant to Security Council Resolutions 1617 (2005) and 1735 (2006) concerning Al-Qaida and the Taliban and associated individuals and entities

UN Doc. S/2008/324 (14 May 2008), Eighth Report of the Analytical Support and Sanctions Monitoring Team pursuant to Resolution 1735 (2006) concerning Al-Qaida and the Taliban and associated individuals and entities

UN Doc. S/2009/245 (13 May 2009), Ninth Report of the Analytical Support and Sanctions Monitoring Team, submitted pursuant to Resolution 1822 (2008) concerning Al-Qaida and the Taliban and associated individuals and entities

UN Doc. S/2009/502 (2 October 2009), Tenth Report of the Analytical Support and Sanctions Implementation Monitoring Team submitted pursuant to Resolution 1822 (2008) concerning Al-Qaida and the Taliban and associated individuals and entities

UN Doc. S/2011/245 (13 April 2011), Eleventh Report of the Analytical Support and Sanctions Implementation Monitoring Team established pursuant to Security Council Resolution 1526 (2004) and extended by Resolution 1904

(2009) concerning Al-Qaida and the Taliban and associated individuals and entities

UN Doc. S/2012/729 (1 October 2012), Twelfth Report of the Analytical Support and Sanctions Implementation Monitoring Team, submitted pursuant to Resolution 1989 (2011) concerning Al-Qaida and associated individuals and entities

UN Doc. S/2012/968 (31 December 2012), Thirteenth Report of the Analytical Support and Sanctions Implementation Monitoring Team submitted pursuant to Resolution 1989 (2011) concerning Al-Qaida and associated individuals and entities

UN Doc. S/2013/467 (2 August 2013), Fourteenth Report of the Analytical Support and Sanctions Monitoring Team submitted pursuant to Resolution 2083 (2012) concerning Al-Qaida and associated individuals and entities

UN Doc. S/2013/71 (31 January 2013), Fifth Report of the Office of the Ombudsperson pursuant to Security Council Resolution 2083 (2012)

UN Doc. S/2013/452 (31 July 2013), Sixth Report of the Office of the Ombudsperson pursuant to Security Council Resolution 2083 (2012)

UN Doc. S/2013/698 (26 November 2013), Report of the Security Council Committee pursuant to resolutions 1267 (1999) and 1989 (2011) concerning Al-Qaida and associated individuals and entities

UN Doc. S/2014/41 (23 January 2014), Fifteenth Report of the Analytical Support and Sanctions Monitoring Team submitted pursuant to Resolution 2083 (2012) concerning Al-Qaida and associated individuals and entities

UN Doc. S/2014/73 (31 January 2014), Seventh Report of the Office of the Ombudsperson pursuant to Security Council Resolution 2083 (2012)

UN Doc. S/2014/286 (21 April 2014), Letter dated 17 April 2014 from the Permanent Representatives of Austria, Belgium, Costa Rica, Denmark, Finland, Germany, Liechtenstein, the Netherlands, Norway, Sweden and Switzerland to the United Nations addressed to the President of the Security Council

UN Doc. S/2014/770 (29 October 2014), Sixteenth Report of the Analytical Support and Sanctions Monitoring Team submitted pursuant to Resolution 2161 (2014) concerning Al-Qaida and associated individuals and entities

UN Doc. S/2014/888 (11 December 2014), Fifth Report of the Analytical Support and Sanctions Monitoring Team, submitted pursuant to Resolution 2160 (2014) concerning the Taliban and other associated individuals and entities constituting a threat to the peace, stability and security of Afghanistan

UN Doc. S/2015/80 (2 February 2015), Ninth Report of the Office of the Ombudsperson pursuant to Security Council Resolution 2161 (2014)

UN Doc. S/2015/533 (14 July 2015), Tenth Report of the Office of the Ombudsperson pursuant to Security Council Resolution 2161 (2014)

UN Doc. S/2015/441 (16 June 2015), Seventeenth Report of the Analytical Support and Sanctions Monitoring Team submitted pursuant to Resolution 2161 (2014) concerning Al-Qaida and associated individuals and entities

UN Doc. S/2016/96 (2 February 2016), Eleventh Report of the Office of the Ombudsperson, submitted pursuant to Security Council Resolution 2253 (2015)

UN Doc. S/2017/35 (13 January 2017), Nineteenth Report of the Analytical Support and Sanctions Monitoring Team submitted pursuant to Resolution 2253 (2015) concerning ISIL (Da'esh), Al-Qaida and associated individuals and entities

UN Doc. S/2018/14/Rev.1 (27 February 2018), Twenty-first Report of the Analytical Support and Sanctions Monitoring Team submitted pursuant to Resolution 2368 (2017) concerning ISIL (Da'esh), Al-Qaida and associated individuals and entities

UN Doc. S/2018/705 (27 July 2018), Twenty-second Report of the Analytical Support and Sanctions Monitoring Team submitted pursuant to Resolution 2368 (2017) concerning ISIL (Da'esh), Al-Qaida and associated individuals and entities

UN Doc. S/2018/1094 (11 December 2018), Letter dated 7 December 2018 from the representatives of Austria, Belgium, Chile, Costa Rica, Denmark, Finland, Germany, Liechtenstein, the Netherlands, Norway, Sweden and Switzerland to the United Nations addressed to the President of the Security Council

UN Doc. S/2019/50 (15 January 2019), Twenty-third Report of the Analytical Support and Sanctions Monitoring Team submitted pursuant to Resolution 2368 (2017) concerning ISIL (Da'esh), Al-Qaida and associated individuals and entities

UN Doc. SC/10252 (16 May 2011), Anti-Terrorism Committees Must Continue to Strengthen Efforts, Despite Death of Osama Bin Laden, Security Council Told. Available at: bit.ly/2H1pzx1

UN Doc. SC/10467 (30 November 2011), Security Council Al-Qaida Sanctions Committee Deletes Entry of Abu Sufian Al-Salamabi Muhammed Ahmed Abd Al-Razziq from Its List. Available at: bit.ly/1DrcIyE

UN Doc. SC/10785 (5 October 2012), Security Council Al-Qaida Sanctions Committee Deletes Entry of Yasin Abdullah Ezzedine Qadi from Its List. Available at: bit.ly/1SInck4

UN Doc. SC/11019 (30 May 2013), Security Council Al-Qaida Sanctions Committee Amends Entry of One Entity on Its Sanctions List. Available at: bit.ly/31BSAXV

UN Doc. SC/11397 (14 May 2014), Security Council Al-Qaida Sanctions Committee Amends Three Entries on Its Sanctions List. Available at: bit.ly /2MZ818B

UN Doc. SG/SM/7360 (17 April 2000), Secretary General Reviews Lessons Learned during 'Sanctions Decade' in Remarks to International Peace Academy Seminar. Available at: bit.ly/2KK1qw7

UN Doc. S/PV.4892 (12 January 2014), UN Security Council, 4892nd meeting, Monday 12 January 2004

UN Office of Counter-Terrorism, UN Countering Terrorist Travel. Available at: bit.ly/2JKfF4F

UNSC ISIL and Al-Qaida Analytical Support and Sanctions Monitoring Team, 'United Nations Security Council travel ban on Al-Qaida and associates: implementation opportunities and challenges' (April 2016). Available at: bit .ly/2ZiJb71

UNSC Counter-Terrorism Committee (CTC), *Country Reports: Reports by Member States pursuant to Security Council Resolution 1373* (2001)

UNSC Counter-Terrorism Committee Executive Directorate (CTED) and UN Office of Counter-Terrorism (UNOCT), *United Nations Compendium of Recommended Practices for the Responsible Use and Sharing of Biometrics in Counter-terrorism* (2018). Available at: bit.ly/2ygyeHf

UNSC S/ RES 232 (1966)

UNSC S/ RES 418 (1977)

UNSC S/ RES 731 (1992)

UNSC S/ RES 1267 (1999)

UNSC S/ RES 1333 (2000)

UNSC S/ RES 1373 (2001)

UNSC S/ RES 1390 (2002)

UNSC S/ RES 1526 (2004)

UNSC S/ RES 1535 (2004)

UNSC S/ RES 1617 (2005)

UNSC S/ RES 1730 (2006)

UNSC S/ RES 1735 (2006)

UNSC S/ RES 1822 (2008)

UNSC S/ RES 1904 (2009)

UNSC S/ RES 1989 (2011)

UNSC S/ RES 2083 (2012)

UNSC S/ RES 2161 (2014)

UNSC S/ RES 2178 (2014)

UNSC S/ RES 2253 (2015)

UNSC S/ RES 2309 (2016)

UNSC S/ RES 2368 (2017)

UNSC S/ RES 2396 (2017)

UN Special Rapporteur on the Promotion and Protection of Human Rights and Fundamental Freedoms while Countering Terrorism, *Submission to the Report of the Office of the United High Commissioner for Human Rights on the Right to Privacy in the Digital Age*. Available at: bit.ly/2JXPebD

US Embassy Cable 06USUNNEWYORK714 (4 April 2006)

US Embassy Cable 06USUNNEWYORK917 (4 May 2006)

US Embassy Cable 06USUNNEWYORK1078 (26 May 2006)

US Embassy Cable 06ROME1708 (7 June 2006)

US Embassy Cable 06USUNNEWYORK1430 (31 July 2006)

US Embassy Cable 06USUNNEWYORK1609 (22 August 2006)

US Embassy Cable 06PARIS5732 (25 August 2006)

US Embassy Cable 06RIYADH8416 (24 October 2006)

US Embassy Cable 07RIYADH305 (13 February 2007)

US Embassy Cable 07ROME2515 (28 December 2007)

US Embassy Cable 08USUNNEWYORK313 (7 April 2008)

US Embassy Cable 08ROME190 (11 February 2008)

US Embassy Cable 08ROME711 (4 June 2008)

US Embassy Cable 08LONDON1690 (24 June 2008)

US Embassy Cable 08STATE69684 (27 June 2008)

US Embassy Cable 08STATE4740 (15 January 2008)

US Embassy Cable 08USUNNEWYORK421 (12 May 2008)

US Embassy Cable 08USUNNEWYORK640 (18 July 2008)

US Embassy Cable 09BRUSSELS41 (13 January 2009)

US Embassy Cable 09LONDON452 (20 February 2009)

US Embassy Cable 09USUNNEWYORK301 (23 March 2009)

US Embassy Cable 09USUNNEWYORK474 (8 May 2009)

US Embassy Cable 09BRUSSELS616 (29 April 2009)

US Embassy Cable 09ROME652 (9 June 2009)

US Embassy Cable 09OTTAWA478 (18 June 2009)

US Embassy Cable 09CAIRO1363 (15 July 2009)

US Embassy Cable 09USUNNEWYORK818 (4 September 2009)

US Embassy Cable 09CAIRO1976 (19 October 2009)

US Embassy Cable 09STATE109494 (22 October 2009)

US Embassy Cable 09BRUSSELS1524 (13 November 2009)

US Embassy Cable 09LONDON2678 (2 December 2009)

US Embassy Cable 09ROME1344 (4 December 2009)

US Embassy Cable 09ROME1404 (23 December 2009)

US Embassy Cable 09ROME1405 (23 December 2009)

US Embassy Cable 10USEUBRUSSELS212 (24 February 2010)

US Embassy Cable 10BRUSSELS219 (dated 25 February 2010)

US Mission to the UN, 'Remarks by Ambassador Susan E. Rice, U.S. Permanent Representative to the United Nations, on Security Council Resolution 1904,

Sudan, and the Middle East, at the Security Council Stakeout', Press Release No. 2009/314 (17 December 2009)

US National Security Strategy (May 2010). Available at: bit.ly/2MUum76

Valverde, M., '"Despotism" and ethical liberal governance' (1996) 25(3) *Economy and Society* 357

Law's Dream of a Common Knowledge (Princeton NJ: Princeton University Press, 2003)

'Authorizing the production of urban moral order: appellate courts and their knowledge games' (2005) 39(2) *Law and Society Review* 419

'Jurisdiction and scale: "legal technicalities" as resources for theory' (2009) 18(2) *Social and Legal Studies* 139

Chronotopes of Law: Jurisdiction, Scale and Governance (London: Routledge, 2015)

Valverde, M., Levi, R. and Moore, D., 'Legal knowledges of risk' in Law Commission of Canada (ed.), *Law and Risk* (Vancouver: University of British Columbia Press, 2005)

Valverde, M. and Mopas, M., 'Insecurity and the dream of targeted governance' in W. Larner and W. Walters (eds.), *Global Governmentality: Governing International Spaces* (London: Routledge, 2004)

Van Brabant, K., 'Can sanctions be smarter? The current debate: report of a conference held in London, 16–17 December 1998' (London: ODI, 1999). Available at: bit.ly/2Or1g1t

Van Den Herik, L., 'Peripheral hegemony in the quest to ensure Security Council accountability for its individualized UN sanctions regimes' (2014) 19(3) *Journal of Conflict and Security Law* 427

'Targeted Sanctions Workshop' (University of Amsterdam, 24 February 2014)

Van Den Meerssche, D., 'Scholars in self-estrangement (again): rethinking the law of international organisations' (2017) 5(3) *London Review of International Law* 455

'International organizations and the performativity of measuring states: discipline through diagnosis' (2018) 15(1) *International Organizations Law Review* 168

'Performing the rule of law in international organizations: Ibrahim Shihata and the World Bank's turn to governance reform' (2019) 32(1) *Leiden Journal of International Law* 47

Vismann, C., *Files: Law and Media Technology* (Stanford CA: University of California Press, 2008)

Vogel, R. J., 'Ending the "drone war" or expanding it? Assessing the legal authority for continued US operations against Al-Qa'ida after Afghanistan' (2015) *Albany Government Law Review* 8

Von Bogdandy, A., 'Pluralism, direct effect and the ultimate say: on the relationship between international and domestic constitutional law' (2008) 6(3–4) *International Journal of Constitutional Law* 397

Von Bogdandy, A., Dann, P. and Goldmann, M., 'Developing the publicness of public international law: towards a legal framework for global governance activities' (2008) 9 *German Law Journal* 1375

Walker, N., 'The idea of constitutional pluralism' (2002) *Modern Law Review* 317

  'Beyond boundary disputes and basic grids: mapping the global disorder of normative orders' (2008) 6 *International Journal of Constitutional Law* 373

  'Out of place and out of time: law's fading co-ordinates', Working Paper No 192009/01 (Edinburgh: University of Edinburgh School of Law, 2009)

  Intimations of Global Law (Cambridge: Cambridge University Press, 2015)

Wallensteen, P. and Staibano, C., *International Sanctions: Between Words and Wars in the Global System* (London: Frank Cass, 2005)

Walters, W., 'Secrecy, Publicity and the Milieu of Security' (2015) 5(3) *Dialogues in Human Geography* 287

Walters, W. and Best, J., 'Translating the sociology of translation' (2013) 7(3) *International Political Sociology* 345

Warren Perry, R. and Maurer, B. (eds.), *Globalization under Construction: Governmentality, Law and Identity* (Minneapolis MN: University of Minnesota Press, 2003)

Watson Institute, *Targeted Financial Sanctions: A Manual for Design and Implementation – Contributions from the Interlaken Process* (Geneva: Watson Institute for International Studies, 2001). Available at: bit.ly /2YZ5VvJ

  Strengthening Targeted Sanctions through Fair and Clear Procedures: White Paper (Geneva: Watson Institute for International Studies, 2006)

WCO Doc. PC0421E1b, Permanent Technical Committee, 209th/210th Sessions, *Summary Document* (6 October 2015)

WCO/IATA/ICAO, 'Guidelines on Advance Passenger Information (API)'. Available at: bit.ly/33pTvfH

Weber, J., 'Keep adding. On kill lists, drone warfare and the politics of databases' (2016) 34(1) *Environment and Planning D: Society and Space* 107

Weiss, T. G., Carayannis, T. and Jolly, R., 'The "third" United Nations' (2009) 15 *Global Governance: A Review of Multilateralism and International Organizations* 123

Weiss, T. G., Cortright, D., Lopez, G. A. and Minear, L. (eds.), *Political Gain and Civilian Pain: The Humanitarian Impacts of Economic Sanctions* (Lanham MD: Rowman & Littlefield, 1997)

Weizman, E., *The Least of All Possible Evils: Humanitarian Violence from Arendt to Gaza* (New York: Verso, 2012)

Wexels-Riser, N., 'The Security Council's ISIL (Da'esh) and Al-Qaida Sanctions Regime: The Human Dimension', paper presented to the Max Planck Institute for Foreign and International Criminal Law (2 December 2017). Available at: bit.ly/2yCOO48

Wikileaks Press Release, 'Secret US Embassy Cables' (28 November 2010). Available at: bit.ly/29H84Du

Wille, T., 'The diplomatic cable' in Mark Salter (ed.), *Making Things International II: Catalysts and Reactions* (Minneapolis MN: University of Minnesota Press, 2015)

Willis, G. L., 'Security Council targeted sanctions, due process and the 1267 Ombudsperson' (2010) 42 *Georgetown Journal of International Law* 673

Wolf, K. D., 'The new raison d'état as a problem for democracy in world society' (1999) 5(3) *European Journal of International Relations* 333

Wolff, A., 'Statement by Ambassador Alejandro Wolff, US Deputy Permanent Representative, in the Security Council, on the 1267, 1373 and 1540 Committee Briefings' (13 November 2009)

Woolgar, S. and Lezaun, J., 'The wrong bin bag: a turn to ontology in science and technology studies?' (2013) 43(3) *Social Studies of Science* 321

Yanow, D., 'Thinking interpretively: philosophical presuppositions and the human sciences' in Dvora Yanow and Schwartz-Shea (eds.), *Interpretation and Method: Empirical Research Methods and the Interpretive turn* (London: Routledge, 2006)

Zagaris, B., 'Somali Swedes challenge terrorism freeze' (2002) 18 *International Enforcement Law Reporter* 277

Zarate, J. C., *Treasury's War: The Unleashing of a New Era of Financial Warfare* (New York: Public Affairs, 2013)

Zedner, L., 'Pre-crime and post-Criminology' (2007) 11(2) *Theoretical Criminology* 261
    'Preventive justice or pre-punishment? The case of control orders' (2007) 60(1) *Current Legal Problems* 174
    'Seeking security by eroding rights: the side-stepping of due process' in Benjamin J. Goold and Liora Lazarus (eds.), *Security and Human Rights* (Oxford: Hart Publishing, 2007)

Zumbansen, P., 'Defining the space for transnational law: legal theory, global governance and legal pluralism' (2012) 21 *Transnational Law and Contemporary Problems* 305
    'How, where and for whom? Interrogating law's forms, locations and purposes', *Inaugural Lecture, King's College London* (28 April 2016)

INDEX